The Fourth Service

The Fourth Service

Merchantmen at War
1939 - 45

John Slader

NEW
GUILD

A New Guild Book

Published by New Era Writer's Guild (UK) Ltd
5 Cogdean Walk, Corfe Mullen
Wimborne Minster, Dorset BH21 3XB

PO Box 11476
Bloubergrant 7443, South Africa
Tel: (+21) 557 6281
Fax (+21) 557 0704

PO Box 100-806
North Shore Mail Centre
Auckland 10, New Zealand
Tel/fax: (+9) 443 8069

ISBN 1-899694-45-5

This book was designed, typeset and produced by
Crispin Goodall Design Ltd
463 Ashley Road
Poole, Dorset BH14 OAX

Printed in the U.K. by
Short Run Press Limited
Bittern Road, Sowton Industrial Estate
Exeter EX2 7LW

Contents

To Gwendoline

Who as a wartime ATS served with the Army
on the Home Front

Illustrations

Between page 256 and 257

PICTURE CREDITS

Acknowledgements

Acknowledgements and thanks are due to the Controller of Her Majesty's Stationery Office for the permission to reproduce copyright material appearing in HMSO books (as listed in the bibliography) and to the Public Record Office for allowing me to reproduce material stored in their records. Every effort has been made to trace the owners of copyright material; where it has unfortunately proved impossible, I offer my apologies.

For much of the background to Chapter 6, 'Atlantic Victory', I have relied largely on some of the many published works of this longest of all maritime battles. A full list of sources are contained in the bibliography.

In addition to those who have contributed information, a list of which follows, I am particularly indebted to the Ministry of Defence (Naval Historical Branch), the Public Record Office, Lloyds Register of Shipping, the Imperial War Museum and the National Maritime Museum. My grateful thanks go to the librarian and staff of Abergavenny Public Library, and to the special projects editor of the *Western Morning News* for his assistance in uncovering material on the loss of the *Khedive Ismail*. Special thanks go to my wife whom I courted as a young deck apprentice during those difficult days a half century ago. Without her help with the typescript and her unfailing patience over the two years taken to complete this work, the book would remain unwritten.

Thanks go to the following people, who kindly provided me with information:

W.D. Abbot, R. Alexander, W.T. Allen, L. Bainborough, P.J. Barber, A.H. Black, T.L. Black, S. Bordell, K.R. Booth, Mrs A.J. Bray, P.J. Bridson, F. Brown, F. Browne, R.A.H. Buck, J. Bulloch, C.J.M. Carter, R.N. Clarabut, P. Clark, J.H. Cochrane, S. Cook, J.E. Cowden, K. Crabtree, G.E. Cregeen, J.A.C. Crowe, S.E. Daniels, A. Dashwood-Howard, L.O. Davies, G.F. Dickinson, W.H. Donner, E. Duckworth, G.B. Evans, K. Eyre, H.C. Fellingham, R. Fenton, H. Ferguson, R. Gardner, J.A. Gilmour, H. Goldsmith, I. Gosling, L.E. Grant, P. Gunson, A. Hague, Admiral Sir J. Hamilton, C. Hatton, R. Hayes, R. Higham, G. Hime, C.H. Holder, E.C. Horrell, R. Howell, T. Hutchinson.

C. Idle, J.F. Jamieson, G.R. Jones, L. Jones, M.W. Jones, A.H. Joyce, T. Kay, L.D. Lasbury, A.R. Lightfoot, J.S. Lingwood, K.P. Lewis, K.T. Lewis, W. Lewis, A. Lloyd, W.E. Loynd, R. Machielsen, D. MacLeod, I.M. Malcolm, R. Manson, L. Matthews, G. May, F.H. May, R.J. May, S. Mayes, J.C. Meddle, R.H. Melbourne, I.A. Millar, A.D. Mills, G.V. Monk, T. Moore, R. Mott, W.H. Moses, F. Moyser, J.K. Mudd, P. Mullan, P. Mummery, G. Musk, W.S. Mutimer, E. Mutter, L. Norbury-Williams, C.H. Nutt, P. Oastler, M. O'Leary, A.W. Owen, G.R. Owen, D.E. Pain, C.T. Pleavin, P.J. Porteous, S.H. Potter, D. Purdon, J. Quinain, K.R. Ray, G.W. Raymond, H. Rees. D. Roberts, M. Roberts, T. Robertson, T. Robson, Professor Dr J. Rohwer, J. Ross, R.P. Roux-Schroder, R.A. Ruegg.

J.G. Smith, W. Smith, Major C.D. Spears, R. Spencer, C.J. Stevens, A. Strickland, H. Stimpson, S. Styles, H.J. Taylor, E.A. Thomas, T. Thomas, W.B. Thomas, R. Travers-Bogusz, A.T. Tubb, J. Tyrrell, V.G.A. Upton, H. Vinall, J. Waggott, C. Walker, G.K. Walker, L. Warman, G. Wauge, A.H. Wells, T.G. Wilson, D. Williams, B. Workman.

Introduction

It was George Bernard Shaw (1856–1950) who once said, 'Reminiscences make one feel so deliciously aged and sad.' There is a certain amount of truth in this statement as I have found over the past two years during the research and writing of this volume. Having studied both the land and air battles of the Second World War in addition to that of the 'killing seas', I often found myself asking the question: 'Where would the Allies have stood without a large and efficient fleet of merchantmen?' It is my hope that this book will put the record straight.

Written during a period of many fiftieth anniversaries it is perhaps an appropriate time to assess what was achieved at a time when it has been claimed (by Captain John Waters, US Coast Guard), that the number of men on both sides, Allied and Axis, who lost their lives at sea was greater than the combined deaths in all the naval battles of the previous five hundred years.

As one of my contemporaries, Roy Melbourne of Wallasey, has said,

> It was an accepted fact of life that the Merchant Navy would go anywhere it was sent, without argument, and it did just that. It received little publicity because it was a 'non-stop' operation. Merchantmen were either loading or sailing, crews snatching a few days leave (two days per month away), or endeavouring to reach our destination wherever in the world that might be. As crew members we sought no publicity but got on with the job. We were never in one place long enough to do otherwise. All the fighting services had their moments of achievements or defeats chronicled with many books and even films to record their deeds.

Few such detailed records have been made of Britain's merchant fleet.

There is no better introduction to the subject of merchantmen at war than declarations made by those in positions of command – the first by Winston Churchill speaking in July 1941:

> The Merchant Navy, with Allied comrades, night and day, in weather fair or foul, faces not only the ordinary perils of the sea but the sudden assaults of war from beneath the waters or from the sky. Your first task is to bring to port the cargoes vital for us at home and for our armies abroad, and we trust your tenacity and resolve to see this stern task through.

Eighteen months later at the conclusion of a New Year's Day message to the officers and men of Allied merchant vessels, Admiral Sir Andrew Cunningham (later Admiral of the Fleet, Viscount Cunningham of Hyndhope) declared, 'Navy, Army and Air Force alike know how much they depend on your efforts.'

On 1 March 1943 after the conclusion of the successful 'Torch' Operation in North Africa, Lord Leathers, at the time Minister of War Transport, said in a speech: 'Merchant ships, carrying troops and equipment, actually sail into the battle line. Merchant shipping has become a fourth service so far as major combined operations are concerned'. The Rt. Hon. Alfred Barnes, successor to Lord Leathers as Minister of War Transport, was to say as Britain once again returned to a peaceful life (30 October 1945), 'The merchant seaman never faltered. To him we owe our preservation and our very lives.'

So it was that the Merchant Navy, the fourth service, or as known by some, the Mercantile Marine, a civilian service on a war footing, became the maritime force on which all the armed services depended. The word 'merchantman' embraces many types of ships: the passenger or cruise liner, the cross-channel ferry; the pleasure steamer; the cargo liner (or intermediate ship); the cargo trampship, sometimes known as the freighter; the tanker; and, by no means the least important, the ubiquitous coaster. Nor must we forget the fishing boat, for the fishing fleet itself became an important part of the service. All are merchant ships as distinct from warships; trading vessels which carry people and merchandise alike.

By tradition British seamen had stood by their homeland whenever the enemy threatened. It was this spirit that inspired seamen to overwhelm the might of Spain in 1588, stand out against the tyranny of the French kings in the eighteenth century, and refuse to bow before Napoleon when he had nearly the whole world at his feet in the nineteenth century. Many who had been sunk by the enemy in the First World War were still at sea during the 1940s. They were to suffer the indignity of being hunted by the same foe all over again. Strategically, the oceans have always served as barriers against invasion, the lifelines of a nation in peril. In the conflict of 1939–45, despite the huge American contribution, 54 per cent of world shipping losses were British, as against the United States' 16 per cent. It was a heavy toll to pay, both in ships and in men.

This is the story of the merchantmen and those men of courage who were proud of their ships and their flag, proud even of their rusty ocean-going 'tramp'. Those who sailed in her were of a certain calmness in facing hazards. Of long apprenticeship, our seamen were inclined to be imperturbable men. Hardy, adventurous and with stout hearts, they faced the peril of the sea and the enemy alike. It is an account of those who kept the foodlines open; brought home the aviation spirit used so magnificently by 'the Few' and the bomber crews who later flew deep into Germany; travelled the deadly lane to Murmansk and 'Bomb Alley' to Malta; brought a reeling, battered but undefeated army back from the beaches of Dunkirk and years later carried them to the beaches of North Africa, of Sicily and Europe's underbelly. Finally in triumph, they sailed to Normandy, the climax of the fleet's involvement in a war which lasted from September 1939 to May 1945. In this day of worldwide television, with immediate access to the world's trouble spots, it is difficult to imagine how remote from the fighting were not only the loved ones left behind but those actually engaged upon sailing their ship across the seven seas.

In the April 1931 prospectus of the *Conway*, the training ship established for Merchant Navy deck officers, there appeared a rousing paragraph which related the maritime heritage of the British Isles. I believe it remains as true today as it did in the 1930s and 1940s: 'In every British man or woman is born the spirit of our sea roving and sea fighting tradition. Take this inheritance, plant it in the right surroundings, nourish it with sound training and you will produce the finest sailor in the world.'

In the final chapter of this book I remark upon the varied parts of the British Isles from which men came to join the ranks of seafarers. Few realize that no place is further than seventy miles from the sea. Unique, perhaps, was the island of Lewis in the Outer Hebrides and in particular the 'Viking' village of North Tolsta, situated on its north-east coast. With just over a hundred houses it was probably the 'heaviest' seafaring village in Britain. Contained in the Roll of Honour, recently published by the Tolsta Community Association, are some 330 names (men and women). The great majority of these belong to men who were already serving in the Merchant Navy or who were Naval Reservists called up for duty before war was declared. Known the world over as among the finest seamen, many saw service in both world wars – in armed merchant cruisers, in armed trawlers, rescue ships, merchantmen loaded to their 'marks' with food and ammunition, tankers and troopships. Many of the vessels on which they served are mentioned in the pages that follow. Herein lies a hope that they and the thousands like them will not be forgotten.

Never a large service in comparison with the armed services, the Merchant Navy numbered some 185,000 with an estimated 144,000 at sea at any given date. This figure comprised around 4,500 masters, 13,000 deck officers, 20,000 engineers, 120,000 seamen, with the remainder made up of radio officers, stewards, cooks, pursers and auxiliary staff.

The inter-war years, even in a world dominated by maritime trade, had not been easy for the British seafarer. After 1928 the slump swept across the Atlantic from the United States with all the power of a storm-force wind. By 1932 there were 40,000 seamen unemployed, and a total of 1,663,000 tons of British shipping was laid up. Freight rates dropped from one all-time low to another. It was in this situation with rumours of war rumbling across the continent of Europe, that preparations for the war at sea were made.

As early as 1936 official discussions took place with the leading shipowners to make certain that their vessels were suitably prepared; the intention was to strengthen many of them so that guns could be mounted aft as part of a national policy. Following the adoption in the same year of the naval rearmament programme, those merchantmen built from 1937 onwards had stiffening incorporated into the stern with the plates and poop-deck strengthened as a result. Later, in June 1939, a special section of the Trade Division was formed to co-ordinate imports and exports and to organize the arming of the whole fleet.

From August 1937 the Admiralty commenced training courses in gunnery for Merchant Navy deck officers. By January 1939, when courses were instituted for ratings, some 60 per cent of deck officers had completed the course. During this period (1938) ration books covering essential foodstuffs were printed and were stored at convenient points throughout Britain. The fate of the large food ships, particularly those trading to Australasia and South America, was to become closely associated with food rationing throughout the war.

In the second month of the war the Ministry of Shipping was established and in November 1939, Sir Vernon Thomson, Chairman of the Union Castle company, was appointed Principal Shipping Adviser and Controller of Commercial Shipping, a full-time appointment which he was to hold until April 1946. His close co-operation and consultation with all the shipowners, the unions and the Shipping Federation ensured the smooth running of an operation which relied upon close harmony with many Government departments.

From the very first day of the war Germany was intent on disrupting Britain's trade and commerce. In spite of the fact that Adolf Hitler later changed his priorities somewhat in favour of the land war, he agreed with Grand-Admiral Dönitz from the outset that there was every possibility that the United Kingdom could be defeated by cutting her overseas supply lines. In a directive to the German forces in February 1941 Hitler set out his aims to concentrate all weapons of air and sea against imports to Britain as well as to hold down the aircraft industry. 'For this purpose it will be necessary', he continued,

   a.   To destroy the most important English harbours for imports, particularly port installations and ships lying in them or building.

b. To attack shipping, especially when homeward bound, by all methods. The sinking of mechantmen is more important than attacking enemy warships.

c. Systematically, to destroy the key points of the aircraft industry, including factories producing anti-aircraft equipment and explosives.

Some 7,000 British seamen were killed by enemy action during 1941 prior to the bombing of Pearl Harbor, which brought the United States into the war; the following year the total was nearly 8,000. Total Allied and Neutral merchantmen casualties for the war reached 62,933 (see Appendix XX). Of those employed under the British Register, approximately 24,000 appear on the Tower Hill Memorial in London; the remainder appear on memorials at Calcutta, Bombay, Halifax (Nova Scotia), and in Australia, New Zealand, Singapore and Hong Kong; a small number appear in the grave registers of the Commonwealth War Graves Commission. Their ships, even though they may still lie at the bottom of the sea, remain listed as war graves by Act of Parliament.

Because of the tremendous strides that have been made during the post-war years in the construction of merchantmen, little of it in United Kingdom shipyards, it is now difficult to believe that in 1939 Britain entered the Second World War with some 27 per cent of world tonnage and a fleet of 6,843 vessels (tonnage: 17,675,404). The majority of these, however, were coal-burners; only 972 were modern motorships, whilst half of the entire fleet was over twenty years old.

Whilst great progress has been made in the design, construction and propulsion of world tonnage, it is important to remember the tragedy which has befallen the British Merchant Navy; likewise the United States Mercantile Marine. A necessity in time of war, a source of independence and strength in time of peace, the British merchant fleet is reduced, at the time of writing, to some 274 vessels of 3.4 million tons, less than 2 per cent of world tonnage. Qualified British seafarers have slumped to less than 5,000. In this uncertain violent world every effort must be made to reverse the present trend.

Experiences during the Falklands War and Operation 'Desert Storm' in the Arabian Gulf have shown how important merchantmen are even given the presence of wide-bodied jet aircraft. Furthermore, the marine losses of recent years indicate that foreign-registered ships, many under the command of and crewed by foreign nationals, are far more vulnerable than those which are British registered and completely manned by British qualified seamen. Whilst successive British governments continue to give lip service to the need for an adequate Merchant fleet and personnel, plus a reserve for war and worldwide emergencies, little has been achieved.

With the increasing size of ships, particularly of tankers, and with the marked reduction in the time necessary to load and discharge cargoes as against the time at sea, it means that the loss of a single ship today is roughly equivalent to the loss of a whole medium-sized convoy of World War II. We have been fortunate that in spite of a troubled post-war period, no large-scale war has broken out in which surface raiders and submarines have been involved.

The tanker situation was brought to the fore during the Falklands War of 1982. After a desperate 'scanning' of the seas and ports, eight British-owned tankers, each of 15,640 tons displacement, were called up. Also requisitioned were Cunard's *Queen Elizabeth II* and P & O's *Canberra* and *Uganda*, the latter a passenger liner ex schools ship converted to a hospital ship. In total thirty-six merchantmen, including fourteen tankers, five fishing trawlers and four ocean tugs, were taken over for war duty. The additional six tankers ranged from the 33,330 ton-displacement *Alvega*, owned by Finance for Shipping Ltd, to the 15,560-ton *Anco Charger*, owned jointly by P & O and Ocean Transport and Trading. Only twenty-three of the thirty-six vessels were wholly British-owned.

Once again British Merchant Navy officers and seamen had the opportunity to confirm their professionalism. During the conflict, Cunard's *Atlantic Conveyer* was sunk by an air-launched Exocet missile with the loss of twelve men. Her cargo included all but one of the available Chinook heavy-lift helicopters. Also engaged were five Royal Fleet Auxiliary tankers and three support vessels; many of their seamen were Merchant-Navy trained.

By the time the Gulf War erupted in 1991, the shipping situation had deteriorated still further. Out of 112 merchantmen chartered from merchant fleets only five were British-registered. Further, extremely high rates were paid by the British Government for chartering suitable tonnage. The 28 January issue of the United States journal *Fortune* reported that at the peak in early January, as many as 100 cargo and passenger aircraft were arriving at Saudi Arabian airfields daily; meanwhile, 130 transport ships were steaming towards the Gulf. The supplies totalled 1.6 million tons; four times as many ton-miles of people and material were moved in one-third as much time as during the Berlin airlift of 1948. As 95 per cent of supplies were carried by sea to Saudi Arabia (95 per cent of personnel by aircraft), it will be seen that shipping played an important part in the operation. It was reported at the time that US shipping resources were so thin that foreign help was heavily relied upon. Their own share of the world's fleet was reduced from 26 per cent in 1950 to 3 per cent in 1991.

In writing this book, a story which is as glorious as any in the annals of the sea, it has been impossible not to be conscious of those of the Senior Service who were lost, and also those of the enemy, in particular those of

Germany's U-boat crews, who paid the supreme sacrifice. In the early years, they had the upper hand at sea. Technical advances on the Allied side, however, meant a dramatic reversal of fortunes. The life expectancy of a German submariner was cut to fifty days; out of 820 U-boats, 718 were destroyed in action; the death toll was some 32,000 out of a total sea-going personnel of 39,000.

Casualties in the Royal Navy, the Senior Service of the realm, amounted to 50,758 men killed, 820 missing and 14,663 wounded.

JOHN SLADER
Abergavenny
April 1993

Unless otherwise indicated, all merchantmen mentioned are British-flag; all tonnages are gross-registered (grt).

1   The Price of Defeat

Winston Churchill described Dunkirk as the greatest military disaster in British history. Some regard it as the greatest escape story in history, one of the most extraordinary exercises in survival ever undertaken. One thing is certain. The evacuation which took place at Dunkirk during that last week of May, and its aftermath, brought the British nation to the brink of defeat.

During that spring of 1940, Winston Churchill faced a crisis within days of his coming to power. After eight months of calm in Europe came the storm. The enemy swept everything before them. First Denmark and Norway, then on 10 May they crossed the frontiers of the Netherlands, Belgium, Luxembourg and then France. Within days much of the British army lay trapped in a triangle based upon Gravelines and Zeebrugge. The remainder fled to Normandy and Brittany, some even to the Atlantic ports of western France.

There was no such calm at sea; no 'phoney war'. Britain's merchant fleet had been in the front line from the first day. The Donaldson liner *Athenia*, sunk in the Atlantic less than nine hours after the declaration (3 September 1939), was followed by an assortment of merchant ships, many of them in convoy. Tankers and tramp steamers, cargo liners and coasters – sunk by U-boats and by dive bombers, surface raiders and underwater mines. Over a period of eight months, 163 British-flag vessels had been sunk.

Masterminded by Vice-Admiral Ramsay from deep in the cliffs of Dover Castle, Operation 'Dynamo', the evacuation from Dunkirk, called for an armada of small ships. The number of merchantmen available was relatively small. A considerable proportion of the fleet was engaged upon their worldwide trade, even though voyages and cargoes carried were made upon orders issued by the Ministry of Shipping. In this already tragic week, the steamship *Sheaf Mead* and the tanker *Telena* were sunk by *U-37* in the North Atlantic, and the steamships *Orangemoor* and *Stanhall* by *U-101* off the coast of Brittany. British forces in Norway were in great peril. In Norwegian waters was the enemy battle cruiser *Admiral Hipper*. In the South Atlantic, German surface raiders were searching for food vessels homeward bound without escort.

21

A number of ships in home waters were either unsuited to the needs of the operation or were in port, loading or discharging cargo. Additionally there were many 'shallows' in the approaches to Dunkirk as well as the ever-increasing possibility of air attack. Nevertheless, from the 1,400 vessels of all types which took part, 216 merchant ships were engaged. In addition there were 230 trawlers, fifty-six Naval destroyers and, proudly flying the Red Ensign, the 'little ships' called up from the estuaries and creeks of the North Sea and Channel coasts. From the Port of London, motor lifeboats lowered into the docks from the merchantmen that lay there.

As late as 19 May the Merchant Navy took part in reinforcing the garrison at Calais. On that day the *Royal Daffodil* carried the Second Battalion of the 60th Rifles, whilst the Irish Guards were brought to Boulogne by the veteran *Queen of the Channel*. That same day both vessels returned to Dover crammed to the gunwales with nurses and wounded. Two days later enemy bombers launched particularly savage attacks on the port area of Dieppe and in the vicinity of Boulogne and Calais. Two Southern Railway cross-Channel ferries, the *Brighton* and the *Maid of Kent*, were sunk at Dieppe. Both were acting as hospital ships bringing out wounded troops. The loss of life was heavy. Monday, 27 May became known as 'Bloody Monday' as the casualties rose. Men stood helplessly around the harbour of Dunkirk and on the nearby beaches awaiting transport. Overhead the activity of the Luftwaffe increased. Ill-equipped RAF fighters faced great danger as they engaged the enemy. Yet over ten days of Operation 'Dynamo' 101 patrols were made, totalling 4,822 flying hours. An estimated 262 enemy aircraft were destroyed. Ships' guns from the beaches accounted for a further thirty-five.

The Royal Navy lost a total of nine destroyers, five armed trawlers, five armed drifters, together with the armed boarding vessel *King Orry*. The destroyers that tasted defeat, some with troops already embarked, were HMS *Grenade* and *Wessex*. HMS *Basilisk, Havant* and *Keith* were lost in the Luftwaffe attack of 1 June when the German Air Force claimed a total of thirty-one ships of various types. The First World War-vintage HMS *Valentine* was bombed, grounded and abandoned in the river Schelde. HMS *Wakeful*, which had loaded troops from the beach at Bray-dunes, was sunk by an E-boat. HMS *Grafton*, one of those who went to her aid, was torpedoed by *U-62* and had to be sunk by the destroyer *Ivanhoe*. HMS *Whitley* was badly damaged and beached.

The merchant ship *Dotterel* was commandeered at short notice to bring out British, French and Dutch refugees from Ijmuiden together with the closely guarded Dutch crown jewels. Under cover of darkness but risking aerial bombardment, the 1,385-ton vessel sailed for Harwich (on 7 March 1941 she was sunk by an E-boat in the North Sea). Also from Ijmuiden sailed *Perseus* with part of the Dutch gold reserve, as did *Phrontis* with 900 prisoners of war.

In addition to the Southern Railway cross-Channel ferries sunk in the evacuation of Dieppe, eight of the forty-five troop transports employed at Dunkirk were sunk. A further eight were so badly damaged they had to be withdrawn.

Three vessels owned by the Isle of Man Steam Packet Company were sunk: *Mona's Queen*, when she set off one of the new magnetic mines; *Mona's Isle*, when she cast off from the harbour mole amidst a cascade of bombs. Twenty-three men were killed and sixty wounded. She was further damaged when attacked by enemy coastal guns off Les Hemmes *en route* for Dover. The third vessel, *Fenella*, was loading stretcher cases when she received a direct hit from a screeching Stuka. Many of the 700 men on board were killed, including fifteen of her crew. Moored close by were *Crested Eagle*, a well-known Thames excursion paddle steamer operating as a special anti-aircraft service ship, together with *Golden Eagle* and *Royal Eagle*. Struck by burning debris the latter vessel quickly became an inferno. Her decks were covered with the dead and the dying.

Southern Railways' *Lorina* broke her back when she was dive-bombed. The small motor-coaster *Spinel* was struck repeatedly by bombs and burned for many hours. The *Worthtown*, dive-bombed at dawn, sank before troops had the opportunity to board her. Destroyed by gunfire from shore batteries was the motor-cruiser *Sequacity*. The coaster *Bullfinch* ran herself up the beach so that troops could climb ladders to board her. When floated off on the rising tide she had 1,500 men on board.

The North Wales excursion steamer *St Seiriol* made seven trips to the beaches. An average of 900 men were brought out each time. On one occasion the Red Funnel *Princess Elizabeth*, acting with *Oriole* as a minesweeper, embarked a total of 3,415 troops and brought them safely to Dover. *Royal Daffodil*, bombed and damaged, and *Royal Sovereign* between them rescued some 20,000 men. *Medway Queen* was credited with saving a total of 7,000 during seven trips. All vessels were dangerously overloaded.

The pleasure steamers requisitioned by the Admiralty, which had been hastily converted into minesweepers, suffered grievous losses. P & A Campbell's *Brighton Queen* was shattered by gunfire and abandoned. The heavily loaded *Brighton Belle* drifted over a submerged wreck, and her bottom was torn out. The survivors were rescued by *Medway Queen*. Campbell's *Devonia*, damaged by Stuka bombings, was beached and abandoned. New Medway Steam Packet Company's *Queen of the Channel* was bombed and sunk as she waited for a suitable moment to approach the harbour. 950 soldiers were already aboard. All were crewed by merchant seamen.

The *Gracie Fields* was bombed after embarking 750 troops from the beach at La Panne. With her upper deck engulfed in steam from broken pipes and with her rudder jammed, she was forced to circle endlessly. Two barges were brought alongside to take off her human cargo. *Pangbourne*, already damaged by near misses which had claimed the lives of thirteen men, lifted off the remainder and attempted in vain to tow the *Gracie Fields* back to England.

The Isle of Man pleasure steamer *Tynwald* brought out 7,500 men over five trips to the beaches. The coaster *Yewdale*, with a crew of eleven and 900 troops aboard, limped to Deal after being bombed. With her wheelhouse completely destroyed, her sides holed in several places and steam pipes fractured, she was steered from the poopdeck, her master plotting his course by coastal objects.

Clan MacAlister of Clan Line Steamers, at 6,787 tons the largest vessel of the operation, had been commandeered in the London docks where she was discharging cargo. Now, she was laden with landing craft to assist in the evacuation. Embarking troops at her anchorage, she was bombed by a Junkers 88 aircraft. A third of her crew and many soldiers were either killed by the explosion or burned to death in the fire that followed.

The 689-ton *Abukir*, with a complement of some 200, sailed from Ostend a few hours before the port was captured. Sunk by a German E-boat she had on board seventy officers, soldiers and airmen of the British mission to the Belgian Army. She also carried some Belgian nuns and a group of British schoolgirls who, only two hours before sailing, had arrived from Bruges after retreating from the advancing Germans. The destroyers *Grenade* and *Codrington* searched for survivors but only twenty-one passengers and five of her crew were found. They included Captain Woolfenden, Master of the *Abukir*, who was awarded the MBE and Lloyds War Medal for his courage and spirit during the attack. For six hours he endured the cold waters of the North Sea before rescue came.

The steamer *Scotia* (London, Midland & Scottish Railway), *en route* for Dover with some 2,000 French soldiers aboard, was savagely attacked by twelve dive-bombers. Whilst the steamer was sinking by the stern, the survivors clambered over the bow onto the deck of HMS *Esk*. As the *Scotia* broke up it could be seen that her superstructure as well as her lifeboats had been destroyed. Thirty crew and over 300 French troops perished.

The following day (2 June), close to where the *Scotia* had found her grave, sank Southern Railway's *Paris*. Coming from out of the sun, the Stuka dive-bomber, machine-guns firing, dropped two bombs in quick succession. The first opening up her port side amidships, the second went down the after-cross bunker trunkway and exploded deep down, blowing out the ship's side to starboard and killing those in the engine room.

The whole ship shivered and trembled violently, taking a list to starboard of fifteen degrees. The forestay and foretopmast stay were carried away and the foremast shook and swung aft. Two more bombs followed, falling into the sea close by and blasting away the propeller. This was high out of the water by now, with the bow churning beneath the water, though the ship was still making headway. The attack, from sighting the aircraft to the survivors' abandoning ship, lasted less than one minute – then, she heeled over and was gone.

The 'little ships' famous action and the fact that the sea was calm were 'the miracles' of Dunkirk. Taking part in the crusade were 700 'little ships', of which 100 perished. Few of their owners accompanied what were, in many cases, precious possessions, having been taken over, commandeered and manned by the Senior Service.

The four services had ensured the rescue of 'the flower' of the British Army from the clutches of the enemy – 338,226 men out of an army of nearly 500,000 were brought out. Sixty-five thousand died before reaching the beaches. Embarrassed and dejected the survivors came home.

Although Dunkirk at the height of its glory gave the impression to many of a magnificent improvisation, the evacuation was at root an operation skilfully planned by the Royal and Merchant Navies. Added protection from the air given by pilots of the Royal Air Force was complemented by daring amateurs bringing up fine support in a great variety of vessels.

With the withdrawal complete, King George VI sent a historic message to the Prime Minister:

I wish to express my admiration of the outstanding skill and bravery shown by the three Services and the Merchant Navy in the evacuation of the British Expeditionary Force from Northern France. So difficult an operation was only made possible by brilliant leadership and an indomitable spirit among all ranks of the Forces. The measure of success – greater than we had dared to hope was due to the unfailing support of the Royal Air Force, and in the final stages the tireless effort of naval units of every kind.

Suddenly, with rumours of an imminent invasion, there was a news blackout. Radio and newspapers were unable to tell the public much about the continuing disaster which was taking place from Narvik in the north to Saint Jean du Luz in the south.

Following the carnage of Dunkirk came the evacuation of Norway, principally from Narvik and Harsted. Over five nights (5–10 June) 25,000 men were brought out along with some of their equipment.

Many of these Army reinforcements had been landed less than three weeks earlier in an effort to assist the Norwegians and stem the advance of the enemy. Ship losses included the aircraft carrier *Glorious*, the destroyers *Acasta* and *Ardent* and the Orient liner *Orama*. Returning to England empty, and surplus to requirements, she was sunk by the cruiser *Admiral Hipper* and the destroyer *Lody*. Nineteen crew were killed and 280, including her master, Captain Sherburne, were taken prisoner.

Many well-known ships of the fleet were called up for the evacuation, including *Atlantis*, *Arandora Star*, *Duchess of York*, *Franconia*, *Georgic*, *Lancastria*, *Monarch of Bermuda*, *Ormonde* and *Oronsay*. Also employed were the Polish *Batory* and *Sobieski*. In great secrecy King Haakon and his Government arrived in London, and made an agreement which ensured that the Norwegian Merchant Navy, with its many modern oil tankers, would forthwith ply the oceans of the world in the cause of freedom.

The evacuation resumed at Le Havre on 9 June when over 11,000 British troops were rescued. The process was to be repeated at the numerous ports along the French coast to the Spanish frontier. On the South Coast of France efforts were being made to extract some Free French servicemen who were intent on reaching the United Kingdom to serve alongside British forces. Unfortunately this resulted in the Orient liner *Orford* being bombed and set on fire between Marseilles and Toulon. She became a total loss.

Employed at Le Havre were nine personnel carriers led by HMS *Codrington*. They included the Channel steamer *Lairds Isle*, the *Amsterdam*, *Brittany*, *Lady of Mann*, *St Briac*, *St Seiriol*, *Tynwald* and *Vienna*. The London and Northeastern Railway's *Bruges* took a direct hit during a bombing attack and had to be abandoned. Among six destroyers protecting the coastline to seaward, HMS *Bulldog* and *Boadicea* were damaged during an air raid. HMS *Ambuscade* was severely damaged by gunfire from the shore as she attempted to assist the Canadian frigates *Restigouch* and *St Laurent*, which were on patrol.

A further withdrawal was proposed from the beaches near Saint-Valery en Caux, when sixty-seven ships and small craft assembled for a Dunkirk-like operation. Fog doomed the operation from the start, however, and apart from some wounded taken off by HMS *Broke* and *Gardenia*, thousands of troops were stranded and became prisoners of war.

There now commenced the 'big ship' evacuation, which employed many large passenger ships and cruise liners. Some of them had just returned from Norway and made a quick turnaround in the Clyde and the Mersey. An estimated 140,000 members of the British armed forces were retreating westward towards Brittany and the Biscay ports. On 15

June evacuation took place from Cherbourg, three days before the enemy entered the port: 30,630 were brought out.

Operation 'Aerial' then looked westward to Saint-Malo and Brest. At Saint Malo thirty-five vessels assembled, including many cross-Channel ferries such as *Autocarrier, Biarritz, Deal,* the hospital ship *St Andrew, Princess Maud* and the Belgian vessels *Princess Marie-Jose* and *Prince Baudouin.* The total number of troops evacuated was 21,474.

At Brest a large-scale operation was mounted. Transports including the 27,000-ton liner *Georgic,* the *Arandora Star, Franconia, Orontes, Otranto* and *Strathaird* were brought in. Several Alfred Holt ships with heavy-lift facilities were in evidence. They included *Bellerophon, Euryades* and *Lycaon,* which had first been engaged in transporting the British Expeditionary Force to France some eight months before. These three vessels had also been called up for the evacuation from Narvik.

So fast was the German advance that when Cunard's *Lancastria* arrived she was directed to Quiberon Bay where she was joined by the *Georgic* and *Oronsay, Batory, Duchess of York, Franconia* and *Sobieski.* A total of 32,584 troops, including 6,500 on board P & O's *Strathaird* alone, were embarked at Brest. She also carried many civilians, 200 cadets from the military school at Brest, gold from British banks in Paris, some Gaullist leaders and even pet dogs.

Whilst all this activity was taking place, with aircraft cover withdrawn so as to protect the English Channel beaches, a decision was made to evacuate all men of military age, women and children from the Channel Islands. During the middle of the month a massive movement of merchantmen took place. Thirty-one sailed from Jersey on 20/21 June, a further thirty from Guernsey and five from Alderney. Some 22,000 Channel Islanders were brought out without casualty. By the end of the month the islands were occupied. For five long years they lay in enemy hands.

The sinking of the French liner *Champlain* by a magnetic mine on 17 June at La Pallice roads (four days later she was torpedoed by *U-65* as she lay on the sea bottom) was overshadowed by the loss of the 16,243-ton *Lancastria* off Saint-Nazaire. This was to become the greatest single shipping casualty of the whole war. In readiness to sail, she had on board between 5,000 and 6,000 service personnel – the exact number was never known. Attacked by Dornier DO17 aircraft on 17 June, the ship was struck by a bomb where a large Air Force contingent had been billeted. Taking a strong list she rolled on her portside a minute later, revealing a gaping hole through which 1,600 tons of fuel oil freely flowed.

Within twenty minutes *Lancastria* sank. Over 3,000 servicemen and many of her crew were lost. Captain Sharp, who later in the war lost his life when the Cunard White Star liner *Laconia* was sunk, swam for some four hours before being rescued. Only the destroyers *Havelock* and *Highlander* were on hand to represent the senior service, though they worked splendidly to rescue survivors, as did many of the merchantmen present. *Fabian*, *Glenaffaric*, *Oronsay*, *Robert L. Holt*, *Teiresias* and *Ulster Prince* were all available. So, too, was the tanker *Cymbula* which, with the *Glenaffaric* and *Robert L. Holt*, was the last to leave the river anchorage. Alfred Holt's *Teiresias*, loaded with military vehicles and stores, was later lost in an enemy air attack outside the port limits.

The trawler *Cambridgeshire* (Captain Easton) received no less than 1,100 survivors from small boats and rafts. They were transferred to the *John Holt*, whose master, Captain Fuller, successfully sailed his lone ship to Plymouth through enemy minefields. Many of those aboard were seriously wounded.

Enemy bombing raids continued to take place in the Loire estuary. *Oronsay* had been damaged the previous day whilst lying at anchor. Now, bcause of the oil in the water, rescue work was becoming increasingly difficult. *Duchess of York*, *Georgic* and *Sobieski* sailed that same night for Liverpool without interference, but a veil of silence was drawn over the loss of the liner *Lancastria*. For thirty-nine days Churchill withheld any announcement fearing questions in Parliament and disquiet among the British public who assumed that many units of the armed forces were trapped in western France.

The south coast ports of Plymouth and Falmouth were kept busy with the arrival of the 'big ships' as they landed their human cargoes. *Franconia* and *Oronsay* made three trips to the evacuation ports. On that hot summer's morning of 19 June, forty-eight hours after the *Lancastria* disaster, the *John Holt*, *Robert L. Holt* and *Glenaffaric* lay at anchor in Plymouth Sound. Later there arrived *Ulster Prince* and Ellerman's *Fabian* (Captain Hocking), the latter vessel disembarking 800 servicemen. The hospital ship *Somersetshire* also arrived from Saint-Nazaire. Some of the tramp-ship carriers, such as Ropner's *Ainderby* and Walmar Shipping's *Marslew*, after calling at Falmouth for drinking water and for orders, proceeded to Barry and Cardiff. *Glenaffaric* landed some 4,000 soldiers, then sailed for Bordeaux accompanied by *Cyclops* and *Clan Ross*.

Marslew was the last British vessel to leave the quayside at Saint-Nazaire. To illustrate how fast had been the advance of the German Army, she had been discharging Welsh steam coal loaded in Barry when her master, Captain Watkins, was told by his owner's agent to prepare for the embarkation of a British Army contingent and to be prepared to sail at two hours' notice. After taking troops aboard she sailed under aerial bombardment and without escort. Upon receipt of radio instructions *Marslew* spent the night off Belle Isle and the next morning sailed close inshore to a point off Brest.

During the crossing to Falmouth, Captain Watkins had to reduce speed from his vessel's nine knots maximum to allow a convoy of twelve submarines to pass ahead. Their sighting sent a 'shock wave' through all those aboard, but they passed peacefully across the bow. Later it was understood that the submarines were French and engaged in taking gold ingots from the Bank of France to the Vichy French West African port of Dakar. Sadly, only eight months later, the steamship *Marslew* was torpedoed and sunk by *U-95* north-west of Scotland with the loss of Captain Watkins and twelve of his crew.

The evacuation continued from Bordeaux and from Le Verdon where the cruiser *Arethusa* and the cargo liners *Madura, Nalon* and *Nariva* brought out many thousands of servicemen and refugees. P & O's newest ship, the *Ettrick*, had been specially built to serve as a 'trooper' for the armed forces. Arriving at Saint-Jean du Luz, she was joined by *Cyclops, Glenaffaric* and the overworked *Arandora Star*, whose crew was exhausted. The *Clan Ross* had returned to the United Kingdom after being bombed and damaged by the Luftwaffe whilst lying off Bayonne awaiting instructions. On 22 June, the day that France fell, *Ettrick* embarked 2,000 Polish, French and British as well as King Zog and his family from Albania.

From the Channel Islands and the Biscay ports a total of over 210,000 servicemen were brought out, as well as several thousand civilians, 2,292 military vehicles, 310 guns and 1,800 tons of stores. The Royal and Merchant Navies had engineered a momentous combined operation as great as any in the long history of the maritime services. Without close co-operation nothing would have stopped the enemy from sealing the ports and coastline and from inflicting much higher casualties. A second military disaster like that of Dunkirk was avoided. Notwithstanding the *Lancastria* tragedy, Operation 'Aerial' far exceeded the most optimistic expectations.

Sea power had saved Britain from the worst consequences of defeat on land, by evacuating an army under heavy attack from the air. With France forced into surrender, the new German 'empire' stretched from the North Cape of Norway to Saint-Jean du Luz, some 3,000 miles of coastline. Never in the long history of European wars had the British Isles faced such a situation. On 2 July, Hitler ordered the planning of the invasion. Only the Dover Straits stood between him and his proposed conquest.

Already across the Atlantic the United States government contemplated annexing British colonies in the Western hemisphere to keep them out of Nazi hands. Would sea power save Britain from invasion and fire the imagination of the free world? Since the year 1066 Britain had stood invincible against European marauders. Britain stood alone against the might of Germany.

At this moment came the clarion call from Prime Minister Churchill:

We shall defend our Islands whatever the cost may be. We shall fight on the beaches, we shall fight on the landing grounds. We shall fight in the fields and in the streets. We shall fight in the hills. We shall never surrender. Britain will fight on, if necessary for years, if necessary alone. We shall go back.

Within days it became increasingly clear that the fear of Britain's fighting alone was, indeed, justified. When the Italians declared their support for Germany, the submarine fleet, flying the Italian tricolour, sailed for ports in Western France, to Bordeaux and Saint-Nazaire. There, underwater craft with names such as *Archimède, Barbarigo, Cappellini, Da Vinci, Malaspina* and *Veniero* came to be based.

During the next twelve months Britain came under siege; this was the price of avoiding defeat. Plans were made for the defence of the country. The Government commandeered large mansions in Wales in case evacuation from London became necessary. Beaches and possible landing sites for gliders along the Channel coast were obstructed. Concrete tank traps were laid. The Home Guard, affectionately known as 'Dad's Army', was formed. A great security screen was thrown around the liners *Batory, Sobieski* and *Monarch of Bermuda* which were lying at anchor off Greenock in the Clyde estuary. On 5 July they sailed in convoy with the battleship *Revenge* and the cruiser *Bonaventure*. They carried £192 million of gold bullion from the Bank of England and arrived in Halifax, Nova Scotia, seven days later.

Those close to the War Cabinet became concerned at what the future held. There was talk in Whitehall that in the event of occupation, the Government in exile would sit in Ottawa. Meanwhile, intelligence had realized that the new highly secret Merchant Navy Code had been unravelled by German forces at Bergen in Norway. Sea war radio intelligence was yet to come, however. Enemy surface raiders were already scoring notable successes in the Atlantic and Indian Oceans, and memories of the armoured cruiser *Admiral Graf Spee* (See Chapter 5), with her destruction of nine merchantmen, were still fresh in the minds of the majority of the British public.

Both Hitler and Grand-Admiral Dönitz were confident that they could sever the lifeline without which the island fortress of Britain could not hope to survive. Already, in January 1940, food rationing had been introduced. As early as July the German construction industry (the Todt organization) completed a new U-boat base at Lorient on the French Atlantic coast. Submarines were protected by pens of solid reinforced concrete sixteen feet thick. On 7 July *U-30* was the first to enter the port for refuelling and rearming prior to attacking homeward-bound convoy SL38.

By August Brest and La Pallice were operational U-boat bases and Grand-Admiral Dönitz had converted the château at Kernével outside Lorient on the north bank of the river Blavet as his command post. Later Saint-Nazaire, Le Baule and Bordeaux also became U-boat bases. Six U-boats sank thirty-one Allied ships totalling 156,420 tons between 9 June and 2 July. No fewer than nineteen boats were operating simultaneously.

Since September 1939 outward ocean convoys had been running down-Channel from the Thames to a point some 200 miles west of Ushant, where the ships bound across the North Atlantic separated from those destined for Gibraltar and more southerly ports. During the first nine months of the war these convoys ran smoothly, with little interference from the enemy. But in the summer of 1940, when the Germans gained possession of air and naval bases on the coasts of the Low Countries and France, the situation changed drastically in the enemy's favour. Heavy air and torpedo-boat attacks began to be launched against traffic passing slowly through the narrow seas.

June 1940 heralded the start of the German E-boat campaign. These powerful torpedo boats were capable of 40 knots and carried a heavy punch in the way of armament. They were to harass coastal shipping even to the end of the war. The following month a total of forty Allied ships (75,698 tons) were sunk in the Channel by air and E-boat attacks. Two outward-bound convoys, OA177 (twenty-two ships) and OA178 (fourteen ships) were particularly badly hit. Again, the problem was lack of air cover; off Portland the Junkers 87 aircraft, based at airfields in Brittany, were coming in waves of six at a time. The situation annoyed Churchill, who ordered the Channel convoys to be provided with a six aeroplane escort, though rarely was such a luxury available.

The coastal convoys were heavily attacked as they negotiated 'Hellfire Corner', that part of the Straits of Dover in range of enemy guns mounted at Sangatte between Calais and Boulogne. It was not only long-range guns, however, but German aircraft and E-boats. Convoy CW8 was met by ninety aircraft, Junker 87s and Junker 88s, during the last week of July. This was precisely the time when RAF fighter aircraft were being held back for what was thought would be the crisis, the invasion force of landing craft and barges. The Battle of Britain was yet to come.

Of the twenty-one colliers and coasters which sailed westward during 'Black Thursday' of that week only eleven passed Dungeness on the Kent coast and of these, only two reached their destination. So heavy and so continuous was the dive-bombing that records do not reveal just how many attacks were made. Two days later the 'Dover' destroyers lost their flotilla leader HMS *Codrington*, and HMS *Walpole* limped back to port badly damaged. Dover, as a base for anti-invasion destroyers, was abandoned. The Luftwaffe and the E-boats appeared to have cleared the way for the Germany Army. Dover itself was bombed on 29 July. For ten days a breathless silence settled upon the invasion coast. The coastal convoys were abandoned.

The men of the coasters and colliers lay waiting at anchor off Southend. They lay low in the water, loaded with flour and sugar, coal and coke from the north-east ports. Twenty-five of them comprised convoy CW9. They were to become part of combined operations, a naval operation to force 'the narrow sea', the Dover Straits. The seamen, many of them Geordies from the Tyne, were anxious to be on the move. The South Coast was dependent upon sea-borne coal. Over 40,000 tons were needed each week. It was the custom for such cargoes as flour and sugar to be discharged from foreign-going vessels in the Port of London there to be transhipped for ports such as Shoreham, Portsmouth, Weymouth and Plymouth. Without fuel the supply of electricity would be cut and essential factories would be unable to maintain full production.

However, the coasters and the colliers were not being sunk because of the cargo they carried, but as a tactical move in the air battle between the Luftwaffe and RAF Fighter Command taking place in the skies above. The air battles which took place when convoy CW9 sailed were a preliminary to the Battle of Britain – which, in turn, was to be a preliminary to Operation 'Sealion', the invasion of Britain.

Convoy CW9 sailed on the afternoon of 7 August and was scheduled to pass Dover at midnight. The 'Coal-Scuttle Brigade', as these convoys became known, crept beneath the white cliffs of Dover towards the shelter of the Isle of Wight. A destroyer escort and a squadron of Hurricane fighter aircraft in a Sussex airfield were standing by. Then suddenly from out of the black night came the snarl of high-powered engines, the E-boats screamed across the water at twenty-five knots, firing their deadly torpedoes at the ships and sending the convoy scattering. At daybreak the steamship *Holme Force* and the motorship *Fife Coast* lay at the bottom of the Channel. In struggling to avoid a torpedo, the steamship *Ouse* sank when she collided with the *Rye*, which though damaged was still afloat. As the remaining twenty-one vessels approached Spithead the Junker 87s came screaming through the cloud cover having fought their way through the scrambled RAF Hurricanes. Meeting the fire of the gunners aboard the escorts and the small ships the enemy aircraft caused great havoc. The colliers *Ajax Coquetdale* and *Empire Crusader* were sunk, and thirteen vessels were damaged by near misses.

The following week saw further attacks on Channel convoys as well as on Dover and Portland. The losses on the convoys were amounting to one ship sunk or damaged beyond repair out of every three that sailed.

On 12 August the Battle of Britain began. The convoys were cancelled and ships from the East Coast ports were routed to Methil in the Firth of Forth and around the north of Scotland, to Loch Ewe, Oban and the Clyde estuary. Could the south coast exist without the 'Coal Scuttle Brigade'? The overburdened railway system, the London Northeastern Railway and the Southern Railway, came to the rescue.

The U-boats based from Narvik in the North to Bordeaux in the South were led by peacetime underwater aces – 'the professionals' – who took command in the deep sea of the North Atlantic. Fritz Julius Lemp, at twenty-six years of age in command of *U-30* had torpedoed *Athenia* on the first day of the conflict. Others included Engelbert Endress, aged twenty-nine in *U-46*; Gunter Prien, the 'old fox', in *U-47*; and Herbert Schultze in *U-48*. The autumn of 1940 became the heyday of the individual U-boat aces, the 'grey wolves' as the enemy propaganda machine called them. Other successful commanders were Otto Kretschmer, known as 'the tonnage king', in *U-99*; Joachim Schephe of *U-100*; and Fritz Frauenheim of *U-101*.

The danger posed by German minelaying, which included the laying of magnetic and acoustic mines, dated from as early as October 1939, seven months before Dunkirk. During that time destroyers and U-boats carried out some eleven undetected operations against North Sea shipping. Mines were also parachuted from Heinkel 59 naval seaplanes. The attacks were aimed to cripple the East Coast ports concentrated on the Tyne, Humber and Thames estuaries, though the area off Cromer, through which North Sea convoys were routed, was also heavily mined.

The magnetic mines, which were triggered when a ship's metal hull passed over them, had a devastating impact upon the river estuaries and coast. Winston Churchill accused the Germans of committing 'an outrage upon the accepted international law. Driven from the gun to the torpedo and from the torpedo to the mine, U-boats have now reached the acme of villainy.' Casualties included HMS *Gipsy*, HMS *Blanche*, the Polish passenger ship *Pilsudski*, the Dutch *Simon Bolivar*, the Japanese liner *Torukumi* and Union Castle's *Dunbar Castle*. By the middle of February sixty-seven merchant ships, three Royal Naval destroyers and six auxiliary naval ships had been sunk by the insidious mines.

The Thames and Mersey mining operations, coupled with the continuing E-boat menace, sent twenty-two merchantmen of 45,685 tons to the seabed in the six months following Dunkirk. At least 300 mines, of which fifty were magnetic, were laid between Southend and the Isle of Sheppey; many were fitted with a $4\frac{1}{2}$-day delayed-actioned fuse and became live simultaneously. On 17 December five ships were sunk. A further five, including the Royal Mail motorship *Araby* (victim of an acoustic mine), were sunk by the end of the year. The War Cabinet and the Admiralty became concerned at the situation lest the East Coast ports should become 'blockaded'.

As Hitler turned his attention eastwards to the Russian frontier, the threat of invasion passed. It was left to the Luftwaffe to convince the nation that they must seek peace with the aggressor. Hitler felt confident that his U-boats and his Air Force, plus the mining activities of the Germany Navy, could blockade Britain into submission. With the U-boats increasing their 'wolf-pack' tactics on Atlantic convoys, the ports bore the brunt of the blitz, particularly London, Liverpool, Hull and Manchester. But the aggressor reckoned without the grit and determination of the British people and of its seamen.

The first fight for survival had been won. Officially lasting sixteen weeks over the skies of southern England, the Battle of Britain was a contest between the Royal Air Force and the German Luftwaffe. It was in that summer of 1940 that Churchill paid his unforgettable tribute to Fighter Command: 'Never in the field of human conflict was so much owed by so many to so few.' The Air Force had won by a narrow margin. Now it became a contest between the ships and the seamen, the dockers, the civil defence, Royal Air Force and the ground anti-aircraft defences against the might of the Luftwaffe. 'The price of defeat' was hard to accept.

The dock area of London was bombed over three successive nights beginning 7 September 1940 and again in Christmas week. Three months later (19/20 March), 370 aircraft laid waste to the port and the surrounding area. On this occasion trade was brought to a complete standstill for over two weeks. The royal group of docks, already crippled because of mines in the river estuary, lay in ruins from which they never really recovered.

In normal peacetime conditions 27 per cent by weight of all Britain's imports came in through the Thames estuary, mainly to the Port of London. Thameshaven was an important oil port: upriver was the site of most of the country's cold storage and entry for more than half of the nation's meat, butter and cheese supplies, imports necessary for the health of the population. The East and South Coast ports accounted for almost 60 per cent of dry cargo imports; in the last quarter of 1940 this dropped to 18 per cent as the merchantmen were switched to the West Coast ports of Merseyside, Clydeside and the Bristol Channel.

During London's September blitz 21,000 tons of shipping was sunk and eighteen vessels of 84,336 tons were damaged. Among those sunk and considered a total loss was Larrinaga's *Minnie de Larrinaga*. Nevertheless after many months of work she was raised from the bed of the dock and sold to the Admiralty, which then towed her to Dover where she became a blockship in February 1941. Larrinaga's, a famous British shipping company, survived into the 1970s and were the last privately owned tramp company operating out of Liverpool. Founded in

1864 by the redoubtable Captain Ramon de Larrinaga, a Basque from Bilbao, it had a colourful history.

Of the five steamers in Victoria Dock only one, the *Duquesa*, was afloat when dawn broke on 9 September. Owned by Houlder Brothers and engaged in the Argentine meat trade she was captured and later sunk by the pocket battleship *Admiral Scheer* (see Chapter 5). Her sister ship *Baronesa*, with general cargo on board, was seriously damaged in the Royal Albert Dock when a bomb fell between the ship's side and the quay. In the West India Dock, Bullard King's *Umtali* fell victim to the bombers on two occasions and received extensive damage. Not until 1942 did she return to service.

The *Glenstrae*, one of the Glen Line fleet owned by Alfred Holt & Company, arrived in the port of London on the first night of the blitz. Passing through the locks in the Royal Albert Dock to berth in the King George V Dock when the raid started, she was hit by a bomb which burst six feet from the port side; another passed through her decks and through No.4 deep tank which was full of copra. An hour later the bomb exploded, causing considerable damage.

Several damaged vessels, *Bennevis, Frumenton* and the cargo liner *Otaio* among them, which had been under repair for many months, were later to succumb to enemy action. *Frumenton* was mined and sunk in the North Sea during March 1942, and *Otaio* was torpedoed and sunk in the North Atlantic by *U-558* less than twelve months after those cruel nights in London. *Bennevis* captured by the Japanese in December 1941 (see Chapter 7), suffered two direct hits from high explosive bombs during the night of 8 September. As one might expect in a home port only a small number of personnel were aboard. The third mate and eight seamen perished aboard the Ben Line steamer. Despite the fact that the vessel was enveloped in flames, Captain Shilton and an able-bodied seaman, the two survivors, together with the help of a few dock police, let go the moorings and secured the merchantman in the middle of the dock by dropping the anchor. Meanwhile fire ravaged the warehouse on the quay from which she had been loading cargo.

Inkosi and *Inanda* were severely damaged by fire, the latter so badly that her owners were unable to bear the capital outlay of repair. Subsequently she was taken over by the Ministry of War Transport, which, after having her superstructure virtually rebuilt, renamed her the *Empire Explorer*. During July 1942 she was torpedoed and sunk by *U-575*. Many merchantmen were in the docks seriously damaged after the March raid. Those seriously damaged were withdrawn from service for over six months. They included *Telesfora de Larrinaga, Nailsea Meadow* and *Lindenhall*. The latter two vessels were later torpedoed and sunk by *U-196* (May 1943) and *U-508* (November 1942).

The emerging importance of the West Coast ports caused the

Luftwaffe to redirect their efforts. The diversion of ships and cargoes, both import and export, brought about a multitude of problems – to the Admiralty Trade Division, the Ministries of War Transport and Supply, and to the Ministry of Food, whose staff were already burdened with food rationing administration. Immediately, in addition to a substantial increase in outward war cargoes, there was an increase of 42 per cent in the dry cargo imports to the West Coast.

A more acute problem was the shortage of warehousing and storage space, particularly open-air space suitable for tanks and the many different types of Army vehicles destined for overseas theatres of war. There was a shortage of labour and equipment for discharging and loading vessels as well as overburdened rail facilities. Of all ports those of the Clyde suffered most, for shipbuilding had to be given every priority and it was difficult to cater for the larger volume. The Clyde estuary had to service the 'troopers' and the many merchantmen assembled for convoy at the 'tail of the bank' anchorage (Gourock). The greater variety of both imports and exports at the docks and quays placed a great strain on facilities. There was a gross lack of shed and storage space and the important rail connections with the South were bad.

To avoid crossing Britain the Luftwaffe utilized the captured airfields of northern and western France; this meant that the greater part of their flight path lay across water. Within six weeks of Dunkirk, Dover, Weymouth, Portland, Plymouth, Falmouth and Cardiff were bombed in daylight. Bristol and Liverpool came under attack in November and December, whilst the first five months of 1941 saw a whole series of night raids upon British west coast ports, together with Hull, still the third largest port of the United Kingdom in terms of volume.

On the west coast, Avonmouth, Cardiff, Glasgow, Manchester, the Merseyside ports of Birkenhead, Liverpool and Stanlow, together with Swansea; the south coast ports of Plymouth, Portsmouth, Southampton; and the port of Belfast in Northern Ireland, with its important shipyard, were all bombed during this period.

Avonmouth and Stanlow were to become two of the most successful oil ports, and became of great significance later in the war. Here tankers discharged their precious cargoes, which had been piped aboard in the Caribbean or at the American refineries. From both ports ran underground oil pipes, ensuring distribution throughout Britain. Both were natural targets for an enemy intent upon crippling the British war economy.

Swansea was another vital west coast oil port with its own refinery and oil tank farm. It was, in addition, a major coal bunkering port, an exporter of anthracite and growing increasingly important for the importation of foodstuffs and raw materials such as iron and manganese ore. It was still a major industrial location involved with the iron and steel, tinplate, aluminium and other metallurgical industries. During 1941/42 many thousands of tons of war materials passed through Swansea docks for the Mediterranean war theatre.

The three consecutive night raids of 19 to 21 February 1941 were particularly vicious, devastating forty-one acres and causing destruction and chaos in the dock area and city centre. Defence against air attack in the Bristol Channel was virtually non-existent. Swansea possessed a mere three heavy anti-aircraft guns compared with London's ninety-two, Coventry's forty-four and Liverpool's sixty-four. The other ports of South Wales fared even worse. Now assuming the status of major war shipping locations with good mainline rail facilities connecting with London and the Midlands, they were choice targets. Barry (coal bunkering and exporting) possessed only one anti-aircraft gun, Newport had six and Cardiff twelve. Most of Wales had no searchlight cover whatsoever.

Merseyside, embracing the ports of Liverpool, Birkenhead, Wallasey, Bootle and Stanlow, bore the brunt of the bombing during that spring. Already magnetic mines in the estuary had sunk five merchantmen, including the *Tacoma City*, off Rock Ferry Light, and the *Ullapool*, close by the Princess Landing Stage.

In February a new headquarters was established at Derby House, Liverpool, for fighting the U-boat war. Admiral Sir Percy Noble was installed as Commander-in-Chief Western Approaches. It was Noble who was responsible for the initiation and defence of Atlantic convoys between 1941 and 1942. Here were elaborate operations rooms and communication networks necessary for fighting the Battle of the Atlantic, which every day threatened the nation as no battle, on land or at sea, had before. Derby House was linked to defence commands including warships, aircraft bases and remote radio stations. More than 400 long-distance private operational circuits covered Britain. Downriver from Bootle's Gladstone Dock operated the Second Support Group of U-boat-killing naval sloops.

Some 21.7 million tons of cargo entered the Mersey river in 1939 and during that year, together with the Thames, accounted for 60 per cent of the nation's trade. It had already become the main gateway to Britain when it assumed the role of the premier convoy port. No fewer than 1,285 convoys arrived in the Mersey during 1939–45. The enemy was conscious of the role it was playing.

The statistics give some idea of its importance as a wartime seaport. Covering 500 acres, the docks and their twenty-nine quays stretched for seven miles, which, at their widest point, were more than half a mile deep. Across the river at Birkenhead stood a further 182 acres of docks and nine miles of quays plus Cammell Laird's shipbuilding and ship repair yard, where many Royal and Merchant Navy vessels were built.

Two months before war was declared, Cunard's *Mauritania* was to sail upon her maiden voyage from the yard. As a troopship she carried more than 350,000 troops and steamed more than 540,000 miles.

Over a period of some fifteen months, Nazi bombers made repeated attempts to destroy the shipyard. During the worst raid a direct hit caused damage to Britain's newest battleship *Prince of Wales*, then in the fitting-out basin. During the Second World War, Cammell Laird built numerous merchant ships and ten Royal Naval vessels. Its repair department dealt with 120 warships, including nine battleships and eleven aircraft carriers, as well as over 2,000 merchantmen. Together with the Gladstone Graving Dock the yard employed some 20,000 workers.

Merseyside's war record is impressive. It outshone every port worldwide. Around 120 million tons of ocean-going shipping, representing an armada of 12,000 ships, each of 10,000 tons, were docked and unloaded, and often repaired, fitted out, loaded and dispatched – all with the utmost speed and urgency. 23 million tons of coastwise shipping was handled, representing 75 million tons of cargo of which 56.5 million tons were vital imports. Some 18.6 million tons of goods were dispatched, mostly war supplies to the battle fronts. More than 4.7 million troops passed through, of whom 1.2 million were American.

From the decks of merchantmen were landed 73,782 aircraft and gliders, some of them later to be reshipped in vessels bound for West Africa and the Middle East. Some 5,513 ships used the graving docks, and many used the oil bunkering facilities at Stanlow and at Ellesmere Port, where the Manchester Ship Canal joined the Mersey. The invasion of North Africa (see Chapter 10) was largely mounted from Birkenhead. The greater part of the munitions, tanks and other supplies were dispatched from its docks.

Speke Airport became a reception and assembly centre for the aircraft being shipped into Liverpool from North America. The processions of such crated or wingless aeroplanes as 'Lightnings', 'Black Widows', 'Thunderbolts' and 'Mustangs' being towed through the city streets from the docks and from Pier Head was a regular wartime scene. At Speke was the Lockheed Overseas Corporation's depot, which became the number one Aircraft Assembly Unit. During the May 1941 blitz week the Merchant Ship Fighter Unit was formed close by.

The 'Fighter Unit' was a highly secret convoy-protection project, whereby fighter aircraft were to be catapulted from the decks of specially equipped merchant ships. Here, during those dark days, hundreds of tests were made using rocket-launched Hurricane aircraft. Many of the aeroplanes were later to be loaded by crane aboard the CAM ships at Liverpool (see Chapter 3). The unit was closed down in September

1943, at which time victory in the Atlantic 'black hole' – that part of the western ocean that up until that time had been without air cover – had been achieved.

During the Merseyside night bombing of Christmas week 1940, ships damaged included such well-known vessels as the *Almeda Star, Eastern Prince, Highland Princess* and *Llangibby Castle*. In the March raid a parachute mine sank the *Myrmidon* in the dock where she was loading. She was later raised and repaired, but remained a particularly unlucky vessel. In June the same year she detonated a magnetic mine upon entering the Mersey. The following December she was attacked off the Butt of Lewis by an enemy aircraft which sprayed her with machine-gun bullets but dropped no bombs. A few days later she collided with a Norwegian ship which had just been launched at Clydebank; both vessels suffered damage. She was finally torpedoed and sunk by *U-506* in September 1942.

Damaged in the March blitz were a total of ten vessels, including Alfred Holt's *Glenartney* and Blue Star's *Imperial Star*, but it was the raids of the first week of May that led to the decimation of Merseyside. For eight successive nights wave after wave of bombers saturated the area with high-explosive and incendiary devices. The ports were closed for over 1,300 hours, and ninety-one ships, excluding Royal Navy vessels, were sunk or seriously damaged within the dock system. Out of 130 deep-sea berths normally available only twelve were usable. Yet by the end of that month, out of 144 berths of all types, ninety-six were again in operation.

The city of Liverpool's outline was altered forever, yet from out of the horror there emerged a major victory in the Battle of Britain. Whilst the May raids were a setback in the conduct of the war at sea, the bustling port and river quickly recovered. The historian John Terraine has said that its recovery was 'a milestone in the Battle of the Atlantic without which it is hard to see how Britain would ever have reached, let alone overcome, the terrible times that lay ahead'.

Winston Churchill realized that if the Merseyside ports became unusable it would not only be a severe setback but a climax to the enemy blockade. The nation's 'larder' was already seriously depleted. Campaigns in North Africa and Europe were already being planned. Could the nation recover? In retrospect it can be seen that the enemy missed a golden opportunity in saturation bombing, as was employed by the Allies in Germany later in the war.

But for the work and leadership of the Civil Defence Services and the skilled salvage work carried out by the Mersey Docks and Harbour Board aided by merchant and Royal Naval crewmen, the result could have been catastrophic. The co-operation of the civilian services ensured a victory of immeasurable value.

It was not only the cost in ships totally lost (39,100 tons) but the greater cost to the war effort of ships damaged (40,400 tons), of ships diverted to other ports (83,600 tons) and the subsequent disorganization to those other ports. Ships delayed in working due to the destruction of wharves and warehouses amounted to 185,000 tons. A tonnage of 66,000 was required to replace lost imports, much of it valuable foodstuffs and raw materials for manufacturing. Several of the merchantmen loading were destined for the Middle East, due to transport equipment and supplies necessary for the British Army and Air Force in North Africa. In the warehouses and upon the quays thousands of tons of military hardware were destroyed or damaged beyond repair.

Over and above the shipping situation, chaos outside the Merseyside dock gates was little better. Railways were paralysed. The telephone system and public transport were non-existent. Some 10,000 dwellings had been destroyed, 184,000 damaged. Fatalities rose to 3,966, with 3,812 seriously injured. A month later, a dark pall of smoke still clung to the air over the port. The smell of smouldering wood and masses of rubble of the devastated city centre buildings, the docks and warehouses, still clung to the nostrils. Army UXB squads were still dealing with the numerous unexploded bombs.

Later during 1941, the monthly average of British vessels, dry cargo of 1,600 tons and over, that were damaged and not in use, rose to 1,450 (1,882 total of British, allied and neutral vessels). This figure was principally due to the Battle of the Atlantic and the bombing of ports in the United Kingdom. The figures for 1942 were similar, that is, 1,472 and 1,935 respectively. The 2.8 million deadweight tons under repair in the spring of 1941 meant a total of 2.8 million tons withdrawn from service. Damaged merchantmen were an item that seriously reduced the carrying capacity of the fleet, and the situation remained thus throughout the Battle of the Atlantic. The Huskisson Dock in Liverpool on the morning of the 4 May 1941 was the scene of utter desolation, a scene reminiscent of a Somme battlefield during the First World War. Few ashore had experienced the detonation of a merchant ship loaded with high explosive. As for the civilian population generally they knew little of such disasters. Censorship in the press and on radio was tight. There was no television.

The *Malakand* and the *Mahout* vessels, owned by T. & J. Brocklebank, had virtually completed loading for the Air Force in the Middle East. By nightfall on 3 May each vessel had about 1,000 tons of high-explosive bombs aboard. Both were hit by a shower of incendiaries and within minutes the whole area was blazing fiercely, the warehouse at the east end of the dock having been obliterated by a parachute mine.

At 2300 hours incendiaries fell again on *Malakand*, setting fire to a small coaster, the *Busiris*, moored next to her. To add fuel to the fire a hydrogen-filled barrage balloon landed on the foredeck of *Malakand*, setting the hatch covers alight. This was followed by two high-explosive bombs, which demolished the warehouse from which the vessels had been loading. Jets of flame roared over the quay. *Malakand* was ablaze from stem to stern. Her master, Captain Kinley, considered scuttling but it was impossible to reach the engine room. Ship's officers joined firemen in putting two or three pumps to work but flames and smoke overcame them.

At 0800 hours the end came. An explosion, followed by a second an hour later, reduced the *Malakand* to a mass of torn and twisted steel on the bottom of the dock. Debris fell over a wide area. *Mahout*, lying close by, was a total loss. Other vessels were damaged and warehouses over a wide area destroyed. The many who spent long hours trying to avert disaster, knowing that every moment could be their last, showed great courage.

The death toll was remarkably light, although Captain Kinley concluded his report to the Admiralty by adding, 'Several men were injured when the explosions took place, myself included, and I regret to have to state that lives were lost.'

During that week, vessels sunk included *Elstree Grange*, *Domino*, the former Danish liner *Europa* and *Tacoma Star*, subsequently raised and repaired. Damaged were *Brittany*, *Baronesa*, *Baron Inchcape*, *Clan MacInnes*, *Cantan Lobos*, *Industria*, *Marton*, *Roxburgh Castle*, *Silversandal*, *Talthybius*, *Trentino* and *Waiwera*. The latter vessel, owned by Shaw Savill & Albion, was raised from the bed of the dock some months later and repaired. Taken up for Middle East munitions service she made more than one run to Malta. She was torpedoed and sunk by *U-754* in the North Atlantic during June 1942.

Baron Inchcape lay partly sunk in Canada Dock with a cargo of grain. It took so long for the salvage men to discharge the cargo that the fumes from the remaining mouldy mass turned the gold braid of the salvage officers' uniforms green. Nearby, the Ben Line steamers *Benlomond* and *Benreoch* were alongside the quay as fully laden sheds filled with inflammable cargo were set on fire. Captain Cuthbertson and Captain Tough were commended for the part they and their crews played in fighting the fires. Shipping offices were laid to waste. Bills of lading, typewriters and office equipment were scattered amongst splintered wood and rubble. The timber yard beneath the overhead railway blazed for a week; a heavy bomb pierced the railway tracks leaving a huge crater in the roadway to the dock.

At the Shell refinery at Stanlow were lying the 'Eagle' oil tankers *San Fabian* and *San Emiliano*. They had been at the mercy of the enemy throughout a particularly difficult Atlantic passage. As part of convoy

HX121 from Halifax, Nova Scotia, they had survived the first daylight wolf-pack attack upon a fully escorted convoy since the summer of 1940. In a daring raid by *U-96*, two motor tankers, the *Caledonia* and the *Oilfield*, along with Port Line's *Port Hardy*, had been sunk. A further modern motor tanker, the *Capulet*, was damaged after being hit by a torpedo from *U-552*.

As the wave of bombers came upriver from the Irish Sea *San Fabian* was hit by a parachute mine. A hole was blown in the main deck. The superstructure and surrounding structures were extensively damaged. *San Emiliano* had to be moved from the jetty when all its pipelines took fire.

Later, as *San Emiliano* was being brought back alongside, the piermaster fell between the tanker and the wharf. One of the deck apprentices (Donald Clarke), although he could not swim jumped over the side. He was able to rescue the piermaster, an act for which the Liverpool Shipwreck and Humane Society gave him their silver medal. He was just one of many who acted in the finest tradition of the service that week. *San Fabian* and *San Emiliano* were both torpedoed and sunk in August 1942 – see Chapter 4.

Because of its strategic position, Merseyside remained unreported, whilst such places as Coventry were given publicity for propaganda purposes. Winston Churchill sent a typically stirring message to the brave people who lived within earshot of the Mersey river – people whom he knew made fine soldiers and superb seamen. 'When I look back on the perils which have been overcome, upon the great mountain waves through which the gallant ship has driven; when I remember all that has gone wrong, and remember all that has gone right, I feel sure we have no need to fear the tempest. Let it roar, let it rage, we shall come through.'

During those anxious days, the 120 acres of docks at Manchester, with its 5½ miles of quays and with its ship canal navigable by vessels of up to 15,000 tons deadweight, became an important port of entry for much of the nation's grain. Like Liverpool the port was centrally situated with good communications to all parts. The giant elevator could accommodate 40,000 tons of grain drawn by suction from the holds of ships at ten to fifteen tons a minute. Here, too, the Luftwaffe concentrated their bombing.

After an interval of fifty years the memory of being beneath the elevator, discharging Canadian wheat shipped in Boston, whilst German aircraft roared overhead dropping their high-explosives indiscriminately, is still vivid. In number 9 dock our deck cargo of green ambulances with white cross motifs had been landed for immediate transport to the blitzed cities. Convoy HX120 had transported the first-priority equipment under the Lease-Lend arrangements recently signed in Washington.

On the North Sea coast, the docks at Hull were on 8 and 9 May turned into an inferno that could be seen fifty miles away. Many warehouses were destroyed and the docks were closed for three weeks. Seriously damaged were the steamships *Dan-y-Bryn* and *Castillian*, and many barges lay wrecked. The town had had forty-nine air-raid alerts, many of them false alarms, since the Battle of Britain began. The bombers returned to the Humber estuary on 29 June (*Silverlaurel* was damaged in the King George Dock) and again during July, long after the rest of the country had been left alone.

Herbert Morrison, writing his memoirs, commiserated with its people for hearing their sufferings reported day after day as those of 'a North-East town'. 'I would say the town that suffered most was Hull,' he wrote, yet Merseysiders and Londoners would disagree. The frequent attacks upon Hull were probably due to the fact that crews on training could be sent to the port; it was easy to find. Kesselring's bomber crews, on the look-out for shipping, would unload on Hull if the seas proved empty or the ships were hidden by bad visibility.

The London raid of 10 May 1941, with a 550 bomber force, was the worst night ever in the capital. There were 1,400 people killed and 2,000 fires; thirty factories and 5,000 houses were destroyed. Fortunately the docks were spared the worst and, in any case, the ocean-going merchantmen were mostly along the west coast.

Towards the end of May, apart from in the port of Hull, there was a lull in the bombing. The reason only became clear on 22 June. On this day Adolf Hitler's 'Operation Barbarossa' was launched. Winston Churchill gave his word 'to give whatever help we can to Russia and the Russian people'. And so commenced another great saga of heroism, endurance and gallantry (see Chapter 4).

'Defeat' led to the closure of the Mediterranean to merchant shipping. Long-haul vessels *en route* for Australasia and the Far East, and ships destined for the North African theatre, and the Arabian Gulf with its oil supplies, were henceforth routed to Freetown, Sierra Leone, and thence via the Cape of Good Hope. For those who undertook this voyage it was a reminder of the great insight of Ferdinand de Lesseps who, eighty-two years before, had formed a company to construct a ship canal connecting the Mediterranean with the Red Sea. Without the Suez Canal the voyage was long and during 1942 and 1943, as we shall see, the South Atlantic and the Indian Ocean could at times be more dangerous than the Mediterranean.

The exception to the long-haul Cape route was granted to those ships engaged upon the relief of Malta. In Chapter 9 I will cover the battles that were fought and the merchantmen and seamen that were lost in the defence of this island. They sailed from Gibraltar in the West and from Alexandria in the East – as glorious a story as any in the annals of

Britain's maritime history.

From the first day of the war, defence of the merchantmen – against aircraft, mines, U-boats, battle cruisers and surface raiders – had been given some sort of priority. But there were many priorities in those days of 'defeat'. Just how and what was achieved is virtually an unknown story. Those who survived the long war, either unscathed or without spectacular adventure, or those whom were sunk and rescued, owe their lives in part to those specialists from the armed services whose work was solely in the defence of ships and their crews. These are the forgotten men of the fourth service and it is only just that half a century later we should remember them and their work.

2   Merchantmen and Defence

Since before the days of Nelson merchantmen had been defensively armed. Defensive armament by tradition was 'abaft the beam'. This meant that merchant ships could, in times of conflict, fire guns broadside and astern but not ahead. During the Second World War this ruling came to be broken. Many of the replacement ships built from 1943 onwards, particularly the 'Liberty' vessels built in North America, were, in addition, armed 'for'ard of the beam'.

Armed forward, the merchantmen served as offensive ships alongside their white-ensign partners. During the latter stage of the war some fourth service vessels flying the red ensign were more heavily armed than certain vessels of the senior service. Such ships lost their civil status and became, to all intents and purposes, warships.

In regard to ships requisitioned by the Ministries of Shipping or War Transport it should be explained that where these were operated by the Ministry's Sea Transport Department or by one of the other Operating Divisions of the Ministry, such vessels continued to serve under the red ensign (or 'red duster' as it has been familiarly known for centuries). Where merchantmen were requisitioned to operate as naval auxiliaries, such as Armed Merchant Cruisers, they were transferred to the Admiralty and flew the white ensign of the senior service.

Many Merchant Navy deck and engineer officers volunteered to remain in vessels requisitioned. In the main these were peacetime passenger and cruise liners and such officers were commissioned into the Royal Naval Reserve; mostly they signed T124 or T124X agreements, pledging themselves to serve under naval command. The Admiralty then brought the crews up to full complement with naval personnel.

From those 'days of defeat', of Dunkirk and the fall of France, there was grave concern for the defence of merchant ships, not only because of daylight air and E-boat attacks on coastal convoys but also because of mines in the shallow waters of the estuaries and the approach channels to the ports. There was also the overwhelming power of the enemy battle cruisers, the surface raiders and, of course, the U-boats.

'This mortal danger to our lifelines gnawed my bowels,' wrote

Churchill, referring to the U-boat menace. It was Churchill's concern and action alone that brought about the recruitment of two sections of the armed services to combat these 'evils'. They were the Royal Navy and the Royal Artillery.

Recruited as Training Development Officer into the Anti-Aircraft Department of the Naval Gunnery School, HMS *Excellent* at Gosport, was Lieutenant John Hamilton, gunnery officer of the 1st Destroyer Flotilla. His ship, HMS *Grenville*, was sunk off the Dutch coast in January 1940 and after a spell in hospital he was plunged head-first with little instruction into the world of DEMS – Defensively Equipped Merchant Ships. In 1942 Lieutenant Hamilton was appointed fleet anti-aircraft officer in the Mediterranean, seeing service with all the Malta convoy operations from Gibraltar. In 1943 as gunnery officer of the battleship HMS *Warspite* he took part in operations for the invasion of Sicily and Italy.

Merchantmen, large and small, needed to be armed with close range anti-aircraft weapons, mainly 20-mm Oerlikon guns and .303-inch machine-guns. This brought with it the requirement to provide facilities for training large numbers of DEMS gunners. Recruited from the ranks of the Royal Navy, they were mainly 'hostilities only' volunteers, called to the colours under the Emergency Powers Act.

To set up anti-aircraft firing ranges at all merchant shipping terminal ports in both the United Kingdom and overseas would have been impracticable. HMS *Excellent* was given the task of providing training in the method of using the open sight fitted to the weapon for engaging aircraft. From the outset anti-aircraft training was given priority. Training in the use of other weapons, such as the Mark 4-inch breech-loading gun, used in the defence against U-boats, came later.

There were three main educational aids in the early days. *The Eyeshooting Pocketbook* was compiled by Lieutenant Hamilton and illustrated by the well-known *Punch* artist Fougasse – a new departure for Government publications. Although written for DEMS trainees the *Pocketbook* was later distributed widely in the Royal Navy. Then came *The Eyeshooting* film, with a script written and delivered by Lieutenant Hamilton; finally, there was the Dome Anti-Aircraft Teacher. (The DEMS 'Pocket Book' would come later.)

The film, widely distributed for use by DEMS and Royal Navy training, was made in conjunction with Technicolor. Animation techniques were combined with live footage from the naval anti-aircraft range at Eastney. The Dome Teacher was the brainchild of Lieutenant Stephens RNVR. As a training device it was exceptionally valuable: the prototype model set up at HMS *Excellent* was so realistic that it attracted the attention of many VIPs, including the King, and Generals Sikorski and de Gaulle. They were set up all over the United Kingdom and at convoy ports and bases in Canada, Australia, Egypt and South Africa.

The 'Teacher' threw the image of a diving aircraft upon a dome-like ceiling and produced the sound of the aircraft's engines. Aim was indicated by a spot of light on the ceiling visible only to the instructor. Admiral Sir Frederic Dreyer made sure that as many Domes as possible came off the production line, so great was the need for this type of training. Later came courses on aircraft and ship recognition. Modern equipment, such as the flash projector, was acquired, and training in instant identification was given by throwing the silhouette on to a screen for as short a time as one fifth of a second.

Admiral Sir Frederic Dreyer, a great gunnery man in his day, was brought back from retirement early in 1941 and made Inspector of Merchant Navy Gunnery. With his high standing in the Navy and particularly in the gunnery world, he had direct access to Winston Churchill. His great drive and experience, his readiness to cut through red tape and his unique position in relation to the Prime Minister, meant that his appointment gave tremendous impetus to DEMS training and the defence of merchantmen. Due to his foresight, merchant ships engaged in the Battle of the Atlantic, whilst equipped with much out-of-date armaments, were manned by many thousands of well-trained gunners.

The old gunnery instructors were men with faith who taught the recruits the art of hose-pipe firing. 'Wait,' they said. 'It will take lots of guts, but don't shoot your stuff while he's circling you. Remember the old saying about shooting when you see the whites of their eyes. Hold your fire until he dives to bomb, until he's 500 yards away. Shoot for the pilot. Spew it right into his face at point-blank range. You can do it if you wait. Let him ride right down your muzzle and his hands will come off the bomb release and onto the joy stick – but fast!'

Admiral Dreyer appointed two gunnery commanders to serve beneath him, one of whom was responsible for interviewing masters or senior officers who had survived sunken ships. This was to ensure that the Admiralty kept continually in touch with German methods of destruction and the effectiveness of counter-measures. This 'feedback' also enabled Merchant Navy officers to recommend certain measures which they knew from experience were necessary. In this way many of the improvements to lifeboats and rafts, to life-saving gear generally, was brought about.

Inspecting officers from the DEMS staff took periodical trips in merchantmen to ensure that standards were being kept up, that naval discipline and dress were being observed and that training in new weapons was being maintained. In 1943 this led to the Department appointing Wrens to carry out some of these duties. They were employed, much to the amusement of some elderly Merchant Navy skippers, as Naval Control Service boarding officers. Their work included boarding merchantmen in harbour, delivering sailing orders, explaining alterations of route and mustering confidential books. They were responsible, too, for 'keeping an eye on the gunners', checking guns, ammunition and armament stores.

An interesting comment on their life was made by the Wrens Director, Dame Vera Laughton Mathews DBE and quoted by John Winton in *Freedom's Battle: Volume One*. Its origin lies in a notice at Officers' Appointments WRNS Headquarters headed, 'Assets Necessary for a Boarding Officer' – perhaps meant in jest but all the same very true. Dame Vera described it as 'a really heavenly job'.

(a) To have been a boat's crew, or some form of maintenance rating working on boats – so that they may know their way about easily and know all the terms of parts of a ship etc.

(b) To have a complete lack of sense of modesty – we see wonderful sights of naked sailors every day as we go round the accommodation.

(c) To be more or less teetotal, to resist continuous offers of drinks.

(d) To be completely impervious to all insults, comments, and compliments from dockers to USA sailors.

(e) Not to mind having perpetually wet feet.

(f) To be more or less elastic and acrobatic and to have a good sense of balance – you should see the ladders and planks we have to climb and walk.

It has been said that, while few Englishmen are born soldiers every one of them is at heart a sailor. The men of the DEMS and those of the Royal Artillery, proved the truth of this. The raw recruit who undertook the course was a seaman gunner after three weeks; after a further five weeks he was a gunlayer, a process that in peacetime would have taken five years. Literally within hours of completing his course he could be drafted to a port where some coal-burning tramp steamer of ageing years lay awaiting the next high tide. Three or four weeks later the ocean convoy, blasted by the tempest and the enemy alike, could land him in North America.

The DEMS 'Pocket Book' (BR 282) gave a little insight as to what was expected of the senior rating 'seconded' for duty aboard a merchantman. Duties included the training of all gunners – both DEMS and Royal Artillery, plus selected members of the Merchant Navy crew. Or as the 'Pocket Book' puts it, 'Training in the use of all the weapons and devices provided by the Admiralty for the defence of the ship when attacked by hostile ships or aircraft.'

He was further responsible for the maintenance of the armament and all naval stores supplied to the master of the ship by the Admiralty; for the welfare and discipline of both Navy and Army personnel serving on board. In addition the 'Pocket Book' served as an instruction to the

Athenia at anchor in the River Mersey prior to sailing, 3 September 1939. At 1945 hours, less than nine hours after Chamberlain had told the nation a state of war existed between Britain and Germany, she was sunk by U-30

The *Belfast Telegraph*'s cameraman's view of a 1939 convoy clearly illustrates the lack of censorship at the time. The merchantmen are still seen in their peacetime colours. The repainting of the fleet in wartime grey took many months

Dummy warships of the Shaw
Savill company. *Centre Pakeha,
Mamari* and *Waimana* as they were
before the war. *Top* as pseudo-
battleships. *Bottom* the *Mamari*
disguised as the aircraft carrier
Hermes

Inverdargle, Trinidad for Avonmouth with aviation spirit, mined off
Lynton, North Devon, 16 January 1940. She detonated one of several
mines laid by U-33 in these waters on 5 November 1939

The 'miracle' of Dunkirk. Many thousands of British servicemen line up on the beaches awaiting transport

Dunkirk – few merchantmen alongside the quay escaped the fury of the Luftwaffe

Units of the British Expeditionary Force being evacuated from Brest.
A total of 32,584 were embarked during early June 1940

The trawler *Cambridgeshire* seen here rescued no less than 1,100
survivors from *Lancastria*, sunk off St Nazaire, 17 June 1940. Between
5,000 and 6,000 service personnel were lost

Defensively armed, merchantmen were equipped with a 4-inch gun seen in the background and an anti-aircraft gun

Nailsea Court seen on arrival at the mouth of the Mersey river, April 1941, is carrying aircraft on deck. They were loaded aboard in Philadelphia. *Nailsea Court* was sunk in March 1943; there were only three survivors

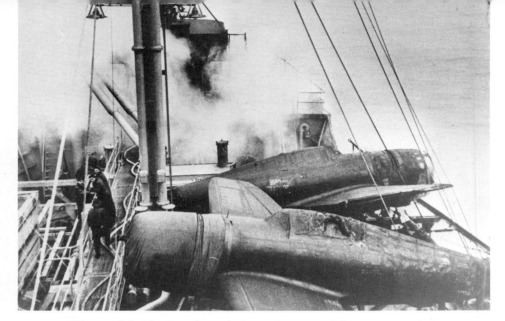

Silversandal with aircraft on deck was just one of the many merchant-men damaged during the disastrous air raids on Liverpool and the river Mersey during the first week of May 1941

Converted as a fighter catapult ship, Elders & Fyffes' twin-screw *Ariguana* carried a Fulmer fighter, one six-inch gun, one twelve-pounder HA gun, two pom-pom anti-aircraft guns, four rocket projectors and two Holman projectors. Seen here with a 1941 convoy she was to be torpedoed and seriously damaged in October of that year

One of the thirty-six vessels designated as catapult armed merchantmen (CAM ships) is seen here being equipped with her sea hurricane
aircraft at Cardiff docks. CAM ships were similarly equipped at
Avonmouth, Clydeside and Liverpool

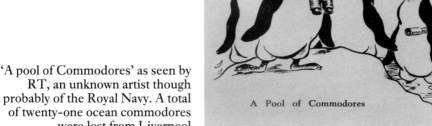

A Pool of Commodores

'A pool of Commodores' as seen by
RT, an unknown artist though
probably of the Royal Navy. A total
of twenty-one ocean commodores
were lost from Liverpool

Above The twin-screw 9,333 ton motorship *Apapa* is bombed by a lone Focke-Wulf aircraft on 15 November 1940. She was the first vessel to be sunk in convoy by the four-engined bombers. *Below* U-97 sailing from Kiel on her first war cruise later attacked convoy OB289. She sunk three British cargo ships and extensively damaged a Norwegian tanker

master mariner to whose ship the gunner had been appointed. It was thus a unique 'command' to smooth the way for the integration of the services aboard a merchantman, something which had not been attempted for over a century.

> Masters of ships, on which DEMS personnel are embarked, are requested to render assistance to their Senior DEMS Naval Rating by encouraging the Chief Engineer and his officers to give any technical assistance which he may require for the efficient maintenance of the ship's armament. Masters are expected to co-operate with the Senior Naval DEMS whenever he requires the services of officers or members of the crew for training in the operation of all the defensive equipment embarked.

As if to emphasize to the captain of a merchantman that he is master of all aboard his domain, the 'pocket book' told him that his ship had the right to resist capture or destruction. It was his responsibility alone for the decision to open fire on an enemy. His Royal Naval superiors told him, however, that experience had shown that he should delegate this responsibility to the senior naval DEMS rating. It does not take a lot of imagination to realize just how a weather-beaten old skipper with over forty years watchkeeping experience reacted to the idea of delegating responsibility to one so junior.

> Every effort must be made to prevent a ship from being captured by a surface raider but if capture is inevitable the raider should be delayed in any way possible to give our Naval forces a better chance of locating her. When opening fire, the national colours [the Red Ensign, first instituted aboard merchantmen in 1707] must be hoisted.

Masters were asked to allocate to the gunners a lifeboat at the stern of the vessel, though few merchantmen were so equipped. This was suggested so that in the event of the main armament being used against a raider or surfaced submarine the boat would be in the immediate vicinity. 'It is the duty of the gun's crew to stand by the gun until the ship is obviously about to sink, or until they receive definite orders to fall out.'

When alteration or repairs to naval equipment was necessary in neutral countries or ports where Admiralty representatives were not available it was essential that invoices were signed by the master and senior naval rating. Reasons for putting the work in hand had to be stated. Such invoices were then countersigned by the British Consul, Lloyds representative or other Government official. None of this admitted Admiralty liability but simply certified that the cost was fair and reasonable.

The heavy responsibility given to the senior naval rating was undertaken after five weeks' instruction in a variety of surface and anti-aircraft weapons. Success on this course was rewarded with promotion from ordinary seaman to able-bodied seaman, with remuneration of fourteen shillings weekly. On embarkation, when he was signed on the ship's articles, an extra sixpence a day was awarded. This was infinitely better than the situation of the Maritime Royal Artillery 'recruit', whose pay was increased by one shilling a month.

To place pay in the right perspective 'board and lodging' must of course be taken into account. It could be said, however, that the Gunners were greatly underpaid. During 1941 Merchant Navy able-bodied seamen were paid ten pounds twelve shillings and sixpence per month, to which was added a war bonus of ten pounds per month.

DEMS, although British at the outset, became an international Allied organization. Training centres were established in Australia, Bombay, Canada, Gibraltar, Port Said and later in the USA. A rating from Melbourne might be brought ashore to the DEMS centre in Halifax, Nova Scotia, for additional training and then be drafted to another ship of any nation for any port. Many tramped the oceans of the world and were away from home for long periods. By 1943, personnel numbered 26,000 men. By the end of the war a total of 2,713 DEMS gunners had given their lives.

The First Lord of the Admiralty, Mr A.V. Alexander, in paying tribute to the Force, said that not less than 100 independently routed merchantmen a year had been saved by the gunners and their equipment. In addition there were the vessels saved in convoy. In total it is estimated that their contribution to defence saved some 1.25 million tons of shipping a year. DEMS personnel earned 841 naval awards, including 263 Distinguished Service Medals (DSMs) and 110 British Empire Medals (BEMs).

The earliest record of soldiers of the British Army aboard merchant ships was that of men from the City of London who, in 1662, banded themselves together to man the 'merchant ships' to fight the Spaniards and the French. They became known as the 1st Maritime Regiment of Foot, later to be called The Royal Marines. In those days the 'merchant ships' were the King's ships and as such were part of the senior service. Ten regiments of the line were subsequently appointed for 'sea service' as marines.

The Maritime Royal Artillery of the Second World War are proud of the fact that they were called to service at sea by none other than Winston Churchill. In fact they became known as Churchill's Sharpshooters and for some reason, Lord Haw Haw, the German radio commentator, once called them 'Churchill's Spies'.

The 'soldiers of the seas' were brought into being in February 1940 when Churchill was First Lord of the Admiralty. Air attacks upon coastal shipping were increasing and North Sea ports were being bombed. During this month 500 two-man teams, taking their own Lewis or Bren guns and ammunition with them, were embarked on coasters carrying priority war material. From this small beginning the Maritime Royal Artillery was gradually developed.

In September that year a request was made by the Admiralty for further volunteers. This was made to extend protection to all coasters and to provide soldiers to man guns on merchantmen in home ports. The men on the coasters were increased to a force of 2,000 whilst 2,000 additional men, trained at the Naval gunnery schools, were provided for the ports.

By February 1941, with an extra 600 soldiers, a total of fourteen home ports were being covered. At this time some were drafted 'deep-sea', giving protection to the Sierra Leone convoys, which were being subjected to attack by enemy Focke-Wulf bombers. A month later, due to the increasing loss of ships in the North Atlantic, the scheme was extended to embrace all merchantmen. Added to the Army armament was the 40-mm Bofors gun along with personnel specially trained in the operation of this weapon.

During the spring of 1941 a 'private army' of some 1,400 men was established under Movement Control for the anti-aircraft protection of troopships. This brought the total MRA personnel to some 12,000. Not everything ran smoothly. There is a case of thirty 'rooky' gunners of the Duke of Wellington's Regiment being 'shanghaied' aboard the *Highland Monarch* while lying at anchor off Greenock. As was often the situation, no one knew the ship's destination.

After some fourteen days at sea the 'rooky' gunners were surprised to find themselves 'put ashore' at Freetown. Yet no one at Military Headquarters, West Africa, knew who they were or what they were doing there. They pitched their tents at Lumley Beach, now a well-known holiday resort. After a few weeks one of them volunteered his services as a clerk at Military HQ. He did quite well for himself – his 'work' included having afternoon tea one day with the Bishop of Sierra Leone. In due course he was shipped as gunner (able-bodied) aboard the Polish steamer *Lewant* bound for Liverpool. The thirty gunners were the forerunners of the MRA, who were to be based at the port for the manning of homeward convoys.

By March 1943 the Maritime Royal Artillery had been reorganized into six regiments. They included twenty-four port detachments in the United Kingdom, with overseas batteries in Halifax, Nova Scotia, and Bermuda; in New York, Freetown, Port Said, Bombay and Simonstown, South Africa. Independent troops were stationed at Sydney, Australia; Haifa; and, after the invasion of Italy, at Naples. Total strength was some 170 officers and over 14,000 other ranks. Of the officers, thirty-six could be at sea at any one time as assistant gunnery officers. Of the other ranks, over 13,000 were regular seagoing gunners.

During Operation 'Torch' (see Chapter 10) a port detachment was established at Algiers. Independent troops were established at Courseulles, Normandy, four weeks after D Day, later in 1944 moving to Ostend and then to Antwerp. Operationally the MRA came under the Royal Navy and the essence of its organization was the close co-operation with that service. They enjoyed the same 'communion' with masters, officers and men of the merchantmen and signed on ship's articles as did their DEMS 'brothers'.

The number of personnel and the amount of equipment on board ship varied with each vessel. On the 'monsters' there might be twenty-five or thirty while in a small coaster only two. The average service detachment aboard a merchantman of the Liberty type was seven men. These could be all naval ratings, all army men or a mixture of both. The general principle was, however, to have mixed detachments roughly in the proportion of six to four. All, as far as possible, were trained in everything a merchantman might carry, from a 6-inch naval gun down to rockets and balloons. Bofor guns, when mounted, were purely an MRA commitment.

Total casualties of the Maritime Royal Artillery were 1,222. For gallantry and distinguished services at sea, MRA personnel were awarded naval and not military decorations. They included five DSMs and four BEMs. An early George Cross, the first to be won at sea, in fact, was awarded to Bombardier Reed for carrying the badly wounded chief mate of the SS *Cormount* from the bridge to safety during an air attack in the North Sea in June 1941.

Bombardier Reed, himself badly wounded by machine-gun fire, later died. The chief mate after many months in hospital recovered and was awarded the MBE for driving off the aircraft and for saving the vessel. Over two years later the *Cormount* finally succumbed to the enemy when she was mined off Harwich in November 1943.

The brave deeds of the men simply known as 'the gunners' would fill a volume by themselves. Many took to the boats on the order 'abandon ship'; only a few are remembered fifty years later. The Scot from Forfar, twenty-eight days adrift. Landed St Bathelmy, West Indies; sent to St Kitts, then by US sloop to St Thomas. From there by Cuban ship to San Juan, Puerto Rica. To get home he joined a vessel which took him to Norfolk, Virginia, to Halifax and Montreal. Then south again to Galveston. At last fully loaded, the merchantman returned to Halifax and an HX convoy homewards.

Two gunners survived an open boat voyage of forty-eight days. Shipwrecked, frostbitten and gangrenous off Spitzbergen, three were largely instrumental in saving the lives of the ship's master and some of the crew. One solitary gunner, though wounded three times, endeavoured for over two hours to shield his companions on a Carley float from machine-gun 'practice' by a Japanese submarine. Another hit and sank an approaching torpedo with an Oerlikon gun, a feat only possible through the torpedo depth being incorrectly set.

On a lighter note, one bombardier recalls the transfer of a gunner back to his Royal Artillery unit. He sailed from Hull on three separate occasions yet each ship struck mines before they had even reached the mouth of the Humber river. 'Gunlayers wanted for service on merchant ships,' said the billboard outside the registration office. On volunteering for that branch of the Royal Navy a recruit recalls the immediate cursory medical examination on the Friday with a railway warrant to report to HMS *Drake*, Devonport, on the following Tuesday. There followed a four-week training period in seamanship after which he was drafted to the Cardiff Merchant Navy Defence Centre.

From Cardiff, after completing a four-week crash course in gunnery and the operation of numerous electrical devices, the recruit was drafted to the SS *Dalfram*. There followed the *Esturia*, the *Bothia*, the *Tower Grange* (sunk 18 November 1942) and then the *Pentridge Hill*, which took him away from home for 422 days. At one time during his service he was disembarked in New York in need of dental treatment. Held there he found himself detailed for escort duties to Indiana with drafts of trainee Fleet Air Arm leading airmen. A variety of jobs was always possible for gunners who found themselves cast ashore in foreign parts.

Probably the worst memory of a Swansea Bombardier was service aboard the steamship *North Devon* during a night-time air-raid on a North Sea convoy. 'There was moonlight and I was able to see the aircraft as it made a classic attack from starboard to port. I emptied my magazine into the aircraft before I was blown into the scuppers, my stand and gun on top of me. The bomb exploded within the engineroom bursting the ship's boilers. Many of the crew were badly scalded by steam; four were taken ashore dead including a fourteen-year-old cabin boy'. The Bombardier was subsequently credited with 'a kill', the Heinkel having crash-landed in the sea. He was commended for his action and given promotion.

During another bombing incident (23 January 1941) the 1,859-ton steamship *Mostyn* was sunk 150 miles west of Ireland. On a bitterly cold day in typical Atlantic wintry weather many lives were saved through the action of the gunlayer. Edward James Butler was later awarded the George Medal and Lloyds War Medal 'for outstanding gallantry and devotion to duty, in safely disposing of damaged high explosive bombs and ammunition during an air attack'.

Drafted to Port Said in the spring of 1941 two gunners found themselves aboard the Mediterranean coaster *Kilbell Kaber* bound for Matrûh. The master was Spanish, the chief mate Chinese, the second mate Polish and the crew Egyptian. Bombed and sunk in Matrûh harbour the vessel was raised and repaired with the help of the Army. It was nearly five months later that the naval gunners arrived back in Port Said. Drafted to different merchantmen, one sailed aboard the *Birchbank* for the Far East. There followed a voyage across the Pacific and around Cape Horn to load meat in Argentina for the United Kingdom. In Buenos Aires he spent two months in hospital due to spinal damage sustained during a hurricane.

Sailing from the river Plate in Lamport & Holt's *Bruyere*, loading corned beef and hides at Rio Grande Sol, Santos and Rio de Janeiro, the gunner found himself set on a homeward course via West Africa. Just north of the Equator the SS *Bruyere* was torpedoed and sunk by *U-125*. Rescued and taken to Freetown he was put aboard the Panamanian *Oriskani*, of convoy SL125, which lost thirteen merchantmen from attacks by U-boats before reaching the United Kingdom. The gunner drafted to the *Kilbell Kaber* had been away from home for nearly two years. After twenty-eight days' leave he was aboard the Dutch trooper *Dempo*. He served aboard the *Samvern* at D-Day and later in the Normandy campaign on the *Sambolt*. Altogether he saw service on nineteen merchant ships.

An anti-aircraft gunner fighting the blitz at Plymouth and Falmouth volunteered for service on high-octane tankers. His most frightening experience, however, was being a survivor of the cargo steamer *Bolton Castle*, one of the vessels sunk from the ill-fated Russian convoy PQ17. 'We were sunk in the icefields and the ship sank in thirteen minutes. Over the following eight days we attempted to row the 480 miles to Murmansk. Fortunately we were picked up by a Russian trawler. We would never have survived that last fifty miles.'

At night in convoy the *Orient City* was attacked by a Focke-Wulf bomber. There was a phosphorescent glow on the sea and each ship was throwing up a bright bow-wave and distributing a broad white wake behind her. The gunlayer trained his gun as the aeroplane approached. All the pilot could have been aware of was a bright flash. He flew straight into the shell-burst. The aircraft's engines stopped as though suddenly switched off. The machine fell into the sea like a giant leaf. As it crashed, its bomb-load, intended for the *Orient City*, exploded. The convoy, once more out of danger, sailed on.

Two gunners cast adrift after their ship sank off the Arabian coast had a unique experience. For one of them, a DEMS leading seaman, it was the third time he had been torpedoed since volunteering in 1941. Together with a British second mate and twenty-six Indian crew they drifted for six days before sighting land. At dawn on the seventh day they were rescued by Arab surf-boats. One of the inhabitants of this remote coast cooked a meal and ordered a clay hut to be given to them for rest. Later two guides led them in the broiling heat over a range of hills, and when civilization was reached, two camels were provided for transporting food and water.

Across waterless desert and rocky hill country they journeyed for nine days, a distance of over 500 miles. At last, physically exhausted, they arrived at the village of Desse from where the headman took them to a British airfield a few miles distant. They were then flown in stages to Aden where they were hospitalized.

Sailing independently with a particularly dangerous cargo of high explosives in June 1942 was the Dutch motor vessel *Alioth*. Virtually on the Equator in longitude 18.52W, she was torpedoed and sunk by the Italian submarine *Da Vinci*. On board were seven British gunners, four MRA and three DEMS. Two lifeboats got away, led by the Dutch second mate. Navigator that he was, he had thought to bring along his sextant. Ten days later he brought them into the river at Freetown.

All hands survived despite the moments of drama which punctuated the voyage. In the words of its gunlayer: 'The tropical storm produced some fantastic sheet and forked lightning. The waves – I don't know which was worse: on top looking down or the bottom of the trough looking up'. They owed their lives to the efficient and disciplined Dutch officers and crew.

One of the saddest tales is connected with British India's *Gairsoppa*, a straggler from the ill-fated SLS64 convoy. Homewards from Freetown she was torpedoed by *U-101*. On the thirteenth day under sail the one lifeboat launched was driven upon the rocks close by the Lizard lighthouse off west Cornwall; the three men aboard were flung into the raging sea. The second mate, the only survivor, was flung on to the rocks unconscious.

In the Lizard peninsula it was for long rumoured that a twenty-year-old gunner was found dead in the boat when it washed ashore. Hearing of the tale, a retired master mariner set about tracking down his name and his burial place. In the little churchyard of St Wynwalloc in the village of Church Cove the mystery was solved. Next to the last resting-place of the ship's radio officer was an unnamed grave. It was dedicated to 'a sailor' of the *Gairsoppa*. Today after fifty years of anonymity, gunner Norman Haskill Thomas of Tenby has his name inscribed on the memorial stone beneath which they laid him to rest.

Without the gunners the history of British and Allied Merchantmen during the Second World War would have been vastly different. They served in all theatres of war and in all climates – from the Arctic winters to the humid tropics of Malaya and West Africa. They provided much of the essential training in defence for merchant seamen. Without the naval and army gunners, the troopships and tankers, the cargo vessels and coasters that secured the vital lifelines would have been much more vulnerable than they were and would have paid an even higher price for ultimate victory.

The gain to the Allied war effort from saving a laden merchantman from destruction are incalculable. Every ship that made port was to aid the war efficiency of men on the battlefield. Even if a cargo ship or tanker was eventually sunk, each completed voyage meant the safe arrival of urgently needed and often vital war materials.

Of course, a gunner is only as good as his armament. In many cases modern equipment was lacking, an example of the unprepared state in which Britain entered the war. It was against attacks by aircraft that the men of the DEMS and MRA were able to show their true worth. Countless Allied merchantmen were saved from destruction by an effective anti-aircraft barrage that kept the attacking aircraft at bay. Even on the perilous Arctic route and in the narrow confines of the Mediterranean, a large number of vessels got safely to their port of discharge simply because of the effectiveness of anti-aircraft defence.

During the eight months of August 1942 to April 1943 – a period which includes Operation 'Torch', the North African landing – as many as 503 of the 529 British and Allied merchantmen assailed by enemy aircraft, successfully fought off their attackers and escaped. In the same period, twenty merchant vessels that were given no opportunity to engage the enemy were sunk.

Principally because of the experience at sea during World War I defence against U-boats and surface raiders had been envisaged during the 1930s. In the twelve months after the outbreak of hostilities in September 1939 some 3,000 merchantmen were armed. The key defence was the 4.7-inch gun, which had lain in store heavily greased since 1919. To complete the task was immense, however, coming at a time when so many ship repairers were busy with a backlog of damaged ships. Vessels were still being armed during the spring of 1941.

A typical 4-inch gun crew comprised seven men plus a number of ammunition-supply personnel. All were under control of a gunnery control officer, usually the ship's second mate, who would have taken shore instruction at a Merchant Navy gunnery school in addition to exercises on board. In addition to the DEMS gunlayer, the senior member of the gun crew, there was the breech-worker and gun-trainer. The breech-worker controlled the actions of the remainder of the gun crew – the rammer, the loader, the shells or cartridge supplier, and the sight setter.

The Japanese 4.7-inch gun, some dated as early as 1894, were much in evidence. Many ships were fitted with a 12-pounder as secondary armament. Troopships, particularly those which had served as armed merchant cruisers in the early part of the war, were equipped with a 6-inch gun on the poopdeck at the stern.

The most famous lone actions utilizing the low-angle 4-inch gun were those of the *Chilean Reefer* (managed by Alfred Holt's), the Royal Mail steamer *Culebra* and the 'Eagle' tanker *San Florentino*. In the case of the action of *Culebra* (Captain Bonner) with the surfaced *U-123*, her commander, Lieutenant Reinhard Hardegen, wrote in his log: 'He manned his gun and machine gun ... he was a tough opponent. Speed was reduced and he was blowing off steam. With astonishing cold-bloodedness he fired on, although we were constantly hitting his after-deck ... I must pay the enemy every respect, they held out and did not leave their stations.'

As *Culebra* sank 'in a mighty cloud of smoke and steam' the survivors, which included her six gunners, took to the remaining lifeboat. Sadly, no one survived the gale which sprang up twenty-four hours later. It was a heroic stand against a superior enemy.

In September 1939, and even during the two weeks prior to the outbreak of war, merchantmen were fitted with the 4-inch gun in shipyards overseas on instructions from the Admiralty in London. The motorship *Derrymore* was so equipped in Melbourne on 30 August; other vessels similarly armed at this time in Australia were Blue Star's *Imperial Star*, Port Line's *Port Gisborne* and the Australian phosphate ship *Triadic*. New Zealand Shipping Co's *Kaituna* was armed as early as 17 August.

By the end of September a further thirty British-flag merchantmen had been armed and manned by the Royal Australian Navy in Sydney and Melbourne. These included P & O's *Strathnaver* and Orient Line's *Otranto* plus a variety of vessels – *City of Manchester*, *City of Perth*, *Port Freemantle*, *Port Townsville*, *Port Wyndham*, *Port Saint John*, *Speybank*, and the trampships *Hoperange*, *Loch Lomond*, *Janeta*, *Tregenna* and *Trewellard*.

Strathnaver was fitted with a 6-inch gun, 1904 vintage, together with a 3-inch high-angle anti-aircraft gun and range finder. Records of Hain Steamship's *Tregenna* indicate that the 4-inch breech-loading gun was manufactured in 1896. Stored in Gibraltar it was test-fired in 1930 and sent to Australia. There it lay in storage until fitted to the *Tregenna* in Sydney. Before sailing, eight of her crew were given one day's instruction in the handling of the gun. Further instruction and practice firing was carried out on the voyage to Durban.

Priority in arming the vessels of the fourth service was given to Australian ports because of the long voyage homewards to Britain. Such vessels were carrying urgent foodstuffs, wool and wheat and would be sailing independently, unlike those from North America, in convoy and with naval escort. In addition to U-boats already on station in the North Atlantic, the German pocket battleships *Admiral Graf Spee* and *Deutschland* had sailed from Wilhelmshaven and Kiel on 21 and 24

August. It was estimated that at the time Prime Minister Neville Chamberlain was preparing Britain for a state of war, both ships were approaching the Equator, far from the German advance into Poland.

The courageous effort of Lieutenant-Commander Ouvry of the mining school HMS *Vernon* at Portsmouth, when he defused a magnetic mine on the mudflats of Shoeburyness, resulted in a system being devised of 'degaussing' a ship's magnetism. This was achieved by passing an electric current through cables wrapped around its hull. This reduced the steel vessel's magnetic field, which could activate the mines' firing mechanism. Vast lengths of special copper cable were laid around the ship's 'tween deck or the upper deck. These were activated by the vessel's generator, which was not really designed for such a load. On each occasion before sailing the system's effectiveness had to be checked against the compass. If working correctly the compass needle would jump to a position at right angles to the lay of the wires. As a rule, 'degaussing' was only switched on in shallow waters or when instructed to do so in convoy or in theatres of war such as the Mediterranean.

In terms of time, labour and materials, degaussing was a colossal task. Every ship, and there were over 10,000 on Lloyds Register, had to be put through a special test to determine its magnetic field. In the first two years 50,000 miles of degaussing cable were fitted, equipment which was estimated at a cost of £20 million. Between May and June 1940 (Dunkirk) 2,000 ships were degaussed and a further 1,000 were 'wiped'.

Formed at the time of Dunkirk was the Directorate of Miscellaneous Weapon Development at Weston-super-Mare. It was led by Vice-Admiral Sir Richard Lane-Poole, who, together with Admiral Sir Frederic Dreyer, was responsible for the degaussing of Allied shipping, new weaponry and for the training of Merchant Navy crews in defence. Surrounding themselves with an array of boffins they together came up with some remarkable new weapons.

Admiral Sir Frederic Dreyer, the Inspector of Merchant Navy Gunnery, suggested a flame-thrower mounted on the poopdeck of ships might be disconcerting to enemy dive-bomber pilots. If the flame thrower was designed to fire directly upwards the pilot would either have to abandon his line of attack or fly straight through a pillar of fire which might destroy him. The first flame thrower was mounted upon a tank for airfield defence, though naval flame throwers were soon in limited production.

The Holman Projector, firing Mills grenades, was developed by Holman's of Camborne in co-operation with the Directorate. After testing was carried out at Victory Inn Moor near Porthtowan on the North Cornish coast an order for 1,000 was placed by the Admiralty. Initially the weapon-fired grenades were fitted in metal containers with open tops. On leaving the muzzle the container fell away, releasing the spring plunger and starting the fuse. Three seconds later the grenade exploded. Maximum range was 600 to 650 feet. By late spring 1941 the Projector, now adapted to use steam instead of compressed air, was beginning to make a name for itself. It was fitted to destroyers, minesweepers and motor torpedo boats as well as hundreds of merchantmen.

In the initial stages the gunners experienced some embarrassing moments with the weapon. The DEMS gunner on a trial run aboard the Trinity House vessel *Vestal*, based at Swansea, well remembers one such occasion: 'With a loud hiss of steam, the can came out of the barrel, fell gracefully out of the end and deposited the armed grenade at my feet. The offending bomb was scooped and hurled over the ship's side where it went off with a very satisfactory bang.'

The Holman Projector quickly achieved some successes. The first spectacular action involved the small steamship *Highlander* (1,216 tons) off the east coast of England in August 1940. During a forty-minute battle with two Dornier bombers she was attacked with aerial torpedoes, bombs and machine guns. As the first Dornier was shot down in flames the gunners obtained further hits on the second as she was making her approach. It was then that a Holman bomb burst in the root of the wing. She lost height and plummeted into the sea, her damaged wing landing on the ship's poopdeck and destroying one of the two lifeboats. Triumphantly *Highlander* made port with part of the crashed aircraft still on deck.

In the first year the Projector claimed over twelve aircraft destroyed. Late in 1941, one thousand of the Mark III version were ordered. This was a semi-automatic and more powerful version which fired two or three grenades simultaneously to a height of 1,000 feet. In all, 4,500 of these unusual guns, powered by compressed air or steam, saw active service in the war at sea.

The Mark III version was successfully used when the SS *Thirlby*, homeward bound in convoy in January 1942, drove off a Focke-Wulf Condor aircraft. No sooner had the plane broken cloud cover than bombs were dropped and a hail of cannon shells shot up the bridge accommodation. Nevertheless the chief mate, on watch on the bridge, bravely manned the Holman Projector and eventually the enemy was driven off. Although badly damaged with one hold open to the sea, the *Thirlby* limped into Loch Ewe with her precious cargo of wheat.

Experiments with rockets as a means of defence were first made in 1940 due to the shortage of guns. The first to be installed in merchantmen was the 'pig trough' and was designed to shoot down dive-bombers. To keep it pointing vertically even when the ship rolled it had a swinging mounting which looked like a large umbrella stand. It carried fourteen rockets each carrying a 2-pounder shell.

The 'pig trough' gave the effect of a monster shotgun laying a vertical barrage into the path of the attacking aircraft. Whilst impressive in action, its success was limited, for the slung mounting was not steady enough to give the required accuracy.

In 1941 came the Pillar Box and the Harvey Projector. The Pillar Box, so called because of its appearance, was operated by the gunner or crew member who shut himself inside the circular, swivelling cabin. Outside the casing on either side of him was a bank of 2-inch rockets, seven a side. A Mark II version was equipped with twenty rockets, ten on each side. The gunner trained and elevated the device by moving levers mounted on a contraption resembling the handlebars of a bicycle. It was fired electrically and was susceptible to malfunction when water entered.

The Army disliked the Harvey Projector. At sea it was mainly fitted to auxiliaries, principally to some of the larger banana boats that were converted to carry out independent patrols aimed at intercepting enemy blockade runners. These vessels were quite heavily armed and their crews did not regard the new rocket device with any great enthusiasm.

The 'Harvey' consisted of several pieces of gas-piping mounted on a pipe pedestal. On either side were metal shields with glass windows with crossed lines to provide a rough and ready sight. It was a powerful weapon not to be handled without taking safety precautions. Consequently it was manned principally by the DEMS and MRA. Few Merchant Navy crews were given instructions in its use.

The single rocket shell of over 9 feet long was carried on two rails. In its nose was an aerodynamic brass fuse carrying nearly 14 pounds of high explosive and cordite. It was capable of travelling at least seven miles. Little used until the fitting of a 'proximity fuse', a top-secret fuse based on a principle akin to radar, the weapon was first fitted on board SS *Alleghany* at Belfast. She was a banana boat flying the white ensign before being converted to an anti-aircraft vessel and heading for the Red Sea.

HMS *Patia*, an auxiliary fighter catapult ship of 5,355 tons, was the first attacked vessel to shoot down an aircraft with a 'Harvey'. A merchantman requisitioned for naval service she was bombed and sunk off the Northumberland coast in April 1941 when 119 of her crew were lost.

The Parachute and Cable (PAC) was first developed for the Air Force. Briefly, it was a rocket that could carry a steel cable up to a height of 500 feet on the end of which was a parachute. At the end of the cable was a Mills bomb. Its use was proven in the Battle of Britain when a Dornier aircraft blew up over Kenley after its port wing had been torn clean off. It was then that Churchill pressed for it to be used as a deterrent to bombers at sea.

Sited on the ship's bridge the weapon was coupled to a lanyard leading into the wheelhouse. What the boffins did not realize was that during fog the officer of the watch could mistake the PAC lanyard for the siren lanyard, which was used to signal to other ships in the convoy. One can imagine the result when the incorrect lanyard was pulled. What if the descent rate of the parachute, with its accompanying bomb, equalled the forward movement of the vessel? Was the mate about to bomb his ship by its own defensive weapon?

After some early failures, mainly due to lack of training in its use, there were successes. Gunners aboard the merchantman *Stanlake* fired the PAC when a Heinkel aircraft was still many yards off. By the time the parachute opened the plane was right on the cable. She sheered violently. For a moment the pilot regained control when some 900 yards from the ship and then, hidden by the approaching dusk of the evening sky, the engines stopped dead.

PACs were also used during the hours of darkness for the firing of Snowflake rockets. These were employed upon instructions from the Convoy Commodore, when attacked by U-boats. These rockets illuminated the sea with a steely grey light in an effort to assist the escorts in hunting the enemy, which was often on the surface between the columns of ships.

Finally from the boffins at Miscellaneous Weapon Development came a more lethal weapon, the Fast Aerial Mine (FAM), a much larger version of the PAC. Its purpose was to lay a curtain of aerial mines on wires in the path of low-flying aircraft or dive-bombers. The projector fired a rocket which carried aloft a canister containing a parachute and aerial mine connected by a long wire to a second parachute and mine. When the canister attained a certain height its parachute was released, leaving the long wire trailing from the top parachute and mine to the bottom unopened parachute. The object was that the impact of an aircraft's wing on the wire opened the bottom parachute, released the top parachute and armed the mine, which was then dragged down on to the wing by the forward movement of the aircraft and the restraining power of the lower parachute.

The fitting of PACs and FAMs led to the enemy abandoning attacks at masthead height. It was said they were much feared by German aircrews. Only in 1943 did these weapons come off the secret list. At the time it was claimed they were responsible for destroying nine enemy aircraft at sea. At least thirty-five merchantmen, some of them troopships, were saved from destruction by these two devices.

In addition to the new weapons there were other devices designed to protect the merchantmen. Smoke floats (for long carried aboard Royal Navy vessels) were ignited when a ship or convoy wanted to make it difficult for the enemy, in particular a surface raider, to locate and obtain the range of her prey. Depth charges were not only carried as a defence against submarines but were, on occasion, stowed low down in the bowels of the vessel and could be detonated from the bridge. In this way the vessel could be destroyed, rather than allowing it and its cargo to fall into enemy hands. They were much carried by merchantmen participating in Mediterranean convoys for the relief of Malta.

During the North African invasion (Operation 'Torch') such troopships as Cunard's *Scythia* carried, in addition to an American 4-inch gun at the stern, four Oerliken guns, a Bofors gun, two 12-pounders forward on the forecastle, a PAC and an FAM. Also carried were smoke floats and depth charges, both at the stern and in the bowels of the vessel, though the latter were never used.

Many fast merchantmen, particularly those engaged on combined operations, carried paravanes at the bow, in much the same way as they were carried by many types of warships. These mine cable-cutters were often a thorn in the side of World War II naval men. Should a mine or mines be caught up in one of these cutters and the ship brought to a standstill, there was the danger of an explosion upon contact amidships. This happened when the cruiser *Neptune* was sunk by four such mines off Tripoli, Libya, in December 1941. With the exception of one leading seaman, all hands were lost.

The paravanes (PVs) resembled a torpedo about nine feet long and when towed from the bows drifted outwards from the ship's side at an angle of 35 degrees. At the nose of the paravane was a pair of serrated cutters. The aim was to sever the mine cable, thereby bringing the mine to the surface to be detonated by small-arms fire. The effectiveness depended upon the speed of the vessel being not less than 15 knots and the bows being rounded and not knife-edged.

Admiralty Net Defence (AND) was initiated as a means of protection against the torpedo, both aerial and underwater types. Captain C.N.E. Currey CBE RN was the expert who worked on the system. The principle was that the 5 feet by 2½ feet diamond mesh was carried on booms amidships lying 90 degrees from the side of the ship. The mesh, being a dynamic (moving) defence, only worked effectively at speeds above 7 knots; this approach contrasted with such static systems as boom defence, when nets were laid across estuaries or rivers leading to docks or naval bases. When not in use the booms were housed aloft against the masts with the nets brailed.

Altogether some 700 vessels were equipped with Admiralty Net Defence during the war. Of these 203 were so equipped in Canada, sixty-eight of them being fitted on new ships of the 'Fort' and 'Park' types. They were by no means popular, as they slowed down loaded merchantmen considerably; this was particularly in heavy seas, when instability was also a problem. Those who sailed in such vessels could offer many tales of hair-raising incidents.

Much of the experimental work on Net Defence was carried out aboard the liner *Arandora Star*, probably one of the best-known ships of the 1930s due to her work as a cruise liner to the northern capitals and the West Indies. In December 1939 she was directed to Avonmouth where she underwent tests and trials to determine whether or not the gear could be used by both merchantmen and warships and what would be the probable reduction in speed.

From Avonmouth the *Arandora Star* went to Portsmouth where, under Admiralty guidance and instruction, the nets were slung from booms and rigged out whenever the state of the English Channel permitted. Nets of various-sized meshes were fitted and trials run. For a vessel of her size they were considered successful and during torpedo-firing trials the nets trapped all that were fired. Admiralty Net Defence was never infallible, however, and covered no more than 60 to 75 per cent of the ship's side. Of the twenty-one ships fitted with AND that were hit by U-boat torpedoes with the nets streamed six were sunk – either because the nets were penetrated or because the torpedoes struck the ship in an uncovered part. On the fifteen other occasions the torpedoes either exploded in the net, causing non-lethal damage, or else failed to pass through it.

With the increasing losses to personnel, ship's crews and gunners, lifesaving became of great importance. Supplies of the red battery-powered lifejacket lights, first issued during the autumn of 1940, became compulsory in March the following year. Successful escape from the sinking ship was studied and recommendations made. During the spring of 1941 all cabins had to be equipped with portholes, through which those trapped could obtain exit. It was to such a newly designed porthole that, later in the war, I would owe my life. New cabin doors with a crash panel in the lower half, were fitted, enabling them to be kicked outwards.

During the autumn of 1941 the Butterfield lifesaving raft, made in three sizes for ten, fifteen and twenty persons was introduced. This was a new type of raft fifteen by eight feet at the largest size, which had been designed by the old established firm of Charles Butterfield of London in conjunction with two surveyors from Lloyds. It was double-sided and ready for immediate use whichever side up it floated; sharp ends were fore and aft to make steering convenient and easy. Equipped with side screens with steel stanchions, storage lockers, mast, yard, oars, and rowlocks as well as water storage tanks, the new raft afforded greater security and better accommodation. Strong in construction and tested to withstand a drop from a height of thirty feet into the water, the new raft was fitted to 138 merchantmen over a period of four months. Subsequently, many more were built.

At the same time the firm of Charles Butterfield built and assembled 730 lifeboat radio masts, so enabling survivors to send distress signals after abandoning ship. In addition, metal lifeboats were introduced for tankers in order to withstand fire, both on board and after launch. Technicians of the tanker shipping company Eagle Oil developed a face-mask to protect crews against the effect of immersion in oil. These four innovations alone were to save many thousands of lives during the years 1942–45.

During the same period, lifesaving rations per man were increased. In January 1942 these stood at 3 quarts of water, 14 ounces of biscuits, 14 ounces of chocolate, 14 ounces of milk tablets and 14 ounces of pemmican (the latter being a specially prepared ration of lean meat, dried, pounded and mixed with fat and other ingredients).

Until such time as sufficient escort ships had been built for the Royal Navy and Royal Canadian Navy much of the defence of merchantmen on Atlantic convoys was provided by peacetime passenger vessels, cruise liners and 'intermediate' ships. At great expense they were converted into armed merchant cruisers at shipyards both in the United Kingdom and the principal ports of the British Empire. Such measures were rendered necessary by the acute lack of proper cruisers. This shortage was aggravated by the need to track enemy surface raiders at large in the South Atlantic and Indian Oceans, and because Royal Navy anti-aircraft cruisers were constantly required in the Mediterranean.

Requisitioning actually began in late August 1939 some eight to ten days before the outbreak of hostilities. Alfred Holt's *Antenor* was ordered to Calcutta for conversion; Peninsular & Oriental's *Cathy*, *Maloja* and *Ranchi* were dispatched to Bombay for the same reason. The Admiralty ordered many of the liner companies to prepare some of their finest vessels for conversion. *Athenia* of the Donaldson Atlantic line, torpedoed and sunk on the first day of the war, had been earmarked for conversion as soon as she arrived in Canada. The sailings of many liners and cruisers were cancelled.

Altogether fifty vessels, some of them famous, some old and obsolete, were summoned for duty. Within two years, fifteen of them were sunk by enemy action – two of them, the *Rawalpindi* and *Jervis Bay*, in epic engagements. It was soon realized that the employment of merchant cruisers was too risky when weighed against the likely benefits. As a stop-gap measure during the 'days of defeat' they were of immeasurable value, but by 1943 those that remained afloat had been converted into troopships. It was just in time, for by that date the shortage was one of troopers to carry the vast armies of men. One must remember that during the Second World War there were no troop-carrying aircraft as such.

The armed merchant cruisers (AMCs) carried out a variety of work. Many of them engaged in patrolling northern waters, a particularly hazardous, exacting and arduous job both from the point of view of the weather conditions – the intense cold and the long and dark nights of those latitudes – and the close proximity to the U-boats based in Norway. The object was to patrol these northern waters and enforce the blockade of Germany by intercepting both enemy and neutral merchantmen. It was necessary for neutral ships to be inspected in case they were carrying contraband cargoes useful to the enemy. Others served as ocean escorts, taking a position in the centre of the convoy like a hen shepherding her chicks around her.

Shaw, Savill and Albion Ltd was a liner company particularly hard hit by the requisition of its vessels. The first to be taken, in what were panic measures, were the *Arawa, Esperance Bay, Jervis Bay* and *Moreton Bay*. The 1922-vintage *Arawa*, a twin-screw steamer of 14,462 tons, with a speed of 15 knots, was commissioned as an armed merchant cruiser in New Zealand on 24 August 1939. She went on patrol in the China Sea. *Esperance Bay* and *Moreton Bay* were converted during the same week at Brisbane and Sydney. *Jervis Bay* was reconstructed and commissioned in London, from where she joined the Northern Patrol. The 'Bay' ships (there was also the *Largs Bay*), were owned by the Aberdeen and Commonwealth Line but were managed by Shaw, Savill and Albion. The *Largs Bay* remained on commercial work until she was converted into a troopship in 1941.

In September 1939 three of the Company's oldest ships, the *Pakeha*, *Mamari* and *Waimana*, were purchased by the Government for conversion into dummy warships. The *Pakeha* and *Waimana* were converted to resemble battleships of the Royal Sovereign class. The *Mamari* was suitably transformed into an imitation of the aircraft carrier *Hermes*. They were anchored in the Firth of Forth and at Scapa Flow during the early part of the war in order to act as decoy ships for enemy aircraft. When the necessity for this form of deception disappeared, the *Pakeha* and *Waimana* were reconverted into refrigerated cargo liners and handed to the company for management. Unfortunately, the *Mamari* was wrecked on the East Anglian coast in July 1941, whilst on passage to Chatham Dockyard to have her naval fittings removed.

In the second half of 1940, nine armed merchant cruisers, with a total tonnage of 143,807, were sunk in the North Atlantic, eight of them by U-boats. They were *Carinthia, Scotstoun* and *Andania*, all in June; and *Transylvania, Dunvegan Castle, Laurentic, Patroclus* and *Forfar*.

HMS *Patroclus* and HMS *Laurentic*, both flying the white ensign and returning from a Western Patrol, were lost within a few hours of each other. (The Western Patrol was established to survey the approaches to the enemy's newly gained bases on the French Biscay coast.) *Patroclus*, an 11,314-ton Blue Funnel (Alfred Holt & Co Ltd) passenger cargo ship, had been converted in January 1940 and armed with six 6-inch and two 3-inch guns. The 18,734-ton Cunard White Star *Laurentic*, converted in October 1939, had been equipped with seven 5.5-inch guns and three 4-inch guns. She became one of the last of the Royal Navy's coalburners.

Late on the evening of 3 November, *U-99*, under the command of 'the tonnage king' Lieutenant Commander Otto Kretschmer, was some 300 miles off Bloody Foreland, Donegal, when he sighted the two cruisers. At 2250 Central European time a torpedo was fired at *Laurentic* from a range of 1,500 yards. Hit abaft the after funnel her engine room was crippled and she came to an abrupt stop. *Patroclus* immediately went to her assistance, and it was whilst she was picking up survivors from the lowered lifeboats that she too was torpedoed.

As with most armed merchant cruisers, the holds were filled with empty barrels, designed to increase buoyancy. The sea surrounding the two vessels was now a mass of such barrels. Radio distress messages were sent when *U-99* surfaced and opened fire with 8.8-centimetre shells. *Patroclus* gallantly returned the gunfire, forcing *U-99* to submerge, but at 0453 hours two additional torpedoes were fired at *Laurentic*, followed thirty-five minutes later by five more at *Patroclus*. Both cruisers sank shortly afterwards.

Thirty-six hours later from mid-Atlantic came the horrifying news of HMS *Jervis Bay*, lost whilst shepherding convoy HX84. The memorable passages in the pages of maritime history written by her 'slaughter' are related in Chapter 5.

The first merchant cruiser to be 'sacrificed in the face of defeat' came as early as November 1939. It was then that P & O's *Rawalpindi* was sunk as she faced the combined power of two of Germany's most modern and powerful battle cruisers. Built in 1925 for the company's service between India and Hongkong, the 16,697-ton *Rawalpindi* had been converted on the Clyde only three weeks before sailing on that fateful November day. Equipped with eight 5.9-inch guns some forty years old, she had no armour plating and her maximum speed was 17 knots. Seventeen months later, her sister ship, AMC *Rajputana*, was sunk by *U-108* whilst on Atlantic patrol.

On Thursday 23 November *Rawalpindi* was on patrol ninety-five miles off Iceland. The time was 1530 hours. The wind was rising and the temperature plummeting as night closed in. In command was sixty-year-old Captain Edward Kennedy, who had been recalled for Royal Naval service after seventeen years ashore. Before the declaration of war he had been leading the uneventful life of a retired naval man in Buckinghamshire. It was said of this white-haired stickler for discipline that when news came that he had been given a ship, the effect was electric. 'Thank God,' he cried and beamed like a happy schoolboy.

The loss of *Rawalpindi* was one of the most gallant actions in the annals of the Navy. Flying the white ensign, not a man on board was drawn from the active list of the Royal Navy. Manned from Devonport she was crewed by officers and men of the Royal Naval Reserve, the Royal Naval Volunteer Reserve and by 129 merchant seamen, sixty-five of whom were from her peacetime crew. Five of these were deck officers, thirty-one were stewards and the remainder, seamen and engine-room hands. Many were seafarers from the island of Lewis in the Outer Hebrides, a particularly tough brand of Scottish seamen who were to be found in great numbers aboard the merchant cruisers.

Captain Kennedy had a fine naval record. In 1900 he had served on the China Station. During the First World War, President Poincaré of France made him a Chevalier of the Legion of Honour for services rendered. As he sighted the outline of the *Scharnhorst* through the mist of that dusk, the huge enemy battle cruiser signalled: 'Stop or we sink you.' 'Sink and be damned to you,' answered Captain Kennedy to his officers on the bridge. He ordered full speed ahead, altered course to bring the enemy on the starboard quarter and ordered the crew to action stations. At this point, the *Gneisenau*, an equally powerful sistership hove into view.

At 1545 hours *Scharnhorst* fired her first salvo from her 11-inch guns at a range of 10,000 yards. It proved a near miss, and Captain Kennedy responded with all four of his starboard 6-inch guns. The enemy's second salvo was again a near miss, but the third destroyed the generating room, leaving the vessel without power or light. The fourth and last salvo shot away *Rawalpindi*'s bridge and radio room along with much of the accommodation.

Amid the squall and rising heavy seas the guns of HMS *Rawalpindi* were out of action. Sixteen minutes after the first salvo had been fired she was ablaze from stem to stern. Despite the seas, thirty-seven men got away from the burning ship, of which twenty-seven were picked up by *Gneisenau*. Captain Edward Kennedy and 248 of his men, 101 of whom were merchant seamen, perished with their ship. Some hours later, *Rawalpindi* sank, her battle flags still flying. A famous merchantman had served her country well, her captain and crew had fought and lost an epic duel. *Gneisenau* and *Scharnhorst*, at the time the finest ships in commission in the German Navy, scurried home to their base, successfully evading the pursuing British fleet units.

The Royal and Merchant Navies, the senior and the fourth services, were more closely integrated than many post-war writers would have us believe. Flying the red ensign, the merchantmen engaged in their role of trade and commerce, went about their work defended as best as possible by the small number of Royal Navy escort vessels. In port and at sea the gunners of the Royal Navy and Royal Artillery worked in close harmony with the merchant seamen. In spite of this close co-operation the loss of ships and of men were of great concern yet the gruesome aspect of total war and the 'happy days' of the U-boat crews was still to come.

3   U-boats: The Early Days

From the week of Dunkirk to the day that Japan bombed Pearl Harbor, Britain was virtually on its own and in dire peril. Early days in the battle for survival, these were eighteen long months for supremacy in the North Atlantic – the so-called 'happy days' of the U-boat crews, the 'era of the grey wolves'. Eight flotillas of U-boats were operating from western France. They had many successes. Working together in numbers, in 'wolf packs', they broke the inadequate escort screen. They sailed the ocean independently, picking off fast merchantmen, those that sailed without escort, at will. Many of them were the cream of Britain's merchant fleet.

In August 1940 Hitler lifted all restrictions on U-boat targets. Neutral as well as enemy shipping would be sunk on sight. The life of those aboard became highly dangerous. There was rarely any warning, just a violent shuddering explosion, often fatal to the engine-room staff. With the rapid tilting of the decks, the water came thundering in.

During the last five months of 1940 a total of 315 British-flag vessels were sunk. In the week ending 22 September twenty-seven British and Allied ships were sunk, more than any seven day total during the First World War. Losses in personnel mounted alarmingly. Of the five British merchantmen lost from homeward-bound convoy HX65 on 25 August, 162 trained officers and men perished. Enemy strength had increased to fifty-seven operational U-boats assisted by twenty-seven submarines of Mussolini's new Italian Atlantic Flotilla.

The commodore ship of HX65 (*Harpalyce*) sank in sixty seconds, taking with her thirty-seven crew as well as Commodore Vice-Admiral B.G. Washington and his staff. On her first war cruise, *U-124*, commanded by Lieutenant Wilhelm Schulz, came up fast, her surface speed of 18 knots catching the slender escort unawares. The crew of forty were all lost from *Fircrest*, which was carrying iron ore from Newfoundland. *U-48* sank *La Brea*, *Empire Merlin* and *Athelcrest*, a tanker delivered from the builder's yard only two months before.

The first successful wolf-pack operation was against convoy SC2, fifty-three ships sailing homewards from Sydney, Nova Scotia, on 25 August. Admiralty route instructions had been decoded by the enemy and, thirteen days later, *U-47* (Prien) and *U-28* (Kuhnke) were making contact. U-boat Command also called up *U-99* (Kretschmer), which, though unable to make contact, was engaged in the assault on convoy HX72 just twelve days later.

SC2's commodore was Rear-Admiral E. Boddam Whetham, on board *Harpoon*; the escorts were HMS *Lowestoft*, *Scarborough*, *Westcott*, *Skeena*, *Scimitar*, *Periwinkle* and the armed trawlers *Apollo* and *Berkshire*. Five merchantmen were lost: *Neptunian*, sunk by *U-47*; *Jose de Larrinaga* (*U-47*); *Mardinian* (*U-28*); the Norwegian *Gro* (*U-47*); and the Greek *Possidon* (*U-47*).

At the time SC2 was under attack an agreement was signed between Churchill and Roosevelt in which fifty veteran destroyers were to be taken out of reserve and delivered to Britain. In exchange a 99-year lease was granted to use bases in Newfoundland, Bermuda and the Bahamas, as well as West Indian islands in the Caribbean. It was a stop-gap measure. Much work was necessary to bring the vessels up to modern standards. It was many months before they were able to play their part in protecting the convoys.

Convoy HX72 was subjected to a twelve-hour battle on 21/22 September, in which eleven ships were sunk. Two more were damaged, although they were able to reach port. A total of over 100,000 tons of American supplies and some 45,000 tons of fuel oil were lost; undoubtedly the worst loss was again the men, particularly those with a lifetime of experience at sea. Unlike the fuel oil and supplies, they were irreplaceable. Later, when nearing the west of Scotland, the merchantmen experienced heavy weather and bombing by the Luftwaffe.

The Commodore was Captain H.H. Rogers RNR flying his standard in *Tregarthen*. Abreast of St John's Newfoundland ships from Bermuda and Sydney, Nova Scotia, joined those from Halifax. In *U-47* Prien, acting as weatherman, sighted the vessels low down on the horizon shortly after the ocean escort AMC *Jervis Bay* had left for other duties. Having only one torpedo left he called up *U-32*, *U-43*, *U-48* and *U-65*. Kretschmer (*U-99*), however, was first upon the scene.

At 22 degrees west the convoy had neither escort nor air cover, and suffered a devastating attack. The modern motor tankers *Invershannon*, torpedoed by *U-99*, and *Torinia* (*U-100*), built in 1938 and 1939 respectively, exploded, with heavy loss of life. *Baron Blythswood*, torpedoed by *U-99*, was another vessel carrying iron ore for the hungry steel industry. She sank like a stone amid a huge sheet of flame. Her master and thirty-four of his crew perished. Joachim Schepke, in command of *U-100*, was to claim a further six vessels, even though at the time a Canadian escort had arrived.

The voyage of convoy SC7 the following month was again disastrous.

As the thirty-five heavily-laden merchantmen, steaming in nine columns abreast, made their way eastward a gale blew up from the north-west. There was little to comfort one. The majority of the merchantmen were old, slow and dirty coalburners – 'old wrecks and barnacled tramps' was one description. Half of them dated back to the First World War and some even to the turn of the century.

Half-way across the wide 'western ocean', with the gale developing into storm, came the escorts – HMS *Scarborough* and *Bluebell; Fowey, Leith* and *Heartsease* – a welcome sight. On the twelfth day the commodore, 57-year-old Admiral Mackinnon, aboard the merchant-man *Assyrian*, became concerned when a small Canadian Lakes steamer was unable to maintain her position. Straggling astern she was sunk by *U-124*. As the day wore on seven U-boats converged. There were six other boats in the vicinity. Then came the massacre. Twenty-one were torpedoed and sunk – nine during the first two hours – and a further two damaged. Yet no submarines were sunk in reply. Kretschmer (*U-99*) made one of his deadly surface dashes through the convoy ranks at 18 knots and sank six vessels.

Among those sunk was *Assyrian*, which earlier had given chase to a U-boat on the surface with the intention of ramming it. The torpedo from *U-101* tore into her side just forward of the engine room. Miraculously Admiral Mackinnon was hauled aboard HMS *Leith*; he was injured. Among the long list of casualties was the vice-commodore ship, the former-French tanker *Languedoc, Scoresby*, the Greek *Aenos, Beatus, Creekirk* and the Swedish *Convallaria*. With the convoy scattered over some thirty square miles it became the turn of the Dutch *Soesterberg*, the Norwegian *Snefjeld*, the British *Sedgepool, Thalia* the Greek and *Boekolo* the Dutchman.

Boekolo, damaged by *U-100* on 18 October, was sunk by *U-123* the following day. When torpedoed the second time she lay wallowing in the sea attempting to rescue survivors from the Cardiff tramp *Beatus*. Over a period of seventy-two hours a further 100,000 tons of cargo lay on the ocean floor: the *Corinthic*, loaded with 8,000 tons of scrap and steel and topped up with railway lines and strip steel for plating aircraft; *Creekirk*, the oldest British vessel, built in 1912 – along with her cargo of iron ore she took her entire crew of thirty-six brave men, including her Jersey-born master and a sixteen-year-old cabin boy; *Assyrian*, with grain loaded in New Orleans; *Somersby*, with grain from the Canadian prairies; and *Sedgepool*, with grain for Manchester.

With the attack on HX 79, which followed only hours later, it was the same violent story: thirteen vessels sunk. Over a period of just two days 327,000 tons of merchant shipping had been lost from two convoys. The late-November convoy, departing from Halifax, Nova Scotia, on the 21st of the month, was another hunted down by 'the professionals', the peacetime commanders drilled in the action of 'wolf-packs'. In this instance seven U-boats, with Prien in *U-47* and Kretschmer in U-99, were at the forefront of the affray. Ernst Mengersen in *U-101* was to torpedo four vessels – three were sunk and one damaged.

The Commodore aboard *Botavon* was governed by two factors: the weather was deteriorating and only AMC *Laconia* was available to protect his 'brood' of forty ships, in nine columns five cables apart. He was therefore content to await the arrival of his destroyer escort. It was then that all hell was let loose. Over a period of thirty hours, a further eight merchantmen were hit by torpedoes. With *Laconia* already departed for other duties, AMC *Forfar* was directed to the scene; but when about to leave for escort OB251 to the north, which was being shadowed by *U-43*, she herself was torpedoed and sunk. Sturdy merchantman that she was, it took five torpedoes from Kretschmer's *U-99* to send *Forfar* to the bottom.

Bibby Line's *Stirlingshire* with a cargo of frozen meat and 'generals' (general provisions) from Australia, was sunk by *U-94*. This U-boat was commanded by the successful Herbert Kuppisch, whose 'tonnage' during the following year brought him his Iron Cross. *Victoria City*, the Vice-Commodore ship, loaded with steel from New York and bound for London, became separated from the convoy owing to the weather. Neither she nor her crew of forty-three were ever seen again.

Of all the convoy battles during the year 1941 special mention must be made of those involving OG71, SC42 and SC52. It was on 17 August in calm seas and beautiful summer weather that *U-201* (Adalbert Schnee) sighted the twenty-two vessels of OG71. Guided by reports from her and from aircraft, *U-559*, *U-564* and *U-204* were called up. The convoy was under continual enemy surveillance from the air, and their activities were reported to U-boats in the region.

One of the escorts, the Flower-class corvette *Campanula*, had on board a raw lieutenant by the name of Nicholas Monsarrat. He went on to command his own corvette, and later, a frigate, but of all his five-and-a-half years spent at sea on Atlantic convoys, OG71 to Gibraltar remained the strongest in his memory. 'That convoy was my worst experience of the war,' he declared. 'It will live with me for ever.' In the pages of *The Cruel Sea* he describes the role of the fictional corvette HMS *Compass Rose* in a convoy to Gibraltar, which left the bombed city of Liverpool at exactly the same time as convoy OG71.

Leading the convoy of twenty-two merchantmen through the Mersey Bar was the Yeoward Line cargo passenger *Aquila*, the commodore vessel with Vice-Admiral Patrick Parker and his staff aboard. The *Ciscar* (Captain Hughes) was to act as vice-commodore. It was the thirteenth day of August. Six days later, in the early hours, the destroyer *Bath*, on loan to the Royal Norwegian Navy, was torpedoed by *U-204*. One of the former US four-funnellers, she was astern of the convoy zigzagging at 12 knots. She sank in a horrific three minutes taking eighty-three men with her including her captain, Lieutenant Commander Frederick Melsom.

A minute later the small (1,584 tons) *Alva* came to a similar end, sunk by *U-559*. Two hours later, 600 miles west of Ushant, course south-west by south, speed 8 knots, *Ciscar* and *Aquila* were hit simultaneously by a four-torpedo salvo fired by *U-201*.

Later the ocean-going tug *Empire Oak*, which had earlier rescued six survivors from *Aquila*, and the Irish merchantman *Clonlara*, were sunk shortly before a further four vessels, one of which was the corvette *Zinnia*. She blew up with an explosion that echoed all round the convoy and submerged in a mere fifteen seconds, leaving hardly a vestige of wreckage. The remaining fourteen merchantmen entered the neutral Tagus river and anchored off Lisbon on the morning of 24 August. They were escorted by the destroyers *Gurkha* and *Lance*, which had been called up from convoy WS10X by Commander-in-Chief Western Approaches (Admiral Sir Percy Noble). That day witnessed 'a cruel sea' indeed – one that no survivor could forget. The following is a summary of the losses that day:

Aquila cargo, 'generals' sunk by *U-201*. Two torpedoes; vanished in 90 seconds, 16 survivors including her master, Captain Frith. 65 crew, five gunners, the Commodore and four of his staff, together with 89 passengers which included 22 WRENS being drafted to Gibraltar were lost. Steward seriously injured.
(The only other occasion during the war which involved the loss of young members of the Women's Services was when the transport *Khedive Ismail* was sunk in 1944 (see Chapter 7. East of Cape Town).)
Ciscar Stores. *U-201*. 13 lost 25 rescued.
Alva Coal/Stores. *U-559*. One lost but later 14 lost from *Clonlara* and 3 from *Empire Oak*.
Empire Oak (tug) *U-564*. 14 lost.
Clonlara Coal. *U-564*. 12 lost.
Aldergrove Patent fuel. *U-201*. One lost.
Stork Petrol in cans. *U-201*. 19 lost, only 3 rescued.
Spind (Norwegian) Coal/Coke. Hit by torpedo and gunfire, *U-564*. Sunk later by *U-552*. All saved.
RNN *Bath* *U-204*. 83 lost from a crew of 130.
HMS *Zinnia* *U-564*. 17 survivors only.

All four active U-boats were later sunk:

U-204 Mediterranean. 19 Oct 1941. HMS *Mallow* & *Rochester*. No survivors.

U-559 Mediterranean. 30 Oct 1942. HMS *Pakenham, Petard, Hero, Dulverton, Hurworth* and British aircraft. 8 killed, 38 captured.

U-201 North Atlantic. 17 Feb 1943. HMS *Fame*. No survivors.

U-564 Biscay. 14 June 1943. Aircraft. Br. Sqdn 10. 28 lost, 18 captured.

The 7½-knot convoy SC42, homeward bound in September, suffered severely. The sixty-five merchantmen in twelve columns were led by Commodore Rear-Admiral W.B. Mackenzie on board *Everleigh*. Escort for the first part of the Atlantic crossing was provided by a Canadian group – HMCS *Skeena, Alberni, Kenogami* and *Orillia*.

After the battle, the biggest in the war to date, the convoy was joined by relief escorts from the United Kingdom. There were no further attacks for five days but upon approaching the north of Scotland, the motorship *Jedmoor* was sunk by *U-98*. She was carrying a valuable cargo of manganese ore used in the manufacture of steel. Loaded at Santos in Brazil she had logged some 8,000 miles. Thirty-one men were lost; only six were saved.

A total of fifteen vessels were sunk, including a straggler, *Empire Springbuck*, loaded with steel and munitions, which was lost with all hands. The tanker *Tahchee*, torpedoed and damaged, was successfully towed to Reykjavik by HMCS *Orillia*. The other merchantmen were:

Muneric Sunk by *U-432*. Rio de Janeiro/Middlesbrough with iron ore. No survivors – 63 including 2 stowaways.

Baron Pentland *U-652*. 39 rescued.

Winterswijk (Dutch) *U-432*. 20 crew lost.

Stargard (Norwegian) *U-432*. 2 men lost.

Sally Maersk (ex-Danish) *U-81*. All saved.

Empire Hudson *U-82*. Recently converted CAM ship carrying grain. 54 saved. Prematurely abandoned.

Thistleglen *U-85*. 3 men lost.

Bulysses (tanker) *U-82*. 4 men lost.

Gypsum Queen *U-82*. Cargo sulphur. 10 lost. 26 rescued by Norwegian *Vestland*.

Stonepool *U-207*. Grain from Canada. 41 lost. 8 rescued.

Berury *U-207*. One man lost.

Scania (Swedish) *U-82/U-202*. All saved.

Empire Crossbill *U-82*. Carrying munitions. No survivors – 48 lost.

Garm (Swedish) *U-432*. 6 lost. 14 saved.

Two U-boats were sunk: *U-501* by HMCS *Chambly* and *Moosejaw*; and *U-207* (no survivors) by HMS *Leamington* and *Veteran*. Both submarines were on their first war cruise. None of the other seven U-boats survived the war:

U-81 Sunk by US aircraft. Pola, Italy. 9 Jan 1944.

U-82 HMS *Rochester* and *Tamarish*. All hands. N. Atlantic. 6 Feb 1942.

U-85 Lost with all hands. USS *Roper*. N. Atlantic. 14 April 1942.

U-98 All hands. Aircraft 608 Sqdn. N. Atlantic. 19 Nov 1942.

U-202 HMS *Starling*. 18 killed, 30 captured. N. Atlantic. 1 June 1943.

U-432 French *Aconit*. 26 killed, 20 captured. N. Atlantic 11 Mar 1943.

U-562 Damaged by aircraft 815 & 203 Sqdn. Crew recovered by *U-81* who then sank her. Aegean. 2 June 1942.

SC52 was sailing from Nova Scotia with a Canadian escort in October 1941. On the last day of the month, trouble arrived whilst the convoy was still off the coast of Newfoundland. The steamer *Rose Schiaffino*, an iron ore carrier bound from Wabana to Cardiff, had no sooner taken up her position than she was torpedoed by *U-569*. All hands – thirty-seven crew and four gunners – perished.

Four hours later there followed *Flynderborg* and *Gretavale*, sunk by *U-202*, and as night fell, so too did *Empire Gemsbuck* and the Latvian steamer *Everoja*, now under British management. Both were sunk by *U-203*. It was at this stage that the commodore, Captain S.N. White RNR, on board *Empire Hartebeeste*, ordered the convoy to return to Sydney for regrouping. This was the furthest west that the U-boats had ventured during this period. The escort had been unable to detect them in advance and loss of life on the merchantmen had been heavy.

As course was set for the mouth of Belle Isle Straits, fog set in and the vessels became scattered over a wide area. Two ships, the *Marouka Pateras* and the *Empire Energy* ran aground where they quickly became a total loss. SC52 won the distinction of being the only transatlantic convoy to be driven back by the enemy during the entire war, this in spite of the local Canadian escort of two destroyers and eight corvettes.

There were many famous pre-war merchantmen lost during the 1940–41 period. Those chosen for mention now are one from each of four companies whose operation was essential to the successful conduct of the war: the Blue Star Line, Canadian Pacific, Ellerman's and the Pacific Steam Navigation Company.

Arandora Star had served her country well even before she sailed on her fateful voyage so early during the conflict. She had been engaged in the Norway fiasco, in the evacuation from Brest and from Saint-Nazaire, Bordeaux and Saint-Jean du Luz. On 29 June her overworked crew were at Liverpool preparing for a transatlantic crossing to St John's, Newfoundland. Three days later, she sailed at about 0400 hours, carrying 1,673 people who were made up of: 174 officers and crew; 200 military guard; 479 German interned males; 86 German prisoners of war; 734 Italian interned males.

During the morning of the same day, proceeding independently at 15 knots and zigzagging in accordance with Admiralty instructions, she was positioned seventy-five miles west of Bloody Foreland, County Donegal. Sighted by Günther Prien in *U-47* the torpedo ripped apart the after-engine room, and the ship was plunged into complete darkness. Two lifeboats were smashed and she took on a twenty-degree list. Panic reigned as many of the Germans and Italians refused to jump to the liferafts which had been thrown from the upper deck; at the same time they overcrowded the ten lifeboats which had been lowered.

With bows raised, *Arandora Star* rolled over on her side and then slid under carrying many with her: 805, including her master, Captain Moulton, twelve of his officers and forty-two crew, perished. Rescue was made by HMCS *St Laurent*, which landed 868 survivors at Greenock the next day.

Even more distressing, perhaps, was the disaster that overcame Ellerman's 1936-built *City of Benares*, which sailed from the Mersey some ten weeks later. It was in fact Friday the thirteenth, a date that seamen, by superstition, would refuse to sail upon in peacetime. However, convoy OB213, nineteen ships strong, departed on Friday, 13 September 1940, bound for Canada. Superstitions are not allowed to interfere with the conduct of war.

City of Benares was commodore ship with Rear-Admiral Mackinnon DSO aboard. Convoy speed was 8½ knots. There were three columns with the Commodore leading the one in the centre; the escort was one destroyer and two sloops. Her loss is remembered in particular for the seventy-seven children who were drowned when she was torpedoed by *U-48* on 17 September. Only thirteen children survived.

During the early hours of that fateful day, the escort vessels left being at the limit of their range. There was a strong north-west wind, a rough confused sea and it was necessary to discontinue zigzagging. At 2205 hours the torpedo struck *City of Benares*. There was a violent explosion and within minutes she began to settle by the stern. The vessel was abandoned at 2220 hours, but there was difficulty in lowering the lifeboats on the weather side. Some of the children in lifeboat number 8 had been seriously injured in the explosion. As the boat cast off, shipping water badly, they were laid flat in the bottom, the blood-tinted sea-water giving indication of their plight.

A total of 255 lost their lives in the disaster:

European crew: 20 including Captain Nicoll.
Asian crew: 101 from a total of 166.
Convoy staff: Rear-Admiral Mackinnon DSO.
Passengers (fare-paying): 51.
CORS Children: 77.

CORS Escorts: 6.
18 September (evening): HMS *Hurricane* picked up 105 survivors.
25 September: HMS *Anthony* rescued 40 survivors.

Under the Children's Overseas Resettlement Scheme (CORS) young children from five to fifteen years were offered homes in British dominions for the duration of the war. The scheme prospered: 1,530 were sent to Canada; 577 to Australia, 353 to South Africa; and 202 to New Zealand. After the loss of *City of Benares* there were no more Children's Overseas Resettlement ships; the sailing of *Llandaff Castle* scheduled to sail for Cape Town on 20 September was cancelled.

Before this tragedy, other merchantmen engaged in the overseas evacuation of children had been *Anselm, Batory, Ceramic, Duchess of York, Hilary, Llanstephen Castle, Rangitata, Ruahine* and the Dutch *Volendam*. The latter, however, was torpedoed and seriously damaged off the west coast of Ireland only fourteen days before *City of Benares* sailed. Fortunately there were no casualties.

Empress of Britain (Captain Sapsworth) owned by Canadian Pacific Steamships Ltd had been charted to carry HM King George VI and Queen Elizabeth and their party eastbound from Canada to Southampton in 1939. Fifteen months later (26 October 1940), travelling independently homeward from Suez via Cape Town, she was bombed by a Focke-Wulf 200 aircraft. On board, in addition to her crew of 419, were 224 military personnel and their families, eagerly awaiting disembarkation in Liverpool the next day.

Receiving a direct hit from two bombs, the ship burst into flame, which spread over the whole midship section; forty-five of her complement were missing. Efforts were made to take her in tow but the following day she was sighted by *U-38*, which had been called up. Trailing the liner and evading the protecting screen of the escorting destroyers, *U-38* fired three torpedoes during the early hours of 28 October. *Empress of Britain* heeled over and quickly disappeared. At 42,348 tons, the largest merchantman to be sunk during the Second World War, she had been requisitioned as a troopship in November 1939. Having travelled 61,000 miles during her eleven months of service, she had carried 9,231 military personnel, 925 civilian passengers and 2,850 tons of cargo.

Oropesa, the second ship of her name, was owned by the Pacific Steam Navigation Company and launched in 1920. She too had been patronized by royalty. In 1931 she was chosen to carry HRH the Prince of Wales and Prince George on a tour from Santander, Spain, to Callao, Peru. Laid up during the worldwide shipping slump of the 1930s, she was converted at the outbreak of war for troop-carrying. At the end of December 1940, *Oropesa* sailed homewards from Cape Town with Royal Navy personnel, 203 crew and 3,000 tons of 'generals'.

In the early hours of 16 January, some 200 miles off the north-west coast of Ireland, the independent 14,118-ton *Oropesa* was torpedoed by *U-96*. (The next day the same submarine was to sink the unescorted 14,935-ton *Almeda Star*. Though severely damaged the PSNC vessel showed little sign of sinking, and no attempt was made to abandon her. Some two hours later, as engineers were making desperate efforts to restart one of the engines, a further two torpedoes hit their target. Immediately she began to heel over and was quickly abandoned. Nine lifeboats got away and soon afterwards *Oropesa* slipped beneath the waves stern first.

With the weather deteriorating into storm-force winds and snow and sleet, the boats became separated, though three were found by HMS *Westcott* within twenty-four hours. Another lifeboat was taken in tow by a naval tug on 24 January, but the other five, containing many seamen from Merseyside, were never seen again. Among those lost was her master, Captain Croft.

During the winter and early spring of 1941 Hitler's blockade was beginning to bite. Sailing with convoy OB289 that February there was a strong sense of setting forth into the unknown. Would we, like our Danish, Dutch and Norwegian compatriots who now sailed in convoy with us, at some stage find ourselves sailing the seas without a home port to call our own?

With the storms of war so much in evidence it was easy to overlook the storms of nature, particularly for one like myself, a youth of seventeen years on his first voyage. As *Nailsea Manor* came abreast a misty Eriskay that day there sat a merchantman high out of the water. Two vessels, intent on salvage, appeared to be assisting her. It was J. & C. Harrison's 7,939-ton *Politician* (Captain Worthington), outward bound for Jamaica. Carrying a general cargo, which included 25,000 cases of Scotch whisky, she had gone aground after being battered by mountainous seas just three weeks before. The incident was immortalized in Compton Mackenzie's novel *Whisky Galore*, from which an Ealing comedy was made for the cinema. Later, a television documentary was produced about the stranding.

Always a navigator's nightmare, particularly so when in convoy, the Minches claimed another victim just days prior to our passage. The iron ore carrier *Thala*, commodore ship of a seven-vessel convoy bound 'north about' for Middlesbrough, struck a rock south of Hartamil Island. Breaking in two she sank twenty fathoms deep. Rocks can cripple a ship just as easily as mines, bombs and torpedoes.

After being joined by eleven merchantmen from the convoy assembly base of Loch Ewe, our convoy (32 vessels) was complete, and forged ahead into the Atlantic. Our escort consisted of two corvettes and two armed trawlers. The 'North-western Approaches' had seldom been busier. Between the Outer Hebrides and the Faroe Islands sailed three outward convoys (OB288, OB289 and OB290). From North America two inward convoys were in close proximity, having been routed to the west of the Outer Hebrides towards the North Channel.

Unbeknown to those who sailed the seas that day, twenty-six vessels had been sunk by U-boats in the North Atlantic over the last ten days. Focke-Wulf Condor aircraft operating from Merignac, near Bordeaux, in co-operation with U-boats, had sunk a further twenty ships and damaged five over a seven-day period. Further west in mid-ocean the heavy cruiser *Admiral Hipper* and the battle cruisers *Scharnhorst* and *Gneisenau* lay in wait. During February these raiders had sunk twelve merchantmen.

In latitude 61, ship's time 0300, wind easterly force 4, barometer 29·56 and falling, Temperature 30 degrees Fahrenheit and falling, the enemy struck. The luminous meteoric phenomenon of the Northern Lights overshadowed the 'snowflakes' fired by the escort. The seven columns of OB289 surged ahead, rolling on beam-ends as an emergency turn to port was executed.

The merchantman *Jonathon Holt* blazed furiously as she dropped astern, her engine room and bridge destroyed. Her master, Captain Stephenson and thirty-eight crew, two gunners and eleven passengers died in the inferno. Shortly afterwards the steamship *Mansepool* was torpedoed and sunk. During the forenoon watch the enemy struck again, sinking the tanker *British Gunner* and seriously damaging the Norwegian motor tanker *G.C. Brovig*. The Flower-class corvette *Petunia*, commissioned some two weeks before and on her first escort duty, rescued seventeen survivors from *Mansepool*. She then stood by the *British Gunner* before escorting the Norwegian tanker to Stornaway where the *Brovig* was beached.

The enemy that day was Udo Heilman in *U-97*. Five days previously he had sailed his submarine from Kiel on her first war cruise. On 22 February he was instructed to search for convoys OB288 and OB289, both of which had been reported by Condor aircraft. Also in the area were *U-95*, *U-108* and *U-552*. The following day *U-97* had been ordered to attack OB290 together with *U-47, U-73* and *U-99* and the submarines *Barbarigo* and *Bianchi*, the farthest north that the Italians ventured in the Atlantic war. Heilman was unable to establish contact, however, and *U-97* was subsequently used as a weather-reporting boat, returning to Western France on 8 March.

On 26 February the U-boats sank five merchantmen and damaged one from convoy OB290. Condor aircraft then sank seven and damaged four. It was K.G.40s (Bordeaux) greatest single success against ships in convoy. Notable also was the fact that of the five ships torpedoed by U-boats, four were credited to Lieutenant-Commander Günther Prien (*U-47*).

The 8,106-ton motor tanker *Diala*, outward bound in ballast for the

United States to load gasoline, was damaged twice during that day: first in the darkness of the early hours by a torpedo from *U-47*; and later, during the afternoon when the Condors struck. One of her crew recalls that momentous raid.

> Six of these large Condor aircraft were sighted and they proceeded to fly once around the convoy before splitting up, one to each column. All hell was then let loose: ships sounding their sirens, guns blazing and the roar of aircraft engines getting louder and louder. I was designated as a loader for the gun so had a pretty good idea of what was happening and was amazed at how low the planes were flying. I could see the wing tips of our particular attacker projecting from each side of the bridge of the ship astern.
>
> I saw the bomb leave the bomb bay. We fired our gun; goodness knows where the shell went. There was a huge explosion, the ship leapt into the air. A mountainous sea rose and crashed over the bridge. We scrambled to our feet, again fully expecting to take to the boats but we kept our convoy position. We were fortunate. It was a 'near miss' which necessitated repair-work when we reached the peace of the Delaware river some sixteen days later.

During January 1942 *Diala* was lost when she was torpedoed in mid-Atlantic by *U-553*. Fifty-seven crew were killed when the bows of the vessel were completely blown off creating a huge amount of superstructure damage.

Four months later (June 1941) *Nailsea Manor* was one of the merchantmen sailing with convoy HX133, homewards from Halifax, Nova Scotia (see Appendix X). Dense fog over five days brought four collisions. This was followed by a submarine attack involving six U-boats, two of which were sunk. It became notable in Admiralty circles for being one of the few convoys drawn to the attention of Winston Churchill. The Prime Minister then asked to be shown the reports of the commodore and those of the ocean escort, HMS *Wolfe* (Captain J.D. Laureworth) (Before being requisitioned HMS *Wolfe* was the former Canadian Pacific liner *Montcalm*.)

Captain Roy Gill RNR, who was later knighted, was commodore aboard the vessel *Glenpark*. His was the first convoy to enjoy a Canadian escort for part of the crossing. This came in the form of RCNS *Ottawa*, *Orillia*, *Collingwood*, *Chambly*, *Annapolis* and four trawlers. Later the escort was provided by the B8 group from Londonderry: HMS *Fleetwood*, *Ripley*, *Celandine*, *Gladiolus*, *Niger*, *Nasturtium*, *Malcolm*, *Icarus*, *Violet*, *Watchman*, *Scimitar*, *Speedwell*, *Arabis* and *Maplin*.

The following merchantmen collided with each other: *Nailsea Manor* and *Dolabella; Tricula* and *Treworlas; Skeldersgate* and *Konsgaard;* and *City of Oxford* and *Primero*. The log book of *Nailsea Manor* (19 June, 1024 hours local time) reveals the necessary entry for her owners. 'While in convoy and carrying out the Commodore's orders to alter course from 084 degrees to 024 degrees during dense fog, *Nailsea Manor* No. 041 and *Dolabella* No. 032 collided.'

Merchantmen torpedoed:

Vigrid   26 lost including 4 passengers (21 picked up after 3 weeks in lifeboat).   *U-371*
Brockley Hill   Crew of 42 all saved.   *U-651*
Tibia   Damaged; rejoined convoy.   *U-79*
Soloy   Crew of 29 all saved   *U-203*
Maasdam   2 passengers lost; 77 survivors.   *U-564*
Malaya II   39 lost; 6 survivors.   *U-564*
Konsgaard   Damaged; rejoined convoy.   *U-564*
Grayburn   35 lost; 18 survivors.   *U-561*

Following her collision *Nailsea Manor* was instructed to head for St John's, Newfoundland, for repairs. The following was written shortly afterwards.

It was the worst weather I had experienced. We rolled on our beam ends; there were occasions when my heart 'missed a beat' as I wondered whether she would stay there. I found great difficulty in trying to sleep; my bunk, the top one of a pair, lay transversely across the cabin. At one moment my head was high in the air with my full weight pressing against the bulkhead, the next moment my feet were much higher than my head.

The waves were curling over the bow as the north-westerly with great gusts of spray flew across the bridge. Visibility was down to 300 yards, the wind increasing from force 9, strong gale, to force 10 storm; for'ard she was white with broken seas overall, the alleyways amidships deep in water. Occasionally the seas were coming aboard 'green', a term which hitherto I had come across only in the great sailing ship sagas of discovery and exploration. Now the sea was rushing and tearing through the scuppers and washports. It was 'dirty weather' said the old hands – the type of weather known to all Western-Ocean men. In 5,000-ton trampships, heavily laden with food and the munitions of war, however, you are much nearer the waterline than in tall ocean liners.

As we altered course in the middle watch she corkscrewed badly. Then, with her bow sinking in the deep troughs, her propeller came high out of the water, racing badly, the propeller shaft beneath the after holds vibrating her every rivet. As her bow rose, *Nailsea Manor* shuddered overall. A pillar of water reared up, the dark purple blue paled into clearest delicate green as it towered, its head white, stood for an instant, and then the mass toppled and fell. There was a huge metallic jar as it hit the ship. She vibrated with springing spasms.

I was anxious to get some sleep. As I turned to wedge my head between the pillow and guard rail, the cabin deck seemed to come to meet me, my head tossed back as if it no longer was part of me. There was a thundering crash of solid water meeting metal outside the porthole. The bulkhead took the full force of the sea, every rivet took the strain as she shook and shivered like a drenched sheepdog. But a Bartram-built ship (of Sunderland) was a tough ship; we had every confidence in her.

By daybreak the wind had backed a little though still the gale blew with gusts of storm-force. And with the change in wind came dense fog with visibility now 30 yards, unusual weather for June even on the treacherous Newfoundland banks. As we towed our fog-buoy, an ingenious little device, the scoop of which threw up a small fountain of water abreast the bow on the port side of the following ship (designed by a clever Second Mate) we lost all sight of our comrades. Each ship now cocooned in a world of its own, its only contact with the Commodore and with her friends, by steam whistle. Each vessel at intervals of three minutes sounded her convoy position in morse code. Five long blasts followed by four short and one long thereafter by one short blast and four long (041) signified the position of *Nailsea-Manor* leading column four.

The Commodore, no doubt receiving a warning of U-boats waiting for us ahead, possibly in clearer seas, sounded an alteration of course by whistle. To the layman it was an impossible action. Yet, without seeing each other, three cables apart, forty odd ships, including our escort, shifted their helms. Those on the starboard side of the rectangle increased speed, those on the port side slowed down. The whole convoy wheeled just like a company of soldiers on the parade ground. It is doubtful whether soldiers could achieve the move safely in such inclement weather.

The gale and the dense fog continued for two whole days and two long nights. At dawn on the third day with Masters and Mates, Helmsmen and look-outs, tired and tense, every hour hoping that the next would bring clear skies and smooth waters, possibly the inevitable happened. *Nailsea Manor* had collided with *Dolabella*.

The long-range four-engined Focke-Wulf 200 (Condor) aircraft, which were able to attack convoys far out in the Atlantic from their bases in Western France, became an increasing menace. The Condor was a wartime conversion of a civil aircraft and a bare 200 were produced. It is difficult to understand why the enemy did not devote more resources to building them. In their Atlantic role they were able to find, shadow and report convoy movements to the U-boat arm.

Bombing ships was a secondary role for the aircraft, but so successful were they, that along with other planes of the Luftwaffe, a total of 323,000 tons of shipping were sunk during the month of April 1941. The corresponding U-boat total was 249,000 tons.

To counteract the activities of the Focke-Wulf 200, the catapult-armed merchantmen, soon to be known as CAM ships and briefly mentioned in Chapter 1, were devised as a stop-gap means of giving convoys some protection from the air. Selected ships, thirty-six in total, and most of new construction, had ramps fitted on their fo'c's'les. The aircraft were there mounted on a trolley driven along rails by rockets for some sixty feet. At this distance, using 30 degree flaps and a 6¼-pound boost, a perfect take-off could be made, without any loss of height, at an air speed usually well over eighty miles per hour. Such vessels continued to fly the red ensign and ply their normal trade as cargo carriers.

Except for the SS *Michael E*, one of the first CAM ships which had a naval pilot and a Sea Hurricane aircraft, the pilots and aircraft were from the Air Force. Sixty pilots, all volunteers, formed the unit in April 1941. In each ship selected, the unit consisted of a pilot, four aircrew, naval ratings for catapult maintenance and a naval flight direction officer to guide the pilot on to his target by radio telephone.

The pilot's job demanded a particularly cold-blooded form of courage as his was literally a one-way trip. The convoy would rarely be within flying range of land, so that after engaging the enemy, the pilot had to choose between ditching in the sea alongside a ship or baling out. Either way he hoped he would be picked up.

Commander M.A. 'Dapper' Birrell was the Navy's catapult fighter pilot. It was he who did the first trials on board the *Michael E* in Belfast Lough on 18 May 1941. Only half the rockets fired, and Birrell's Hurricane actually touched the water after it left the ship. The general noise and smoke of the launch caused an air-raid alert in Belfast. The trial was considered a success, however. More successful perhaps were the Air Force trials on 31 May, which took place from *Empire Rainbow* in the Clyde estuary.

The *Michael E* sailed from the Mersey on 27 May in convoy OB236 but only six days later fell victim to *U-108*. The convoy had dispersed the previous day, each vessel having been instructed to proceed direct under Admiralty routeing to their destination. The torpedo caused immense damage to the ship which began to break up. Birrell was aboard, and he argued with the master to let him launch the aircraft so that at least something of the ship would be saved. He argued in vain. The next day, along with some members of the ship's crew, he was picked up after twenty hours in a lifeboat.

In spite of losses – twelve were sunk by enemy action – the CAM ships were considered a success. They sailed 170 convoy voyages round-trip, across the Atlantic, the Arctic and over to Gibraltar. Six enemy aircraft were destroyed and three damaged.

After his rescue from *Michael E*, Birrell joined 804 Squadron, which provided pilots and aircraft for the auxiliary fighter catapult ships. These were converted merchantmen commissioned as warships under the white ensign. One of these, HMS *Ariguani* – a twin-screw 6,746-ton vessel, built for Elders & Fyffes Ltd as a banana boat in 1926 – Birrell joined as pilot of the Fairey Fulmar aircraft.

Bound in convoy for Sierra Leone, Birrell was launched from *Ariguani* in pursuit of a Focke-Wulf 200 aircraft some 275 miles west of Bantry Bay, Southern Ireland. He drove it off after a long chase, but lost the convoy in bad weather and decided to try and make land. He found a long sandy beach at Ardara, County Donegal, in neutral Eire, where he would have been interned. However, a total stranger with an English accent came up and offered him petrol. He was thus able to take off in time to evade the local Garda, who was approaching on his bicycle. Birrell later landed on an airfield under construction in Northern Ireland.

Two months later (26 October 1941) *Ariguani*, with Birrell aboard, was torpedoed by *U-83* when with convoy HG75 homewards from Gibraltar, some 400 miles west of Cape St Vincent. Maurice Birrell was rescued by the corvette *Campion* but as *Ariguani* did not sink, she was reboarded and towed into Gibraltar.

The enemy attack on convoy HG75, which lasted for five days, was particularly vicious. It opened when the destroyer *Cossack* was destroyed by *U-563*; there was heavy loss of life. Later, after four merchantmen had been lost, two Italian submarines were sunk: *Ferraris* during a gun battle with the destroyer *Lamerton*; and *Marconi* through unknown causes.

The CAM ships, the fighter catapult ships and the merchant aircraft carriers, designated MAC ships, which were to follow, all rendered valuable service. Then, during early 1943, came the escort aircraft carriers, which made them redundant. There is no doubt that without these carriers of fighter aircraft, during the dark days of 1941, ship losses would have been far greater.

Of the Royal Navy staff employed upon merchantmen, probably the commodore and his convoy signallers were closer to the master and officers than just about anyone. Generally speaking, they all got on well together. There were two categories of commodores: 'ocean', based at Liverpool under Captain Goff RN (naval control senior officer); and 'coastal', based at Southend, under Captain Champion RN (NCSO). Under their control were the routeing and boarding staff, who were in turn responsible for producing and distributing convoy orders and organizing the timetables.

The commodores were Royal Navy admirals, rear-admirals and captains, Royal Navy Reserve, from the major shipping lines. All were aged between sixty and seventy years, and were mainly retired men who had served with distinction during the First World War. A typical Atlantic convoy would start with the conference of ships' masters where the NCSO and commodore would brief everyone on the latest details relevant to the ocean crossing. Sometimes the senior officers of the escort would attend and usually the convoy yeoman of signals. He was in charge of the commodore's staff, which consisted of the yeoman, petty officer radio telegraphist, leading signaller and three signalmen watchkeepers. Signalmen would also be placed in merchantmen designated Vice- and Rear-Commodore ships. They were necessary in the event of the commodore ship being sunk.

The yeomen would attend the bridge of the ship whilst the commodore was present and at all times during manoeuvres and important signal activity. The radio telegraphist 'sat in' with the ship's radio officer and, in the latter years of the war, operated a portable radio telephone (VHF) for use in emergencies.

Twenty-one commodores were lost from Liverpool during the war, twelve admirals RN and nine captains RNR. In addition, three 'coastal' convoy commodores (Southend) were lost. The top two ocean commodores were Rear-Admiral Sir E. Manners, fifty-two convoys, and Rear-Admiral E.W. Leir, forty-eight convoys. In the coastal organization, Commander F.A.C. Hunter DSC, RD came top, having sailed in no less than 197 convoys; Commander R.V. Rutley OBE, RD came a close second, with 187 convoys to his credit.

Losses among signalmen totalled 138, the highest number of fatalities of any specialist branch of all four services. In addition to the hostilities-only (HO) signalmen, twenty-six Royal Naval men were lost, and this includes twelve yeomen who 'went down' with their commodores. As one would expect, being in virtually continuous action, bravery awards were hard-earned. Even though the Royal Navy had only 17 per cent of all World War Two decorations, this branch is unique among all the services in having the highest proportion of decorated men.

From the intake of 500 men selected for training for convoy signalling work in September 1939 (at HMS *Royal Arthur*, Skegness – the Butlins holiday camp) fifty-five eventually passed as convoy yeomen and had their own staffs. By 1942 they were fully in control of Atlantic, Mediterranean, African and Russian convoys. As the Allies advanced, they widened their scope to take in the landings in North Africa, Sicily and eventually Normandy. They were as much a part of the fourth service as they were of the senior service. Of the fifty-five men, thirty-eight were decorated, many of them more than once. In addition, there were thirty-one Distinguished Service Medals (DSM) and forty-one 'Mentioned in Despatches' (MID) among the signalmen.

The commodore was in charge of the convoy – the navigation, the zigzagging and stationing of vessels, the course, speed and liaison with the escort. Often there were changes of destination signalled by the Admiralty, dictated both by port congestion and where the cargo was required and such orders necessitated a change of station.

Often called 'the elders of the sea' the commodores were weathered and grizzled men with the look of command. They sailed in one of the larger ships, with suitable accommodation for staff, at the head of one of the centre columns. It was essential that the merchantman was well equipped for communication with the other vessels; even a convoy of forty-five ships (the largest comprised 167 ships) covered five square miles of sea with nine columns of five merchantmen.

In the early days the average number was about fifty merchantmen sailing six or seven to a column. They were numbered from port to starboard in the line of advance. With the commodore leading the centre column he could see all his ships and they could see his flag signals. There was a code book, 'Mersigs', for the flag hoists. This covered most eventualities, the major ones relating to alteration of course. The Commodore was in constant touch by light with the SO (senior officer) escort, which would pass on submarine dispositions, course changes received from the Admiralty, weather reports, and so on.

There would be at least one practice emergency turn during the voyage, when all ships would together be required to rotate 90 degrees to port or starboard. This could be hair-raising, especially at night or in poor visibility. Given an anticipated enemy U-boat attack or an actual attack, the course change could be dangerous in itself, as I have illustrated with convoy HX133. Fog buoy exercises were also carried out at intervals, which entailed vessels repeating their convoy position numbers by foghorn.

The ship's master on the commodore vessel remained in charge of the safety of his own vessel, but had the benefit of knowing more about the conduct of the convoy than the rest. Merchantmen did well in maintaining formation, whether different of size or speed, whether in ballast or loaded down to 'the marks'. Often there were difficulties at night or in fog, because of the ships' close proximity to one another. The greatest peril, however, was for ships to straggle astern, for they then became an easy target for prowling submarines.

'Romping ahead' could be as great a peril as straggling. Belching smoke from the coal-burners always brought a word of protest from the commodore. Bad smoke from a convoy could be seen some sixty miles distant on a clear day, and this was something which the U-boat commander, scanning the horizon through his Zeiss binoculars, was always on the lookout for.

Much was required of the ship's master. Many of them were middle aged, some elderly, and had been brought back from retirement due to the depletion of experienced men. Some found the strain too great at times. It was his responsibility to keep station and maintain the number of revolutions on his engines, by instructions to the engine room from the ship's 'telegraph' on the bridge. Only in this way could he preserve his allotted cable's length from the ship ahead. He had to watch for the commodore's signal by flag or Aldis lamp and be ready to react accordingly. In fog or wretched visibility, for many hours or sometimes days, his presence was required on the bridge. No navigation lights could be shone. No bells could be rung during the hours of darkness. The blackout on portholes and doors was always to be observed.

The weather, particularly in the case of Russian convoys in the northern latitudes, remained a major hazard. To re-route in order to avoid the enemy would often take the merchantmen to areas which would never be sailed in peacetime. The presence of icebergs in bad visibility was always a danger.

Night signalling would only be used in an emergency; before daylight faded, any alteration of course, or of clocks, would be signalled by the commodore ship: 'Alter course to 291 at 0100 hours;' 'Clocks to be advanced one hour at 0202 hours.' Sometimes course would be altered more than once during the night, such changes being instructed from Derby House, Liverpool, via the senior officer of the escort.

The yeoman on board the commodore ship would have his signalmen organized into three watches and be up on the bridge himself at dawn and dusk, the favourite times for enemy action. During the summer he would rarely leave the bridge in daylight hours. Some commodores never left the bridge, being very conscious of their responsibilities. They relied absolutely on their yeomen. On such combined operations as the North African landings, Sicily and Normandy, signalling lamps would be continually in use, receiving from the destroyer leader and distributing instructions to all merchantmen, be they troopships or colliers.

A certain amount of confusion sometimes arose as to whom the gunners should take their instructions from. During a submarine alert aboard the commodore ship *Pentridge Hill* (Birkenhead to Bone, North Africa, 1943) the gunlayer closed up his 4-inch gun crew upon a crew member, calling out 'submarine gunner' at the same time as he pointed in the direction of an underwater craft breaking surface. The gun crew went into action, and the shell fell close to the target. No sooner had a correction been made to the sight-setter than the commodore's yeoman ordered the gunlayer to the bridge.

Upon the bridge an elderly and agitated rear-admiral wanted to know who had given the gunlayer permission to open fire. The target had, in fact, been an Allied submarine. The master immediately intervened to say the gunlayer always had his permission to open fire on his own initiative – an instruction he had given when the gunlayer was appointed to his vessel. To be gunned down by one's own is unfortunately a fact of war; 'friendly fire' is a sensitive subject in any conflict.

The principal ocean convoy ports in the United Kingdom were Liverpool, the Gourock anchorage in the Clyde estuary (the 'tail of the bank'), Loch Ewe, Oban and Milford Haven. Overseas they were Halifax and Sydney, Cape Breton, both important transatlantic ports, New York, Bermuda and Hvalfjordhur, Iceland, principally used by Russian convoys. Gibraltar, despite its close proximity to the Mediterranean war theatre and its prime use as a Royal Navy base, came to be used increasingly as a convoy port.

Freetown, Sierra Leone, the best harbour in West Africa became important after the closure of the Mediterranean to merchant shipping in June 1940. Placed under the control of the Army, it was they who conscripted local labour to work the port. Much of the equipment there, including lighters, was supplied by the Elder Dempster Company. Surrounded by low-lying mangrove-fringed tidal areas of the coastal malarious plain, it was known as 'the white man's grave'. 'Deadly to Europeans,' pronounced a book on West Africa published in the 1930s.

The tremendous increase in traffic as a result of being both a convoy and bunkering port as well as a naval base, brought with it all sorts of logistical problems. Visiting troopships required vast quantities of fresh water, and, owing to a local shortage, much was brought from Britain in tankers. This in a land with an annual rainfall of some 135 inches – all within seven months of a hot summer. The port having virtually no foreshore there was little room to store coal. That required as bunkers for cargo ships (which unlike the oil-fired troopships were largely coal burning) had to be delivered to ships at anchor in canvas bags by local labour. The steam coal, mainly imported from South Wales, was often in short supply, leading to delays in ships' movements. Only from early 1942 were mechanical coal hulks organized. The Royal Navy employed Union Castle's *Edinburgh Castle* as their base ship.

Mechanical defects in shipping often delayed departures, resulting in a shortage of anchorages. Military cargo for the port itself increased continually; and the facilities for dealing with it proved increasingly inadequate. For shipowners, masters and crews there were endless troubles. As enemy submarines moved south in the summer of 1941, there were the shipwrecked survivors to be provided for. Every sort of trouble that can afflict wartime ships and sailors descended upon the unhappy, overworked Army administrators and the Elder Dempster employees. In 1942 the port was disturbed by enemy reconnaissance aircraft, which flew in from Vichy-French Dakar taking photographs of convoy arrivals and departures. 'The most soul-destroying place in the world,' said those who were posted to Freetown.

No wonder it was known as 'Hitler's secret weapon' by many who passed through – many who, at one time or another could be found at the 'City Hostelry'. The owner and manager Freddie Ferrarie would tell you that he had the largest collection of 'bouncing cheques' ever. Many who handed over their cheques in return for liquid refreshment never in fact reached their homeland again. The jovial and generous Freddie was only too glad to assist servicemen who arrived in the port without ready cash.

A typical 1941 convoy was HX133, already referred to on page 79. Much of the cargo had been supplied under Lease-Lend arrangements with the US Government. Including those ships which joined from Bermuda and from Sydney on the sixth day, twenty-five were tankers. Of these, nine were of Norwegian registry, two of Danish and two Dutch. These figures indicate the importance attached to the European tanker fleet, which joined the ranks of the British merchant fleet after Dunkirk. They carried a variety of oil products, and the twin-screw *Cliona* (Anglo-Saxon Petroleum Company), carrying 'Admiralty Fuel', was instructed to proceed to Reykjavik on the twelfth day.

Grain ships, principally wheat, totalled fifteen. There were four whose cargo was flour, four carrying steel with trucks in the 'tween decks, one with iron ore from Wabana, Newfoundland, and the remainder 'generals' – a shipping term covering a multitude of products, including fresh and canned food.

Supplies of iron ore from Wabana were increasing at this time, as they were from Pepel, up-river from Freetown. Mining became concentrated here, because of the loss of ore from Swedish mines, when Norway was occupied by the German forces in April 1940. Narvik was the ice-free port for the export of Swedish ore. However, the loss of iron-ore vessels was so great during 1941 that there arose a serious threat to supplies destined for the steelworks of South Wales and the north-esat coast. There was little opportunity for stockpiling. During the month of June, six British-flag iron-ore vessels, in convoy from Sierra Leone, were sunk. Between them they were carrying some 50,000 tons of ore.

Many of the fleet of Hain Steamships, which lost their entire pre-war fleet of twenty-four merchantmen during the conflict, were engaged in this traffic. In October 1941 they lost the 5,218-ton *Treverbyn* (convoy SL89), bound from Pepel to Cardiff, when her crew of thirty-eight and ten gunners perished. Its lost cargo, intended for rail transport to the steelworks of Richard Thomas and Baldwin's, Ebbw Vale, placed the plant in immediate jeopardy.

During the first six months of 1941 there arose a deficit of 7 million tons of imports of ore and war materials plus 2 million tons of food. The latter resulted in a reduction of food rations, a situation which was reviewed weekly by the Ministry of Food and the Ministry of War Transport. Certainly no new military operations using sea passages could be contemplated.

In the 1930s the United Kingdom depended upon imports for well over half her supplies of food – 55 per cent in the case of meat (including bacon), much of it from Argentina, a long-haul voyage. Fats (butter, lard, margarine) were 93 per cent imports; flour (from wheat and other cereals), 88 per cent; sugar, 82 per cent; cheese, 76 per cent; and fruit, 74 per cent.

Every day between the two world wars, ten or fifteen food ships reached British ports with a cargo of some 22 million tons of food and animal foodstuffs in the course of a year. The sources from which these supplies were drawn varied from year to year, according to changes of price and production in the exporting countries. On average about $4\frac{1}{2}$ million tons came from Argentina; nearly 3 million tons from Canada; $2\frac{3}{4}$ million tons from Australia and New Zealand; $1\frac{1}{4}$ million tons from India and Burma; with one million tons coming from the United States. Crucially, about 4 million tons came from countries which during 1941–43 were enemy or enemy-occupied.

The 'price of defeat' in June 1940 included a loss of food from Europe and from Mediterranean countries amounting to some 2 million tons annually. These included supplies of bacon and ham, butter, condensed milk and milk powder, as well as eggs in shell. With the Mediterranean closed to merchant shipping, it was necessary for much food to take the long-haul route around the Cape of Good Hope or across the Pacific and through the Panama Canal. The convoy system meant slower transit times. Ships were being diverted to the Middle East and to the carriage of cargoes other than food. Refrigerated ships, such as Elders & Fyffes's *Ariguani*, were transferred to naval duties because of their speed.

With the catastrophic shipping losses throughout 1941, during which 717 British-flag merchantmen were sunk with a tonnage of 2,824,056 (accompanied by the horrific loss of 8,848 personnel), the diet of the British population dropped to the lowest average of the war. The supply of meat was particularly difficult; and the ration was halved at the beginning of 1941. Even fish was in short supply as an alternative; most of the trawler fleet had by then been requisitioned by the Royal Navy, and many that remained had been mined or bombed by the Luftwaffe.

In May 1941 food rationing per week was set as follows: butter, 4ozs (increased from 2ozs); sugar, 12oz; tea, 2oz; preserves, 2oz; cheese, 1oz; margarine/fats 6oz; plus meat to the value of one shilling and tenpence.

In addition to the reduction of the meat ration, there were shortages of cheese, milk and many such minor foods as jam and onions. Imports of fresh and canned fruit had already been cut to vanishing point in December 1940. Whilst the home agricultural industry was made to produce progressively more, this led to other problems, for example a heavy decline in the number of livestock due to a large reduction in the imports of feeding stuffs for animals. The rationing of animal feeding stuffs was introduced in February 1941. First priority was given to the feeding of diary cows for milk, followed by fattening cattle and sheep, then pigs and poultry.

In those dark days of 1941, when Hitler's U-boats and Condor aircraft were slowly throttling the nation and when British dollar resources were nearly exhausted, the US Lease-Lend Act, passed in March empowered the President to lease or provide goods and services to any nation whose defence he thought vital to the defence of the United States. The act enabled the United Kingdom to postpone payment for munitions and food until after the war. It also enabled valuable foods to be imported from North America that could not be had elsewhere.

The Lease-Lend Act made possible a sorely needed improvement in the national diet. At the same time Axis ships in American ports were seized and the US Government announced it was taking over Greenland as a caretaker for Denmark, whose territory it was. The Act was a saviour for democracy.

After the inevitable initial delays, supplies of such foods as cheese, lard and canned goods began to arrive in summer 1941 – thanks to merchantmen and their crews. By the late autumn, sufficient stocks of canned meat and fish had been accumulated to begin a restricted rationed distribution. Corned beef and spam (supply pressed american meat) were brought in to supplement the loss of South American meat.

When in December that year Japan attacked Pearl Harbor (see Chapter 7) the food problems of the United Kingdom again multiplied. The southward sweep of Japanese conquest eliminated for the time being the normal sources of all its sago and tapioca, nearly all of the pepper, 50 per cent of the copra and 30 per cent of coconut oil. With the fall of Indo-China, Thailand and Burma, 80 per cent of the pre-war supplies of rice were lost. The occupation of the Dutch East Indies cut off sources of sugar, tea and vegetable oils, and the fall of the Philippines denied the country yet another source of sugar. The presence of the Japanese fleet, and more particularly that of submarines in the Pacific and Indian oceans, seriously threatened the passage of food supplies from Australasia and India.

The greater part of the meat imports from Argentina and Brazil were carried by two shipping companies traditionally engaged in this trade. They were the Blue Star Line, part of the great 'Vestey' empire, and Houlder Brothers and Company. During the war the former lost twenty-nine of its pre-war fleet of thirty-eight, including all its passenger liners. Some 646 personnel, including eleven master mariners, forty-seven navigating officers and eighty-eight engineers, gave their lives.

Houlder Brothers lost fifteen of their pre-war fleet of twenty-two, with personnel killed totalling 113; a further ninety-four were taken prisoner, of whom three died in captivity. The Blue Star Line was also engaged in meat shipments from Australasia as were the New Zealand Shipping Company. Records detailing the losses of the refrigerated fleets give some indication of the seriousness of the situation during 1940/41.

BLUE STAR LINE
Doric Star 2 Dec 1939. Mutton, lamb, cheese, butter; from Australasia.
Sultan Star 14 Feb 1940. Meat and butter; from Argentina.
Wellington Star 16 June 1940. Refrigerated foodstuffs; from Australasia.
Avelona Star 30 June 1940. Meat; from Argentina.
Auckland Star 28 July 1940. Meat; from Australia. (*Auckland Star* was the
    largest refrigerated ship in the world at the time.)
Afric Star 29 Jan 1941. Meat; from Brazil.
Rodney Star 16 May 1941. Meat; from Argentina.

HOULDER BROTHERS
Royston Grange 25 Nov 1939. Meat; from Argentina.
Upwey Grange 8 Aug 1940. Meat; from Argentina.
Duquesa 18 Dec 1940. Meat and 15 million eggs; from Argentina.
Oswestry Grange 12 Feb 1941. Meat; from Argentina.

NEW ZEALAND SHIPPING CO.
Turakina 20 Aug 1940. Meat; from Australasia.
Rangitane 26 Nov 1940. Meat and dairy produce; from New Zealand.
Rotorua 11 Dec 1940. Meat and dairy produce; from New Zealand.
Piako 18 May 1941. Refrigerated general foodstuffs; from Australasia

Other important refrigerated ship losses were as follows:

SHAW, SAVILL & ALBION CO LTD.
Tairoa 3 Dec 1939. Meat and butter; from Australia.
Maimoa 20 Nov 1940. Meat, eggs and butter; from Australia.
Waiotira 26 Dec 1940. Refrigerated cargo; from New Zealand.

ROYAL MAIL LINE
Highland –
Patriot 1 Oct 1940. Meat; from Argentina.

A few days after the passing of the Lease-Lend Act the first meeting was held of an Atlantic Committee, led by Winston Churchill, with the Chiefs of Naval and Air Staffs and their scientific advisers in attendance. Five months later Churchill was to board the battle cruiser *Prince of Wales* to cross the Atlantic to Newfoundland for his Atlantic Charter meeting with President Roosevelt.

Upon his return Prime Minister Churchill spoke to the nation of his achievement. 'This was a meeting which marks forever in the pages of history the taking of the English-speaking nations amid all this peril ... back to the broad high road of freedom and justice.' The historian Martin Gilbert has described the meeting as 'one of the great moments of history'.

What a proud man was Churchill. He was just as proud when on Friday 15 August whilst homeward bound on board HMS *Prince of Wales* he passed convoy HX143, of seventy-three merchantmen, heavily laden with foodstuffs and the munitions of war. The battleship altered course so that Mr Churchill could get a closer view. 'I ran out and saw an amazing sight,' wrote H.V. Morton, sailing as an official war correspondent.

> We were racing through the middle of the convoy. There were tramps, tankers, liners and whalers, salty old tubs and cargo boats of every type and size on each side of us, the nearest only two hundred yards away, the crews clustered on decks and fo'c'sles, waving their caps in the air and cheering like mad.
>
> As he looked over the sea from the altitude of the bridge he [Churchill] could see the whole convoy moving towards England. He saw it spread out for miles over the Atlantic, moving in six columns. He saw ships with aeroplanes tied to their decks, he saw cargo-boats wallowing to the plimsoll line with food and munitions, liners deep in the water with every kind of war material and tankers heavy with petrol; a stupendous and heartening sight for the leader of an island at war ... 'a delectable sight,' said Mr Churchill.
>
> They saw in us the majesty of British sea power as we saw in them the gallantry of the Merchant Navy. It was a grand meeting on the high seas in wartime. I doubt if there has ever been a finer one. It symbolised the two great forces which have made Britain and her Empire great and powerful in the world; the two forces we must thank when we eat our bread in freedom at this hour ... No one, seeing those brave ships loaded with help for us passing through the battlefield of the North Atlantic, could ever again waste a crust of bread or think it smart to scrounge a pint of petrol.

When the fifty-strong convoy HX150 (Commodore Rear-Admiral E. Manners RN, Rtd) sailed from Halifax on 16 September with its local Canadian escort, it was met the next day by four US Navy destroyers, the first convoy to have American escort. Although that 'day of infamy' was still many weeks away, the Atlantic Charter was working. Merchant seamen of many nations gave their new escort, flying the 'stars and stripes' at the gaff, a big welcome.

4   U-boats: The Holocausts

Although the number of British merchantmen sunk during 1942 fell to 645 (still a high figure and one that could not at the time be met by new building), the tonnage lost jumped to 3,459,923. In November the total was seventy-six ships of 474,606 tons, the highest monthly total of the war.

On Sunday 7 December 1941 the Japanese attacked the American fleet at Pearl Harbor. The following day Japan declared war on Britain and the British Empire, launching a heavy assault upon Hong Kong. Three days later as Hitler declared war on the United States, the Battle of the Atlantic was intensified. How better to eliminate Britain from the war than to sever the oil pipeline that led from the Caribbean – that endless trail of tankers, whose task it was to transport precious fuels, benzol, high-octane petrol and lubricating oil over a dangerous 5,000-mile sea passage.

It was oil and oil products from the refineries of Aruba, Curaçao, Mexico, Trinidad and Venezuela that Britain now relied upon for the conduct of the war. Japan quickly came into possession of oil resources in Borneo and the Dutch East Indies. German surface raiders and Japanese submarines in the Indian Ocean threatened supplies from the Persian Gulf. The provision of fuel to Britain from the East in long voyages around the Cape of Good Hope was precarious in the extreme and totally insufficient for our needs.

By bringing the United States into the Atlantic war Hitler provided the German U-boat Command with a new and welcome theatre of operation. No fewer than 260 U-boats were now available and more were coming into service at the rate of about twenty a month.

Some twenty underwater craft sailed for the American east coast; twelve were type-VIIC boats which arrived off the Newfoundland Banks on 8 January. They were followed by five larger submarines, type IXC, of 1,100 tons, *en route* for the Caribbean. Allowing for the time spent in crossing the Atlantic the newer-type U-boats could spend at least three weeks off the east coast of the United States and about the same period in the Caribbean. Type IXC could operate as far away as Trinidad. They had an endurance of 16,300 miles at 10 knots on diesel-electric drive or 13,450 miles at 10 knots cruising. Upon passing 40 degrees West, they sent a short signal to base reporting the quantity of fuel remaining.

The most serious of the many disquieting features of the new campaign were the holocausts and the loss of so many trained tankermen. A high percentage of loaded tankers went up in flames. During the last nineteen days of January in these waters, the enemy destroyed thirty-nine vessels of nearly 250,000 tons. Sixteen were tankers, five of them flying the British flag.

There were many tragedies and few survivors. *Empire Gem*, a few months from the builder's yard, was torpedoed by *U-66* off Cape Hatteras on 24 January. Heavily laden, she exploded in a mass of flames. Her master, Captain Broad, and one of his radio officers were the only survivors. Forty-seven crew lost their lives.

Of the sixty-eight British-flag tankers sunk in the Atlantic war during the first six months of 1942, sixteen were sunk off the east coast of the United States and seventeen in the Caribbean. During the year as a whole 222 Allied tankers of almost 2.7 million deadweight tons were lost in the Atlantic. Seventy-three of these were American lost between January and June, twenty-five of which were torpedoed off the US eastern seaboard.

In February, owing to the worldwide oil supply situation, the British Government had been compelled to send forty-nine tankers to the Indian Ocean region. The British Oil Executive calculated that their end-year stock level would be nearly 2 million tons below requirements unless they received tanker reinforcements. They put their need at seventy 10-knot tankers each capable of 10,000 tons of cargo.

Winston Churchill expressed grave concern at the situation. Four large tankers a day were needed to keep the British war economy going. No oil and there would be no bomber offensive against German cities and German industry; there would be no attacks against U-boat pens in Western France, or against U-boats in the Atlantic by RAF Coastal Command. Certainly no overseas military campaigns could be contemplated. The invasion of North Africa, Operation 'Torch', already in the advanced planning stage, had to be postponed from the spring until the late autumn.

On 23 June 1942, the Naval Staff (Admiralty) in a paper to Air Chief Marshal Sir Charles Portal, Commander Air Staff, stated that we had lost a measure of control over sea communications. The supply of raw materials and food for Britain was in jeopardy. We had lost the ability to take the offensive, and ships alone were unable to maintain command at sea. Some 800 aircraft of all types were required, the bulk from RAF Coastal Command, in order that aircraft could 'search, find and kill' the U-boats.

Yet the argument of the need for aircraft to kill the U-boat menace had already raged for many months. Graphs and statistics put forward by the Admiralty achieved little, however, and the bombing of German cities was given priority. The views of 'Bomber' Harris, supported by the Prime Minister's scientific adviser, Professor Lindemann, won the day. Yet what if the bombers were grounded through lack of fuel? It was this distinct possibility that persuaded the United States to supply forty-five tankers for the Atlantic 'pipeline'. The Second World War would indeed be won or lost in the North Atlantic.

In the Caribbean the enemy mounted Operation 'Neuland', a carefully planned series of strikes at tankers off the Caribbean islands. Installations in Curaçao, where five tankers were loading, were shelled. Told to sail, their masters, with one exception, refused to do so without escort.

The exception, the motor tanker *Daronia*, loaded with 8,000 tons of high octane for fighter aircraft took a chance, joined a convoy off Iceland and reached Stanlow in safety. In the immediate vicinity of Curaçao a number of tankers were sunk during the first few days. Later, however, all traffic was suspended for a time, a delay which seriously hindered the supply of oil to Britain. Leading the operation in the region were six U-boats commanded by experienced peace-time professionals:

U-156, sailed from France 19.1.42. Returned 17.3.42.
U-502, sailed from France 19.1.42. Returned 16.3.42.
U-67, sailed from France 19.1.42. Returned 30.3.42.
U-129, sailed from France 26.1.42. Returned 5.4.42.
U-161, sailed from France 24.1.42. Returned 2.4.42.
U-126, sailed from France 2.2.42. Returned 29.3.42.

U-126, commanded by Lieutenant Ernst Bauer, was called up later as a relief boat though she returned home after the first wave. Over a period of fourteen days he sank nine ships. I myself had seen *U-126* at close quarters off the coast of West Africa just four months earlier when Bauer torpedoed and sank the merchantman *Nailsea Manor* upon which I was serving.

After returning home from the Caribbean, his third patrol, Lieutenant Bauer was awarded the *Ritterkreuz* (Knights Cross). He had been engaged in rescuing survivors from the German raider *Atlantis*, sunk by HMS *Devonshire* in November 1941. In April 1943 he became training officer of the 27th Submarine Flotilla. Later, in March 1945, he was promoted to chief of the 26th Flotilla. One of the five tankers torpedoed and sunk by *U-520* was the unlucky Norwegian *Kongsgaard*. The previous year, whilst with convoy HX133, she was first damaged by collision in fog only to be torpedoed and damaged by *U-564* (see page 79–80).

During April and early May, a fifth wave of U-boats arrived in the oil region. On 19 April *U-130* shelled oil installations at Curaçao. Three weeks later *U-161* entered the port of Castries, St Lucia, and sank the Canadian *Lady Nelson* and the British *Umtata*. Both merchantmen were later salvaged and repaired, though less than three months later, on 7 July 1942, *Umtata* was sunk by *U-571* close inshore off the south-western tip of Florida.

Two heroic actions by tankers of the British fleet during 1942 were those of the 12,910-ton *San Gaspar*, torpedoed by *U-575* 100 miles east of Trinidad on 18 July and the 8,671-ton *San Emiliano* sunk by *U-155* 100 miles north of Dutch Guyana (now Surinam) on 9 August. The latter was two days out of Trinidad with a cargo of petrol.

San Gaspar was set on fire after being torpedoed during the night. Whilst most of the crew got away in the lifeboats her master, Captain Blyth, and eight others were cut off by the flames and forced to jump overboard. Guided by the master they swam away from the ship and after about eleven hours were sighted by a seaplane which dropped two rubber dinghies. Although suffering from burns, from which one subsequently died, the men, led by their Captain, were later rescued by one of the vessel's lifeboats and landed the following day.

Captain Blyth was awarded the OBE and Lloyds War Medal, and the citation refers to his conspicuous courage. Before he jumped into the water, he had to remove his artificial leg, which had been damaged by the explosion. Despite being handicapped, he was the first to reach the dinghies and there helped to rescue his companions. His brave leadership and wonderful example were responsible for most of the party reaching safety.

In Chapter 2, I described how the *San Emiliano* came under aerial bombardment in the Mersey. Her end came here in the Caribbean. Captain Tozer was still aboard, as was nineteen-year-old Apprentice Clarke with twenty-seven Atlantic crossings to his credit. Carrying 12,000 tons of high octane petrol the Eagle tanker was struck by two torpedoes and immediately swept by flames. Clarke was trapped in his cabin. Fighting his way out on to the deck and boarding the only lifeboat that was left intact, he was severely burned on his face, hands and legs. Also in the boat were the chief mate, the chief radio officer and five others. Later four more were picked up from the sea. Many were seriously injured.

Only three men were fit to man the oars. With the boat drifting back towards the flaming tanker Apprentice Clarke seized one of the oars and, although terribly burnt and near to exhaustion, he pulled for two hours without a murmur. As he collapsed, with the lifeboat now out of danger, it was seen that his hands were stuck to the oar – for two hours he had been rowing on his bare bones. His hands had to be cut away

Little is left of the 10,455 ton motor tanker *Edwin R. Brown* carrying aviation fuel as she explodes after being struck by a torpedo from U-103. A straggler from convoy HX107 (17 February 1941) all hands, forty-nine persons, perished. The photograph was taken by German war correspondent P.K. Weib on board the submarine

The gunner aboard the *Montreal City* in the North Atlantic, September 1941 is from the Maritime Royal Artillery; they became known as Churchill's Sharpshooters

U-126 here seen sailing for the South Atlantic was one of Germany's most successful submarines with twenty-six 'kills' to her credit. She was sunk in the North Atlantic 3 July 1943 by Br Sqdn 172. There were no survivors

U-124, Lieutenant Commander Johann Mohr, Knight's Cross with Oak Leaves, returns to base after her June 1942 patrol. Another successful submarine with fifty-one 'kills' to her credit, she was sunk in the North Atlantic 2 April 1943 by HMS *Stonecrop* and *Black Swan*. All on board including Johann Mohr perished

Lieutenant Ernst Bauer, Knight's Cross, commander of U-126 from July 1941 until November 1942. He was not aboard at the time the submarine was lost, command having been transferred to Siegfried-Kietz

A submarine Type VII-C is seen on her trials in 1942. On her foredeck is one 88 mm gun with 20 mm anti-aircraft gun on the 'winter garden'

A boatload of survivors from the 7,798 ton motor vessel *Richmond Castle*, sunk in the North Atlantic by U-176 on 4 August 1942 are about to be rescued by HMS *Snowflake*. A further eighteen survivors were picked up by the *Hororata* then on her homeward maiden voyage

The 1,600 ton U-cruiser U-178 is seen sailing for the South Atlantic, 8 September 1942 on her first war cruise. On 10 October west of Ascencion Island, she sank the 20,119 ton liner *Duchess of Atholl* (serving as a troopship) on which the author was travelling as passenger. U-178 was scuttled at Bordeaux, 20 August 1944

Captain Hans Ibbeken, commander of U-178 who continued his war cruise through the Mozambique Channel and Indian Ocean to Penang, at the time a Japanese naval base

Not a particularly successful submarine, U-217 was only credited with three 'kills'. She was sunk by an aircraft from USS *Bogue* in the North Atlantic on 5 June 1943. Her commander, Reichenbach-Klinke and his complete crew perished

The 7,957 ton *Rhexenor* sunk by U-217 was both torpedoed and shelled. Her complete crew (except her fourth mate) survived epic lifeboat voyages. That shown is believed to be number three with the second mate and sixteen men which covered 1,236 miles in twenty-one days

Rhexenor's fourth mate taken prisoner by U-217 was landed at Brest where he was interrogated before being sent to Milag Nord POW camp near Bremen

ninety merchantmen were lost in Russian convoys.

As convoy PQ17 was in transit for Archangel in July 1942, Sir Archibald Southby, Conservative MP for Epsom, spoke in the House of Commons in protest about the slaughter of Allied ships running the Arctic convoy routes to Northern Russia.

> It is true to say that upon the merchant navies of the Allies rests our hope of victory, and the hope of salvation of all those who are now enslaved under the Axis. The world will never be able to repay the debt it owes to the officers and men of the Merchant Navy.
>
> If then, by foolish strategy, we suffer reverse after reverse which not only involve us in military defeats but dissipate the seapower upon which the whole of our war effort is built, we render impossible the fulfilment of the task of guarding those merchantmen upon which we all depend.

Three days later convoy PQ17 lost two-thirds of its ships, 158 Allied merchant seamen, 1,700 million dollars' worth of armaments (99,316 tons), which included 297 aircraft, 594 tanks, 4,246 lorries and gun carriers. No wonder the 1,500 or so weary and embittered British and American survivors, assembled at St Andrew's Hall, Glasgow, at the request of Mr Philip Noel Baker MP, gave him such an icy reception. Speaking in his capacity as under-secretary to the Minister of War Transport, he was howled down when he told them, 'We know what the convoy cost us but I want to tell you whatever the cost, it was well worth it.'

The civic welcome provided for the brave men by the Glasgow dignatories was a farce. Those who know the Arctic waters and who know and understand the story of PQ17 will realize why both officers and men were angry. It was the worst convoy disaster of the war. In total sixty-three merchantmen were sunk by enemy action in Russian convoys during 1942.

Prior to the July disaster, PQ13 and PQ16 had faced the might of the enemy in those waters. Six of the nineteen merchantmen of PQ13 which sailed during March were lost. Upon reaching Murmansk a further three, the *Empire Starlight*, *Lancaster Castle* and *New Westminster City*, were sunk during heavy bombing raids on the port. The German base at Petsamo was only fifty miles away.

At the time, in the face of increasing German pressure and the growing hours of daylight, Admiral Sir Dudley Pound argued that the Russian convoys were becoming too risky. 'These Arctic convoys are becoming a regular millstone round our necks,' he wrote to Admiral King of the US Navy. Allied leaders insisted, however, that the convoys continue. President Roosevelt sent 'Task Force 39', which included the battleship USS *Washington* and the aircraft carrier *Wasp* as reinforcements for the Home Fleet.

During May convoy PQ16 and the homeward convoy QP12 in the same area were met by 108 successive waves of bombers. Seven of the thirty-five heavily laden vessels were sunk, including the CAM ship *Empire Lawrence*, whose second mate was the only surviving deck officer. During a raid by sixty high-level bombers, the ammunition ship *Empire Purcell*, on her maiden voyage, blew up in a mighty holocaust of flame and black smoke. The commodore ship *Ocean Voice* was seriously damaged.

The thirty-five merchantmen of PQ17, twenty-two of which were American, sailed from Hvalfjordhur, Iceland, together with three rescue ships, *Zaafaran*, *Rathlin*, and *Zamalek*, on 27 June 1942. Only eleven of the merchant vessels and two of the rescue ships survived. The escort, under Commander Broome in the destroyer *Keppel*, consisted of a considerable array of warships: six destroyers, two anti-aircraft ships, two submarines and eleven corvettes, minesweepers and armed trawlers. There was a support force of four cruisers, HMS *London* and *Norfolk* and the American USS *Tuscaloosa* and *Wichita*, accompanied by three destroyers. The force was commanded by Rear-Admiral Hamilton. A distant heavy support force consisted of the battleship *Duke of York* with Sir John Tovey, Commander-in-Chief Home Fleet on board, the USS *Washington*, the cruisers *Cumberland* and *Nigeria*, the aircraft carrier *Victorious* plus fourteen destroyers. There were more warships than merchantmen. Broom's instruction from the Admiralty stated, 'Our primary object is to get as much of the convoy through as possible and the best way to do it is to keep moving to the eastward, even though it is suffering damage.'

Two merchantmen turned back after sailing: one ran aground; the other was damaged by drift ice. By 30 June the thirty-three ships and a fleet oiler were some 100 miles south-south-west of Jan Mayen Island with a close escort of six destroyers, four corvettes, the two submarines and the two anti-aircraft vessels. The following day PQ17 and homeward convoy QP13 passed each other. By 5 July convoy PQ17, with Commodore J.C.K. Dowding RNR, DSO, RD sailing in *River Afton*, had lost twenty merchantmen, ten to bombing and ten sunk by U-boats. What caused the massacre and why were the 1,500 survivors landed in Glasgow so angry?

On 29 June in the Trondheim area of Norway lay the battleship *Tirpitz*, the 8-inch cruiser *Admiral Hipper* and five destroyers. Stationed in the Narvik area were the pocket battleships *Admiral Scheer* and *Lutzow* (ex *Deutschland*) together with six destroyers. Admiralty intelligence knew that *Tirpitz* was ready to strike. Although special intelligence had no firm indications to show that the battleship was at sea, Admiral Pound in London acted on his own judgement and signalled to Broome at 0923 on 4 July: 'Immediate. Owing to the threat of surface ships convoy is to disperse and proceed to Russian ports.' Thirteen minutes later, the First Sea Lord's urgency was apparent from his signal: 'Most immediate. My 9.23 of the 4th. Convoy is to scatter.'

It was a fatal error. The threat of the array of enemy naval power was enough to win Germany a resounding a naval victory. *Tirpitz* was still in Alten Fjord awaiting Hitler's approval to sail. As the merchantmen scattered over the wild Arctic Sea, many of which were racing for the pack-ice, the Luftwaffe and the U-boats remorselessly hunted them down.

Sunk by Junkers 88 aircraft from Captain Hajo Hermann's notorious third squadron of KG30 were the *Navarino* and *Bolton Castle*. In the attack on the latter vessel the second of three bombs penetrated number 2 hold, which contained hundreds of tons of cordite. The cargo ignited 'like a giant Roman candle'. Also sunk by the Luftwaffe was the rescue ship *Zaafaran*, a former Cypriot and Syrian coastal cargo and passenger boat. Ninety-seven men, including her master Captain McGowan, were rescued by *Zamalek*. McGowan and his chief engineer were both awarded the DSO for heroism as were Captain Morris of *Zamalek*, Captain Banning of *Rathlin* and Captains Walker and Harvey of *Ocean Freedom* and *Empire Tide* respectively. This military decoration had not hitherto been awarded to any officers or seamen of the Merchant Navy.

Sunk by U-boats were the commodore ship *River Afton*, the vice-commodore ship *Hartlebury* and the rear-commodore *Empire Byron*, which was carrying tanks for Archangel. Commodore Dowding survived, being found on a raft with the ship's chief engineer. Only twenty survived from *Hartlebury*'s crew of fifty-six. A year later her master Captain Stephenson died of his head injuries, the only ship's master of convoy PQ17 to perish as a result of the attack. The *Earlsdon* and the fleet oiler *Aldersdale*, first bombed by Junkers 88s and Heinkel 111s, were later sunk by U-boats. Sixteen US flag vessels and one Dutch ship were lost. Of the survivors only two were British, the CAM ship *Empire Tide* and the *Ocean Freedom*. The remainder which finally reached Archangel consisted of six American, two Russian and one Panamanian flag. There were no warship losses.

'The most shameful episode in naval history,' commented Captain Charlton, master of the commodore ship *River Afton*. A half century later the reasons behind the 'scatter' order are still difficult to understand. Rear-Admiral Hamilton was instructed that he was not to go beyond Bear Island unless he was confronted by surface ships he could fight. In effect this meant that he was not to sacrifice his naval ships in conflict with the *Tirpitz*. Were the British and American capital ships more valuable than the convoy, the war material carried and the seamen who perished? The controversy over PQ17 rumbles on to this day.

It was not until the autumn of 1941 that convoy escorts were being delivered in sufficient numbers. The delivery time of the small flower-class corvettes from such a reputable yard as Harland & Wolff, Belfast, had been as long as twelve months. This timescale was due to the backlog of repairs and the full programme of merchantmen and naval ships under construction. Meanwhile protection had been afforded both by pre-war Castle-class corvettes of 1,010 tons and 16½ knots, the first of which were laid down in 1934, and the sloops, which consisted of the 19-knot Black Swan class and the Grimsby and Sandwich class. The first of the successful Black Swan class was commissioned soon after the outbreak of war.

From the first day of the war the brunt of convoy work fell upon the 25-knot Hunt class and Tribal class destroyers. These were in short supply, however, being in demand for all sorts of worldwide naval duties. There were, of course, the fifty US 'four-stackers' already mentioned, but the true saviours of the merchantmen in convoy were the armed trawlers and the Flower-class corvettes. Ninety-nine 'Flowers' were in commission by June 1941 with ninety-six building, forty-four of them in Britain and fifty-two in Canada.

The 'fighting trawlers', sadly missed by the British housewife, reinforced the hard-worked destroyers and sloops from 'the day of defeat'. Called up from the fishing ports of the West of England, and from Wales, Hull, the north-east coast and Scotland, they took their place as members of the senior service.

Further and further out into the Atlantic went the little trawlers. Many a master mariner proudly nursing his damaged merchantmen, his 'red duster' still hoisted high, was thankful to the trawler which took him in tow until the ship could be beached or the rescue tugs took over. It was in this work particularly that the trawlers showed their seaworthiness. In the heaviest weather of the North Atlantic they rode out a gale better than the destroyers and the sloops. In the Arctic they depth-charged the U-boats and rescued the merchant seamen from the icy waters.

Always ready for sea and to engage the enemy, the trawlers were manned by the Royal Volunteer Reserve (RNVR), a great proportion of them Scots from the Hebrides. 'Stornorwegian' many of them liked to be called. Conscientious, hardworking and fearless men, without fear of the sea or the enemy alike, they claimed to know more about the waters, the shoals and the anchorages from Cape Wrath to the Clyde than any Admiralty hydrographer. Many had sailed aboard the pre-war Antarctic whaling fleet; many served in the armed merchant cruisers (AMCs) and continued their service in them when they became troopers. There were other fearless trawlermen – the Welsh, the Irish, the Westcountrymen and the Geordies – but speak to any master mariner at the time and he had nothing but praise for the seamen of the Western Isles.

The trawlers were the great training ground for both skippers and ratings. Many, groomed for promotion, were moved to the larger escort vessels of the fleet, including the armed merchant cruisers. The trawlers, equipped with depth charges and Asdic gear, became anti-submarine vessels. But, also equipped with stretchers and first aid, they became rescue vessels. In doing such work they left the better-equipped escorts free to hunt and attack the enemy. Of those requisitioned, 169 were sunk.

The Flower-class corvette was the workhorse of the convoy escorts. Captain Roskill, in his masterful work *The War at Sea*, said, 'It is hard to see how Britain could have survived without them.' My own memory serves to tell me they were the 'jack-of-all-trades' escorting convoys, ramming U-boats, acting as rescue vessels, sweeping mines, towing merchant ships and, on one occasion, towing a Sunderland flying boat. 'Flogged to death' as one former chief petty officer remembers. They were the smallest British warship to regularly sail the world's oceans. Of all senior service escorts, they and their crews remained closest in spirit to those aboard the merchantmen.

Named after flowers in the English garden a total of 262 were built, of which thirty-three were lost. Chunky and broad-beamed, they were designed by the British Admiralty to resemble whale-catchers. Their great strength was their seaworthiness and relative cheapness to produce (some £120,000). Their vital statistics were: tonnages, 950 and 1,010; length 205 feet with a beam of 33 feet. Their draught was shallow, only 16 feet 6 inches.

Only after April 1939, when Hitler denounced the naval treaty which had strictly limited the size of the Germany Navy, was serious thought given to the escort of merchant ships in convoy in time of war. Britain alone possessed 3,000 deep-sea merchantmen as well as some 1,000 coasters, totalling 21 million tons. The average number of British-flag ships at sea in any one day was 2,500. Only 150 escort craft were available. RAF Coastal Command was in its infancy and hardly any thought had been given to aircraft available to hunt the U-boats.

The first order for the Flower class was placed in Britain in July 1939. Designed originally for coastal work, the ships' plans were sent to Canada and the first sixteen were laid down in Canadian shipyards early in 1940. A total of 111 were built in Canada for the Royal Canadian Navy and fifteen for the US Navy. Redesigned with lengthened forecastles they were splendid sea-boats though uncomfortable for those who served in them.

With a range of 4,000 miles they were able to accompany a convoy across the Atlantic without refuelling. Powered by single reciprocating engines they had a maximum speed of 16 knots. Whilst limited in speed and armament in comparison with the destroyers they mounted a 4-inch breech-loading gun, albeit of 1917/18 vintage, together with Oerlikon guns as anti-aircraft defence. Later, two 6-pounder Hotchkiss guns were fitted on the bridge. The large number of depth charges carried aft constituted the main method of attack. They could be thrown in patterns of up to ten at a time. Later in the war came 'hedgehog' mortars which threw spigot-type bombs ahead of the corvette and which exploded only on contact.

Originally designed for a crew of thirty, the ship was soon increased to berth fifty, then sixty and, at times, seventy. In 1943, when crews included three telegraphists, three coders and three radar operators, the total complement became some eighty personnel. When loaded with survivors it was not unknown for them to arrive in port with 300 people aboard.

The first contracts were placed with a variety of small shipyards including Smith's Dock, Middlesbrough, out of which *Gladiolus*, pendant number K34, was completed in April 1940, five months and eighteen days from the date the keel was laid. At the time this was an incredible feat. It was at Smith's Dock that much of the initial design work was carried out. Harland & Wolff, Belfast, claimed the record building time. This was five months exactly in respect of *Gentian*, completed on 20 September 1940.

HMS *Gladiolus*, the first to sail, was also the first to make a kill when *U-26* was sunk 1 July 1940 south-south-west of Ireland. *Gladiolus* was herself sunk thirteen months later (by *U-558*) in the North Atlantic whilst under the command of Lieutenant-Commander Harry M. Sanders DSO, DSC, RD. All hands perished whilst she was searching for survivors from a torpedoed merchantman during the attack on convoy SC48.

The officers were fully trained men of the sea. The commanding officer was either a Royal Navy Reserve (RNR) lieutenant commander who had been a master mariner of a merchantman in pre-war days or an RNR first lieutenant with senior service training. The Royal Navy Volunteer Officers (RNVR) were as well trained as was possible, and they quickly acquired the necessary skills. Selected from civilian life they were mainly those of good education who were able to learn quickly and to accept responsibility. The naval discipline at the shore training establishment HMS *Alfred* was a vital part in the training.

During 1991 two famous corvette commanders passed from us. Captain Richard Case DSO, DSC was a *Worcester* cadet who served his apprenticeship with the Pacific Steam Navigation Company. He then sailed with Elder Dempster Ltd and in 1937 as second officer with Coast Lines Ltd. He joined the RNR and was called up with the rank of Lieutenant Commander on the first day of the war. Becoming commanding officer of the trawler *Stella Capella* he later took command of *Campanula*. In 1942 he commissioned the new River class frigate *Rother* and took part in the 'Torch' landings in North Africa.

Captain Ronald Freaker DSO, DSC was one of the most successful of the professional sea officers. He too went to sea as a deck apprentice and upon joining the RNR he served first as chief officer and then as master of the royal research ship *William Scoresby*. In June 1941 (convoy HX133) as commanding officer *Nasturtium* he, with the help of *Gladiolus* and *Celandine*, sank *U-556*. Commanding the frigate *Jed* during 1943 he defended such critical convoys as ONS5 and SC130 (see Chapter 6). He contributed to the great victory that came in May of that year. In escorting ONS10 one month later *Jed* was credited with the sinking of *U-334*.

Crews of the Flower class had a smattering of regulars and time-serving petty officers, but in the main they were hostilities-only ratings. This mixture of regular and hostilities-only men was what made the corvettes work under what at times were the most dreadful conditions. It was naval discipline such as that experienced at shore-based HMS *Ganges* and elsewhere which made these little ships into a real fighting force.

Those serving in the fourth service had the greatest admiration for the fighting men of the Flower class. Rarely did they meet ashore for the escort's Atlantic ports were 'Derry' and 'Newfy Johns'. The facilities at Londonderry had been extended, making the Northern Ireland port an important Anglo-American base, the home of the B7 Escort Group from July 1942 until the Normandy landings. St John's Newfoundland, familiarly known to all sailors as 'Newfy John's', and nearby Placentia Bay became the busy western terminals. Tobermory in the Western Isles was much used by the corvettes as a 'working up' base. The majority were brought here after completion at the shipyards.

The history of HMS *Pink* (K137) epitomizes the history of the B7 Escort Group. She was to stay with this successful group of U-boat hunters until just before Operation 'Neptune'. Engaged in the North Atlantic during the critical period from early autumn 1942 to late spring 1943 she saw action with many convoys attacked by the enemy. In early December 1942, whilst with convoy HX216, she was reported as heading for 'Derry' with a raft carrying an aircraft in tow – no doubt a reference to deck cargo floated off from a torpedoed merchantman. She rescued many survivors from ON153, a convoy battle lasting several days in gale conditions.

During the crisis days of January to April 1943 the B7 Group escorted convoys SC115, ON164, ON173 and HX231. The Group, which included *Alisma*, *Loosestrife*, *Snowflake* and *Sunflower*, added immeasurably to its experience when escorting convoy HX231. Its passage provided all the tough ingredients of sea warfare: the presence of seventeen U-boats, heavy weather, oiling at sea. Their difficulties were alleviated somewhat by co-operation with air escorts of RAF Coastal Command, of the RCAF from Newfoundland and with 'support groups' of sea escorts. The action around convoy HX231, combined with the strenuous training and drills which the Group carried out, both in port and at sea, brought 'the flowers' to a high standard of efficiency.

HMS *Snowflake* (K67) became a member of the B1 Escort Group under the leadership of HMS *Hurricane*. Together with *Saxifrage*, *Oxlip* and *Campanula* she saw service with convoy PQ14 to the northern USSR. Having experienced enemy action from U-boats and aircraft and further bombing raids whilst at Murmansk, it was *Snowflake* that rescued three survivors from the commodore ship *Empire Howard*, sunk by *U-403*.

Empire Howard, heavily laden with tanks and trucks bound for the Soviet army, broke up and sank within sixty seconds. There was no time to launch lifeboats. Some thirty-eight crew survived in the water being somewhat protected by oil which had been released from the ruptured fuel tanks. Suddenly from out of the mist came the anti-submarine trawler *Northern Wave* firing depth charges in an effort to trap the attackers. Only those at some distance lived to tell their story. The remainder died instantly of broken necks or from internal injuries. The hunt for the enemy, it seemed, was more important than those officers and men engaged in helping the Soviet people. It was probably the saddest moment of all the sagas of Russian convoys.

Further survivors of the horrific event were brought aboard the trawler *Lord Middleton* barely conscious, some seriously injured. From a crew of fifty-four only eighteen were saved and of these nine died aboard the trawler. There was no sign of the convoy commodore, Captain Rees RNR. Miraculously the master of the *Empire Howard*, Captain Downie, was one of the fortunate ones.

Whilst on duty with Russian convoys the Flower-class crews had great difficulty sleeping due to the intense cold. There was no heating below deck other than a coal burning stove on the mess-deck, for which it was necessary for the funnel to be erected on the foredeck. Apart from shipping seas, such stoves had a tendency to smoke badly. Condensation below, which built up into ice six inches thick on the bare steel of the mess deck, was a big problem. Kapok suits with zips were the order of the day. When worn on the upper deck it was necessary to use the oilskin outer cover. In such conditions it was a continual fight to keep guns and depth-charge throwers ice-free.

During August 1942 *Snowflake* rescued seventeen survivors from *Richmond Castle*, which had been torpedoed twelve days previously by *U-176*. Brought aboard in a weak condition they needed immediate attention. It was on such occasions that the sick berth attendant showed his true value; that of *Snowflake* was no exception. Every bunk was commandeered, and he looked after the survivors like a mother hen with her young chicks. For two days and two nights he never left them.

The injuries and the illnesses of men adrift in open boats in the North Atlantic for long periods of time were many. Among those rescued from the *Richmond Castle* one had pneumonia and pleurisy, another a badly wounded leg which was going gangrenous. All suffered from exhaustion and exposure. In the days before antibiotics it was often a case of common sense and 'grandma's remedies'. The pneumonia case was treated with aspirin and mustard poultices (the cook's entire stock of mustard was exhausted); the leg wound greatly improved after a course of Epsom salts and Glycerine paste. After a couple of days the necrosed part came away, leaving a deep but clean wound. Five days after the rescue the survivors were landed in Londonderry, still damaged but very much alive. All were handed over to the civilian services and hospitalized.

When recalling the commissioning of HMS *Snowflake* at the Teeside yard a sick berth attendant indicates just how basic the medical stores were: 'a good supply of dressings, bandages etc., aspirins, Number 9s (the services cure-all for all constipation problems) liniment, "white mixture" for indigestion and a few other simple medicaments. Additionally dozens of arm splints, though none for legs. Further, they were all right-handed ones.' After *Snowflake* became established with the B7 Group in Derry she was able to stock up with a more comprehensive supply from the local American base.

HMS *Hyacinth* held the Flower-class record for 'kills' against submarines. Based in the western Mediterranean she sank the Italian submarine *Fisalla* in September 1941, and followed this with the capture of *Perla* in July the next year. On 11 September 1943 the loss of the German *U-617* was officially shared between *Hyacinth*, the naval trawler *Haarlem*, the Australian minesweeper *Woolongong* and 179 Squadron, RAF Coastal Command, based in Gibraltar.

U-617 had sunk seven Allied ships in the Mediterranean: the destroyer HMS *Puckeridge*, the minelayer HMS *Welshman*, the Norwegian merchantmen *Henrik*, *Corona* and *Harboe Jensen*, and the Greek *Annitsa*. Her commander, Albrecht Brandi, received the Knight's Cross with Oak Leaves and later commanded *U-380* and *U-967*.

The corvettes had exciting careers and long service escorting merchantmen worldwide. The majority were involved in a variety of battles with the enemy. Those 'Flowers' engaged in the rescue of merchant seamen, often at great danger to themselves, rendered valuable service in the saving of life. Possibly three stand above all others in this work. *Petunia* rescued 252 from *Andalucia Star* in October 1942, followed by some 450 from *Empress of Canada* the next March. *Cyclamen* saved some 300 seamen from *Adda* on 8 June 1941; and *Starwort* picked up 240 from the troop transport *Anselm* in July 1941.

In addition to the corvette-building programme the development and operation of Merchant Aircraft Carriers (MACs) was equally important and one of the most guarded secrets of the war. Plans were put in hand during the early spring of 1942 and they first entered the Battle of the Atlantic with convoy ONS9 in May 1943. The 'baby flat-tops' were either grain ships or tankers converted into aircraft carriers by having flight decks, small island superstructures, arrester wires, crash barriers, safety nets and highly developed fire-extinguishing facilities fitted on top of their hulls.

The MACs operated three to five Swordfish aircraft, carried 80 per cent of their usual cargo, flew the red ensign and became a powerful addition to the defence of convoys during 1943 and 1944. The grainers were equipped with a hangar aft; in the tankers, as provision could not be made for hydraulic lifts or below-deck hangars, the aircraft were lashed snugly on the flight-deck when not in use.

The first two grainers, *Empire MacKendrick* and *Empire MacAlpine*, were laid down in August 1942 at the Burntisland Shipbuilding Company's yard. They were commissioned in 14 April 1943, eight months later, and made ready for service. Flying trials were held in the Clyde estuary. Carrying some 7,000 tons of grain, their length was 434 feet, the flight deck was 414 by 62 feet with a beam of 57 feet, and their speed was 12½ knots. The full crew comprised 107, half of whom were Merchant Navy personnel and half Royal Navy, Fleet Air Arm. Both vessels were managed by Ben Line Steamers on behalf of the Ministry of War Transport.

Sailing with convoy ONS9, the *Empire MacAlpine* was commanded by Captain Riddle, whilst the Fleet Air Arm personnel were under the control of Commander L.G. Wilson RN, an officer with wide experience as an observer operating from Fleet carriers. Earlier in the war he had flown in Hurricane aircraft catapulted from CAM ships. The two Ben Line MACs became well known in Liverpool and in Halifax, which were their main terminal points. Between them they carried almost a quarter of a million tons of grain from Canada to the United Kingdom before the end of the war.

The tankers were managed by the Anglo-Saxon Petroleum Company and the British Petroleum Company, their flight decks measured 461 by 62 feet, maximum speed 11 knots with a complement of 110. Nineteen in total (see Appendix VIII) the red duster MACs were part of the replacement programme, but served as dual-purpose merchantmen. Created by the Admiralty, the tanker companies and the shipbuilders in association with the Ministry of War Transport, the idea was entirely novel and was most successful in practice. They made 170 round trips with Atlantic convoys, comprising 4,447 days at sea, 3,057 of them in convoy, and amassed 9,016 flying hours on 4,177 sorties. No MAC ship was sunk and because of their presence many U-boats were kept below surface. Only one out of the 217 convoys which enjoyed their protection was successfully attacked by U-boats.

The air staff of the MAC ship consisted of pilots, air gunners, observers and maintenance men. Each aircraft was armed with two depth charges and four small bombs or, alternatively, with the new rockets. Extra DEMS were carried in order to help man the ship's additional armament. On-board armament consisted of the 4-inch gun housed under the flight deck aft, two Bofors and six Oerlikons. A well-equipped sick bay and operating theatre for casualties was provided.

A further all-British escort carrier class for the protection of trade (the others, American-built, I will refer to in Chapter 6), were the three vessels *Nairana, Vindex* and *Campania*, which became known as the Nairana class. Here, 17-knot vessels, ordered under Admiralty licence as meat and refrigerated ships, were taken over by the Royal Navy when construction was well advanced. In 1943 victory in the Atlantic was required at all costs, even though it could mean reductions in the British meat ration.

The escort carrier *Campania* was laid down in the yard of Harland & Wolff, Belfast, as a motor meat carrier of the Waiwera class for her owners Shaw, Savill & Albion Ltd. Launched in June 1943 and commissioned in March the following year, she carried eighteen aircraft. During 1944 she distinguished herself on convoy protection, particularly on Russian convoys in which her aircraft were involved in a number of actions with enemy aircraft based in Norway.

Whilst the convoy escort situation was improving throughout 1942, despite the fact that the number of merchantmen sunk reached its peak at this time, the import situation was deteriorating. Moreover, every ship that could be spared was needed for the vast military operations then being planned. It became vital to reduce further the amount of shipping used for food. In March 1942 the extraction rate of flour, already increased from 70 per cent or less to 75 per cent of the wheat grain, was further raised to 85 per cent. The increase was a nutritional gain, for the new flour supplied certain minerals and vitamins lacking in the national diet; against this there was a loss in quantity and quality of feeding stuffs for animals.

In the autumn it was decided to eke out the wheat supply by mixing in with the miller's grist a proportion of barley, as well as small quantities of rye and oats. Later this policy was revised, for it was found that the compulsory sale of barley by farmers merely resulted in reduced sales of oats. The Ministry of Food, working in close association with the

Ministry of War Transport, then embarked upon a publicity campaign to stimulate the consumption of potatoes instead of bread. At the same time there was intensive propaganda to prevent wastage of food, especially bread.

In the course of 1942 inter-Allied machinery was established for the combined planning of all supplies, material and shipping. Part of this machinery became the Combined Food Board, the nucleus of which already existed in the Anglo-American Food Committee. The loss of heavily laden merchantmen homewards from Australia, India and South Africa, particularly those lost in the tropical climes of the Atlantic, south and west of Freetown, was causing many problems. There became an acute timber shortage, particularly of hardwoods – hence the 'utility' furniture, manufactured with less timber and with ranges reduced to twenty-two, simplified articles in standard designs. More and more hardwood was being imported from West Africa due to the loss of Malaya and Burma to the Japanese.

On the whole, the liner shipping companies were allowed to continue in their customary trades but the movement of U-boats from the transatlantic convoys to the African and South American trade routes particularly hit such companies as the Blue Star Line and the long-established West African traders, Elder Dempster.

The motor ship *Dagomba*, built for Elder Dempster in 1928, completed loading at Takoradi on 29 October 1942. She had loaded at various West African ports as was the custom and had on board 5,000 tons of produce, consisting of palm oil in bulk, palm kernels, timber and tin ore. Five days later, proceeding in convoy towards Freetown (convoy TS23), she was instructed to sail independently to the West Indies and from thence to Halifax, Nova Scotia, to join an HX convoy for Liverpool. This was an Admiralty routeing for all vessels then in the southern hemisphere, owing to the build-up for Operation 'Torch'. Three days later *Dagomba* was sunk by the Italian submarine *Cagni* with the loss of seven lives.

Elder Dempster's motorship *William Wilberforce*, which entered the company's service during 1930, departed from Takoradi on 31 December. With 5,000 tons of West African produce for Liverpool she received a similar routeing. She was to proceed to Hampton Roads on the eastern seaboard of the United States *en route* for Halifax. Maintaining a zigzag course in a north-westerly direction the *William Wilberforce* was struck by two torpedoes from *U-511* on 9 January. She was about 500 miles west of the Canary Islands. A second tragedy befell the chief and second mates four weeks later. Having been allocated berths aboard Elder Dempster's *Mary Slessor*, homewards from Gibraltar, the men were drowned when she struck a mine and sank within five hours of sailing with convoy MKS7. According to German records the mine had been laid by *U-118*.

During August 1943 the *New Columbia* (formerly *War Pageant*), a First World War 'standard' vessel, was loading up on the coast north of Matadi. Included in her cargo were 1,500 tons of copper, 15 tons of Wolfram ore, baled cotton, gum arabic and timber – all commodities of great value to the UK war economy. Sailing independently from Libreville on a course based on the Admiralty route towards Lagos, the *New Columbia* was torpedoed and sunk by *U-739*. The copper was so valuable at the time that officials gave serious thought to recovering it from the bottom of the ocean. But because of the cost involved and the lack of equipment the project was cancelled.

In spite of ship losses the majority of sailings from the west coast of Africa were without mishap, and the colonies of that coast – British, French and Belgian – contributed significantly to the British war effort. A typical homeward voyage of Elder Dempster merchantmen was that of the SS *Cochrane*, voyage forty-eight, loading homewards from Matadi and arriving at Liverpool on 4 August 1943. Her cargo included 11,691 bags of coffee, 20,334 bags of copal, 75,560 copper ingots, 480 bags wolfram, 5,597 bags palm kernels, 11,200 bags of cocoa and bulk palm kernels to the value of £1,771. All were items in short supply in Britain. On the outward voyage *Cochrane* had carried Welsh coal loaded at Swansea for discharge at Takoradi.

Blue Star losses continued throughout 1942. Between 25 August and 27 October of that year five vessels were lost of which four – *Viking Star, Tuscan Star, Andalucia Star* and *Pacific Star*, with a total tonnage of 32,551 – were torpedoed by U-boats whilst homeward bound. All were laden with South American frozen meat.

Viking Star, carrying 4,500 tons of meat, was sunk by *U-130* 180 miles south of Freetown. Her master, Captain Mills and eight of her crew perished. The only lifeboat that remained intact was launched with thirty-six aboard. The little craft sailed for six days before capsizing in heavy breakears on a lonely part of the Sierra Leone coast. All hands survived though they then had to undergo several days of walking through the jungle before reaching civilization. Eighteen of her crew managed to scramble aboard a raft when the vessel sank. The men, using blankets as sails, took eighteen days to reach the coast, and one of them was drowned upon landing.

Tuscan Star, with a total on board of 113, including twenty-five passengers, women and children amongst them, was laden with 7,300 tons of meat. On 6 September, just north of the Equator, she was torpedoed twice in quick succession by *U-109*. The Blue Star merchantman listed heavily to starboard and began to settle immediately by the stern; nine of her crew were killed by the explosions. The lifeboats were sighted by the transport ship *Otranto* on the second day, though a roll-call, taken upon landing in Freetown, showed that forty-one crew, eight gunners and three passengers had gone missing.

On 6 October, during the hours of darkness, *Andalucia Star* was proceeding at 16 knots, 180 miles south-west of Freetown, when she was torpedoed and sunk by *U-107*. She had on board a crew of 170 and eighty-three passengers, most of whom were British volunteers coming home from Argentina to take part in the war. They included twenty-two women and three children. The survivors were landed by HMS *Petunia* at Freetown forty-eight hours after the attack. Two members of the crew and one passenger were missing.

One of the crew lost was Ms Green, a stewardess, who received a posthumous commendation – the Merchant Navy equivalent of a 'mention in despatches' – for her coolness, foresight and devotion to duty in caring for the women and children. One of her last acts was to switch on the red waistcoat light of a four-year-old girl, who was later thrown into the water when one of the lifeboats being lowered was up-ended. The cry of the small child was heard by lamptrimmer William Wheeler who, guided by the red light, swam through wreckage for a distance of about 600 yards towards her. For his gallant action in saving the child's life, Wheeler was awarded the Bronze Medal for Gallantry.

The loss of the *Pacific Star* came at the end of October 1942, a disastrous month in the annals of the wartime merchant fleet. Her loss, with that of twelve other merchantmen from convoy SL125 during a five-day battle, was accepted by Winston Churchill as the price which had to be borne. What of the valuable cargoes of food and raw materials? What of the officers and men? I will return to the battle in Chapter 9, for it was to aid Operation 'Torch' that the sacrifices were made – so that the North African invasion could take place without interruption.

5 Surface Raiders

The pocket battleship raider *Admiral Graf Spee* met her end when she was scuttled after the River Plate battle, which I have already briefly mentioned. Her toll of shipping was nine merchantmen of 50,000 tons. In all, however, the German warships, in conjunction with nine skilfully disguised and heavily armed converted merchant ships, sank 133 Allied merchantmen of some 830,000 tons. Whilst this was far less than the destruction achieved by the U-boats, bombers and mines, 7 per cent of the U-boat total in fact, the raiders caused considerable dislocation of traffic and extended the resources of the senior service at a time when they were already hard-pressed. There was the additional loss of the valuable cargoes of foodstuffs, raw materials and arms, and the loss of thousands of trained seamen, most of them taken prisoners of war – lost at a time when they were most needed.

The *Graf Spee* was the least effective of all the commerce raiders. As a force, with much of their concentration in the southern hemisphere, they were vastly important and formed a key part of the overall German naval threat during the early years of 1940 and 1941. Even with the fifty armed merchant cruisers the Royal Navy was stretched to tearing point by the ever-widening war – and the slightest additional pressure brought severe dislocation. A force of naval cruisers, many of them drawn from the Mediterranean war theatre, was on station south of the Equator. At various times they included such vessels as HMS *Colombo*, *Cornwall*, *Cumberland*, *Devonshire*, *Dorsetshire*, *Dunedin*, *Durban*, *Glasgow*, *London*, *Neptune*, *Newcastle*, and *Norfolk*.

During the winter of 1940/41 there were as many as ten cruisers on station in African and South American waters. Far better if they had been in the Mediterranean when war erupted at Tobruk and when the important 'Excess' convoy was *en route* for Malta and Piraeus. In April 1941 Force V, based at Mombasa, comprised the heavy cruiser *Cornwall*, the light cruiser *Hawkins* and the aircraft carrier *Eagle*. How they would have been welcomed in the evacuations from Greece and from Crete, or in Operation 'Tiger', if they had been sent to reinforce the garrison of Malta. In the first five months of 1941 five cruisers were sunk in the eastern Mediterranean – *Bonaventure*, *Fiji*, *Gloucester*,

Southampton and *York* – yet the Admiralty still felt it necessary to send the light cruiser *Enterprise* and the aircraft carrier *Hermes* to reinforce Force T, based at Trincomalee.

Among the AMCs called up to defend merchantmen in the southern seas were *Alcantara, Antenor, Arawa, Bulolo, Caernarvon Castle, Canton, Cheshire, Hector, Kanimbla, Queen of Bermuda* and *Voltaire*. During the same period three were lost in the North Atlantic: *Comorin, Rajputana* and *Salopian*.

The gallant fight of the armed merchant cruiser *Jervis Bay* excited the admiration of the whole world, yet her story is just one small part of the combined struggle of the Royal and Merchant Navy in defending a Britain in great peril. Her end came as she fought the powerful warship raider *Admiral Scheer*.

From the outbreak of war the former Aberdeen & Commonwealth Line passenger vessel of 14,164 tons was employed escorting convoys to and fro across the Atlantic. *Jervis Bay* was commanded by Captain E.S. Fogarty Fegen RN, an officer with a fine record in the First World War and two life-saving medals in time of peace. A 48-year-old bachelor, he was the fifth generation of his family to serve with distinction in the Navy.

The merchantmen of convoy HX84 had sailed eastwards from Canada, the majority from Halifax with a section from Sydney, Cape Breton, joining during the afternoon of 29 October. As dawn broke on 5 November 1940, the thirty-seven ships in nine columns made a speed of 8 knots on a course of N52E. The Canadian escort had left the previous night and there was now a day's steaming before the escort vessels from an outward convoy would rendezvous. The commodore was Rear-Admiral H. Maltby aboard *Cornish City*.

The largest ship was the 16,698-ton *Rangitiki*, carrying a crew of 223 and seventy-five passengers, as well as a cargo of butter, cheese, meat and wool. There were eleven tankers carrying precious oil fuel and aviation spirit. The remainder carried a variety of foodstuffs – grain, timber, steel, munitions and war materials. *Trefusis*, a World War One 'standard'-type trampship, carrying steel bars and dressed timber, had discharged Anson aircraft and spares at Montreal. Such westbound cargoes were of great value to the war effort. Many thousands of Air Force pilots, carried by merchant transports, were trained in Canada during the war.

One hundred miles to the north steamed the 10,000-ton pocket battleship *Admiral Scheer*. She had been dispatched 'to relieve pressure on German operations in the North Sea and English Channel by rapid action which would tend to upset normal dispositions of the British escort forces'. Guided by intelligence reports, she was on course to intercept 'a large convoy ETD Halifax, Nova Scotia, 28 October'.

Launched in 1933, the *Admiral Scheer*, commanded by Captain Theodor Krancke had been designed to 'raid and run'. Her draught of twenty-three feet allowed her to enter shallow harbours and river estuaries, and was ideal for hiding from her enemy or refuelling and victualling from her supply tanker. With a maximum speed of over 26 knots, she had a range of 19,000 miles at 15 knots cruising. Equipped with two spotter aircraft her six 11-inch guns could throw a shell weighing 670 lbs nearly 12 miles. She was also fitted with eight 5.9-inch and six 4.1-inch high-angle guns, eight torpedo tubes, radar, range-finding equipment and gun-control systems.

The *Jervis Bay* was, of course, no match for such a warship – a warship with as many 5.9-inch guns of the most modern type in a secondary battery as the total armament of the Aberdeen & Commonwealth liner. With her speed and her 11-inch guns there was no doubt that it was within the capability of the *Admiral Scheer* to annihilate the convoy. At 1240 hours her Arada reconnaissance seaplane sighted HX84 at 88 miles' distance; the small seaplane was actually observed during a break in the clouds by the third mate of the *Trefusis*, who reported the sighting to the commodore ship by Aldis lamp. After acknowledgement he was asked to confirm that the aircraft was in fact a seaplane. This fact would seem to indicate that an enemy surface vessel of some sort was in the vicinity.

Captain Krancke set full speed and altered course so as to engage the convoy. Speed was essential, as his aim was to destroy the convoy and then steam 150 miles during the hours of darkness. Soon, however, he sighted Elders & Fyffes's banana boat *Mopan* proceeding independently from Kingston, Jamaica, bound for Garston. Though Krancke did not wish to delay, he knew he was unable to let *Mopan* proceed nor could he allow her to use her radio. As Captain Sapsworth, her master, was about to give the alarm, the *Admiral Scheer* despatched a warning shell at close range. Without making the usual distress signal, Captain Sapsworth abandoned ship, the enemy taking him and his crew aboard.

After the *Mopan* had been sunk by a couple of well-placed shells Krancke set course for HX84. To delay his attack until dawn the next day would have meant the convoy would have been 100 miles nearer to the Western Approaches, where British naval units would be on hand.

At 1545 hours *Rangitiki* alerted the commodore after smoke (from the burning *Mopan*) was seen on the horizon. A few minutes later *Empire Penguin* signalled that a ship was approaching from a northerly direction and *Jervis Bay* was informed. At 1635 hours Captain Fegen himself sighted the battleship's hamper and within ten minutes he identified her as an enemy. He immediately hauled his ship out of line towards her. *Jervis Bay* was headed straight towards the enemy and worked up to her maximum speed of 15 knots. Trailing a smoke screen she sent up red rockets, a signal for the merchantmen to set off smoke flares, following which Rear-Admiral Maltby, aboard *Cornish City*, signalled an emergency turn, 40 degrees starboard. At 1710 hours, at a range of ten miles, Krancke turned his ship round to bring all six 11-inch guns on target and opened fire.

The *Admiral Scheer* now paid all its attention to the *Jervis Bay*, whose every gun that would bear forwards was firing rapidly at its maximum elevation. The crews serving and laying them proceeded as though they were at drill; two-thirds of them were fourth service seamen with a minimum of gunnery training and no battle experience whatsoever.

The first salvo from the enemy smashed the bridge and the radio room of the merchant cruiser, seriously wounding Captain Fegen. With her power steering wrecked *Jervis Bay* was steered on her twin screws until a party, calmly working in the open, could ship the hand emergency gear aft. Shells set fire to her decks in several places, and soon the bridge was blazing fiercely and the midship guns were destroyed. One shell completely blew to pieces a whole gun, its mounting and its crew. Amazingly Captain Fegen crawled from the blazing inferno calling for the ship's surgeon to bandage his badly injured leg and an arm which had been almost shot away. He remained in command and although outgunned and outranged, with watertight doors buckled and jammed, and with the decks littered by the dead and the dying, he dragged himself to the stern gun to direct its fire. For twenty-two minutes he stood between the might of the German Navy and the merchantmen he was protecting.

As *Jervis Bay* rolled over and sank, her colours still flying, Captain Fegen and 185 of his men were dead. As darkness was falling and the enemy transferred his fire to the merchantmen, survivors were miraculously plucked from the water by the Swedish *Stureholm*. With a good deal of difficulty and peril to his own crew her master, Captain Olander, found a lifeboat and four rafts. Sixty-five officers and men, including the third and fourth mates, were saved.

As the merchantmen attempted their escape, the *Admiral Scheer* was at close quarters, her 5.9-inch guns blazing. For a while there was chaos as each vessel turned their bows away from the gunflashes; at a maximum rate of knots they sought the darkness of the night. *Lancaster Castle* came dangerously close to *Rangatiki* sailing in the opposite direction. Both were to escape under cover of a smokescreen, as was *Andalusian*, in spite of damage amidships caused by an enemy shell.

Blazing furiously was the tanker *San Demetrio*, loaded with petrol from the refinery in Aruba. *Kenbane Head* took the full force of a salvo from *Scheer* which blew gaping holes in her cargo holds. Repeatedly hit in the engine room her funnel casing was smashed, her starboard lifeboat reduced to matchwood and her radio aerials carried away. With her 4-inch gun useless and her steering gear damaged, she was abandoned.

The 10,042-ton *Beaverford*, which was loaded with munitions, timber and foodstuffs, in an effort to take some of the fire and allow the smaller vessels to escape, opened up with her two guns. Later, amid a tremendous roar she exploded and burst into flames. She sank with all hands, seventy-seven officers and men. She had taken twelve rounds from the main armament of the *Admiral Scheer* and seventy-one rounds from her secondary armament. Three direct hits by main and sixteen by secondary guns were recorded to sink her. To finish her off Krancke despatched a torpedo. *Maidan* was another that day carrying a valuable war cargo: munitions, iron, steel, brass, trucks, timber and tobacco. Escaping on a southerly course she was struck by a salvo of shells which ripped her apart; transformed into a ball of fire, she heeled over and sank. Her complement of ninety officers and men perished.

Trewellard, carrying steel and pig iron, sank within minutes after *Scheer* used her whole armament on her. Seventeen of her crew were killed, although three of her lifeboats got away. Seven shells were sent crashing into *Fresno City* after she was illuminated by powerful searchlights from a distance of some 3,000 yards. With her cargo of grain burning fiercely she was the last to succumb to the raider. As the enemy sped away from the scene at midnight, six merchantmen had been sunk and two damaged. Some 206 merchant seamen had perished, yet thanks to HMS *Jervis Bay* thirty-two ships of convoy HX84 were able to proceed on their voyage towards Britain.

Captain Edward Stephen Fogarty Fegen was awarded the posthumous Victoria Cross 'for valour in challenging hopeless odds and giving his life to save the many ships it was his duty to protect'. Third Officer Wood was awarded the Distinguished Service Order for his courage and devotion to duty. There were other crew members decorated or mentioned in despatches. In detailing the awards the *London Gazette* took the unusual course of amplifying the citation with the words: 'Among those who went down in the *Jervis Bay* there must have been many, and among the survivors others, whose gallantry, were the whole truth known, deserved decoration. The appointment of awards should be taken as an honour to their ship as well as to those who earned them.'

Andalusian and *San Demetrio* limped to port in spite of their 'wounds'. The latter was reboarded when the fire subsided, two days after the attack, and brought to the Clyde estuary by the fashion known to seamen and aviators as 'by guess and by God'. Thirty-seven hours after the battle, responding to the 'attacked by raider' distress call radioed by *Rangitiki*, came the *Gloucester City*. Her master, Captain Smith, rescued seven boatloads of survivors spread over a fifteen-mile radius.

Ninety-two exhausted merchant seamen were landed at St John's, Newfoundland, on 13 November.

Captain Sven Olander, who landed his survivors from the *Jervis Bay* at Halifax, Nova Scotia, found little relief from the war. Some four weeks later he and his Swedish crew found themselves again at the mercy of the naval might of Germany. Their neutral ship, the *Stureholm*, was sunk by *U-96* on 12 December whilst making a second attempt to cross the Atlantic. She was one of four ships sunk from convoy HX92.

The master mariners of convoy HX84 were full of admiration for the way *Jervis Bay* had drawn fire away from their ships. Perhaps the finest tribute came from Captain Piekarski, of the small Polish steamer *Puck*, who wrote to *The Times* newspaper upon docking in London. 'The fine example set to us by the British crew of this ship, who through their sacrifice saved a lot of valuable tonnage and very valuable cargo, filled both myself and my crew with deep admiration and made us their spiritual debtors. This fresh example of British valour on the high seas is sufficient to give renewed confidence in the British Navy and in British victory.'

In the many tributes made to the officers and men of the merchantmen who fought their way out of battle, and who saved their own tonnage and precious cargoes, perhaps there is none better than that made by F. Tennyson Jesse in his HMSO book, *The Saga of San Demetrio* (1942).

'These men of *San Demetrio* would be the last to say that they were in any way exceptional. And indeed we may be thankful that the Merchant Service is full of men as brave and as knowledgeable as these, who are fighting for us night and day the battle of the Western Ocean.'

A question that remains unanswered over fifty years after the event is why the naval staff on board *Cornish City* or *Jervis Bay* apparently failed to advise the Admiralty of the seaplane sighted. If, in fact, they did so, why was no action taken? Such an aircraft in mid-Atlantic was every proof that a surface raider of some type was in the vicinity. Captain F.H. Parmee of the *Trefusis* again reported the sighting upon his de-briefing by a naval officer on arrival in Rothesay Bay. As a consequence, the officer called the third mate of the vessel to give his personal account. No more was heard of the incident.

With Captain Sapsworth of the *Mopan* and his crew of sixty-seven huddled together below deck aboard the *Admiral Scheer*, the battleship set course for tropical waters. *Port Hobart* was sunk off Bermuda, as was *Tribesman* in position 15.00N, 35.00W. Seven days before Christmas on the Equator, Houlder's coal-burning refrigerator ship *Duquesa* met the same end.

The break-out through the Denmark Straits of the German cruiser *Admiral Hipper* (Captain Meisel) in December 1940 heralded a series of actions by enemy warships directed against merchantmen over twelve weeks of a wintry North Atlantic. The damage wrought by the *Admiral Scheer*, and the fact that she was now south of the Equator sinking ships at will without being sighted by Allied naval forces, gave encouragement to the German high command. *Admiral Hipper* was followed in February by *Scharnhorst* and *Gneisenau*.

Prior to the Norwegian campaign in April 1940 the German heavy cruiser *Lutzow* (soon to be renamed *Deutschland*), and the new heavy cruiser *Blücher*, were being fitted out for mercantile raiding in the North Atlantic. Both were pressed into operations in the German invasion of Norway. Both were torpedoed: the *Lutzow* by the British submarine *Spearfish*, and the *Blücher* from shore batteries in Oslo Fjord. With all hope gone for their future role, Grand-Admiral Raeder was most bitter. Had they been available during the autumn and winter of 1940/41 much greater havoc could have been wrought amidst the convoys.

Admiral Hipper's foray was against the 'Winston Special' convoy WS5A, bound for India and the Middle East, which was carrying some 4,000 troops. The convoy had sailed from Liverpool on 10 December and included such well-known vessels as the *Empire Trooper* (the former German liner *Cap Norte* that had been boarded and taken as a prize by HMS *Belfast*); the two Belgium transports *Elizabethville* and *Leopoldville*; *Anselm, Llandaff Castle, Orbita, Rangitiki*; the Dutch *Volendam*; and three 'City' boats, *City of Canterbury, City of Derby* and *City of London*. The commodore flew his standard in *Tamaroa* and the escort was provided by the cruisers *Berwick, Bonaventure* and *Dunedin* along with the flower-class corvette *Clematis*. Also within the convoy were the carriers *Argus* and *Furious*, destined for Takoradi, with aircraft for overland transfer to Egypt.

Around 700 miles west of Cape Finisterre, just before dawn on Christmas morning, the strong escort took Captain Meisel by surprise. There was a brief engagement as *Hipper* shelled HMS *Berwick*, the 13,994-ton transport *Empire Trooper* and the merchantman *Arabistan*. The latter was damaged by a shell which struck the fo'c's'le. The *Trooper*, which had been straggling with engine problems, was struck on the waterline. Later she was taken into the neutral harbour of San Miguel in the Azores for repairs, whence she was escorted to Gibraltar.

Because of the convoy escort the *Admiral Hipper* broke off the engagement only to be chased by the cruisers *Berwick and Bonaventure*. However, these having lost sight of the enemy due to poor visibility, the chase was called off. Captain Meisel of the German cruiser wrote in his log at 0810 hours:

I have decided to break off the operation and to sail to Brest as fast as possible before measures are taken by the enemy, provoked by the attack on the convoy, take effect. If I continued at sea I would have to refuel to-morrow at the latest in order to remain in operation. This has been the task which was set me. I feel the moment has come where the limit of the efficiency of ship and crew is in sight.

At 1010 hours, 450 miles west of Ushant, Captain Meisel enters in his log, 'In rain a shadow at 340 degrees. Speed approach. Medium size freighter.' Heavy armament and two torpedoes were employed. Within minutes the merchantman *Jumna*, bound for Freetown and Calcutta after serving as commodore ship for convoy OB260, which dispersed on 19 December, was ruthlessly destroyed. She had been proceeding to Freetown independently as was normal practice for OB convoys at the time, there to land the commodore and his staff. All on board, including the commodore, Rear-Admiral H.B. Maltby, and his staff, were killed; only six weeks previously the Rear-Admiral had led the *Jervis Bay* convoy. Forty-three of the 111 dead were Lascar merchant seamen being repatriated after their steamship *Planter* had been torpedoed on 16 November.

There is a postscript to the records of convoy OB260. On 20 December a merchantman was sunk within hours of the dispersing. This was the *Carlton*, torpedoed and shelled by the Italian submarine *Calvi*. Shelling continued even though the lifeboats were being launched. One of the two successfully launched contained eighteen seamen, though none of them survived their ordeal. The second lifeboat arrived at a Canadian port after an eighteen day voyage. Led by the chief mate, only four survived the wintry weather; twelve, including two sixteen-year-old boys, died from exposure.

Admiral Hipper returned to the high seas in February, sailing from Brest on the first day of the month. Whilst the important Winston Special convoy had the benefit of 'cruiser' support, convoy SLS64, homewards from Freetown, reflected the more typical situation. Thirteen days after sailing from the Sierra Leone river on 30 January, the convoy of eight British and one foreign vessel found itself 200 miles south-east of the Azores, without any escort whatsoever. It was then that the 8-inch-gun cruiser *Hipper* came up fast from astern. Sailing 'peacefully' between the centre columns she suddenly declared her identity. No sooner had the swastika been hoisted aloft than the first salvo of shells devastated the *Warlaby* at close range.

A further six merchantmen were quickly blasted from the sea: *Borgestad*, *Derryname*, *Oswestry Grange*, *Perseus*, *Shrewsbury* and *Westbury*. Damaged were the *Ainderby* and *Lornaston*. The steamer *Clunepark*, partly abandoned in confusion due to damage, transferred some of her crew to *Blairathol* but eight men were lost in the process. Both vessels later arrived in Madeira. *Admiral Hipper*, in case distress signals had alerted the Royal Navy that she was in the vicinity, and low on fuel, left the scene of destruction as fast as she had arrived and returned to Brest.

A total of 122 merchant seamen died, including the masters of four of the vessels. Valuable cargoes, including frozen Argentine beef aboard *Oswestry Grange*, were destroyed. *Lornaston* and *Ainderby*, the former carrying many survivors, arrived at Funchal in the Azores a few days later, where they spent over three months under repair. The *Ainderby* was never to reach her home port. On 10 June *en route* from Funchal she was sunk by *U-552*. Twenty-one of her crew lost their lives.

Three merchantmen, *Empire Energy*, *Dartford* and the *Nailsea Lass*, fell behind SLS64 soon after sailing from Freetown – the first two with engine trouble, the *Nailsea Lass* because her bottom was so badly fouled with weed that she was unable to maintain the convoy speed of 7½ knots. *Empire Energy* eventually docked at Avonmouth on 28 February, the local paper announcing her arrival as the first, if not the only, ship to arrive in the United Kingdom after the *Hipper* attack. *Nailsea Lass*, for fourteen days struggling to reach friendly shores unaided, was torpedoed and sunk by *U-48* within sixty miles of Fastnet Rock. Her master (Captain Bradford) and chief mate taken prisoner, five of her crew were to die in the lifeboats. The remaining vessel to survive the *Hipper* onslaught was the coal-burning *Gairsoppa*, to which I made reference in Chapter 2. Loaded with pig iron from India, bad weather made her low on bunkers, and in an effort to conserve fuel her speed was reduced to 5 knots. It was then that she was torpedoed and sunk.

The battle cruisers *Scharnhorst* and *Gneisenau*, two of the most powerful raiders in the German fleet, crept undetected through the Skagerrak on 24 January 1941. An attempt to pass through the Iceland–Faroes passage was foiled by the Home Fleet though they successfully cut across the North Atlantic shipping lanes by breaking out through the Denmark Strait. The enemy was again determined to harass the convoys with the big guns of its navy. However, their attempts to molest several convoys were frustrated by the presence of a single escorting battleship; on 8 February, upon sighting HX106, they withdrew when they found it escorted by HMS *Ramillies*. Sailing westward they chose to cruise in waters where it was usual at the time for convoys to disperse and proceed independently to their destinations, and where escorts would rendezvous with inward convoys from North America.

The day after *Admiral Scheer*, still on her destructive voyage in southern waters, sank the steamship *Canadian Cruiser*, the two raiders sank five merchantmen which had sailed from the Clyde and Mersey estuaries on 15 February (OB287) and dispersed five days later. During the afternoon of the dispersal morning, the merchantman *Harlesden* was machine-gunned and bombed by a seaplane, killing the second mate and destroying the radio aerial. At dusk *Gneisenau* was in close contact and shelling the vessel unmercifully. There followed the destruction of *Trelawney, Lustrous, Kantara* and *A.D. Huff*. All five vessels were abandoned; there were many casualties and the survivors were taken prisoner.

One can appreciate why the two following westbound convoys, OB288 and OB289, were routed so far to the north (to latitude 60 degrees). Only by so doing did they avoid the ravages of the enemy. At the time, my introduction to the Atlantic war (aboard *Nailsea Manor*, convoy OB289) was just beginning. A common phenomenon at the time was that the men in one particular ship could never tell what was going on beyond the wide sea horizon. Radio officers on watch would often pick up distress signals along with the positions of the vessels concerned. But whilst such information was shared with the captain, 'their lips were sealed'; rarely was such news passed down the line.

After a southerly cruise into the quieter latitude of the Tropic of Cancer *Scharnhorst* and *Gneisenau* returned to the shipping lanes, this time to latitude 42/46 degrees North (longitude 43 degrees West). Here two merchantmen, the British *San Casimiro* and the Norwegian *Bianca*, were captured and prize crews taken prisoner. Meanwhile twelve others from dispersed convoys OB292 and OB294 were shelled and sunk. In addition, a lone independent, the former Danish *Chilean Reefer*, managed by the Alfred Holt Company, was caught. Captain S.W. Roskill has described her action (in *A Merchant Fleet in War*) as one of the most gallant single-ship actions ever fought by a British merchant ship against a vastly superior adversary.

The German prize crews failed in their efforts to get the tankers *San Casimiro* and *Bianca* into Brest without being sighted. On 20 March they were observed by aircraft from the carrier *Ark Royal*. Closing up fast was the battleship *Renown*. With HMS *Sheffield* called up from Force H, under the command of Admiral Sir James Somerville, both vessels were scuttled and abandoned.

Demeterton, bound from the Mersey for Halifax (in convoy OB292), was stopped for ten hours during the night of 14/15 March on account of engine repairs. Resuming full speed she intercepted a raider warning from the tanker *Simnia*. Then came a further warning from the tanker *Athelfoam*, the two being some 200 miles apart. At noon that day a third warning signal was heard. *Sardinian Prince* was under shellfire not more than 50 miles to the south-east.

Captain Morris of the 5,251-ton *Demeterton* made the following report at the subsequent Admiralty inquiry, held after he had been repatriated from the Milag POW camp in Germany during October 1943.

At 1545 hours the second officer reported sighting the masts of a ship on the port beam ... on looking through my glasses I saw she was a warship. The unknown ship, which turned out to be the *Scharnhorst*, then ordered me to stop using my radio. Within 15 minutes her bow wave was clearly visible and she then opened fire ... The first shell went over the ship and fell about 20 yards from the side forward. I think the Raider was firing her big guns to begin with, as she was 10/11 miles away at the time. We had the 4 inch gun manned and, as the Raider closed, this could evidently be seen, as she commenced firing at our gun. By this time the smaller guns were firing and shells were screaming across the poop. I did not stop the ship and a direct hit was not scored for some time.

The Raider was closing rapidly so I decided it was time to abandon ship, the boats being ready for slipping. I turned one side of the ship away from the gunfire until one boat was lowered, then in the opposite direction for the other one to be lowered. All the crew got into the boats except the chief officer, chief engineer, second officer, wireless operator, helmsman and myself. The Raider now started shelling furiously. The port boat, in the charge of the third mate, was swamped by the main discharge and although the boat's crew bailed vigorously, they could not get the boat dry so I had to send the chief engineer to stop the pump. Meanwhile the ship was stopped, with both boats alongside.

I told the chief purser to throw all his papers overboard and get off the ship, then I went on the bridge, tore up the chart and threw it over the side. I then went to my room, collected an overcoat and 500 cigarettes before making my way to the boats. As I arrived in the alleyway, the Raider scored her first shot on the bridge; the next shell hit the starboard boiler which burst and started a fire in the stokehold. All the crew having abandoned ship I went aft and jumped over the side and was picked up by the starboard boat; by 1710 hours the ship was finally abandoned.

When the Raider saw the lifeboats in the water, she closed to within 200 yards and opened rapid fire. The first salvo missed the hull but hit the superstructure, carrying away the awnings between the after end of the bridge and the funnel. She then fired into the shear strake continuing to do so until, at 1745 hours, the ship sank. ... The Raider had evidently sunk several ships as she had between 400/500 prisoners on board.

The merchantman *Sardinian Prince* (Captain Millikan) sailed from the Mersey on 11 March, with convoy OB294, her destination Philadelphia. Only two days later the convoy was ordered to disperse, an indication of the shortage of escort vessels at the time. She too intercepted the 'attacked by raider' signal from the oil tanker *Simnia* on 15 March. Before dawn broke the following day the *Sardinian Prince* observed gun flashes to the south-west; the Dutch ship *Mankim*, also of convoy OB294, was under attack. Shortly afterwards gunfire from the same quarter was again heard. This time it was the *Silverfir*. Neither merchantmen managed to transmit a distress or 'attacked by raider' radio message.

Although *Sardinian Prince* altered course, steering away from the sound of the gunfire, Captain Millikan sighted a 'man-of-war' off the starboard quarter steaming at a high speed from the eastward. The time was about 0730 hours. The British master also made his report upon his return from Germany (17 November 1943). His Admiralty report continues:

> As I was unable to identify the vessel I gave instruction for a wireless message to be transmitted giving our position and stating 'suspicious vessel closing us'. Immediately the Wireless Operator commenced transmitting, the Raider, which was then about 6 miles away, opened fire with three big guns. The first shot fell well ahead, the second one close behind and the third one just short of the bridge.
>
> After the first salvo from the Raider I stopped the ship and threw the confidential books and the wireless codes overboard. The Raider continued firing and one shell of his second salvo struck the ship in the after end of No.2 hold, a little forward of the bridge. A splinter from this shell pierced my leg ... the crew abandoned ship in the remaining three lifeboats and by 0900 hours everyone was clear of the ship. As we pulled clear the *Scharnhorst* resumed shelling; at approximately 0930 *Sardinian Prince* rolled over to starboard and sank. After about half an hour in the boats all survivors were taken on board the Raider. I was immediately taken below to the hospital.

At the time *Demeterton* was being shelled by the *Scharnhorst* the lookout on the independent outward-bound *Chilean Reefer* reported a vessel on the port beam. This was the *Gneisenau* bearing south, distance about twelve miles. Within minutes she was endeavouring to intercept. On breaking radio silence the Raider opened fire. Captain Bell of the *Chilean Reefer* reported: 'at about 1720 hours our vessel having been hit by one salvo and being on fire forward, the raider was at a distance of about 4 miles and seemed within 4 inch gun range so I opened fire hoping that with the rapidly decreasing range some damage might perhaps result.'

Even though *Gneisenau* closed to within half a cable, pounding 82 rounds into her quarry (a small vessel of only 1,739 tons), Captain Bell, calm in command, tried to zigzag his way out of trouble, releasing smoke floats in a desperate attempt to confuse his attacker and save his ship. Alas! she became a burning hulk, her brave master and his men only abandoning her when it became impossible to stay aboard.

Later that same night Captain Bell and his crew, with the exception of the second mate, were picked up by the battleship *Rodney*, called up from a homeward-bound convoy in the vicinity. Second mate Collett, like the survivors from the other vessels, was taken prisoner. Weeks later they arrived at the prison camp near Bremen. The remaining merchantmen sunk were the *Rio Dorada*, in which Captain Clare and his crew of thirty-nine all perished as she blew up amidst a sheet of flame;

the *Empire Industry*; the former French *Myson; Royal Crown*; and the tanker *British Strength*. The two battle cruisers returned to base after sinking a total tonnage of 115,600, by far the heaviest damage ever inflicted on merchantmen by German surface warships.

During May 1941 the sortie led by the giant battleship *Bismarck* and the heavy cruiser *Prinz Eugen* led to one of the most dramatic series of fights in the entire annals of sea warfare. The interception, and sinking, of the *Bismarck* (despite the loss of HMS *Hood* the pride of the British fleet) was to end the commerce raiding by German warships except on a small scale against convoys to Russia. Had *Bismarck* and *Prinz Eugen* been allowed to decimate the homeward HX convoys, laden with foodstuffs and war materials, the horror wrought by the German Navy in the North Atlantic would have been complete. Even so, Britain's convoy cycles were completely dislocated. In the first quarter of 1941, warship raiders had sunk thirty-seven valuable ships; the six merchant raiders, twenty-five ships.

In spite of the success of *Scharnhorst* and *Gneisenau*, that achieved by the German armed merchant raiders was far greater. The merchant raider *Widder* (formerly *Neumark*) of 7,800 tons, equipped with six 5.9-inch guns, two twin 21-inch torpedo tubes and auxiliary equipment, sailed from Kiel on 5 May 1940, the month of 'Dunkirk'. Her captain, a 49-year-old naval reservist, was Lieutenant-Commander Hellmuth von Ruckteschell, who had been recalled to the colours in 1939. He became the only enemy naval captain, including those of the Japanese Navy, to be brought to trial and convicted as a war criminal in 1947. *Widder* was the third of nine converted merchantmen, all brilliantly disguised ocean marauders. *Atlantis* had sailed on 31 March and *Orion* a week later.

With orders to raid in the central North Atlantic von Ruckteschell was in the Trinidad–Azores region on 13 June when he sighted the tanker *British Petrol*, sailing in ballast and requisitioned by the Admiralty as a Royal Fleet Auxiliary. Flying the red ensign at the stern she was still a member of the fourth service and fully crewed by Merchant Navy personnel. Without any warning *Widder* quickly brought her guns to bear and destroyed the tanker 20 degrees north of the Equator.

The sighting of the merchantman *Davisian* north of the Leeward Islands a month later brought the raider's six 5.9-inch guns immediately into action. The radio aerial was torn down and considerable damage was done to the superstructure. Preparations were made by her master to abandon ship. Claiming that men were seen running aft and making their way to the 4-inch gun – something which, together with the radio, von Ruckteschell instructed was on no account to be used – the German captain ordered his men to open fire with the 37mm and 20mm cannon; three of *Davisian*'s seamen were killed. This was the first of several charges of brutal behaviour brought against von Ruckteschell, not only by the victorious Allies but by his associates, who claimed he was unfit emotionally to command a raider. In contrast to Japanese brutality on the high seas, the shooting-down of enemy seamen was obnoxious to the peacetime officers of the German Navy.

In the case of the steamer *King John*, brought to a standstill three days later, Captain Smith instructed his radio officer to send the distress call. Immediately the ship was shelled into submission. Subsequently von Ruckteschell sent on board a boarding party, including his doctor, to assist with the survivors and report on the situation. Three crew were dead, six seriously injured and fifty-nine crew were to be taken as prisoners. These included twenty-one survivors from a ship sunk by a U-boat – Yugoslavs, Portuguese, Maltese and Spaniards amongst them; 'dirty, lousy folk,' von Ruckteschell observed.

The third account upon which *Widder*'s captain was found guilty was related to his failure to provide for the safety of the crew and those survivors from the 5,596-ton coal carrier *Anglo Saxon*. *En route* from Newport for Bahia Blanca she had dispersed from her outward convoy. Then as dusk fell on 21 August 1940 in mid-Atlantic she was sunk within a few minutes by heavy shelling. The first salvo virtually destroyed the stern of the vessel. With her steering gear and 4-inch armament swept away the magazine blew up. After a torpedo had been sent into her she disappeared in the growing darkness of the night. Upon instructions from von Ruckteschell the raider *Widder* steamed off. At the subsequent trial of her captain it was claimed that the British merchantman radioed after being told to hold silence.

The next morning the chief mate and six others found that they appeared to be the only survivors of the horrific action. They were alone in the lifeboat. There was no sign of their ship or of the raider. By September 10 seamen Wilbert Widdicombe and Robert Tapscott were the only survivors. They were to survive in the boat for a total of seventy days, after which they were cast ashore in an exhausted condition on Eleuthera Island. Found on 30 October by a native farmer they were taken to Nassau's Bahamas General Hospital.

Sir Etienne Dupuch, editor proprietor of Nassau's *Tribune*, commenting on the survival of the two seamen, wrote in his newspaper, 'their only sign of life was the haunted eyes shifting from side to side'. The Duke and Duchess of Windsor, at the time residents of Nassau, paid them a visit, but otherwise they received little attention nor did they seek it. When the *Siamese Prince* was sunk with all hands by *U-69* some 180 miles north-west of the Hebrides only three months later no one mentioned that one of its seamen was Wilbert Widdicombe, late of the trampship *Anglo Saxon*. His name had already been forgotten.

Robert Tapscott took longer to recover, but later signed an affidavit saying that the German raider had turned its guns on the men in the boats. This was denied at the war trial and as Karl August Muggenthaler has rightly written in his brilliant survey, *German Raiders of World War II*, 'it was an impression many frightened survivors in many wars, shocked by their ordeal, ducking from flying fragments of steel and deadly ricochets, retained even after much of their hatred had worn off, but it was usually one impossible to substantiate'.

Hellmuth von Ruckteschell was listed as a war criminal in 1947 and found guilty on three counts. He received a seven-year jail sentence, one which excited much controversy over the years. One can only reflect on the remarks of Captain Roskill in the history *The War at Sea* ... 'It is only fair to mention that the captains of German armed merchant raiders generally behaved with reasonable humanity towards the crews of intercepted ships, tried to avoid unnecessary loss of life and treated their prisoners tolerably.'

How very different were Captain Bernhard Rogge of the raider *Atlantis* and Captain Ernst-Felix Krüder of the *Pinguin*. Both were of the old school. Krüder had served in the German Imperial Navy with distinction during the First World War and afterwards he had volunteered for the dangerous job of clearing mines – just for the sheer joy and excitement of it.

Pinguin, equipped with six 5.9-inch guns and an Arado seaplane, sailed from Germany on 15 June 1940 with 300 mines for her own use together with twenty-five torpedoes and eighty mines for transfer to U-boats in mid-ocean. Her first action was against the homeward-bound British tramp steamer *Domingo de Larrinaga*, laden with grain from Bahia Blanca. Spotted on 31 June, west of Ascension Island, the steamer flouted the enemy's instructions by radioing her position, describing the appearance of her attacker, failing to stop as requested and making ready her gun for action. Captain Krüder however showed great patience; only the bridge of the merchantman was destroyed after three warning shots had been fired.

As flames spread and leapt high from the *Larrinaga* trampship, Captain Chalmers, her master, had to admit defeat. Eight of his crew had been killed, and the remaining thirty survivors were taken aboard *Pinguin*. With the enemy boarding party, Krüder sent his ship's surgeon and two sick bay attendants to examine the injured. Among lives that were saved that day were those of the wireless operator Jock Morrison and the second mate C.A. Plummer. Both were safely landed in Bordeaux from the prison ship *Storstad* on 6 February 1941. Captain Chalmers and crew were transferred to the *Nordvaard*, which docked in France on 22 November 1940.

Pinguin's trail of destruction included the merchantman *Benavon*, loaded with rubber, jute and hemp, and bound from Singapore to London; and the *Maimoa*, with her refrigerated cargo of 1,500 tons of

Australian butter, 170,000 cases of eggs (over 16 million eggs), 5,000 tons of meat and 1,500 tons of grain; the *Port Brisbane*, another refrigerated vessel, carrying frozen meat, butter and cheese; the *Port Wellington*, with a cargo of lead ingots, baled wool (also carried as deck cargo four bales high), frozen lamb, cheese and butter.

The distress calls made by *Clan Buchanan* and *British Emperor* led to the destruction of *Pinguin* on 8 May 1941 by HMS *Cornwall*. She still had 130 mines on board as well as prisoners of war, 200 of whom perished. Ninety-seven were from the Clan Line steamer, all but one member of the crew of the steamer *Empire Light*, and most of the forty-five crew of the tanker *British Emperor*. Only twenty-two survivors were picked up by *Cornwall*.

The raider *Pinguin* had sailed 59,188 miles, sunk or captured twenty-eight vessels, including sixteen prizes totalling 136,551 tons, as well as 18,068 tons sunk by mines. Taking into account the losses of cargo destined for the 'siege island' of Britain she was one of the most successful of the merchant raiders. Thanks largely to the humanity of Captain Krüder, casualties in the wake of his achievements were not heavy.

Orion, commanded by Lieutenant-Commander Kurt Weyher, sailed for the Pacific by way of the Indian Ocean; the only vessel she sunk *en route* was the British-flag *Haxby*. After laying 228 mines in New Zealand waters (as a result of which the 13,415-ton liner *Niagara* was sunk) she sighted New Zealand Shipping Company's *Turakinia* rolling heavily due to bad weather in the Tasman Sea. She was *en route* from Sydney to Wellington, there to finish loading up with frozen lamb before proceeding on her way to the United Kingdom. There followed one of the most famous fights between a merchantman and an enemy raider. Captain Laird of the *Turakinia* brought his sole 4-inch gun to bear upon the enemy in reply to a salvo from her 6-inch armament. For twenty minutes the battle raged.

To quote from the *London Gazette*:

Third Officer Mallett was the gunnery officer and his splendid example of courage and determination inspired the guns crews. Later, when the chief radio officer was blown from his post, he went to his rescue and carried him down to the boat. Chief Radio Officer Jones displayed great courage and devotion to duty, thereby sacrificing his life. He remained on board to send out distress messages until he was blown from his desk through a wooden bulkhead. Able Seaman McGowan displayed conspicuous bravery and a high sense of duty while serving the guns throughout the action.

All three cited were awarded Lloyds War Medals.

With valiant *Turakinia* badly battered and blazing fiercely, *Orion* approached to within a mile and sank her prey with two torpedoes. Captain Laird and thirty-four of his officers and crew were taken down with her. Twenty-one men survived to be picked up by the raider, though one later died from his injuries. On board, in reply to one of his men who questioned the risk he was taking in searching for further survivors, Kurt Weyher explained what war was and what one seaman's duty to another was. It was sad, he said, to sink ships, and horrible to kill. 'Once that was over, one fought man's common enemy, the sea, to save as many souls as possible.'

Orion's last victim before returning to Bordeaux on 23 August 1941 (510 days at sea with 127,337 miles to her credit) was the outward-bound *Chaucer*, sighted at dusk 800 miles west of the Cape Verde Islands. In reply to a spread of torpedoes and shelling, her master, Captain Bradley, courageously ordered the firing of his 4-inch and 40-mm Bofors gun. Yet still *Orion* closed, her powerful searchlight illuminating the red-duster vessel. With two more torpedoes sent into her all was lost and she was abandoned. Miraculously, all forty-eight crew survived and were taken aboard the raider, though thirteen were suffering from injuries.

Captain Roskill records in *The War at Sea* that *Orion* was an old ship (built in 1930) and, although not a very successful raider, had performed a remarkable feat in maintaining herself in seagoing condition for so long a period away from a proper base. When awarded the Iron Cross, Weyher said, 'I led my ship with common sense and luck, my men with my heart.'

Brilliant and honourable were the epithets ascribed to the name of Captain Rogge, who sailed his raider *Atlantis* through the southern oceans until 22 November 1941, when she was sunk by HMS *Devonshire*. Her tally of ships totalled twenty-two, including three prizes, a tonnage of 145,697. *Atlantis* sank two vessels in the Indian Ocean during July of her first year; both were British – *City of Baghdad* and *Kemmendine*. Ellerman's 'City' boat, a First World War reparations prize, sailed from Lourenço Marques for Penang on 28 June with a full cargo loaded in the United Kingdom. On the Equator in longitude 90.00E the merchantman under the command of Captain Armstrong White was stopped by four warning shots from the raider's 3-inch guns.

At the time *Atlantis* was flying signals indicating that no radio was to be used nor the vessel abandoned, but that her engines were to be stopped. Armstrong White insisted, however, that the signals could not be understood. 'The flags were flying in such a manner', he said in his report, 'that they could not be distinguished by either the chief mate or myself.' The sending of the recognized distress call by radio immediately brought the heavy guns into action, and the radio room and part of the superstructure were smashed. A total of forty-two rounds were fired, many of them being directed at the foredeck – this to avoid heavy casualties amongst the crew.

Nevertheless, the shelling brought about the deaths of three native crewmen and serious injuries to the radio operator and the quartermaster. *City of Baghdad* was later to sink by the explosion of time bombs brought aboard and by a shell fired on the waterline abaft the engineroom. Subsequently Captain Armstrong White, OBE, was to say of his former captor, the postwar Admiral Rogge, 'a nice fellow with good human qualities of decency'.

The survivors, with the exception of the chief engineer and those injured, spent 108 days on *Atlantis*, twenty-eight days on the Yugoslav prize ship *Durmitor* and ninety-six days in the Italian prison camp at Mogadishu in Somaliland. Here the fourth and fifth engineers died of dysentery in appalling conditions. By contrast, the treatment accorded to all prisoners on board the raider was good; for example, all received the same food, whether British or German.

The chief engineer (because of his age) and the injured were transferred to the prize ship *Tirranna*, a Norwegian merchantman captured on 10 June, for the voyage back to Europe. But the 'chief', along with eighty-six others were drowned, when the *Tirranna* was torpedoed and sunk by the submarine HMS *Tuna* in the Bay of Biscay.

The Alfred Holt merchantman *Automedon*, outward bound for the Far East, was sunk by *Atlantis* in the Indian Ocean during November 1940. Her loss is remembered firstly for the deaths of her master, Captain Ewan, and the third mate. They were killed during the first engagement, when there was appalling destruction on the bridge and the officers' accommodation. In the second instance, it is notable for the officers' unsuccessful attempt to destroy the ship's documents, some of which were highly secret. During the attempt the chief mate sustained serious injuries and was found unconscious by the second mate. Later, the German boarding officer reported:

> We found all the Admiralty's instructions, course directions and secret log books and after breaking into the master's safe we found the Merchant Navy code, conversion tables etc. In the mail room we found a number of bags marked 'Safe Hand. By British Master only.' These contained material surpassing our expectations – the whole of the top secret mail for the High Command Far East; new code tables for the fleet; secret notices to mariners: information about minefields and swept areas, plans and maps: a War Cabinet report giving a summary of defence of the Far East; Intelligence Service material and many other documents.

Subsequently all merchantmen were provided with an electrically detonated destruction device to prevent secret documents falling into enemy hands. Over fifty years later, it is difficult to understand why such secret material was dispatched over 12,000 miles by sea; yet in 1940 there were no long-haul air services, and transit by a 'blue funnel' vessel was therefore considered the fastest and safest method.

Under international law the immunity of a merchant ship from attack depended on her not 'resisting' capture. The Germans always held that to use radio constituted offering resistance and therefore justified their action in shelling ships which acted in that manner. The difficulty in which master mariners were placed was due to the fact that no proper guidelines were issued by the Admiralty and in any case, the master, under his contract with his shipowner, was responsible for bringing his vessel safely to port. 'Resisting capture' was a matter of controversy throughout the war. The Allies put forward the view that to sail merchantmen in convoy escorted by warships was in fact to offer 'resistance'.

There were many casualties during the attack by *Atlantis* on the steamer *Mandasor* (24 January 1941), a perfect example of a ship resisting capture. Even after the radio aerial had been carried away by the spotter seaplane (by dragging a wire across the beam of the vessel), an emergency aerial was erected under the orders of Captain Hill, her master, and the 'attacked by raider' signal was radioed. This brought a bombing raid from the aircraft and two salvoes from the heavy armament of *Atlantis*. Immense damage resulted and much of the vessel took fire. The citation accompanying the Lloyds War Medal awarded to the British master concludes with this tribute: 'Captain Hill showed outstanding courage and resolution. His determination in refusing to abandon his ship until she was sinking deprived the enemy of her stores and provisions which were badly needed by the Germans.' Homeward bound from Calcutta the *Mandasor* was down to her 'marks', loaded with tea, hessian and pig iron.

The raider *Komet*, commanded by Captain Eyssen, sailed for the Pacific Ocean by the 3,300-mile voyage through the mostly impassable north-east passage to the north of Russia, a risky undertaking which was only possible with the assistance of Russian icebreakers. In his personal war diary Eyssen wrote 'I passed the Bering Strait between 0200 and 0230 this morning (a voyage of 23 days). This trip has been enough for me; I would not do it voluntarily a second time.'

In the Pacific *Komet* joined forces with *Orion* and there on 26 November 1940 they blasted *Rangitane* from the high seas. Briefly mentioned in Chapter 3 for the valuable cargo which she carried, it was her thirty-first New Zealand/UK voyage and her seventh made during wartime. Carrying 111 passengers, including some women and children, her master was Captain H.L. Upton DSC, RD, RNR. During the darkness of the night the two raiders confronted their prey from ahead, one on the port bow, the other to starboard. Captain Upton at once instructed his radio officer to send the 'suspicious ship' message – the 'raider' message – and immediately the enemy opened fire. The attack by *Orion* and *Komet* was both savage and ruthless. It was the first time that two of Germany's ocean merchant raiders worked in harmony. There is no doubt that it also proved highly successful.

Four hours after the first attack, *Rangitane* was heavily on fire, and flames and smoke added to the horror of the scene. She was holed in a number of places below the waterline, her steering gear was disabled and her superstructure riddled and torn about by shellfire. As the ship was abandoned, one of the lifeboats capsized and many were thrown into the sea. There were many acts of bravery in the highest traditions of Britain's Merchant Navy; three members of the crew were awarded the British Empire Medal and Lloyds War Medal. As torpedoes sent the 16,712-ton *Rangitane*, crammed with food for the British housewife's table, to the bottom of the ocean, 295 souls drifted helplessly amidst the wreckage. Distributed among *Orion, Komet* and a supply ship, the *Kulmerland*, some were put ashore on Emiran Island on 20 December. The remainder, transferred to the *Ermland*, another Germany supply vessel, were prisoners at sea for six months before reaching Bordeaux.

Several of the raiders had narrow escapes. The disguised *Thor*, (formerly *Santa Cruz*), the smallest of the nine raiders, a 17-knot vessel commanded by Otto Kähler, engaged AMCs on three occasions. After successfully fighting off the attentions of the British cruisers *Alcantara* and *Caernarvon Castle* she sank *Voltaire* in April 1941. It was after the loss of the *Voltaire* (seventy-five of her crew perished) that the Admiralty decided finally to take the AMCs off convoy work.

In March 1941 *Thor* destroyed *Britannia*, Anchor Lines' comfortable 14-knot merchantman belonging to the days of the Indian Raj. The diary kept by an officer of the Royal Navy who was a passenger for Bombay, records for all time how eighty-two survivors set out in a lifeboat built and certified for fifty-six, and how after 23 days they had covered 1,535 miles of a stormy Atlantic. At the close of this dramatic tale only thirty-eight were cast ashore upon the coast of Brazil. Now in the care of the National Maritime Museum, the diary is a sad tale of wartime at sea.

Britannia had sailed from Liverpool with a total complement of 484, of whom altogether 235 survived. For over an hour, beneath the heat of a tropical sun, she put up a stiff fight with her single 4-inch gun. The terrible bombardment meted out by the raider (159 shells in total) was provoked, as in so many cases, by the bravery and defiant action of her captain. In her endeavour to escape behind smoke flares and skilful helmsmanship she radioed 'RRRR *Britannia*', giving her position, then QQQQ (the merchant raider signal). Even when the order had been given to abandon ship, *Thor* came up close to continue the bombardment.

After a cruise of 329 days, with ten merchantmen and one prize sunk, *Thor* returned to Germany at the end of April. After re-equipping with, among other featurees, new 5.9-inch guns and a modern radar set, she sailed again under Günther Gumprich. Although a new commander, he adopted the well-tried and successful procedure of: 'Sight ship, tear down radio aerial, stop ship and shell.' For the young 37-year-old 'Denholm' skipper, master of the steamer *Wellpark*, it all happened so quickly. Captain Cant was following Admiralty independently routed instructions from Canada for Alexandria via 'the Cape'. Only the fact that his enthusiastic gunners started to fight back led Gumprich to shell the merchantman. Even then, at close range, the shelling was limited to parts of the vessel where casualties would be light. One shell penetrated No 1 hold whilst a second pierced the boiler casing under the funnel, exploding over the engine room. Salvo after salvo followed until the enemy observed Captain Cant preparing to abandon ship. Seven of *Wellpark*'s crew of forty-eight were killed.

The 1938-vintage *Kormoran*, originally the Hamburg–Amerika Line's 18-knot *Steiermark*, sailed from Germany fully equipped as a raider on 3 December 1940. Her captain was Lieutenant-Commander Theodor Detmers, who joined the German Navy in 1921, and who in 1938 became captain of the large new destroyer *Hermann Schoemann*. Sailing in the Atlantic tropics nearly two months later – her range at 10 knots cruising was 70,000 miles – she sighted her fourth victim. This time it was a night attack using starshells instead of the seaplane with her towing wire.

The thirty-year-old 'blue funnel' *Eurylochus*, commanded by an Alfred Holt stalwart, Captain A.M. Caird, dispersed from her southbound convoy on 19 January and ten days later was about 500 miles south of the Cape Verde Islands. Bound for Takoradi on the Gold Coast she was carrying sixteen aircraft, a valuable cargo which was to be assembled and serviced before onward flight to Egypt – see Chapter 9.

Immediately the starshell illuminated his ship, Captain Caird ordered a radio attack signal to be sent. With hindsight it could be considered a fatal error. *Kormoran* opened fire with one of her 6-inch guns, blasting sixty-seven rounds into *Eurylochus* in a murderous attack. Although the British gun crew replied with some five rounds from their only heavy armament the odds were hopeless. As anticipated by Detmers, the radio signal was picked up at Freetown, from where the armed merchant cruiser *Bulolo* was ordered to the scene; the cruisers HMS *Norfolk* and *Devonshire*, which were already at sea, were similarly instructed. Those aboard *Kormoran* were anxious to sink their prey and escape to quieter waters.

With his steering gear out of action, and eleven of his crew lying dead with the chief mate seriously injured, Captain Caird had no alternative but to abandon ship. The raider then raked the merchantman with machine guns, fired a torpedo into her, sent a boarding party to place time bombs in her engine-room and then waited whilst she broke up. Three Europeans and thirty-nine Chinese crew were taken as prisoners of war, whilst Captain Caird and twenty-seven others escaped on rafts, a no mean achievement even though the enemy was in a hurry to depart. Captain Caird and his survivors were rescued the following day by the Spanish ship, the *Monte Teide*.

The story of the German mercantile raiders and their commanders is a fascinating one. There is no doubt that no other wartime maritime nation could have mounted such a disciplined and hard-fought campaign; theirs was the final climax to the long and romantic era of ocean raiding. No longer in any modern war can such a campaign be repeated.

6 Atlantic Victory

The Battle of the Atlantic was one of the most momentous ever fought in all the annals of war. Historical works of the twentieth century will forever relate its significance in the overthrow of Hitler and Nazi Germany. Never before had the British islands faced such a situation. Without victory there could be no Second Front, no victory in North Africa nor the Mediterranean. Unless the U-boat could be overcome the invasion of mainland Europe could never take place. Unless the German armies could be driven from the lands they had conquered between 1939 and 1941, Hitler could not be defeated in the west. Unless the U-boat and the Norwegian-based enemy aircraft could be overcome, the Russians would without doubt be starved of the vital supplies needed to stop the German armies in their drive to the east.

This was a desperate battle for survival, so desperate in fact that had the Allies lost the battle, the British nation would have been isolated and the Axis powers would have dominated the world. History would have repeated itself; a third World War would have taken place within twenty-five years.

The Atlantic battle was fought for three years in an ocean over 3,000 miles wide and stretched from the Arctic Sea in the north to south of the Equator. It proved the most prolonged and complex battle in the history of naval warfare, fought most of the time whilst Britain stood alone. Victory meant Britain would not starve; British industry would not wither for lack of raw materials; the RAF Bomber Command's offensive would not halt for want of oil; and Coastal Command's Liberator aircraft, engaged in the hunt for U-boats in mid-ocean, would not be grounded for want of aviation fuel. Perhaps the most important factor of all, the invasion of Europe's underbelly and the landings in Normandy, would go ahead as planned.

Even three months before victory there were doubters in the War Cabinet and the Admiralty. 'If we lose the war at sea,' they said, 'we lose the war'. In March 1943, barely six weeks before victory was assured, there was concern about military supplies. With 116 U-boats at sea, the United Kingdom was consuming 750,000 tons more oil and military equipment than was being imported. Already landings on the beaches of

Normandy had secretly reached an advanced planning stage, with General Eisenhower appointed supreme commander.

To those who manned the merchantmen, particularly those slow coal-burning 'trampships' of uncertain age, it was the faith they had in one man that gave them hope of victory. War and the elements alike impressed upon them all the horrors of the deep; many saw their comrades crushed by the war machine of the enemy; yet the former naval man, the former First Lord of the Admiralty was their Commander-in-Chief. Historians will forever wonder whether the Atlantic battle could have been won for the Allies without Winston Spencer Churchill.

Though Churchill was well aware of the situation few were aware of the immensity of the task that faced the operational commands. Without imports of high-octane fuel the fighters could not fly, the bombers could not drop their bombs, whether on Dresden or the U-boat pens at Lorient. Without the raw materials for steelmaking, neither ships nor tanks, nor a vast array of heavy military equipment, could be built. Without imports of certain foodstuffs to maintain the diet of citizens and military personnel alike, malnutrition was a distinct possibility. Islands in war are dependent upon mastery of its seas and of its merchant fleet and personnel, a fact as true today as it was fifty years ago. Further, survival of islands depends upon exports of finished goods and the wherewithal to fight wars overseas.

The convoy battles were as important as any land battle, whether they were fought in the desert of North Africa, the mountains of Italy or upon the banks of the Rhine. The convoy battles were many: in the treacherous 'black hole', amidst the ice floes of the far north and in warmer climes south of the Equator. 'Battles might be won or lost, enterprises might succeed or miscarry, territories might be gained or quitted,' wrote Churchill, 'but dominating all our power to carry on the war, or even keep ourselves alive, lay our mastery of the ocean routes and the free approach and entry to our ports ... The only thing that ever really frightened me during the war was the U-boat peril.'

As Donald MacIntyre has written (in *The Battle of the Atlantic*, 1961), the so-called 'battle' – first given public expression by Churchill himself though some attribute the phrase to a Fleet Street journalist during 1940 – 'concentrated attention upon an aspect of naval warfare, which, on account of its often humdrum nature, is apt to be looked upon as a side-show, a backwater of the main stream of naval operations, yet which is in fact the whole purpose of seapower and in which an island power must either decisively win or be driven to abject surrender.'

Commander Donald MacIntyre was there, to protect the merchantmen and hunt the enemy as leader of the 5th escort. My war had a different course. A lowly seventeen-year-old deck apprentice straight from public school, by the end of the war I had passed my Board of Trade second mate's foreign-going certificate and was serving my company as third mate of the steamship *Nailsea Moor*. From the time that I first crossed the wide ocean – a month that coincided with the first meeting of the Atlantic Committee – to the time that the enemy at sea had to admit defeat was just over two years. Like the Battle of Britain in September 1940, it was won by a narrow margin. As Captain Roskill has written, it was 'won perhaps above all by the fortitude and endurance of our merchant seamen – much of the price was, inevitably, paid by the Merchant Navy'. It was this superior staying power of merchant crews, witnessed by my own eyes when *Gazcon* ploughed under, that will always remain with those who served and survived those years. Relatively few succumbed to the unremitting strain and at the point of victory everyone concerned redoubled their efforts.

Those who survived the battle, however, particularly those of more mature years, believe that the demand it placed upon the endurance of man was higher than any other – higher than the stab of terror and elation of the fighter pilot; higher than the slow build-up towards crisis of the bomber crews over Germany and the sound, fury and concussion of being bombed or shelled; and higher than the animal terror and fury of close infantry combat. The Battle of the Atlantic had something of the character of all these experiences. 'A heroic fight which knows no equal,' said Grand-Admiral Karl Dönitz.

With inadequate naval forces, necessary if only to forestall invasion and maintain hold upon the Mediterranean, trade protection had to take priority above everything. The crisis which the War Cabinet and the Admiralty were forced to face had never been envisaged when war plans were framed. How therefore was victory in the 'western ocean' achieved? What was it that tipped the scales in the greatest battle at sea of all time? Some have given credit to the introduction of very long-range (VLR) aircraft, such as the Liberator; others to the build-up of naval escorts, particularly of the Flower-class corvettes. It was in fact a combination of many factors. In the words of the Commander-in-Chief himself, this was a war 'of groping and drowning, of ambuscade and stratagem, of science and seamanship'.

An increase in the number of escort vessels and VLR aircraft certainly played a large part. But let us not forget the CAM ships, the MAC ships, the fighter catapult ships and the carrier-borne aircraft of the US fleet during the latter stages of the battle. Then, too, there was the formation of the integrated escort groups and the brilliant leadership of Admiral Sir Percy Noble, a former submarine officer, who was finally responsible for their introduction. When his successor as Commander-in-Chief, Western Approaches, Admiral Sir Max Horton, took over in November 1942, he was able to win one of the most decisive victories of the war.

There was, in addition, the replacement ship programme, including the shipbuilding feats of the United States and Canada. Without merchantmen to replace those sunk there could be no victory. The development of bases in Northern Ireland and Bermuda, in Nova Scotia, Newfoundland, Iceland and Greenland, all played their part. Important, too, were the 'back-room boys' of Bletchley Park: the Government Code and Cipher School headed by Roger Winn, its hard-working director, who was a barrister in civilian life. To the re-routeing of convoys, the so-called 'evasive action', and the development of U-boat tracking, many a merchant seaman owed his life. Admiral Edelsten, Assistant Chief of Staff (U-boats & trade) from December 1942, said of Roger Winn, 'his experience, wisdom and sound appreciation of the U-boat war has saved this country vast amounts of shipping tonnage and enabled a heavy toll of U-boats on many occasions'.

Bletchley Park in close co-operation with the Operational Intelligence Centre, a team headed by Vice-Admiral Sir Norman Denning and his deputy, Admiral Jock Clayton, played a significant part in the victory. The movements of enemy ships and underwater craft were betrayed by 'ultra' special intelligence. From the beginning, the Merchant fleet faced the U-boat campaign with no sure method of concealing its communications. The British and Allied Merchant Ship Code (BAMS) was most vulnerable.

Without the introduction of new weapons, particularly that of the mark 24 mine, victory would have been postponed for many months. Valuable, too, was the Leigh Light, which was employed by aircraft at night. The key to many convoy battles was radar, the 10-cm radar and the high-frequency finder (HF/DF), commonly known as 'Huff-Duff' and used by the new escorts.

As with many conflicts of arms a contribution towards a victorious enemy is often made by a misguided leader. Unlike Churchill, Hitler, after his invasion of Russia, failed to recognize the life-and-death struggle of the Atlantic. Dönitz estimated a force totalling 300 operational U-boats was necessary in the North Atlantic to strangle Britain's ocean lifelines, but this was never achieved. Further, due to Hitler's insistence that twenty U-boats be kept in Norway for fear the Allies would invade his 'northern frontier', and his fanatical attention to the land war in the east and in North Africa to the south, Dönitz was unable to exploit his successful 'second happy time' in February 1942, when so many tankers were sunk in the Gulf of Mexico and the Caribbean.

What became known as one of the biggest scandals in the history of the German Navy was the failure of so many of the early torpedoes. What began at Scapa Flow in October 1939, when Günther Prien penetrated all the defences of the 'lion's den', was still a problem in March 1941. German records indicate that torpedo failures prevented even greater results against convoys OB288 and OB289. A year earlier Dönitz estimated that at least 30 per cent of all torpedoes were duds – 'without doubt the torpedo inspectors have fallen down on their job,' he wrote in his diary.

Historically the countdown to victory can be considered as dating from as early as March 1941. The loss of *U-551*, sunk with all hands by HMS *Visenda* on 21 March, was the fifth U-boat loss within sixteen days. In that short space of time the U-boat arm had lost one fifth of its current fighting strength. This was felt all the more because for three months there had been no losses. The scuttled U-boats were, in addition, significant individually: *U-47, U-99* and *U-100*, commanded by such outstanding commanders as Prien, Kretschmer and Schepke respectively. Few who followed were their equals in ruthless ability and daring. These losses coincided with a lack of fully trained and experienced crews – many were wartime Nazi recruits.

The nerves of the enemy were further shattered only seven weeks later, just two weeks before the *Bismarck* sailed on her last voyage. On 9 May, 400 miles south-west of Reykjavik, *U-110* (Commander Fritz-Julius Lemp) was seriously damaged as convoy OB318 dispersed. Involved in the action were HMS *Aubrietia, Bulldog* and *Broadway*. Lemp had, when 26 years old, been the commander of *U-30* when she had sunk the liner *Athenia* on the first day of the war – a passenger ship which Lemp had sunk in violation of both international law and his strict instructions. Further, he left the scene of the crime without attempting to offer the assistance demanded by the submarine protocol. It was said that he was never forgiven, either by Grand-Admiral Dönitz or by his fellow commanders, for the lack of attention to orders. But on this summer like day of May 1941, seeing that his U-boat was about to be boarded and her capture imminent, Lemp made a desperate attempt to get back aboard and scuttle her.

As the merchantmen of OB318 passed on their way westward thirty-four bedraggled Germans were rescued. There was no sign of her Commander. It is believed that Fritz-Julius Lemp committed suicide when he realized what had happened, for the capture of the code-books and Enigma machine from *U-110* would give the British cryptanalysts the first chance to penetrate the complicated U-boat codes. The capture of this prize was to remain a closely guarded secret for a period of thirty years.

The code-breaking advantage which the enemy had so far enjoyed began to crumble. The short-signal code books and Enigma machine enabled the cryptanalysts to read from May 1941 onwards the *Kurzsignale*, the short signals in which the U-boats transmitted their sighting reports and weather information. It enabled them to read all traffic for June and July, including 'officer-only' signals. By the beginning of August mastery over the home waters settings had been established – a mastery which enabled the 'back-room boys' to read the whole of the traffic for the rest of the war except for occasional days in the second half of 1941. It was then that there was some delay, though the maximum was seventy-two hours.

Such a coup was priceless. It is no wild imagining to believe that without such a capture the Atlantic war would have been lost. King George VI, when decorating one of the naval officers who accomplished the capture, was heard to remark that it was 'perhaps the most important single event in the whole war at sea'.

In April the enemy had extended the war westward, to longitude 28 degrees. Reports of ten merchantmen lost out of twenty-two, with only one U-boat destroyed, were being received as Churchill addressed his War Cabinet. This was homeward convoy SC26, about which he became very concerned. 'Our losses in ships and tonnage are very heavy, and, vast as are our shipping resources which we control, the losses cannot continue indefinitely without seriously affecting our war effort and our means of subsistence.' 'With Southern Ireland ports denied us, only a few of our flotilla escorts could reach them. With air protection impossible effective protection was only possible over about a quarter of the route to Halifax.'

The neutrality of Eire, and its consequent lack of available ports, was a great disappointment to both Churchill and Roosevelt. It was a factor which contributed to the crippling losses, and President Roosevelt personally involved himself in sending American technicians to Northern Ireland to build the Londonderry naval base and nearby airfields. The naval base at Lough Swilly had been handed back to the Dublin government during the 1930s on the understanding that in the event of another war this and other bases would again be available. At the outbreak in September 1939 they were, however, denied to the British Government. As a result of this decision RAF Coastal Command and the naval escorts, with their limited fuel supplies, were forced to rely solely on the English and Northern Irish bases.

No one can relate the situation better than Rear-Admiral Sir Kenelm Creighton has done in his *Convoy Commodore* (1956):

This supposedly Christian country was entirely dependent on British ships to bring the coal, oil and countless different manufactured goods to her shores. Merchantmen sailing under the Irish flag and registered in such ports as Dublin and Cork carried their cargoes under the protection of British convoys and Royal Navy escorts. But, in a war of right against intolerable oppression, she chose to handicap those behind whose shield she was able to hide.

Thankfully the criticism did not apply to many of the young men of Eire who flocked to England in their thousands, not only to fight in the many British armed forces but to join the Merchant Navy. At sea on board the red duster merchantmen, they took their place alongside their brother mariners. Many with whom I sailed gave their utmost in helping to deliver the goods, both to Britain and to the various theatres of war. Many gave their lives in the cause of freedom.

Churchill became so concerned at the Atlantic situation during the late winter and spring of 1941 that he directly involved himself in the day-to-day administration of ships and shipping. It was an involvement that was to last for over two years.

18 February 1941. PM to Minister of Transport.
I am shocked to learn that those who had to take the decision to unload or divert the *New Toronto* were ignorant of the cargo which she carried. I always keep check myself personally of the approaching ships which are carrying large consignments of munitions.

28 February 1941. PM to First Lord and First Sea Lord.
City of Calcutta due Loch Ewe 2 March is reported to be going to Hull arriving 9 March. This ship must on no account be sent to the East Coast. It contains 1,700 machine guns, 44 aeroplane engines and no fewer than 14,000,000 cartridges. These cartridges are absolutely vital to the defence of Great Britain ... That it should be proposed to send such a ship round to the East Coast with all the additional risk is abominable ... Another ship now of great importance is the *Euryades* due Liverpool 3 March; she has over 9,000,000 cartridges.

The cartridge situation was critical during the winter of 1941. The Prime Minister had found it necessary to write to the First Lord and the First Sea Lord the previous month (with copies to the Minister of Supply and the Minister of Shipping), regarding the loss of the merchantman *City of Bedford* – a loss caused not by the enemy but by collision of two vessels. 'I was greatly distressed at the loss of the cargo of the *City of Bedford*. It is the heaviest munitions loss we have sustained. Seven and a half million cartridges is a grievous blow. It would be better to disperse these cargoes among more ships. I presume you have inquired into the causes of this collision ... I must again emphasize the gravity of the loss.'

The tragedy occurred west of Ireland on 30 December 1940 as the eastbound convoy HX97 and the westbound OB264 found themselves proceeding on almost directly opposite courses. The night was dark, a force 7 wind was blowing and there was thick fog. Both vessels sank as the commodore ship *City of Bedford* was struck on the port side by the steamer *Bodnant*. Heavily laden, the *Bedford* went down in a mere twenty seconds, taking with her the commodore, Rear-Admiral Hamilton, and many of the ship's crew.

1 March 1941. PM to Secretary of State for War.
I am relieved to hear that the 250,000 rifles and the 50,000,000 rounds of ammunition have arrived safely with the Canadian troop convoy.

15 March 1941. PM to General Ismay.
I agreed that the 50th Division should go with convoy WS8 and that the convoy should have additional ships.... Let me know what this will involve in extra drain on shipping.

15 March 1941. PM to Controller Admiralty.
Give me a report on the progress of ships to carry and disgorge tanks. How many are there? What is their tonnage? How many tanks can they take? When will each one be ready? Where are they being built? What mark of tank can they carry?

Churchill concerned himself with a wide variety of subjects: the loss of masters and navigating officers; recruitment for more labour at the ports; another 40,000 men required for shipbuilding and ship-repairing; congestion at the quays; attention to development of fuelling escorts at sea; flying boats for employment in the Freetown area; how many refrigerated meat ships have been requisitioned by the War Office and Middle East, and where and how are they employed?; is it true that the War Office demand provision for eight gallons of water a day per man on a troopship?; might it not be feasible to place a radar station on Rockall?

The losses of convoy SC26, mauled by a pack of nine U-boats in longitude 40 degrees West, covered a period of two days and two nights as the twenty-two merchantmen steamed at 8 knots south of the Denmark Strait. 'Somehow,' wrote Churchill, 'we had to contrive to extend our reach or our days would be numbered.' Seriously damaged was the AMC *Worcestershire* struck by a torpedo from *U-74* at a time when she was the only escort. Fire took hold in the fo'c's'le, the steering gear jammed and two forward holds and the magazine were flooded. With the fire put out and the steering restored she steamed 1,000 miles to Liverpool for repairs.

Three eastbound convoys later, HX129 received surface escort the whole way; subsequently, OB331 was the first westbound to be escorted likewise. This was achieved by the formation of a Newfoundland escort force and an ocean escort for the western Atlantic – both provided by the Royal Canadian Navy based at St John's. In mid-ocean (35 degrees West) a British escort from Iceland took over. Another meeting point was in 18 degrees West, where a Western Approaches escort group assumed control. The 36th Group was led by Captain F.J. Walker, whose aggressive and novel tactics brought him fame as the foremost U-boat killer of the war.

Although the Royal Canadian Air Force extended air cover in the western Atlantic by the use of long-range Catalina flying boats, there was still a 'black hole' in mid-ocean which air cover could not reach, but it was reduced to some 300 miles. The situation was eased in the Western Approaches during the summer of 1941 by the delivery of sixty-five Catalina aircraft and many Sunderland flying boats to RAF Coastal Command.

It was the auxiliary aircraft carrier which was to provide convoys with continuous air cover. The first of these was *Audacity*, equipped with Grumman 'Martlet' fighters, which sailed in September 1941 (convoy OG74) for Gibraltar. Converted by the Blyth Drydock and Shipbuilding Company, the 5,587-ton *Audacity* (the former German *Hannover*) was captured by HMS *Dunedin* in March 1940 between Dominica and Puerto Rico. She had a short life, being sunk by *U-751* during the passage of HG76 on 21 December 1941.

The auxiliary aircraft carrier was to become a decisive development in the Battle of the Atlantic. Five vessels similar to *Audacity* were converted in British yards and six ordered from the United States under Lease-Lend arrangements. The captain, deck officers and key technicians were from the Royal Navy, but most of the seamen and all the engine room staff were engaged from Britain's fourth service under T124X articles.

In September the submarines returned to the offensive. In addition to SC42, homewards from North America, convoys on the southern route, to and from Gibraltar and Freetown, suffered heavy losses, both in ships and men. Further deliveries of corvettes and frigates were, however, being made after superhuman efforts by the shipyard workers, and ninety-nine were ordered from American yards. Delivery of these began in 1942 with four of the Captain class (1,085 tons); a total of sixty-three were commissioned during 1943.

The passage of SL87 from Sierra Leone was an unhappy one. Seven days after disastrous losses from SC42 came the attack on the small convoy of thirteen ships which set sail from Freetown on 14 September. It was an unlucky thirteen, for seven of them, carrying important food supplies and precious timber, were sunk. U-boat Command had switched many boats to warmer climes and calmer seas knowing full well that fewer escorts would be encountered.

Owing to the distances involved and the few naval bases available, the Southern Irish question being the main problem, only escort vessels with considerable endurance could be employed. Here in the seas west of the Canary Islands and Madeira, SL87 was accompanied by the old sloop *Bideford*, the *Gorleston*, one of the former American Coastguard cutters, the corvette *Gardenia* and the small Free French *Commandant Duboc*. It was an inexpert and ill-organized escort. After four days of enemy action the convoy split into two groups. At the subsequent Admiralty board of inquiry the leadership was criticized for heading an escort untrained in affording maximum protection.

The next large German onslaught in the Atlantic battle was against SC48, north of latitude 53 degrees, on 15 October. Thurmann, Krech and Schultze (*U-553, U-558* and *U-432*) showed that despite the cryptanalysts and weather conditions they could still cruise through the convoy columns torpedoing merchantmen at will.

The fifty-ship SC48 lost a total of nine merchantmen from enemy action; a further eleven lost contact owing to stormy weather and high seas. The first to be sunk (by *U-553*) was the motor vessel *Silvercedar*. Usually a sugar carrier, she had this time been loaded in New York with high explosives; on deck, above each hatch, she carried Beaufort bombers. Amidst the gale, of force 8–9, the torpedo struck at No. 3, the only hold not loaded with explosives, it was in fact filled with cases of condensed milk. Nevertheless, *Silvercedar* blew up with a mighty explosion and sank in less than two minutes; the survivors were plucked from the sea by HMS *Gladiolus*.

Carrying explosives, as I will relate from first-hand experience (Chapter 7) was highly dangerous, particularly when carried in the forward holds. In these cases the inevitable destruction of the bridge and the officers' accommodation added to the high death toll amongst master mariners, certificated navigators and radio officers. In every homeward transatlantic convoy there were always two or three 'ammo merchantmen'. Churchill had every reason to be worried about the high density of explosives loaded aboard any one ship.

Attacking from inside the convoy between the seventh and eighth columns, *U-432* torpedoed the Norwegian tanker *Barfonn*. *U-558* destroyed the British *W.C. Teagle* and the Norwegian *Erviken*, tankers weighed down with aviation spirit. The merit of those on watch on the bridge was not only in navigating perilous seas and coping with the difficulties of sailing in convoy, but in combating the enemy when the need arose. Sailing under such conditions, the tanker like the ammunition ship, could merit the description of a 'floating volcano'.

Great damage was recorded by Atlantic storms during the last three months of 1941. Gales of Force 7 or more were recorded on fifty-three days and stragglers brought many problems for the escorts. From one convoy of forty-three ships there were a reported twenty-six stragglers; from another, of forty-six ships, as many as twenty-three stragglers. Many merchantmen arrived in port with heavy weather damage, necessitating repair and subsequent delay. Whilst the atrocious weather curtailed, to some extent, the activities of the U-boats, those ships

Above A convoy is seen forming at Freetown, Sierra Leone, a port which became known as 'the most soul- and energy-destroying place in the world'. *Below* The captured Norwegian tanker *Storstadt* is seen here with survivors from merchantmen sunk by the commerce raider *Pinguin*. Taken at the end of January 1941 near the equator when the prison ship was refuelling other German vessels, it shows captured seamen exercising on deck. Captured officers are locked away under the foc'sle-head. POWs aboard numbered 424 men and women, including eight ladies of the Salvation Army, ex *Port Wellington*. The Gironde estuary (SW France) was reached on 4 February 1941

Convoy HX143 as seen from HMS *Prince of Wales*. On the return voyage from Churchill's historic meeting with President Roosevelt, *Prince of Wales*, with the Prime Minister on board (15 August 1941), passed convoy HX143 of seventy-three merchantmen. The battleship altered course so that Mr Churchill could get a closer view

During a snow-squall, late afternoon 24 March 1942, Russian homeward convoy QP9, the minesweeper HMS *Sharpshooter* caught U-655 on the surface, rammed and sank her. There were no survivors. (*From a painting by T.F.J. Rogers*)

A homeward bound 1943 Atlantic convoy. Many newly built 'replacement ships' are included

The Flower Class corvette HMS *Orchis* is seen on Atlantic convoy duty. The 'Flowers' accounted for more than fifty German and Italian submarines, in some cases participating with other naval ships in the sinking, either in a primary role or a supporting one. (*From a painting by T.F.J. Rogers*)

HMS *Pink* is seen here off Iceland in October 1943 picking up survivors from a Liberator aircraft shot down by a U-boat (*From a painting by T.F.J. Rogers*)

Otranto with *Orcades* lying astern are seen embarking troops at Sydney, Australia, January 1940. They were just two of the liners which made up troop convoy US1

The Anzac convoy US1 in the Indian Ocean. In the foreground, the battleship HMS *Ramillies*. Behind, from left to right, Orient Steamship's *Orford* and Canadian Pacific's *Empress of Japan* and *Empress of Canada*

Highland Monarch, Royal Mail Line, seen here at Durban was kept busy as a troopship throughout the war. At the time of the armistice she was engaged with other British liners in the evacuation of 33,303 Allied POWs through the Russian port of Odessa

The gun crew of the 1910 built 10,048 ton *Ascanius* 'on parade' in South African waters. *Ascanius* served for a variety of purposes at different times culminating in her service at Normandy when she was damaged after being torpedoed

A burial in the South Atlantic. The ship's master at the far right. Even in wartime, death from natural causes cast a gloom over the whole vessel

The ship's company of HMS *Snowflake*, a Flower Class corvette, is seen assembled on a rare occasion for the photographer at the naval base of Londonderry

Convoy duty, North Atlantic. Many a Merchant Navy crewman owed his life to the escort vessels

A tanker low in the water homeward bound. She carries the 'lifeblood' of the Allied fighter and bomber aircraft

The CAM ship homeward bound. On her foredeck, the fighter aircraft to protect her convoy. In her holds, precious grain to feed those at home

caught suffered heavy casualties.

Churchill at this time, prior to the Japanese attack on Pearl Harbor, became concerned at the low sinkings of U-boats – less than two per month – whilst their numbers were increasing by nearly twenty a month. Ever since the historic Newfoundland 'Atlantic Charter', however, Churchill and Roosevelt had co-operated closely; and the first 'hot line' between two heads of state was established. Both leaders had a naval background: Roosevelt had effectively run the US Navy from 1913 until 1921 as Assistant Secretary.

During the passage of convoy SC48 through the western Atlantic a situation of undeclared war developed between the United States and Germany. The American destroyer *Kearny*, directed to assist the Canadian escort group, was torpedoed by *U-568* during the night of 17 October; damaged, she was able to make St John's for repair. The next night *U-101* torpedoed and sunk HMS *Broadwater*, with heavy loss of life. Two weeks later, in longitude 27 degrees West, the American destroyer *Reuben James* was lost when torpedoed by *U-552*. At the time she was escorting eastbound HX156, which found a safe passage; no merchantmen were lost.

During 1942 few Atlantic and Russian convoys sailed without rescue ships. Manned by master mariners and merchant seamen, and Royal Naval medical and nursing staff, tremendous feats in saving lives were achieved. The work called for courage and seamanship of a high order. Equipped with sickbays and operating theatres, with comfortable cabins for survivors, they carried special rescue gear. Additionally, rescue ships often carried anti-submarine weaponry in the form of detection equipment and, as such, operated closely with the convoy escort.

Special vessels were selected for the rescue operation. Of less than 2,000 tons, these sturdy vessels were in the main former cross-Channel steamers. Of the eleven so equipped four were lost in the cause of saving life: *Bury, Copeland, Gothland, Perth, Rathlin, Stockport* – (lost with convoy ON166); *Toward* (lost with convoy SC118), *St Sunniva. Walmer Castle* – bombed and sunk with heavy loss of life, OG74; *Zaafaran, Zamalek.*

Copeland, Rathlin and *Zamalek* sailed in a total of ten outward and nine homeward Russian convoys. *Zamalek* herself sailed with sixty-four convoys and saved 611 lives. In January 1943 *St Sunniva*, on her first Atlantic convoy rescue duty, was lost in bad weather and ice conditions (longitude 60 degrees west). There were no survivors.

During August and September 1942 U-boats located twenty-one out of sixty-three convoys. Seven were attacked, during which the enemy sank forty-three merchantmen. By November there were 200 operational U-boats plus a further 170 on trials or training. British and American strategists feared the Allies were losing the Battle.

Submarines were being sunk – the loss now totalled 135 German and 53 Italian – but German yards, aided by pre-fabrication at inland factories, were producing new ones, many of them new types of longer-range submarines, twice as fast. More tanker U-boats or 'Milch Cows', as they were called, were also being built, to extend their range still further. Would Dönitz achieve his magical 300 in operation in the North Atlantic?

The 'happy days' might be past but the enemy still had the initiative. His energy and resourcefulness were immense. In spite of his increasing losses, our experience had already made clear that his swelling U-boat fleet would be used with even greater originality and strategic skill.

Counter-measures against submarine warfare were steadily improving. New escort destroyers, the principal U-boat killer, were on order; eight were due during the latter weeks of 1942, fifteen in 1943. Fifty frigates were on order, thirty of them due to be commissioned during 1942. More flower-class corvettes, the mainstay of the escort forces, were due for delivery. A system of refuelling escorts at sea from tankers which sailed with convoys for this purpose was introduced. Depth-charges, which could explode at a depth of 500 feet, were in use. There was also the 'Hedgehog bomb', fired by a multi-barrelled mortar and filled with Torpex, a much higher-powered explosive. Its range was 250 yards ahead of the escort vessel. War at sea can be cruel. The destruction of a U-boat leaves no survivors. How then could Dönitz hope to man his new constructions?

Convoys SC104, SC107 and ONS154 were near disasters, on which large packs of U-boats converged. Thirty-eight merchantmen were sunk and valuable cargoes lost. Casualties were high due to the wintry Atlantic weather – in the case of ONS154 a total of 486 died, of whom 131 were Allied merchant seamen. During the same period, the previously mentioned SL125, northbound from Sierra Leone, lost twelve merchantmen with a heavy toll of life.

The forty-four vessels of SC104 were menaced by thirteen U-boats over a period of five days. With only two destroyers and four corvettes the escort was hardly capable of attacking as well as protecting. Two ships, the *Empire Lightning* and the *Millcrest*, were in collision. Commodore Taylor DSC (Captain RN retired), aboard *Merchant Royal*, reported her losing steerageway and drifting out of control on one occasion. On a second occasion the engines stopped, creating much confusion. It was an unhappy ship. Her master, under the influence of alcohol, was ordered off the bridge; responsibility and war fatigue had taken its toll. Commodore Taylor reported the vessel unfit for the duties of a commodore and his staff.

In spite of all the problems with convoy SC104 and the loss of eight merchantmen, the brave escort evened the score by sinking three submarines (*U-619*, *U-353* and *U-661*). The fact that all three were on their first war patrol – *U-353* had failed to record a 'kill' and both *U-619* and *U-661* were lost with all hands – would seem to indicate the mark of inexperience. Two further U-boats were damaged.

U-661, commanded by Erich von Lilienfeld, along with nine other submarines were sunk by aircraft in the Atlantic during October 1942. These successes were proof that the long-range aircraft were necessary to support the overworked destroyers and corvettes. The senior Coastal Command pilot, the first and most successful leader of the airborne offensive, was Squadron Leader T.M. Bulloch DSO, DFC. As early as December 1941 his VLR Liberator sighted three U-boats positioning themselves for an attack on convoy HG76. All submerged before he could bring his aircraft into an assailable position; he was aloft over Atlantic convoys for almost sixteen hours before returning to base at Limavady, near Londonderry.

Submarines damaged generally meant an immediate return to base for repairs, which often kept them out of action for many weeks. *U-653*, while pursuing Convoy SL118, was badly damaged when bombed by Squadron Leader Bulloch in August 1942. The U-boat was under repair at Brest for three months. The fact that aircraft were now beginning to patrol convoys meant that the U-boats preferred to keep below the surface. The main problem in the early days was Coastal Command's lack of a suitable weapon. Depth charges and 'anti-sub' bombs had little effect on the tough steel hull of Germany's submarines.

On patrol over convoy ONS136 in October, Bulloch sank *U-597* with the loss of all aboard. Eight depth charges were used in the assault. Later in the month he broke up a wolf-pack converging on HX212. The main gain was that the convoy sailed on whilst the enemy kept out of sight below. During the previous twenty-four hours HX212 had lost two merchantmen, and a further two had been damaged.

Royal Air Force and Royal Navy liaison was now reaching a high standard, something never achieved before. Convoy losses were fewer when provided with air cover. The new U-boat commanders and their young, inexperienced crews came to be fearful of the approach of aircraft. It would appear that this development in the Atlantic battle took U-boat Command by surprise.

To the south-west of Ireland convoy SC107 lost fifteen merchantmen from its forty-two vessels during the last week of November. The attack came from a pack of sixteen U-boats. Though one was sunk, this was unlikely to have been the escorts' fault, who were few in number. After sinking *Hobbema*, *Hatimore* and the *Empire Linx*, *U-132* was on target for being bombed by a Liberator of 120 Squadron. Then from beneath the water came a tremendous explosion as *Empire Linx*, an ammunition ship, blew up. It is assumed that *U-132* was within lethal range and thus became a victim of her own victory. There were no survivors.

The December homeward convoys SC111 and HX217, with only a day's sailing between them, met twenty-two U-boats, which were strung out in mid-Atlantic and prepared for a co-ordinated onslaught. With naval escorts far too few in numbers they fared surprisingly well; only two merchantmen were sunk and one damaged. However, at the end of the month, the North America-bound ONS154 lost sixteen merchantmen, many of them stragglers. It was simply the powerful air support given to HX217 which kept the U-boats under, coupled with the fact that the escorts were at last showing signs of gaining the upper hand. *U-254* was attacked by Squadron 120, then mistakenly rammed by *U-221*, after which she was finally sunk by HMS *Wrestler*.

By the end of 1942 U-boat losses were rising. The escorts were gathering skill in strengthening convoy screens and in organizing support groups. More effective detection equipment and anti-submarine weapons were being employed. The means of electronic warfare were greatly improved. The VHF radio-telephone had become a standard fitting in all escorts. This allowed reliable and rapid intercommunication – so essential to co-ordinated team-work. Yet, as many realized, the battle was far from won.

During this critical year of 1942 Allied shipping losses were no fewer than 1,664 ships, totalling 7¾ million tons. Of these, 1,160 (6¼ million tons) were lost by U-boat action. The deaths of trained British seamen alone mounted to nearly 8,000 lives. Whilst eighty-seven submarines had been sunk during the year, enemy strength had increased from 249 to 393.

The American B-24 aircraft, christened 'Liberator' by the Air Force, was still in short supply. The Pacific war claimed the majority as they came off the production line, and whilst by Christmas 1942 the US Navy possessed fifty-two, RAF Coastal Command had to make do with only eighteen for Atlantic convoy routes. It was, however, an improvement on the five available in August of that year. Only a personal plea from Churchill to Roosevelt saved the day, though even by mid-summer 1943 the number of aircraft allocated to Coastal Command was fewer than fifty.

The Liberator had a range of 2,400 miles, far beyond that of any other military aircraft, carried 2,500 gallons of fuel and could operate up to heights of 30,000 feet. New airfields with long runways were constructed for its operation: in Northern Ireland at Nutts Corner, Ballykelly and Limavady; at Predannack and St Eval in Cornwall; and at Benbecula in Scotland. The airfield at Reykjavik was able to accept the B-24 as early as September 1942. The existence of this facility in Iceland offered great security to those pilots who roamed the mid-ocean in search of the underwater enemy.

Early in 1943 a vastly improved version of the VLR Liberator was delivered. The Mark III was equipped with a really effective centrimetric radar system. This operated in a frequency range that the Germans could not even credit as possible, because they had not yet conceived the magnetron valve. The system could detect convoys at forty miles and surfaced submarines at twelve miles.

Coastal Command aircraft were now fitted with an airborne searchlight called the Leigh Light, which was named after the officer responsible for its operational development. Developed by 172 Squadron, based at Chivenor in North Devon, it was first fitted in the under-turrets of Wellington bombers, and later in Liberators and Catalinas; of 22 million candlepower it was fitted with its own generator. By the end of the war the Leigh Light, used in conjunction with the new ultra shortwave radar, enabled 218 U-boats to be attacked at night, of which twenty-seven were sunk and thirty-one damaged.

With the new weaponry of 1943, aircraft became devastatingly destructive: the mark 24 mine – it was, in fact, an air-launched torpedo with an acoustic homing head; torpex-filled depth charges – these could fracture, damage or crush the hull of a U-boat if dropped close; MAD (Magnetic Anomaly Detector), developed by the United States – a submarine could be detected under water by its magnetic field; the retro-bomb – rocket-propelled bombs, launched backwards from rails beneath the aircraft's wing, which attained speeds of well over 1,000 m.p.h., an unheard-of velocity at the time; sonobuoys – these were floating radio transmitters from which a hydrophone was suspended. This picked up any underwater sounds and passed them through the transmitter to the circling aircraft's special receiver.

Much of the work on new weaponry and improved versions of aircraft was carried out in great secrecy. Largely on account of military scientists and engineers, the aircraft came to be a bigger menace to the U-boat than the warship. Those at sea had little idea of the progress being made. Patrolling aircraft were rarely seen, for much of their reconnaissance work was carried out far from the course of the convoy.

January 1943 saw the commencement of the crisis. This was the dawn of the great battle of the seas which was to last over four months, a battle fought in some of the worst weather of the western Atlantic. Eastbound convoy HX223 lost two modern Norwegian motor tankers on 26 January, both of which were stragglers in a heavy storm. On the same day the tanker *Kollbjorg*, also registered in Norway, broke in two whilst still with the convoy. The stern part sank while the fore part drifted astern, only to be sunk by two torpedoes, one from *U-607* and the second from *U-594*.

The thirty-eight merchantmen of HX224 sailed from New York on 24 January. Ten days later in mid-ocean three vessels were lost; one, the tanker *Cordelia*, had straggled because of the stormy weather and lost protection of the escort. She was sunk by *U-632*. The commander of the U-boat discovered in conversation with one of the survivors that there was a larger and slower convoy just forty-eight hours behind. The information was quickly passed to U-boat headquarters. 'Careless talk costs lives', as the dockland poster said.

The slower SC118 (64 ships) was then running into a U-boat trap. The convoy was sighted by *U-456*, which nine months before had torpedoed the cruiser *Edinburgh* in the Arctic. On 2 February, the day that the German army was turned back at Stalingrad, the merchantmen passed north of latitude 50; a heavy sea was running and the convoy was scattered over fifty-two square miles. Sixteen U-boats were called up from a reported sixty in the area. By 5 February the escort had been reinforced by the arrival of two US destroyers and a coastguard cutter. Incredible feats of navigation enabled VLR Liberator aircraft from Northern Ireland to give daylight air support. Seldom had a convoy been so strongly guarded.

Ranked as one of the most ferocious, the SC118 battle raged. Thirteen ships were sunk, including the rescue vessel *Toward* and two stragglers. Three U-boats were lost and four severely damaged; Grand-Admiral Dönitz recorded it as the hardest convoy battle of the whole war. However, of the twenty U-boats concentrated against the convoy only two succeeded in breaking through the defence and torpedoing ships from inside the columns. One of these was *U-402*, commanded by the experienced Lieutenant-Commander Siegfried Freiherr von Forstner, a recipient of the Knight's Cross, who on the night of 6–7 February sank six merchantmen. The American 6063-ton *Henry R. Mallory*, which was carrying Army personnel, suffered great loss of life due to confusion and poor lifeboat drill, something that later Churchill went on to criticize. Many bodies were washed ashore on the beaches of Greenland.

On 7 February, *U-624*, a type VIIC submarine, was spotted on the surface by a VLR Liberator of 220 Squadron. She was nine miles from the aeroplane and fifty-five miles from SC118. Her second war cruise quickly came to an end as she was depth-charged and sunk; there were no survivors. The Liberator aircraft was airborne that day from 1230 hours until 2308 hours. Two days later *U-614* was badly damaged when attacked by an aircraft of 206 Squadron on Atlantic patrol from 0655 hours until 1720 hours. It was the first war cruise for *U-614*.

Westbound convoy ONS166, comprising sixty-three merchantmen with six escort vessels, was hit by constant north-west gales. Over a period of four days the convoy averaged 4 knots and by 20 February nine stragglers were reported. Thereafter, a five-day battle commenced, which covered over 1,000 miles of ocean. Seventeen U-boats were in contact and fourteen ships, including the rescue vessel *Stockport*, were sunk. Yet another submarine, *U-623* (on its second war cruise), was sunk by a Liberator of 120 Squadron.

Of great benefit on this occasion was the refuelling of escorts from tankers in the convoy. This was a dangerous operation in heavy weather with U-boats in the vicinity, as was seen when *U-225* torpedoed and badly damaged the tanker *Scottish Heather* whilst she was refuelling HMCS *Chilliwack* during the passage of ONS154 (27 December 1942). *Scottish Heather* was subsequently towed to the Clyde estuary.

The month of February 1943 puzzled the German U-boat command. Whilst thirty-four ships in convoy had been sunk, representing 14 per cent of all ships in convoy attacked, twelve U-boats had been lost, half of which were engaged upon their first or second war patrols. During March came the climax as five convoys, two slow (SC121 and SC122) and three fast (HX228, HX229 and 229A), all heavily laden, ploughed their way towards the British Isles through a succession of storms. With 116 U-boats at sea, total losses were 108 merchantmen of 627,377 tons, two-thirds of these from ocean convoys. The situation was critical.

The sixty-one-strong SC121 sailed from New York on 23 February. Meeting up with forty U-boats north-east of Newfoundland during 6/7 March a battle raged for five days, from longitude 31 west to longitude 21 west. Twelve ships were sunk in exceptionally bad weather – a Force 10 storm, blinding snow blizzards, hail and rain. A depleted escort consisted only of a US destroyer, a coastguard cutter and four corvettes. The latter were reported to be badly maintained, with many HF/DF and radar sets out of action. Those merchantmen sunk included the Norwegian *Bonneville*, with Commodore Captain Birnie DSO, RD, RNR aboard; all hands were to perish. Loss of life in all vessels sunk was heavy (see Appendix XI).

The sixty-strong HX228 from Halifax was diverted to a more southerly route and fell upon a group of thirteen U-boats. However, with four destroyers and five corvettes the defence was much better, though the convoy was unfortunate to lose HMS *Harvester*, torpedoed and sunk by *U-432* with heavy loss of life. At the time the destroyer *Harvester* had been directed from assisting SC121 and was carrying fifty merchant ship survivors. Just previously she had been crippled by ramming *U-444*, which subsequently sank. *U-444* was yet another first-patrol submarine. For Lieutenant Albert Langfeld, it was his first (and only) submarine command. *U-432* was sunk the same day by the Free French corvette *Aconit*.

During the period 5–14 March the HX228 escort was reinforced by the escort carrier USS *Bogue*, her first voyage in convoy, and two destroyers. Four merchantmen were sunk and two damaged. Three of those sunk were ammunition ships: the British *Tucurinca*, the American

Andrea F. Luckenbach and the Norwegian *Brant County*. The latter blew up with an explosion so violent that her attacker *U-757* was herself damaged.

The slow convoy SC122 (52 ships) and the two fast convoys HX229 (40 ships) and HX229A (39 ships) sailed from New York on 5, 8 and 9 March respectively. Of these 131 merchantmen, flying the flags of ten different nations, eighty-one were British and twenty-nine American. Their combined gross weight was 860,000 tons and they carried 920,000 tons of cargo – petroleum fuels, frozen meat, food, tobacco, grain, lumber, minerals, steel, gunpowder, detonators, bombs, shells, lorries, locomotives, invasion barges, aircraft and tanks. The most valuable of the three convoys was HX229A. It included thirteen tankers, eight refrigerated ships and four cargo liners.

No battle fought at sea during the Second World War had to contend with such difficulties. The exceptionally bad weather and sea conditions created problems for both sea and air patrols; there were Force 11 storms, forty feet waves, fog, pack-ice and icebergs. The problems were compounded by the concentration of convoys. SC122, with an escort of two destroyers, five corvettes and a frigate, was diverted to the south where it closed upon HX229 with an escort of four destroyers and one corvette. With only 100 miles between the convoys they met forty-four U-boats head-on, the greatest concentration of submarines ever experienced. Fifteen were on their first patrol, and seventeen were engaged on their second or third patrols.

During a three-day battle twenty-three merchantmen were sunk from the two convoys and 292 merchant seamen perished; there was no rescue vessel available to accompany HX229. During the first day the Liberators were on patrol – one was airborne for eighteen hours 50 minutes, the second for over twenty hours. Only one submarine was sunk. A Sunderland flying boat of 201 Squadron, sent out to reinforce the patrol, subsequently sank *U-384*. During the affray the surface escorts damaged seven of the enemy underwater craft.

Taking evasive action, HX229A was routed north-east towards Greenland. There they came upon Arctic conditions. Five merchantmen had to return to St John's with ice damage and the *Svend Foyn*, an ex-whaling factory ship converted to carrying oil products, struck an iceberg. Remaining afloat for two days she suddenly sank in a terrific gale which sprang up. Forty-three lives were lost.

During the following two weeks, with outward-bound convoys increasing the concentration of ships to 525 within the Atlantic danger zone, only twenty of these were sunk; but no less than twenty-two U-boats were sent to their watery grave. Finally, tactical superiority had triumphed. With convoys HX231 and SC123 sailing from New York during the last week of March, and with additional protection from the aircraft of the escort carriers USS *Bogue* and HMS *Biter*, the Atlantic battle shifted in the Allies favour.

The March successes had given new confidence to the escort groups with their aircraft support. In the view of the Admiralty, however, convoy defence still appeared helpless against massive concentrations of submarines. They were to report: 'the Germans never came so near to disrupting communications between the New World and the Old as in the first twenty days of March'. Was it really as bad as they suggested? Was victory within the Allies' grasp or not?

Of the twenty-three vessels lost from HX229 and SC122, fifteen were sunk during a twenty-four hour period when the convoys were without air cover. When HX231 met twenty-one U-boats in mid-ocean during the first week of a wintry April only six merchantmen were sunk. The sixty-one vessels, which had sailed from New York on 25 March, thirty-six of which were British registry, were carrying 600,000 tons of cargo. Some 523,000 tons arrived safely in Britain. Its defence marked 'the beginning of the end'. *U-632* and *U-635* were both sunk by patrolling aircraft from Iceland, and *U-594* was damaged. Dönitz was to write, 'radar and particularly radar location by aircraft had to all practical purposes robbed the U-boats of their power to fight on the surface'. Kept under by the presence of carrier-borne aircraft it was particularly difficult for the enemy to obtain attacking positions.

The final battle of the great struggle for supremacy amidst the cruel sea came as westbound convoy ONS5 battled its way towards the New World during the last week of April and the first week of May. The forty-three ships, thirty of them British, sailed on 21 April for Halifax, Nova Scotia, being routed to the north so as to avoid the concentration of U-boats lying in wait for them.

An estimated 193 boats were now operating, 128 of them at sea in the North Atlantic. Ninety-eight had sailed from Norway and Western France in April, most in the second half of the month, and all were eager to participate in this great battle. Experiencing heavy weather, the merchantmen were hove-to for long periods; two collided on 26 April; two days later a sighting was made by *U-650*. Only the elements were holding the attack at bay. With the convoy in disarray and making only twenty miles progress in twenty-four hours, thirty-one U-boats lay submerged ahead, and a further thirteen were spreading themselves east of Newfoundland. As the merchantmen changed to a south-westerly course, twenty-seven U-boats straddled ONS5's line of advance.

By the morning of 6 May thirteen merchantmen had been sunk, but the tally of U-boats was seven with two damaged; a further two, *U-659* and *U-439*, had been lost in collision in the vicinity of the convoy. It was the fiercest battle yet, and a resounding victory for both the escorts and the aircraft. Once again radar had paved the way.

Convoy ONS5. U-boats sunk

24 April	*U-710*. Aircraft of 206 Squadron RAF.
4 May	*U-630*. Aircraft of 5 Squadron RCAF.
5 May	*U-192*. HMS *Pink*
	U-638. HMS *Loosestrife*
6 May	*U-125*. HMS *Vidette*
	U-531. HMS *Oribi*
	U-438. HMS *Pelican*

(A total of 15 U-boats were sunk in April and 41 during May).

Convoys SC127, SC128, ONS4 and HX235; at sea at the same time, were successfully diverted. None of these four convoys suffered losses. I was myself serving aboard the *Fort Fitzgerald* of convoy HX235, as twenty U-boats lay to the north. On 28 April aircraft from USS *Bogue* drove off five of them. With the red ensign merchant carriers (MACs) caring for the ships inside the convoy columns, the white ensign escort carriers could co-operate with the special escort hunter-killer support groups and be used as fleet carriers in their own right. Little did we realize at the time that victory would be ours.

In an article in the *Sunday Times* (5 February 1959) Captain S.W. Roskill RN wrote, 'The seven-day battle (of ONS5) fought ... has no name by which it will be remembered; but it was, in its own way, as decisive as Quiberon Bay or the Nile.' In his official history of *The War at Sea* Roskill added, 'After forty-five months of increasing battle of a more exacting and arduous nature than posterity may easily realize, our convoy escorts had won the triumph they so richly merited.'

Admiral Sir Max Horton KCB, DSO, Commander-in-Chief Western Approaches, upon reading the dispatches relating to ONS5, said, 'it may well be that the heavy casualties inflicted on the enemy have gravely affected morale and will prove to have been a turning point in the Battle of the Atlantic'. Despite the losses sustained by the convoy it was an undoubted victory for the escorts.

A turning point it proved to be. Writing his memoirs Grand-Admiral Dönitz concluded his report on the battle thus: 'Wolf-pack operations against convoys in the North Atlantic, the main theatre of operations, were no longer possible. They could only be resumed if we succeeded in radically increasing the fighting power of the U-boats. This was the logical conclusion to which I came.... We had lost the Battle of the Atlantic.'

The Allied forces, led by the Royal Navy, had won a great victory. A thousand years of maritime heritage had proved that Britain, fighting for freedom, could still hold the flag high. On 24 May each year for many years to come, the peoples of the English-speaking world will remember this occasion in the long line of battles fought at sea.

One cannot pass from 'the Atlantic victory' without mentioning the 'independents', those merchantmen which, on account of their speed, could proceed without escort to Admiralty routing. They too paid the price, and they two contributed to final victory. Suffering a loss rate more than double those which sailed in convoy, those that came under actual attack lost no less than 80 per cent of their number. Those that follow are just a few of the many that, alone on the high seas, met up with the enemy.

Calchas, Beacon Grange and *Nerissa* were sunk during the last ten days of April 1941 – a month when seventy-five merchantmen of British registry were sunk. *Calchas*, heavily laden from the Far East, was torpedoed by *U-107*, a type 1X 'Atlantic' boat commanded by Lieutenant-Commander Günther Hessler. He was Dönitz's son-in-law. Those who got away in the lifeboats survived an epic voyage of 650 miles over a period of sixteen days, achieved without navigators (her master and deck officers had perished), without instruments other than compasses, and under the leadership of the ship's bosun, the carpenter, an able-bodied seaman and the chief steward.

The *Beacon Grange*, a meat-carrier outward bound in ballast, was sunk by *U-552*. At the time, grave doubts were expressed in Parliament as to whether the meat ration was in jeopardy. Altogether four torpedoes were fired. Four days later on 1 May, the chief mate's lifeboat was sighted by a Catalina flying boat – the thirty-nine occupants included five young Royal Artillery gunners and four deck boys aged sixteen. Her master, Captain Friend, in the second lifeboat with forty of his men, was rescued by the corvette *Gladiolus* the following day.

Nerissa, lost 35 miles west of St Kilda, was laden with war supplies and 175 North-West Mounted Police together with their horses. She too was torpedoed by *U-552*, captained by Lieutenant Commander Erich Topp. He subsequently became the third highest-scoring submarine ace of the Second World War. August 1941 saw the sinking of another meat-carrier, the *Otaio*, the thirteenth vessel owned by the New Zealand Shipping Company to be lost in twelve months. Bound for Australian ports she had dispersed from convoy OS4 (Outward Sierra Leone). It was the first 'kill' for Lieutenant Günther Krech (*U-558*). Fifty-eight survivors were later rescued by the destroyers *Vanoc* and *Walker*; thirteen crew were missing and five injured.

In November 1941 came the tragedy of the new motorship *Nottingham*, the fourteenth ship of the Federal Steam Navigation's fleet to be sunk by the enemy. Proceeding from Glasgow for New York on her maiden voyage she was torpedoed in mid-Atlantic by *U-74*. No distress call was sent and it is not known whether any lifeboats were launched. There were no survivors.

One of the many attacks on 'independents' during 1942 was that directed against the *Hertford* of the Federal Steam Navigation Company. Sunk by *U-571* 200 miles south of Halifax, Nova Scotia, she was carrying 175,550 carcasses of lamb and mutton, 8,250 sides of pork and 5,670 packages of beef loaded in New Zealand. Those rescued had suffered bitterly from the cold and gale-force winds. Yet another refrigerated cargo was lost when the *Avila Star* was torpedoed (*U-201*). Homeward bound from Buenos Aires, sixty-two died in the disaster, many of them in the lifeboats which had been launched.

Following her Admiralty-routed course off the Azores in December 1942 was the 18,713-ton *Ceramic*, bound for the Middle East. Owned by Shaw, Savill & Albion Ltd, she was not required for trooping but was left to maintain a passenger and cargo service to Australia. During the night of 6 December *Ceramic*, carrying bombs and ammunition in two of her holds, mysteriously disappeared. It was not known until much later that she had been torpedoed by *U-515*. From her crew of 273 and 378 passengers there was only one survivor, a sapper of the Royal Engineers. Dragged from the sea, he was taken on board the submarine and remained a prisoner of war for the rest of the war.

The 12,090-ton *Hororata*, a replacement merchantman built by John Brown & Co Ltd at Clydebank, was torpedoed on her second voyage (13 December 1942). At the time she was the largest refrigerated cargo carrier in the world. She had been loaded in New Zealand with a valuable cargo bound for Liverpool: 3,760 tons of butter, 7,294 crates of cheese, 3,870 tons of frozen meat, 4,369 bales of wool, 500 bales of flax, 3,000 cases of dried milk, 500 cases of tallow and 750 tons of lead.

Torpedoed by *U-103*, she was one 'independent' that survived. Miraculously brought into Santa Cruz Bay, Flores Island, in the Azores by her master and crew, her condition was critical. Three days later she was 'nursed' into Horta, Fayal Island, a voyage of some 150 miles. There wooden patches were placed over the damaged areas, the largest measuring 23 by 21 feet. This was later strengthened by a three-feet-thick cement box and 320 tons of sand, gravel and cement. Three months later she sailed for the Mersey accompanied by HMS *Burwell*. Arriving on 23 March 1943 nearly 10,000 tons of her cargo was then discharged. One of the largest and most valuable cargo vessels had been saved.

Winston Churchill in one of his rallying war cries celebrated the safe homecoming of *Hororata* by declaiming, 'a ship saved is better than a ship built'. Repaired by Cammell Laird at Birkenhead it was not until the following September that she was ready for sea again.

The greater the speed of our merchant ships the safer they proved to be. This was amply borne out by the record of the troopers of the North Atlantic Seaway, including such monsters as the *Queen Mary, Queen Elizabeth* and *Aquitania*. Not one of these 'independents' was sunk – my own wartime voyages to the New World on the *Andes* and the *Queen Mary* are still locked in my memory as two of the greatest moments of my career at sea. Only in tropical waters were the troopers at risk, as I shall relate in Chapter 9.

Though U-boats were to carry on the fight against shipping in the North Atlantic to the last day of the war, never again were they seriously to threaten the lifeline between Britain and North America. They had a brief resurgence with the acoustic homing torpedo. In addition, they ran trials in inshore waters with the 'schnorkel' breathing tube. This enabled them to recharge batteries whilst remaining submerged; but it proved a failure. In the dying days of the war, eighty of the new type XXI boat were ready for a new offensive. Of 1,600 tons, the submarine's range of 15,000 miles and submerged speed of 17 knots – this capable of being maintained for one hour – was impressive. Yet it was all too late. Since that spring of 1943 the enemy had lost the initiative.

7   East of Cape Town

It was not until seventeen days before Christmas 1941 that the war suddenly became a world war. It was then that the Japanese attacked the American fleet at Pearl Harbor and the next day (8 December) declared war on Britain and the British Empire. The situation changed dramatically. Previously it had been the exploits of the German armed merchant raiders east of Cape Town. Now virtually overnight merchantmen and their crews were at risk as never before. The fall of Hong Kong, for long an important outpost for Britain's merchant fleet, was a heavy blow.

On 10 December the two capital ships *Prince of Wales* and *Repulse* were sunk off the north-east coast of Malaya by Japanese naval aircraft, with the loss of 605 officers and men. The next day came Hitler's declaration of war on the United States. This signalled the beginning of a terrible period, during which Allied resistance disintegrated and the Japanese became masters of the China Sea and the whole of South-east Asia.

Following the evacuation of Kowloon, this to avoid annihilation by the Japanese 38th Infantry Division, shipping was in disarray. Some merchantmen were engaged upon coastal work, others, deep sea, were on charter to Far Eastern governments. Seven of British registry were even on charter to Japan; others had reached various stages of their voyages, both from east and west. Those such as the 'blue funnel' *Tantalus* and *Ulysses*, owned by the Alfred Holt company, were under repair, or refitting. There were many Holt ships in the region, as one would expect, given their experience as a Far East trader. In 1939 their fleet consisted of eighty-seven merchantmen, and they were an important factor in the British war effort. The *Antenor* and *Hector*, which served as AMCs, were employed on ocean escort duty; *Ascanius* was carrying troops from India and East Africa to Suez; *Dolius* and *Bellerophon* were on passage westward from Panama; *Gorgon, Phrontis, Centaur* and *Charon* were plying between Australia and the East Indies; whilst *Talthybius, Orestes* and *Polyhemus* were all in the region at various stages of their voyages.

Tantalus, towed by the tug *Keswick*, sailed from Hong Kong on 5

December. Her main engine parts, which had been ashore under repair, were now stowed in the hold. Her instructions were to make for Singapore, but after the Japanese declaration of war, with the vessel barely able to maintain a speed of 5 knots, her master decided to put into Manila where she arrived on 11 December. The city and harbour were bombed almost daily and on Boxing Day, with her crew watching from on shore, *Tantalus* was hit at least four times. Listing heavily she caught fire and later the same evening capsized.

Meanwhile *Ulysses*, at 14,646 tons, the largest of the Holt fleet, which had sailed from Hong Kong a few hours before the Japanese invaded, arrived in Singapore. Her escape was due, in no small measure, to the untiring efforts of her crew. She had been carrying the engines and boilers for the *Empire Blossom* and other machinery for merchantmen being built at the shipbuilding yard of the Hong Kong & Whampoa Dock Company. They were discharged at Singapore. The master of the *Tantalus* and his men were taken prisoner during the capture of Manila on 3 January 1942. Subsequently, her third mate and a seaman were caught trying to escape from the internment camp and later executed in flagrant violation of international law.

Ordered out of Hong Kong on 6 December was the *Bennevis*, with instructions to tow an 800-ton lighter to Singapore. She was two days on passage – which, because of the presence of the lighter, had to be made at reduced speed – when two destroyers approached. With no report of the opening of hostilities, her master was not unduly suspicious until the leading destroyer signalled that on no account was he to use his radio. Whilst both had their guns trained on *Bennevis*, one instructed the merchantman to follow and the other signalled 'captured and strike colours'. Taken to Hainan Island a Japanese party then boarded and took over the vessel. The master and crew became prisoners of war and remained so until released by the Allies in September 1945: four died during internment, three from malnutrition.

With the enemy advance down the Malay peninsula, and the landing of amphibious forces in Borneo and the Celebes, in Sumatra, Bali and Timor, came the rush to send all possible reinforcements to Singapore, at the time the fifth greatest port in the world. Its subsequent surrender, like that of Dunkirk, was a military disaster but, unlike Dunkirk, there was no homecoming to fight again for those who took part. It is a story of lack of reinforcements, of ships, troops and armour; a lack of preparedness, of air cover and naval escorts. The four services were overstretched. There was news of defeat on all fronts – the Atlantic, the American east coast, the Mediterranean, the Indian Ocean – and now the whole of the Far East was virtually in flames.

Seen by Churchill as 'the worst disaster and largest capitulation in British history' it was an anxious time for him as Prime Minister. In

Parliament he faced a censure motion; it was claimed that half the British nation were dissatisfied with his conduct of the war. Few had forgotten his Gallipoli disaster of 1915.

Between New Year's Day and 8 February seven small convoys of merchantmen arrived at Singapore but further inward movements were then stopped. By 12 February, when the Japanese had gained a secure foothold on Singapore island, the order was given to clear the harbour of all shipping that could be got away.

Convoy ZK5 from Sydney had sailed as early as 28 December to reinforce Port Moresby (considered a stepping-stone to Australia) and the other islands of South-east Asia. Included were the *Aquitania*, *Herstein* and *Sarpedon*, carrying 4,250 Australian troops and 10,000 tons of equipment. The *Anglo Indian* from this convoy lay in Singapore harbour for some two weeks, discharging 25-pounder guns and ammunition. Time and time again she was damaged by bombs and by fire but there was never a direct hit. She eventually escaped by way of Batavia and Colombo and thence to Karachi for repairs. Convoy MS1, including the merchantmen *Gorgon* and *Phrontis* already mentioned, arrived in Singapore from Australia but were subjected to heavy bombing on arrival and during discharge of cargo. On 2 January, convoy BM9A arrived from Colombo with troop reinforcements in the transports *Devonshire*, *Ethiopia*, *Lancashire*, *Rajula* and *Varsova*.

Talthybius arrived loaded with tanks, lorries and other military equipment on 25 January. Like many other vessels she had been *en route* to Suez with supplies for Middle East forces when, after being diverted to Bombay, she was convoyed to Singapore. Discharged by her crew and men of the New Zealand Air Force, she afterwards sustained two direct hits during a heavy assault from the air; fires broke out in several parts of the ship.

Whilst *Talthybius* was moved into the Empire Dock there was no way that she could be made seaworthy. Further, no assistance was available as the wharves and godowns were now deserted. Although air raids were heavy and frequent, attempts were still being made by her crew on 10 February to save her. Tragically *Talthybius*, at 10,253 tons the largest cargo merchantman lost in the Far Eastern theatre, rested on the bottom and had to be abandoned. However, although forty years old, it was not to be her final day. Salved by the Japanese and renamed *Taruyasu Maru*, she was found scuttled after the war in Maizuru harbour on the north coast of Honshu. Later raised and repaired at Hong Kong during 1946 she sailed under Ministry of Transport ownership under the name of *Empire Evenlode*.

Arriving early in January with reinforcements was the 27,155-ton *Dominion Monarch*, flagship of the liner company Shaw Savill. Built in 1939, the newest and largest ship regularly employed in the Australian and New Zealand trades, she was requisitioned by the Government as a troopship in August 1940. Overdue for drydocking and engine overhaul, with her owners eager to take advantage of the facilities that Singapore offered, the necessary work was put in hand even though the situation was serious.

As air raids intensified so the position became more precarious. *Dominion Monarch* was partially dismantled and many considered her case helpless and doomed. Yet the Chief Engineer and the whole crew did a magnificent job in the face of the greatest difficulties. With her engines restarted she sailed for New Zealand about 8 February.

Up to the end of her fifth year of trooping the *Dominion Monarch* travelled some 350,000 miles and carried nearly 90,000 service personnel, of which about 29,000 were American and nearly 8,000 were from the Dominions. Whilst cargo space was restricted she brought to Britain 70,000 tons of food supplies, of which 51,500 tons consisted of butter, cheese and meat.

Sailing during the last days of January was the merchantman *Loch Ranza*. Loaded with important radio equipment and anti-aircraft guns for the defence of Palembang in Sumatra, she was bombed and later beached on Abang Island following a heavy attack by aircraft on 3 February. The wreck – she was a total loss – was found by HMAS *Toowooma*. (During December 1940 *Loch Ranza* had been torpedoed by *U-101* in the North Atlantic when with convoy HX90. Badly damaged she limped to port where she was under repair for some six months.)

Prior to Japan's declaration of war, as early as 12 November, convoy WS12A was sailing from Halifax, Nova Scotia, under US naval escort. This comprised the US troopships *Mount Vernon, Leonard Wood, Orizaba, Joseph T. Dickman, West Point* and the *Wakefield* – the last three named carrying units of the British Army's Royal Artillery. On board the *Joseph T. Dickman* were units of the 125th Anti-Tank Regiment who had been in transit since 28 October when they boarded the transport *Oronsay* at Avonmouth bound for 'an unknown destination'. It was in fact to be North Africa.

At Durban the 125th Anti-Tank Regiment transferred to the *Empress of Asia*, again for 'an unknown destination'. Whilst *West Point* and *Wakefield* were diverted to Singapore along with Canadian Pacific's *Duchess of Bedford*, the *Empress* put into Bombay. It was from there that, escorted by HMS *Exeter*, she sailed in convoy together with the *Empress of Japan* (her name was changed to *Empress of Scotland* at Colombo on her homeward voyage), the *Felix Roussel* and *City of Canterbury*.

Attacked by a Japanese bomber force on the approaches to Singapore on 4 February, followed by a second assault the following day, the 16,909-ton coal-burning *Empress of Asia* was dive-bombed and set on fire, the flames getting out of control in a matter of minutes. Brought to anchor close to Sultan Shoal lighthouse she burnt out during the next day and was broken up for scrap in 1952.

The end came swiftly for the *Empress* but miraculously only fifteen military personnel were unaccounted for and only one member of the crew died as a result of injuries sustained in the bombing. Much credit for this was due to the rescue operation mounted by the Australian sloop *Yarra*, which came alongside aft and took off well over 1,000 troops and crew. Others swam to the shore close to the lighthouse. Many of the crew later helped in 'the small ship' evacuation, some never to see their native land again. Those of the catering staff who volunteered for duty in the hospitals later found themselves condemned to prison camps. During her war service the *Empress of Asia* travelled 46,993 miles, carried 6,839 troops, some 1,000 prisoners of war, eighty-four civilians and 3,495 tons of cargo.

The French-flag *Felix Roussel*, a hired transport under the control of the Sea Transport Office and managed by the Bibby Line, was also hit in the assault on the convoy. Carrying a full complement of troops, the ship suffered twelve fatalities, mainly from the 11th Northumberland Fusiliers. Most who landed from this convoy arrived just in time to walk into a prison camp without firing a shot. Many never survived the ordeal.

Two days after arrival *Felix Roussel* embarked 1,100 refugees, mainly women and children for Bombay. These were accompanied by some survivors from the *Prince of Wales* and *Repulse*, some non-combatant service personnel and forty members of the *Empress* crew. On 8 February, the day that the Japanese first established amphibious landings on Singapore island, *Felix Roussel* sailed in company with the *Devonshire, Duchess of Bedford, Empress of Japan, Plancius, Wakefield* and *West Point*. Indian soldiers were unloading ammunition from the *Duchess* until the moment she sailed.

All seven ships, carrying in total some 6,000 European and Asiatic women and children, were pursued and attacked by high-level bombers; ultimately they reached their destination in safety. Sailing in the last convoy with HMS *Durban* as escort, were the merchantmen *Gorgon*, half of whose inward cargo was still in her holds, the *Empire Star* and *Kedah*, the Singapore/Penang ferry steamer. Requisitioned by the Admiralty as an armed auxiliary, *Kedah* was undergoing repairs at the time; already she had ferried several hundred survivors from *Repulse* and *Prince of Wales* and 600 Air Force personnel to Palembang. Thereafter she returned to Singapore where she embarked several hundred more Air Force men for Batavia. On 26 February *Kedah* was engaged in a mission to evacuate General Wavell (later Field Marshal Lord Wavell) and his staff as well as 400 refugees from Cilacap for Colombo, where she arrived on 7 March.

Departure of the last convoy was made under aerial attack, the whole time marred by much confusion in the port area. Some people missed their allotted ship, others jumped aboard the first they came upon, some tragically lost their places altogether. Regardless of embarkation slips, passports and inventories, women and children clambered aboard. *Gorgon*, cleared for Freemantle, sailed with 358; her companion *Phrontis*, sailing independently for Melbourne the day before, was similarly overloaded.

Empire Star, with cabin accommodation for only sixteen passengers, embarked a total of 2,154, most of whom were Australian, Indian and British nurses from the Military Hospital. Carrying a considerable quantity of Air Force equipment and stores in her holds, she was a crowded vessel. Four hours after sailing she sustained three direct hits as six dive-bombers came out of the tropical dawn: fourteen were killed and seventeen badly injured. As the raid continued there were a large number of near misses, and the ship was on fire in three places.

To extinguish the fires was difficult and dangerous in a ship thronged with so many, yet in due course the chief officer led his party in doing just that and forty hours later *Empire Star* arrived at Batavia. After a short stay she continued her voyage for Freemantle. She was not to survive the war, however. Torpedoed by *U-615* on 23 October 1942, she sank 570 miles north of the Azores. Forty-two persons, including her master, were unaccounted for.

Some 223 souls from a total of 245, mostly women and children, perished aboard the 1,646-ton *Giang Bee*. She was bombed and sunk in the Banka Strait. Close by the 4,433-ton freighter *Norah Moller* was caught and four miles from Palembang Bar light vessel, the *Katong*. There were heavy casualties in both instances.

The merchantman *Derrymore*, sunk north of Batavia by the Japanese submarine *I-25* on Friday 13 February, still had the same cargo aboard with which it left the United Kingdom five months before. It included 2,000 tons of explosives and Spitfire aircraft in packing cases on deck, ordered for the defence of Singapore. She had voyaged 16,000 miles via Jamaica, the Panama Canal and Melbourne. It was all too late; too late even to unload her cargo. Instead she received orders for the Middle East via Batavia, where she was to land defeated airmen and soldiers who boarded her whilst laying at anchor.

Only one lifeboat was left undamaged, and *Derrymore* was a doomed vessel. She took a heavy list to starboard, with the cased aircraft smashed and the accommodation amidships badly damaged. The sea was calm, the night was clear and starlit as the crew raced against time. Led by their chief mate, they set about making rafts out of hatch covers and empty oil drums. Later, the vessel was successfully abandoned, and the survivors were picked up by HMAS *Ballarat*. Only nine Australian Air Force personnel were missing.

As with Dunkirk, the fall of Singapore demanded a small-ship operation. After General Percival surrendered his army on Sunday 15 February, about 100 local ships of small tonnage evacuated some 10,000 servicemen and civilians. From an army of 85,000, which included 33,000 British and 17,000 Australians, an estimated 7,000 made their own bid to escape. Some never fled further than the islands surrounding Singapore harbour; many died in the attempt. The fortunate ones, with the help of the Dutch, crossed Sumatra to the port of Padang, from where they were shipped by Allied merchantmen.

One of the largest of the small ships was the *Wu Sueh*. Dressed in white, with a green stripe and a red Geneva cross, she was the best Singapore could manage in the way of a hospital ship. Narrowly avoiding the last of the bombing she ferried the wounded to Java. As many as fifty vessels of small tonnage sailed that last day – those such as the *Pinnia*, the *Ping Wo, Redang, Subadar* and *Vyner Brooke*. The latter, packed with over 300 hospital patients and nurses, raked with gunfire and straddled with bombs, sank off Banka Straits. Many, mostly women and children, were drowned. On board *Ping Wo*, which safely escaped to Batavia, were the master and crew of *Talthybius*.

The *Sing-Keng-Seng* and the *Am Pang* carried survivors from *Prince of Wales, Repulse* and *Empress of Asia*. Arriving in Palembang they were confronted by the sight of over 100 Japanese aircraft dropping paratroops. With the help of the Dutch military they reached Batavia where, after being housed in the Netherlands Bank, they were taken to the port. There, they secured passage in the steamship *Marella*, some of whose crew had deserted. Landing in Australia they were later shipped homewards.

On 19 February the Japanese again struck at Allied merchantmen. Far to the south, the port of Darwin on the north coast of Australia was the target of 188 aircraft, just one less than the number which had attacked Pearl Harbor. Was it the softening-up process for another amphibious invasion?

To the west of Sumatra steamed convoy SU1, consisting of twelve vessels with some 10,900 troops and military equipment from Colombo. This was being moved south to defend a possible attack on the Australian continent. The convoy totalled 97,541 gross tons and included such important merchantmen as *Esperance Bay, Eastern Prince, Mathura, City of London* and *City of Paris*. Some of these, including the 14,204-ton *Esperance Bay*, now returned to the Shaw Savill company after two years service as an auxiliary cruiser, had been on their way to Singapore with Australian troops when the fortress fell and they were ordered to Colombo.

Twelve merchantmen were sunk during the devastating raid on Port Darwin as well as the US destroyer *Peary*. In addition, the Australian sloop *Swan*, the US aircraft tender *William B. Preston* and seven merchant ships were damaged; four small defence and harbour craft lay wrecked. It was a bombing operation of great intensity and accuracy.

Casualties on board ships totalled 172 and another nineteen died of wounds aboard the hospital ship *Manunda*, which happened to be berthed in the port. In the harbour area were another 330 wounded, 200 of them seriously. In the first minutes the motorship *Neptuna*, requisitioned by the Admiralty, was struck by two bombs. Suddenly the 200 tons of depth-charges she was carrying were detonated. The explosion rocked the harbour and the town. Her master and fifteen crew were killed.

Carrying a valuable oil cargo, the tanker *British Motorist* was struck, which led to uncontrollable fires. Blazing fuel oil swept across the harbour, engulfing men and rescue boats. Both the merchantmen *Barossa* and *Zealandia*, partly unloaded, were seriously damaged and sank at their moorings. As with all the hospital ships the 9,115-ton *Manunda* was readily recognisable as such, in her livery of gleaming white with prominent red crosses. She excelled herself as a saver of life at a time of extreme danger. Damaged from the effects of two bombs, fires erupted throughout the vessel and water mains were severed. Sixteen personnel lay dead; her radio equipment, direction finder and echo sounder destroyed. In spite of the situation *Manunda* was still in service at nightfall. She took on seventy-six stretcher cases and 190 patients from shore hospitals, and sailed in the early hours of the 20th for Freemantle.

On the day of surrender in Java (7 March) the great port of Rangoon fell to the advancing enemy in Burma; the occupation of the Dutch East Indies was completed the following day. During the evacuation from Burma, of both military personnel and refugees, there was considerable confusion in the administration and direction of shipping. Panic measures, due to the swift advance of the Japanese, were the order of the day.

During the last week of February 1942 a sergeant in the Australian Air Force, a navigator/bomb aimer on Blenheim Mark I light bombers, and his comrades were ordered at short notice to the dockside in Rangoon. There they boarded the 23-year-old 5,930-ton *Clan Murdoch*. Fifty years later he still holds vivid memories of their escapade. Deep down in her holds the Scottish merchantman was carrying 1,200 tons of bombs and 1,000 tons of soda. Her master was instructed by the port officials to immediately embark 1,200 personnel, mainly airmen but with some Indian Army privates, and sail for Calcutta. Also taken aboard were their stores and equipment.

There was no food on board *Clan Murdoch* for so many and only accommodation for ten or twelve passengers. Conditions on board were naturally crowded, those occupying the 'tween deck 'camped' above the bombs. It was somewhat insanitary, toilet arrangements being by way of buckets on the stern which after use were slung over the side attached to lines – only most did not bother. I had neither occasion nor desire to make use of this facility but hung on for the duration of the voyage – apart from the odd 'piddle' over the lee side of the boat deck where my friends and I were established. To be near the boats in emergency we thought; how innocent and naive. What a shambles it would have been if a torpedo had come up. We could not have survived the rush.

Clan Murdoch sailed from Rangoon on 21 February passing another merchantman proceeding up river. Her decks too were crowded, only this time they were units of the 7th Armoured Brigade ready for disembarkation. They were greeted by shouts of 'eeh tha's headin' wrong f---ing way.' Calling at the port of Akyab the *Clan* steamer took on board four smashed aircraft, 100 tons of spares and a further 250 military personnel. Landing her human cargo at Calcutta on 26 February she was back at Akyab six days later, where she discharged 900 tons of her bombs and then loaded 2,400 tons of rice and 1,000 evacuees for Colombo.

The *Clan Murdoch* led a charmed life and survived the war, but twenty-seven of the forty-six Clan Line fleet were lost. It is estimated that 79 per cent of personnel aboard those sunk did not survive the war years.

The Japanese surface campaign against merchant shipping in the region was coupled with a threat to the whole Indian sub-continent. Its climax came when news was received that Admiral Nagumo's celebrated carrier force, along with four battleships, were heading for Ceylon (now Sri Lanka) and the naval bases of Trincomalee and Colombo. During their passage across the Bay of Bengal the Japanese squadron was to sink twenty-three merchantmen of over 112,000 tons, whilst on the west coast of India submarines added five more of 32,000 tons.

Shipping in all the ports of India's east coast and at Colombo – in all, fifty-five merchantmen – were ordered to sea to avoid capture in the event of invasion. Those that were unable to sail through, being damaged or under engine repair, were ordered to prepare for scuttling. In retrospect such orders were unnecessary and indirectly led to the loss of ships and lives; but the hospital ship *Vita* (formerly of P & O) did valuable work in the region.

The War Cabinet in London viewed the Japanese moves with great concern. Churchill considered it to be one of the most dangerous moments of the whole war. If Ceylon and eastern India were lost the Allies' link with China would have been cut. The collapse of the Middle East; the interruption of oil supplies; the cutting of the Cape route for supplies to Egypt and the Mediterranean; the capture of Madagascar, with its important naval base of Diego Suarez – all were within the realms of possibility. Only with the thoughts of overstretching his communications did Nagumo turn his fleet eastward again. He was never given a second chance in the region.

On 27 March the second radio officer of *Magican*, sailing from Colombo, wrote in his diary: 'Received orders to proceed on our way – Calcutta I believe. This will be a risky trip as the Japs have captured the Andaman Islands only 600 miles east.' The following day he entered, 'keeping close to shore as Jap subs are as plentiful as peas. Passed a naval signal station and got orders to proceed to nearest anchorage.'

On Palm Sunday, 29 March, the *Magican* was anchored at a secret naval base – 'reason for this is that the Jap Navy is on the rampage. Received orders to proceed to Calcutta at 4pm.' On Wednesday 1 April – 'received radio message early hours morning saying ship must turn about and make for Vizagapatam, a little-known base some 300 miles south of Calcutta where we will be safe from Jap prowlers.' On Easter Sunday (5 April), when Japanese bombers raided Colombo harbour, the merchantman *Magican* was still held at Vizagapatam.

That Easter weekend witnessed the Battle of the Bay of Bengal. In the confusion of the moment the *Harpasa*, unlike some which were formed into (unescorted) small convoys, was ordered to sail from Calcutta alone with instructions for East Africa. Attacked by enemy aircraft she was set afire by a large incendiary device. After abandoning ship the survivors were later picked up by the British-registered, Hong Kong-owned *Taksang*. She had been dispatched from a Colombo-bound convoy of seven merchantmen.

Next morning *Taksang* herself was sunk when the convoy was overhauled by the Japanese squadron. Her British master was badly injured, and fifteen crew and the senior radio officer from *Harpasa* lay dead upon deck. Two serviceable lifeboats were launched, and after two days adrift the survivors landed upon an open sandy beach. Others aboard a raft were rescued by a Catalina flying boat.

Other merchantmen lost during that tragic weekend were *Autolycus*, *Ganges* and *Malda*, the latter having just been fitted out as a troopship and whose master, Captain Edmundson of the British India Shipping Company, was acting as convoy commodore. British India's *Indora*, which was also sunk, was carrying some of the crew of both *Autolycus* and *Malda*, whom she had plucked from the water. There followed *Silksworth*, *Shinkuang* and *Sinkiang*.

Further south on the same day, enemy warships overhauled the remnants of another convoy. *Dardanus*, in ballast for Colombo and following the coastal route near Vizagapatam, was attacked by two carrier-based aircraft; two bombs exploded in the engine-room. In no danger of sinking, she was towed by the steamship *Gandara* towards Madras. Unfortunately, both vessels were then bombed by aircraft, then shelled by Japanese cruisers.

The bombing of Colombo harbour on Easter Sunday morning was expected and the few Hurricane fighters detailed for its defence were quickly airborne. They were completely overwhelmed. From out of the tropical sky came ninety-one Japanese bombers and thirty-six fighter aircraft. Most of the shipping had been ordered to sea, but Alfred Holt's 1924-built *Hector*, at buoys in the middle of the harbour, was in the process of decommissioning after two-and-a-half years' service as an armed merchant cruiser. Sustaining six direct hits, from which 114 personnel were killed, she took the brunt of the attack. All the bombs exploded in the fuel tanks and *Hector* was a raging furnace within minutes – this, in spite of fire-fighting assistance given by officers and men of the tanker *British Sergeant*. The 11,198-ton merchant cruiser, resting on the harbour bottom, burned for fourteen days.

Damaged at Colombo were the destroyer *Tenedos*, the submarine depot ship *Lucia* and the merchantman *Clan Murdoch*, still with her evacuees from Akyab on board. *Benledi* was also set afire though the flames were quickly extinguished. *British Judge*, which was under repair, escaped further serious damage; she had limped into Colombo just two weeks after being first bombed and machine-gunned in the Sundra Straits then torpedoed by I-158, one of Japan's newest submarines. The tanker *British Judge* was one of the lucky ones, and she went on to survive the war.

The experiences of *British Judge* after Colombo do illustrate well the difficulties of repair in the southern hemisphere. Sailing for Cape Town, where she could drydock, she was struck by a monsoon causing damage to her hull. She made for Mombasa where she lay for nine months being patched up. After calls at Durban and Cape Town she then steered a course for Bahia in Brazil, alone and unescorted. On many occasions she was hove-to because of the weather. Not until the tanker reached Mobile, Texas, after a 20,000 mile voyage, was she drydocked for repairs.

Shipping congestion and delays in the region were acute. This was principally due to the volume on passage to and from the Middle East. At Durban it was not unusual to find twenty to twenty-five merchantmen lying at anchor awaiting berths; at Cape Town there were twelve to fifteen, with similar numbers at Bombay and Calcutta. Worst hit was Colombo, where some 100 vessels of all types and tonnages could often be seen, the majority of them berthed; the harbour's official berthing capacity was forty-five. It was fortunate that steps had been taken to empty the port that fateful Easter, yet the knock-on effect made for chaos and confusion.

On Good Friday HMS *Dorsetshire* and *Cornwall*, with bands playing, had sailed from Colombo. Forty-eight hours later both were sunk in the

Indian Ocean by dive-bombers. Four days later the same fate befell the aircraft carrier *Hermes* east of Ceylon. In another air-raid on Colombo harbour (9 April) the *Empire Moonrise* was hit by a bomb and damaged.

During the first week of May the Allies occupied Madagascar, which had been controlled by the Vichy French (Operation 'Ironclad'). The Germans had earmarked Diego Suarez as a U-boat base early in the war and urged Japan to take over the island. Led by HMS *Keren*, a former P & O vessel and now an assault and landing ship headquarters (later designated LSHQ), the task force included *Karanja, Royal Ulsterman, Winchester Castle*, nine other transports, and landing craft; also present were the aircraft carriers *Illustrious* and *Indomitable*, the battleship *Ramillies* and other assorted destroyers and frigates. It was the largest co-ordinated amphibious operation since the Dardanelles landings of the First World War. There was little resistance and the campaign was completed within forty-eight hours.

Submarine warfare is often overlooked east of Cape Town but from the time of Pearl Harbor until February 1945 some 271 merchantmen were sunk in the Indian Ocean and fifty in Pacific waters. The majority of these were sailing independently. It was only when one or more troopships were involved, such as those northward from Durban or Persian Gulf/Aden, that convoys were organized. Even on such occasions the shortage of escort vessels was so serious that the most to be expected was two corvettes. Although far from base in Europe, from October 1942 as many as 175 of the notified merchantmen losses in the Indian Ocean were the result of German U-boat activity. In addition to refuelling from 'Milch Cows' they were now using the Japanese naval base established at Penang in Malaya.

During August 1942 my service took me north from Durban, sailing independently aboard the merchantman *Gazcon*. She was a 'replacement' vessel, former Vichy-French freighter whose capture is related in Chapter 8. Loaded with 6,500 tons of military supplies, including high explosives in the forward holds taken on in New York, we were bound for Alexandria. Alas! north of Cape Guardafui entering the Gulf of Aden, the *Gazcon* was torpedoed and sunk by the Japanese submarine *I-29*. The whole forward part disintegrated as the high explosives were detonated. As she ploughed under she took her master and twelve crew with her. To sum up this loss I quote from my book *The Red Duster at War* (1988).

> The dark object proved to be a raft and together with some other members of the crew, I clambered aboard; for the first time in my seagoing career I felt an element of fear. I was clad only in shorts, hastily pulled on amidst the confusion of the moment. In the darkness there had been no time to search for my lifejacket. Yet it was not the sea, or fear of drowning or being attacked by sharks, of thirst or of being burnt to a

cinder by the mid-day sun of which I was afraid, but the cruelty of man. The cruelty of the Eastern enemy was already known in these waters. And the enemy knew no distress signal had been radioed. They alone knew of our plight.

It was the first war cruise for *I-29* (Lieutenant-Commander Juichi Izu) and apart from the Russian *Uëlen*, torpedoed (not fatally) off the east coast of Australia on 16 May, the *Gazcon* was her first 'kill'. During the following three weeks *I-29* was to sink a further three ships, *Haresfield*, *Ocean Honour* and the American *Paul Luckenbach*. Fortunately for the crews of merchantmen sunk by Juichi Izu, unlike some of his compatriots, there was no question of survivors being machine-gunned, of lifeboats and rafts being rammed, or of defenceless merchant seamen being murdered.

Constructed in February 1942, and one of nineteen patrol class submarines, *I-29* was attached to the 8th Japanese squadron under the command of Captain Sasaki. Of 1,950 tons, she carried a small (one-man) reconnaissance aircraft, seventeen torpedoes, one 14-cm gun and a crew of ninety-four. Her surface speed was 24 knots with a range of 16,000 miles at 16 knots. Technologically, Japan was in the lead with large-type underwater craft.

Apart from the possibility that her aircraft may have spotted us the day before (1 September), her speed was the likely reason why she caught the *Gazcon*. On that day we received a radio signal that a submarine had been located about twenty-five miles south of Cape Guardafui. As we were then the same distance north of the Cape, we continued without taking avoiding action. A month beforehand (4 August 1942) the German *U-155* had been active close by. Here she torpedoed and sank the *Empire Arnold* (launched January 1942), which had been loaded with military stores, and bound from the United States to the Middle East.

During the UN trials of Japanese war crimes (May 1946 to November 1948) 5,500 were accused of killing, torturing or otherwise ill-treating Allied servicemen and civilians. Some 4,450 were found guilty. A thousand suffered execution by hanging; yet the deaths of the men who lost their lives after abandoning ship went almost unnoticed and unavenged. Fifty years later the controversy continues. It is difficult to understand why, unlike the Germans and the Italians, the Japanese, members of a maritime nation, ignored the bond of comradeship which has existed for centuries during times of peace *and* war between seamen of different nationalities. The barbaric behaviour shown by certain Japanese mariners would not have been tolerated by the German High Command. Indeed, in the main, German U-boat and surface raider commanders were helpful to those seamen, who, through no fault of their own, found themselves at the mercy of the elements.

The record of the Japanese does not make for happy reading:

10 December 1941. *Donerail* (Panamanian); submarine *I-10*; Commander Kayahara. 27 machine-gunned in lifeboats.

3 January 1942. *Langkoeas* (Dutch); *I-158*; Kitamura. 79 murdered.

25 February 1942. *Boero* (Dutch); *I-158*; Kitamura. No survivors, cause of deaths unknown.

20 March 1943. *Fort Mumford* (British): *I-27*; Fukumura. Only one survivor; cause of deaths unknown.

14 May 1943. *Centaur* (British hospital ship), *I-177*; Nakagawa. 270 lost.

18 November 1943. *Sambridge* (British); *I-27*; Fukumura. Boat and raft machine-gunned (*I-27*. Lost with all hands 12 February 1944.)

14 December 1943. *Daisy Moller* (British); *RO-110*; Ebato. 55 survivors machine gunned and killed. Rafts and boats rammed. (*RO-110* lost with all hands two months later.)

22 February 1944. *British Chivalry* (British); I-37; Nakagawa. Crew of 103 on rafts and boats machine-gunned.

26 February 1944. *Sutlej*. Details as above.

29 February 1944. *Ascot*. Details as above.

9 March 1944. *Behar* (British); surface cruiser *Tone*; 108 souls in four lifeboats taken prisoner. 72 of these murdered.

18 March 1944. *Nancy Moller* (British); *I-165*; Shimizu. More than 20 murdered.

26 March 1944. *Tjisalak* (Dutch); *I-8*; Ariizumi. 98 survivors, including one woman, killed by the submarine crew.

29 March 1944. *Richard Hovey* (US); *I-26*; Kusaki. Machine guns used on men in water, on boats and on rafts.

2 July 1944. *Jean Nicolet* (US); *I-8*; Ariizumi. 96 crew picked up by the submarine and were on deck when the enemy suddenly dived. 13 drowned, 23 survived.

30 October 1944. *John A. Johnson* (US); *I-12*; Kudo. Lifeboats and survivors machine-gunned. 10 lost.

The loss of the *Fort Mumford* is one of the mysteries of the shark-infested seas east of Cape Town. On her maiden voyage, the Canadian-built merchantman had crossed the Pacific with war supplies for the Mediterranean. Having completed loading at Lyttleton (New Zealand) she took on bunkers at Colombo on 15 March 1943; five days later, *en route* for Aden, she was torpedoed by *I-27*. The only survivor, one of the gun crew, was rescued by an Indian dhow bound for Tanganyika.

Eight months later *I-27* was to sink the Liberty ship *Sambridge*, also on her maiden voyage. Bound from Madras for Aden she was fitted with

AND nets, though they were not streamed at the time. Sailing independently she had of necessity to keep to Admiralty positions at agreed times and the net defence would have reduced her speed by at least 2 knots. Torpedoed and sunk due West, on virtually the same latitude as *Fort Mumford*, her rafts were machine-gunned by the enemy. 'An act of deliberate terrorism,' her master declared at the Admiralty inquiry into her loss. Were there other survivors from that fateful day of 20 March when the *Fort Mumford* broke up? We can only surmise what happened in those seas some 200 miles from land.

The second mate of the *Sambridge* was taken prisoner by *I-27*, which landed him in Penang. Nothing was heard of him for over fourteen months. On New Year's Day 1945 his mother received a postcard saying he was alive and well in a prison camp in Japan.

In February of the following year *I-27*, still with Fukumara in command, was responsible for one of the greatest maritime disasters of the Second World War. On the 12th of the month the *Khedive Ismail*, managed by the British India Steam Navigation Company was blasted from the ocean, with the loss of 1,383 lives, including 137 of her 183 crew. Those saved totalled 201 men and six women. Only in two other instances (*Lancastria* and *Laconia*) was the loss of life aboard red ensign ships greater.

A combined operation of the two maritime services, it is one of the saddest and most horrific of war stories. KR8, a convoy of five troopships with their escort sailed for Colombo from Kilindini in East Africa. The periscope of *I-27* was so close to *Varsova* that her gun crew were unable to depress the Bofors gun sufficiently. To port steamed *City of Paris*, helpless to assist. Immediately astern was *Ekma*, which had to alter course to avoid the wreckage.

When Fukumura unleashed his two torpedoes he triggered a triple horror. Most of the 1,600 men and women aboard the *Khedive Ismail* were drowned. She sank beneath the waves in thirty-nine seconds. Three hours later, Fukumura and his crew joined their victims at the bottom of the Indian Ocean. The third element of this tragedy became a recurrent nightmare for Commander Rupert Egan, captain of HMS *Petard*, the only destroyer to sink a submarine from all three enemy navies.

Carrying a matron and sixty nurses on their way to staff a military hospital, as well as twenty-six women from the WRNS, *Khedive Ismail* was the convoy commodore's ship. She was also carrying a battalion of African infantry and parties of British soldiers, sailors and airmen.

It was Commander Egan who depth charged the Japanese submarine as she tried to hide beneath a group of survivors. They were swimming for their lives, and their cries for help changed to screams of horror as HMS *Petard* made her attack. It was another case, not unknown to merchant seamen survivors in the North Atlantic and the Arctic, in which the sinking of an enemy took priority over helpless victims. The fact that Commander Egan had to carry out the depth-charging disturbed him so much that he later took his own life in the United States. He was transfixed with the horror and dilemma of his duty, and his ship's company was numbed by the sure knowledge that the attacks were destroying the lives of the few who survived.

HMS *Paladin*, the other senior service escort, had lowered boats in an effort to rescue survivors when *Petard*, the senior escort, began her attack. Some from *Paladin* risked their own lives by jumping over the side to save those drowning, as *Petard* made her final runs. At the third attempt *I-27* was blasted to the surface but came up still full of fight. As her gunners tried to reach the 5-inch gun they were shot down. Zig-zagging in an effort to make good her escape the submarine was rammed by HMS *Paladin*, which itself was now badly damaged. In a final action HMS *Petard* fired six torpedoes, which unfortunately were all near misses. The seventh was on target and at last *I-27* plunged to the bottom. There were no survivors.

The torpedoing off Brisbane of the hospital ship *Centaur*, a 3,222-ton vessel of the Alfred Holt fleet, was one of the most tragic incidents involving Australians during World War Two. The US destroyer *Mugford* picked up sixty-four soaked and wounded survivors – one nurse and sixty-three men – from the rafts, which were surrounded by many vicious sharks.

With the sinking of *Centaur* Lieutenant-Commander Nakagawa (submarine *I-177*) committed one of the most cold-blooded atrocities of the war. The Australian Prime Minister John Curtis described it as a 'deliberate wanton act, violating all the principles of common decency'. Painted white with a wide green band, the traditional colours of a non-combatant ship, large red crosses were painted on both sides of her hull and funnel with another on deck for aerial identification.

With blazing floodlights illuminating her hull during the night of 14 May 1943 *I-177* committed a dastardly crime. With *Centaur* sinking in less than three minutes, no distress signals could be sent, no boats could be launched; only rafts and some hatch boards gave the necessary buoyancy to save life. Those lost were forty-five of the ship's crew, including her master, the ship's padre, and 223 medical personnel.

By the end of 1943 Nakagawa had transferred to the submarine *I-37* and during February of 1944 torpedoed and sank *British Chivalry*, *Sutlej* and *Ascot* with the fatalities that I have already listed. It was *I-37* (under Commander Otani) that on 16 June 1943 sank the motor tanker *San Ernesto*, in ballast from Sydney for Bahrain. The wreck was sighted on two occasions during August; the derelict ship drifted 2,000 miles before running aground on Pulua Nias Island, where it was dismantled by the Japanese. The boat containing the second mate and eight men was adrift for twenty-eight days, during which time they suffered great thirst and terrible sunburn. The master of the *San Ernesto* was Captain Waite, who commanded *San Alberto* (sunk by *U-48* in December 1939), and *San Demetrio* of *Jervis Bay* fame.

Only four men appeared before the court in Tokyo charged with crimes against Allied merchant seamen. Vice-Admiral Naomasi Sakanju and Captain Haruo Mayazumi were charged with, and found guilty of, murder by beheading seventy-two of the *Behar*'s crew and passengers. Sakanju was sentenced to death and hanged. Mayazumi, whose Christian upbringing prompted him to protest against the mass execution, received only seven years in jail. Two officers who served in the submarine *I-8* at the time of the *Tjisalak* massacre, Lieutenant Sadao Monontaka and Lieutenant Masanori Hattori, also stood trial and were given seven and five years imprisonment respectively.

During October 1942 twenty-five merchantmen were sunk in the Indian Ocean and waters off the coast of South Africa. Only six were destroyed by the Japanese; the rest were torpedoed by German U-boats, who found the waters more congenial than those of the North Atlantic. The new 1,600-ton *U-178*, which sailed from Kiel on her first war cruise on 8 September 1942, did not return to Europe for fourteen months. She was based for part of this time at the Japanese victualling port of Penang. Her biggest 'prize' was the trooper *Duchess of Atholl* – see Chapter 9.

Merchantmen away from home ports for a long period took on a glowing, homely atmosphere as soon as news was spread that the ship was UK-bound. So it was with *Clan MacTavish*, which had been trading in the Middle East and Indian Ocean for twelve months – and particularly so after she had picked up thirty-five survivors from the former Danish *Boringia*, sunk by *U-159*. Nine hours later, however, and some 100 miles off the Cape of Good Hope, the Clan Line steamer was torpedoed and sunk by the same *U-159*. Fifty-four of her crew including the master, Captain Arthur, and seven survivors from *Boringia* perished. The next day, 9 October, *U-159* sank the American *Coloradan* and followed up with the British *Empire Nomad* four days later.

On 17 October *U-504* (Commander Fitz Poske, Knight's Cross) was surfaced 450 miles south of Cape Town when the merchantman *Empire Chaucer* was sighted; she was homeward bound with tea for Calcutta. Poske fired two torpedoes, which immediately crippled the '*Chaucer*'. In the process, several were killed and her master was seriously injured. Nevertheless, three lifeboats were successfully launched and fifty-four of her crew survived epic voyages. Boat No. 3, which contained the senior radio officer, the ship's carpenter and thirteen others, survived for twenty-three days and covered nearly 1,000 miles. They were saved chiefly by a shark, which they tempted aboard by trailing their arms in the sea, and then killed it with a large axe. The fish's flesh kept them alive until they were rescued by the SS *Nebraska*.

South African waters are well stocked with sharks, and therefore potentially treacherous. In November 1942 the 6,796-ton *Nova Scotia* was returning from Port Tewfik (Egypt), where she had disembarked troops for service in 'the desert'. In the Mozambique Channel she was torpedoed and sunk by *U-181*. In addition to Italian prisoners of war she had on board 765 Italian civilian internees. Loss of life was heavy.

There was little censorship in South Africa at the time, and newspapers in Durban and in Cape Province gave details of the many mutilated bodies picked up on the beaches north of Durban. It was suggested that more people had been attacked and killed by sharks in the *Nova Scotia* disaster than during any previous maritime loss in South African waters.

As in the Atlantic the U-boat commander's favourite target was the tanker. The Persian Gulf with its refineries became increasingly important during 1942–43 as a supplier of oil and oil products; the 'Cape route' carried a steady stream of independent, loaded tankers. The *Corbis*, 500 miles east of Port Elizabeth on 18 April 1943, loaded 'to the marks' with high octane, was just such a tanker. The night was dark yet the outline of her superstructure could be clearly seen by Commander Werner Musenberg, on his first war cruise. *U-180* fired two torpedoes in quick succession, followed by a third ten minutes later.

Only one lifeboat got away from the *Corbis*; her master and many of the crew jumped overboard into the blazing sea never to be seen again. Flames reached into the sky as the tanker broke up and the sea was ablaze for over two square miles. Yet miraculously, that one lifeboat remained afloat, and its thirty-two crew alive. As the sun rose that morning, the seamen, forever superstitious in the tradition of seafarers, noticed a white albatross dead in the water. She was one of a pair which had been following the tanker for three days. The brown male bird, which the crew named 'Captain Brown', remained with the lifeboat through calm and storm until rescue came.

For ten days and ten nights the boat survived bad weather. Then came disaster. Four times during a period of twenty-four hours the boat overturned. Two days later only eight survivors remained, their rations and fresh water lost in the rough sea. It was on the fourteenth day, with land on the horizon, that they were sighted by an aircraft. A rescue launch, which put out from the coast, brought them to safety.

The sinking of the *Leana* by *U-198* as she was sailing the East African coastal routeing, 175 miles east-north-east of Lourenço Marques, is notable for the tenacity of her (the ship's) gun crew. At dawn on 7 July 1943, with the bright sun rising just above the horizon, fought the submarine round for round until the latter dived for cover. It was to be a short respite, however. Three hours later, *U-198* attacked by torpedo.

U-198's commander, the experienced Captain Werner Hartmann, who was later awarded the Knight's Cross with Oak Leaves, had positioned his boat so that the sun was directly astern of him. As the gunlayer that day has said, 'I looked into the sun and sure enough there was the outline of the enemy. I and my mates loaded the twelve pounder and made the sun our target; we let fire, the sun was too bad for our sight but we kept on firing.'

With the *Leana* abandoned, her crew, many of them in the water, found sharks were everywhere. Her gunlayer continues his report in the typically nonchalant style of the Royal Navy DEMS: 'we were not worried about sharks but so upset to see our ship sunk into the depth of the ocean'. Taking the master of the *Leana* prisoner, the U-boat sped off and then crash-dived as an aircraft was observed. Adrift in the lifeboats for five days the crew then found themselves thrown out by the surf as they approached a beach north of Lourenço Marques. Their captain, put ashore at Bordeaux upon the arrival of *U-198* on 24 September, spent the rest of the war in the German prisoner of war camp at Milag Nord, near Bremen.

Another Indian Ocean loss for the Clan Line was that of *Clan MacArthur*, torpedoed and sunk on the night of 11 August 1943 by *U-181*. At the time this submarine was commanded by one of Germany's most celebrated and decorated submariners, Commander Wolfgang Lüth, who later received the Knight's Cross with Oak Leaves, Swords and Diamonds. Earlier in the war he had been in command of *U-9*, *U-138* and *U-43*; during 1940 and 1941, he gained many successes against transatlantic convoys. Upon his return from the Indian Ocean he was promoted to commanding officer of the 22nd Submarine Flotilla.

The twin-screw *Clan MacArthur*, the largest and fastest of the Clan Line fleet, was alone and zigzagging at 17 knots on passage to India when she was struck; two torpedoes immediately disabled the 10,528-ton merchantman. Lights were extinguished, both propellers were blown off by the explosions, and many of her Asian crew were trapped in their quarters. Struck by a third torpedo this fine ship, built in 1936, went under amidst a terrifying noise of crushing bulkheads and steam. From a complement of 151, ninety-nine survivors were rescued the next day by a French sloop.

One cannot leave the war east of Cape Town without mentioning the fate of the only two survivors of the Canadian-built *Fort Longueuil*, which was torpedoed and sunk by *U-532* south of Chagos Island in the Indian Ocean on 19 September 1943. The U-boat commander had last been in action in the Battle of the Atlantic when, in April of that year, he had been engaged in the action against convoy ONS5.

The raft of the two survivors of the *Longueuil* landed them on a beach in

Sumatra 134 days later, the fate of their comrades unknown. After this most remarkable feat in all the records of shipwreck survival, they then suffered the ordeal of being taken prisoner by the Japanese, who found them washed up upon the beach. In passing I should add that this record surpasses by only one day that of the Chinese steward, the only survivor of the *Benlomond*, which was torpedoed by *U-172* in the South Atlantic (23 November 1942).

In Chapter 3 I mentioned some of the commodities made scarce by the Japanese advance and the presence of their submarines in Eastern waters. Probably the greatest loss to the Allied war effort was linked to the rubber plantations, which had fallen into enemy hands. But war in the Pacific brought another problem. In addition to the logistical nightmare of transporting war material over water there was the added problem of feeding the armed forces engaged there.

Merchantmen were at a premium. Australian and New Zealand food, previously destined for the United Kingdom, was needed on the spot for US and Imperial troops. This new demand particularly affected meat and dairy produce. To compensate, large Lease-Lend supplies were directed from North America across the Atlantic with notable economies in shipping from Australasia. Moreover, this came at a time during those crisis weeks of the Battle of the Atlantic. So much was at stake in the wake of those crucial convoys.

Because of the increase in American Lease-Lend supplies, it follows that the Japanese conquest indirectly augmented the food ration of the British public during the later years of the war. Nevertheless, at the same time, the North Atlantic convoys became more and more dependent upon the construction of new merchantmen and the repair of damaged vessels. Without them it is doubtful whether the increase in food supplies would have been possible. In 1944, food shipments across the Atlantic represented about 10 per cent of all British requirements, the most typical commodities being canned meat and fish, bacon, cheese, dried egg (in the absence of shell eggs), and condensed and dried milk.

It is to the replacement ships that we now turn, for, with the forthcoming combined operations in the Mediterranean and at Normandy (1943 and 1944), a great deal depended upon them.

8 The Replacement Ships

As in the First World War, it soon became necessary to replace losses of merchantmen by new building. From the early months of 1941 there was much activity in the traditional shipyards of Britain, those of the north-east coast of England, the Mersey on the west coast, the Scottish yards of the river Clyde and at the head of Belfast Loch in Northern Ireland. The building of ships had been the chief industry of these estuaries and rivers since the days of sail.

To those involved in convoy battles, who had seen merchantmen blasted from the seas, it was obvious that replacement ships were essential if Britain was to become victorious in a war which spanned the world. Why was it that the Luftwaffe did not annihilate such hives of maritime industry? How misguided they were to believe that the bombing of London and the cathedral cities would bring Britain to the peace table. Whilst there were air-raids on the shipbuilding and shiprepairing rivers they were, in the main, of the hit-and-run type and the damage caused was small.

Some have led us to believe that it was the North American shipyards that saved the day. Whilst this was true to a certain extent, it is also true that without the yards of the United Kingdom the Allies would have fallen far short of requirements, particularly those shipping requirements for the invasion of the Normandy beaches and of northern Europe.

The so-called 'Liberty' ships, a name taken up by the Henry Kaiser organization on the west coast of the United States, were in fact brought about by the design staff of the Joseph L. Thompson shipyard of North Sands, Sunderland, on the banks of the river Wear. Here, as early as 1935, was constructed the standardized wartime cargo vessel. The prototype *Embassage* became the design on which the wartime merchantmen were to be built. Built to the order of Hall Brothers of Newcastle upon Tyne, she was a 4,954-ton coal-burner with a raked stem and a rounded stern, powered by three North East Marine triple-expansion engines. Twenty-four other standard ships were built during the period 1935–39.

The first of the British 'Libertys', based upon the *Embassage* and

178

commissioned by the British Government, was the *Empire Liberty*, which sailed early in 1941 under the management of R. Chapman and Company of Newcastle. It was fitting that she should set sail on her first voyage during that dreadful year of 1941, as at dawn on 27 August, some 200 miles west of Ireland, the *Embassage* (convoy OS4), destined for Pepel, Sierra Leone, in ballast to load iron ore for the steel-making plants of Britain, had been torpedoed and sunk by *U-557*.

Two torpedoes were fired by *U-557* at the ship ahead but missed their target, and one struck *Embassage* forward of the bridge; a westerly gale was blowing with a rough sea and heavy swell. Her master, Captain Kiddie, and thirty-eight of her crew were already dead as she ploughed under; the bosun and two seamen, the only survivors, jumped overboard to cling to an upturned boat. Convoy OS4 lost a total of five merchantmen, four of them to U-boat *557*.

In September 1940 Mr R. Cyril Thompson, joint managing director of Joseph L. Thompson headed a British shipbuilding mission to the United States at the request of the Admiralty. The object was to order sixty ships from American builders. Mr Harry Hunter of the North-Eastern Marine Engineering Company headed the engineering side of the mission. They took with them plans and designs of their own firm's standard ships and engines and it was from these that Henry Kaiser built ships and engines at such a record pace. They were constructed in new shipyards which Cyril Thompson himself helped to lay out.

Returning home after his first trip to North America Mr Thompson sailed in the *Western Prince*, which was torpedoed in mid Atlantic in rough weather (see Chapter 12). He spent nine hours at the oars in one of the lifeboats, with his precious documents, blueprints, and so on, beneath his seat, before he and his fellow passengers were rescued. For his success in this mission Cyril Thompson was awarded the CBE.

With the Lease-Lend Act, passed in March 1941, the dollar problem largely disappeared. There was then an urgent need to persuade the Americans to build ships as fast as possible to replace British losses. They were also requested to hand over merchantmen at once, for a building programme is slow to yield returns. Even the most optimistic forecasts did not assume that the rate of new Allied building would overtake the loss rate before the middle of 1942. President Roosevelt was to comment at this time: 'the blunt truth is that the present rate of Nazi sinkings of merchant ships is more than three times as high as the capacity of British shipyards to replace them; it is more than twice the combined British and American output of merchant ships to-day'.

During the month of April Sir Arthur Salter arrived in Washington as head of the British Merchant Shipping Mission in the United States to press Britain's claims for merchantmen. He was instructed to request for: large numbers of tankers; some fast troopships; enough cargo carriers to bring in some 7 million tons of imports a year; and, in addition, 100 cargo ships to be delivered at a rate of twenty a month.

Laid up in the rivers and backwaters of the New World was a large fleet of merchantmen. Owned by the US Government they had been built at the end of the First World War but had been completed too late to take part in that conflict. Along with other vessels which private owners had been forced to lay up due to the Neutrality Act, this fleet totalled some 400,000 tons, with a carrying capacity of 600,000 tons.

Of considerable help to the United Kingdom during the seven months after the passing of the Lease-Lend Act was the American and American-controlled dry-cargo merchantmen. These were allocated to carry Lease-Lend cargoes to both British ports and the Middle East. This allocation included some Norwegian flag vessels, the hire of which was paid by the United States in dollars. They were provided to carry cargoes on the outward voyage only, so they were not fully in the service of the British Government.

Early in the war (February 1940) some 178,000 tons of shipping had been purchased from the US Government by the British Ministry of Shipping; at the same time, additional American tonnage was purchased by other neutral governments. After France fell in June 1940 another large purchase was made by Britain, though many were in a deplorable condition. Half of the former US tonnage sailing under the British flag were lost during the war.

Owing to high dollar costs of the US repair yards, these merchantmen were brought to Britain for repair though this seriously aggravated the backlog of work in British ports and shipyards. By December 1940 this was as high as 2 million tons, or 13 per cent of the whole British merchant fleet. In February 1941 a total of 2,593 merchantmen were under repair, and 1,585 were immobilized altogether.

The repair situation remained a problem throughout the war, and the total from all causes never fell below 1,506 vessels (March 1944). The lowest number of totally immobilized vessels was 576 during July 1943. Only by calling upon the repair facilities offered by shipyards and drydocks in the United States was the situation eased. When the damaged tanker situation became desperate during 1942 it was repair yards in Galveston, Texas, Mobile, Alabama and Tampa, Florida that cleared the backlog of this specialized work. At the time it was a question of paying high costs in US dollars or else Air Force aircraft would grind to a halt on the runways.

The repair crisis was only mitigated by the 3 million deadweight tons of foreign shipping acquired from countries overrun by the enemy. In addition to those from Greece, Norway and Poland, they included 684 of French registry, 915 Dutch and eighty-seven Belgian; later, when

Yugoslavia was overrun by German forces, more vessels were acquired. The German and Italian shipping captured in port and on the high seas was a further plus.

With those merchantmen from enemy-occupied countries came their officers and crews, eager to carry on the struggle for the liberation of their countries. Some of these vessels were already chartered to the British; in this way their continued service was guaranteed. As soon as such ships abandoned their neutral status they were run under the aegis of the British Ministry of Shipping, later the Ministry of War Transport. Their remuneration was considerably less than they had earned hitherto, but, on the other hand, there were all the advantages of additional protection and the benefit of the British Government's scheme of war-risk insurance.

These additions to the Allied shipping strength in 1940 may have saved an otherwise disastrous situation, but it did not alter the new strategic advantages for attack, which the Germans had gained by the occupation of the European coastline from the North Cape of Norway to Franco's Spanish frontier; rather it increased the number of their targets. This is exemplified by the figures for Allied merchant ship losses during the ninety-two days of March, April and May 1941: by U-boats, 142 vessels; by aircraft, 179; by surface raiders, 44; and by mines, 33 vessels.

The chartering of merchantmen became an essential part of the replacement ship programme, involving as it did many neutral vessels. Even the chartered US tonnage was neutral, until that nation came into the war in December 1941. As we have seen in Chapter 7, troop transports were chartered from the United States in the autumn of 1941. This became necessary because of the decision to send a reinforcement of 40,000 men to the Middle East, in addition to the movement of 150,000 already in hand. Some 20,000 were, in fact, carried by convoy WS12A from Halifax. Additionally, during the period October 1941 to February 1942, nine fast US cargo merchantmen were placed on the Atlantic service. One of these was the *Almeria Lykes*, which was later chartered for Operation 'Pedestal', the relief of Malta in August 1942 – see Chapter 9.

With the Board of Trade organization as a nucleus, the Ministry of Shipping was established on the outbreak of war. In part, this department was responsible for controlling the chartering and employment of merchantmen in the best interests of the country. Under the requisitioning scheme the Government became the virtual owners of British ships, and left to the actual owners only the feeding, storing, upkeep and provision of officers and crews; as regards the latter, the shipowners had the assistance of the Shipping Federation. The owners also arranged the bunkering of vessels, although the Government paid for it. In return for the use of ships, the owners received an agreed monthly rate of hire, based on the total deadweight tonnage. They were in fact chartered at rates of freight that allowed the Ministry of Shipping a handsome profit.

So far as the Government as a whole was concerned the profits existed mainly on paper, as most of the transactions were, in effect, between one ministry and another. The Ministry of Shipping was acting on behalf of various purchasing bodies, be they the Ministry of Food, Ministry of Supply, the Timber Control or the British Iron and Steel Federation. One concession to the shipowners was that they retained the right to fix any outward cargoes. These 'fixtures', however, were always subject to direction from the Ministry.

Neutral-flag vessels, particularly those of Portuguese, Spanish, Swedish and Swiss registry, were able to obtain charters from the British Ministries of Food and Supply at rates of freight much in excess of those placed to the credit of British-flag merchantmen. In addition, many neutral vessels were taken up by the British Government on time-charter (that is, at a monthly rate of hire) at high rates. A similar scheme subsequently came into being for British shipowners, whereby a set management fee was received with no part of the individual vessels being involved.

No effort was more important in the whole field of war production than that of the British shipyards – and none was more creditable. One must remember, however, that the production in British yards was not only determined by those shipyards' resources but by the availability of imported raw materials – not only iron ore, but manganese, nickel, chrome and wolfram.

The output per man of the British shipyard worker at the time was the highest in the world, something which is often overlooked in the world of wartime statistics. Reckoned in man hours the building of a British ship was a quicker job than in the United States, and less expensive. Due to the world economic situation and to Britain's policy of disarmament during the 1930s many shipyards were closed. By mid-1942 twenty-three of those closed were again in commission and the industry re-equipped with an investment of £6 million. Whilst manning became a problem, many women were taken on to replace those men serving in the armed forces.

A remarkable performance was achieved by the Wear shipbuilders. Between September 1939 and the end of 1944 the total output from the nine yards (not including ship-repairing) was 249 merchant vessels. This total of 1,534,980 gross tons amounted to 27 per cent of the output of 1,240 merchant vessels (5,722,532 tons) from all UK shipyards. Sunderland shipyard led the way in the highest production per man hour.

The Tyne's contribution to this total output was 130 ships of 709,317 tons; the Tees', forty-nine of 269,330 tons; and Hartlepool's, seventy-eight of 369,387 tons: A number of tramp-like cargo carriers were given insulated space of 250,000 to 300,000 cubic feet, arranged in two or three holds and 'tween decks. This was an important innovation in view of the number of meat carriers and general refrigeration vessels sunk during the years 1940–42.

Orders for wartime merchantmen were placed by the Ministry of Shipping or Ministry of War Transport on behalf of the Government and the vessels would be managed by one of the many British shipping companies to make up for the vessels which they had lost. As from 1 May 1941 the Ministry of Transport, which incorporated the Ministry of Supply (Import Executive), was combined with the Ministry of Shipping to form the Ministry of War Transport.

Comments are often made about the speed of American shipyard mass-production during the war, chiefly in regard to the remarkable success of Henry Kaiser. But he had many advantages which were not available in war-torn Britain. Chief of these was that he started from scratch, with unlimited room for laying out spacious yards, and for handling, prefabricating and assembling parts. He had an ample supply of labour, one which could be quickly trained in the welding process. Steel and other supplies were easily obtainable. His shipyards were free of bombing and air-raid precautions. There was no blackout and, consequently, long hours could be worked. The free time of workers in the United States was not taken up with Home Guard and Civil Defence duties. In Britain, whilst undertaken cheerfully and in most cases enthusiastically, these jobs were to some extent a drain on the energy of men engaged upon such heavy and vital work. Repairing and converting merchantmen were also carried out on a tremendous scale in Britain; such work was not classified as shipbuilding.

The north-east coast shipyards, those in the Tyne, Wear, Teeside and Hartlepool, once dominated world shipbuilding. The area was typical of the UK shipbuilding facilities, which, after the long slump of the 1930s, were fortunately already in full swing when Germany broke the uneasy peace in September 1939. On the river Wear the shortage of labour, and also of steel, prevented the authorities adopting a policy of opening new shipyards or reopening those that had been closed; instead, production was concentrated on existing yards.

In three of the Wear shipyards, Bartram's, Crown's and Laing's, a new berth was constructed and, in fact, during 1942 J.L. Thompson's began laying out a shipyard for the newly established National Shipbuilding Corporation. The onus of opening and managing the new yard fell on Messrs Thompson, whose chairman, Major (later Sir) Norman Thompson, was a director of the Corporation. In August 1943 the first ship, the *Empire Trail*, was launched from the Wear yard.

The output of merchantmen was not spectacular by comparison with the peak years of peacetime construction. This was because so much was demanded by warship construction and by repairs to both naval and merchant vessels. The naval programme made considerable inroads on the production from berths that would otherwise have been filled with merchantmen.

A host of subsidiary industries and trades contributed to the success achieved – blacksmiths, anchor-makers, boat-builders, manufacturers of electrical equipment and winches, and ropemakers. In marine engineering the Wear companies were responsible for the supply of machinery to 30 per cent of the total tonnage built in the United Kingdom, mainly reciprocating engines and cylindrical boilers. During 1939–45 there was no major stoppage of any kind on the river Wear; the amount of time lost by any trade dispute was quite negligible.

William Doxford and Sons headed the list of Wear firms with an output of seventy-five merchantmen of more than 500,000 tons. They were engaged almost exclusively in building their own standard type of motor ship, such as the 425-foot-long and 7,359 ton *Empire Earl* and *Empire General* built in 1944, both of which served the 'Mulberry' harbour at Normandy.

Joseph L. Thompson had the second highest output on the river, and built forty-three merchant ships of nearly 300,000 tons. The figure would have been higher but for enemy bomb damage during two air raids in the spring of 1943. Ten of these vessels were 10,000-ton single-screw steamers of Thompson's own design, a development of the earlier standard *Embassage*. Examples were the *Empire Brutus* (damaged by a mine at Normandy); the CAM ship *Empire Wave* (convoy ON19), sunk by *U-562*; and the *Empire Sunrise* (convoy SC107), torpedoed and sunk by *U-402* and *U-84*.

The Thompson shipyard also built three standard fast cargo liners (of 12,000 tons), which had a speed of 15 knots and could accommodate thirty-six passengers. Thompson-built vessels at the Normandy landings included the *Empire Barrie* of 1942, the *Empire Duke* (1943) and the *Empire Pitt* (1944). Other Thompson vessels which served as CAM ships, both were sunk, were the *Empire Hudson* (convoy SC42) and *Empire Lawrence*, dive-bombed during the passage of PQ16 to northern Russia.

Oil tankers were the main product of the Deptford yard (Sunderland) of Sir James Laing and Sons. Their record year was 1942, when they launched eight vessels, seven of them tankers. They were also engaged in tanker repair work. It was to the north-east coast that in 1944 half of the Norwegian tanker *Vardefjell* was towed, after she had broken in two in the North Atlantic. At the Deptford yard workers built a new fore-end, which was then towed round to the Tyne where the two parts were joined together.

Among the various types of tankers under construction were fifteen of the large Norwegian-type 14,500-ton class, and five of the 'standard fast' type; these were of 12,000 tons with a speed of 15 knots. The other builders of tankers were Furness Shipbuilding at their Haverton on Tees yard and Harland and Wolff of Belfast. The latter launched thirty-four tankers during the war years; eleven of them were 'ocean' tankers of 12,000 tons, built to a pre-war 'Shell' design.

Other shipbuilders of the river Wear were S.P. Austin and Sons, William Pickersgill and Sons, Short Brothers and Bartram and Sons. The latter had been builders of fine trampships for many years; during my service I sailed aboard their *Nailsea Manor* of 1938 and *Nailsea Moor* built in 1937. On 24 May 1943 they were unfortunate to have the 6,766-ton *Empire Deed* damaged whilst still on the stocks during a hit-and-run air raid. The *Denewood*, lying in the fitting basin of J.L. Thompson, was damaged in the same raid.

Bartram's carried out specialized work on merchantmen to fit them for the Russian convoys. It was necessary to strengthen bows and fore-ends to withstand the ice packs in Arctic waters. Extra ballast tanks and heavy-lift derricks were often required to enable vessels to discharge tanks and heavy equipment at Murmansk. The jacket illustration shows *Empire Kinsman* of 6,640 tons, launched by Bartram's on 29 August 1942, complete with heavy-lift derricks and Admiralty Net Defence (booms housed owing to rough weather). On arrival at Murmansk, 6 March 1943, she was damaged by aircraft bombing.

Harland and Wolff of Belfast, one of the leaders in specialized shipbuilding, constructed six of the fast refrigerated ships, including the 12,688-ton *Empire Hope*, sunk in Operation 'Pedestal' in August 1942, and the *Empire Grace*, with accommodation for 112 passengers, launched on 25 August 1941. Managed by Shaw, Savill and Albion, she was a motorship of the *Waimarama* type, somewht simplified to meet wartime conditions.

A special mention should be made of the war effort of the Harland and Wolff organization, which was established in Belfast, on the Clyde, in Liverpool, London and Southampton. Not only were they engaged in shipbuilding and shiprepairing, but in the production of tanks, anti-aircraft guns, aircraft parts, gun-mountings and so on. In shipping, they constructed 132 fourth service merchantmen and 139 vessels for the senior service; these included corvettes, minesweepers, frigates and landing craft.

Three further special refrigerated merchantmen, including the twin-screw 9,228-ton *Empire Song*, were built by the Greenock Dockyard Company in the Clyde. This was indeed a river of many great shipbuilders, whose speciality throughout the war were 'Empire' vessels. They included Barclay Curle, C. Cornell, William Denny, William Hamilton and Lithgow's.

It was Barclay Curle and Company which in 1940–41 built the fast cargo liner (special) *Empire Trust*, renamed *Rembrandt* in 1942 when she was transferred to the Government of Netherlands. They also constructed the 15-knot *Empire Pride*, laid down as a cargo liner but converted on the stocks to a troop transport. Owned by the Ministry of War Transport, she was managed by the Bibby Line and saw service in Madagascar, North Africa, Sicily and the southern France landings. She had accommodation for 1,600 troops. Merchantmen which could cruise at 15 knots had the advantage of being able to sail independently without escort. Both *Rembrandt* and *Empire Pride* survived the war.

The Reardon Smith Line of Cardiff was a typical British tramp shipping company of the 1930s. Entering the war with a fleet of twenty-four vessels, they then lost, through enemy action, a total of thirty-three owned or managed by them. It was a horrific situation experienced by the many operators of this type of cargo ship. During 1940 Reardon Smith took over the management of nine former US vessels, plus a further five from a defeated France. The laid-up American vessels, six of which had been sunk, were all built during the years 1918–19:

Eastern Glade (renamed *Empire Jaguar*). Sunk by *U-103*; 9.12.1940 (master and entire crew lost).
Freeport Sulphur No 5 (renamed *Empire Toucan*). Sunk by *U-47*; 29.6.1940.
Texas Trader (renamed *Empire Kestrel*). Sunk by German aircraft; 16.8.1943.
Defacto (renamed *Empire Caribou*). Sunk by *U-556*; 10.5.1941. (Entire crew of 28 lost.)
Kisnop (renamed *Empire Dabchick*). Sunk by *U-183*; 3.12.1942. (Master and entire crew of 36, plus 11 gunners, lost.)
West Amargosa (renamed *Empire Crossbill*). Sunk by *U-82*; 11.9.1941. (Master and entire crew of 37, plus 10 gunners and 1 passenger, lost.)

The Reardon Smith British-built replacement ships came from a variety of shipyards. As with all new 'Empire' construction they were built to the order of the Ministry of War Transport, which remained their owners. Licences could, however, be issued to firms to construct ships for private owners (built to specifications of wartime requirements). Reardon Smith's the *Madras City* (1940), *Atlantic City* (1941) and *Vancouver City* (1942) were in this category.

'Empire' ships:

Empire Sunbeam (1941) Builders: William Gray and Company, West Hartlepool 1942 – management transferred to Sir R. Ropner and Company.

Empire Rennie (1941) Builders: C. Connell and Company, Glasgow. 1942 – transferred to Netherlands Government and renamed *Frans Hals*; as such she was attacked by the Italian submarine *Da Vinci* on 3 November 1942 in the South Atlantic. Her master reported five torpedoes, all of which were near misses.

Empire Rhodes (1941) Builders: Caledon Shipbuilding and Engineering Company, Dundee. Served the Normandy Mulberry harbour, 6–9 June 1944.

Empire Cheer (1943) Builders: William Doxford & Sons, Sunderland.

Empire Baxter (1943) Builders: Vickers Armstrong, Barrow.

Empire Rangoon (1944) Builders: Harland and Wolff, Belfast.

Convoy rescue ships, which I have briefly mentioned, were specially equipped for their job and considerable work was entailed in converting them; many were passenger-carrying merchantmen with a speed of 12 knots. In all there were twenty-nine such vessels requisitioned from shipowners by the Admiralty. They covered 2¼ million miles on 796 voyages, and saved the lives of some 4,200 British and Allied seamen. All eleven vessels of the 1939 fleet of the Clyde Shipping Company were requisitioned: they included *Beachy*, *Copeland*, *Goodwin*, *Rathlin* and *Toward*. Six vessels of the General Steam Navigation Company were taken up, including the managed *Zamalek* and *Zaafaran* of the Egyptian Pharoanic Mail Line.

The design and construction of merchantmen and other special craft for the invasion for northern Europe, the climax to the Allied campaign, was initiated at an early date. The British-built contribution consisted mainly of the tanker and coaster classes, as well as various types of tugs. The tanker *Empire Russell* of 3,738 tons, managed by the Bulk Oil-Steamship Company and built in early 1944 by Sir J. Laing and Sons, was one of ten such tankers built by Laing's and Thompson's of Sunderland. They were designed for quick access to French ports.

The *Empire Pym*, intermediate type tanker class, of 2,370 tons (with a draft of only eighteen feet); the *Empire Cadet*, coastal tanker class, of 797 tons; and the Chant class (an abbreviation of channel tanker), of 400 tons – all were important merchantmen types during the invasion and serviced the ports of northern France, Belgium and Holland during the period June 1944 to May 1945.

The first three of the intermediate 2,370-ton tankers, *Empire Pym*, *Empire Jewel* and *Empire Jumna*, were built by Grangemouth Dockyard Company; the fourth, *Empire Rosebery*, by Blythswood Shipbuilding of Glasgow. The *Empire Cadet* and eleven of her class were also constructed by the Grangemouth company, and a further nine were launched from the yard of A. & J. Inglis of Glasgow.

Forty-three of the Chant class of coastal tankers were built during 1944: sixteen of these by Furness Shipbuilding of Haverton Hill on Tees; twelve by H. Scarr of Hessle; nine by Goole Shipbuilding and Repairing Company; four by Burntisland Shipbuilding and two by J. Readhead and Sons of South Shields.

Orders for coasters from the Ministry of War Transport, most of them in use in northern Europe between 1944–45, totalled some 170 vessels of around 100,000 deadweight tons; seventy dry cargo coasters of 60,000 deadweight tons, were constructed to private account. Built for a variety of work, the vessels' construction took place in many of the smaller shipyards – Blyth Shipbuilding and Drydock, G. Brown of Greenock, Cleland's of Willington, Cochrane and Sons of Selby and Gemmell's of Beverley; Crown's of Sunderland, Ferguson Brothers of Glasgow, Goole Shipbuilding, A. Hall and Company of Aberdeen, Hall Russell and Company, Aberdeen; H. Scarr of Hessle, Scott and Sons of Bowling and J.S. Watson of Gainsborough.

The Rescue type was the largest tug built during the war. These were under Admiralty control and did not bear 'Empire' names; in other words, they were of Bustler, Envoy or Assurance class. It was the Deep Sea, Coastwise and Estuary types which bore the 'Empire' prefix and flew the red ensign. Fourteen of the Deep Sea class (135 feet long) were built by Goole Shipbuilding and Cleland's of Willington.

The former French merchantman *Gazcon*, upon which I served – see Chapter 7 – was in a different category to those managed by the Reardon Smith company; they were taken over in British ports in June 1940 at the fall of France. During the twelve months which followed, *Gazcon* had been operated by the Vichy French east of Cape Town. She was under the command of Vichy French Captain Briot, with a rabid Nazi as her chief mate. Only seven of her crew were anti-Vichy.

The 4,224-ton vessel, built in 1932 for Cie de Nav d'Orbigny of La Rochelle, by the Clyde shipbuilders of H. Stephens and Sons, sailed from Tamatave, Madagascar, on 19 May 1941 bound for Dakar. She was carrying a valuable cargo of chromium and timber which combined with the ship was worth £406,000. Because of bad weather she lay trapped in Lobito harbour in mid June, short of coal bunkers; the Portuguese were reluctant to assist.

The *Gazcon* gained fame after the war when it was revealed that her capture was the single-handed work of Major Len Maderstam, a Russian by birth who hailed from Riga in Latvia. Recruited as a spy by the Special Operations Executive (SOE) in 1939 he first headed the Russian Section and then the newly formed Angola Section. Working from Luanda he was involved in clandestine missions to blow up

German supply stores and sabotage U-boat fuel which was delivered offshore to visiting submarines at Ambrizète.

Having reported the presence of the French-flag *Gazcon* to his superiors in London, Mandestam received orders to seek out General de Gaulle, who happened to be visiting Brazzaville in the French Congo. There he obtained permission to recruit and arm the seven anti-Vichy seamen as members of the Free French forces. Back in Lobito he then persuaded the Portuguese authorities to allow the *Gazcon* 600 tons of bunkers, gave Captain Briot a cheque on an American bank for $40,000 (£10,000), as a bribe, and armed the seven seamen.

On 30 August 1941 the *Gazcon*, still flying her French flag, sailed for a secret rendezvous with HMS *Albatross*, a repair ship and seaplane carrier based at Freetown. With the Nazi mate knocked out and thrown overboard, the rendezvous was kept as arranged with the Admiralty in London. The crew of the *Albatross* received £50,000 in prize money for boarding and taking the ship though, Manderstam received not a penny. After the war, however, he was awarded the MBE (Military Division), 'in recognition of gallant and distinguished services in the field'. The recommendation added 'throughout the whole of the planning (of the capture of the steamship *Gazcon*) Major Manderstam exercised great skill, judgement, tact and balance of mind, with the result that the operation was completely successful'.

The *Gazcon* was just one of the 502 enemy vessels seized or confiscated between September 1939 and May 1945 when Germany was overrun; much Italian shipping was also seized or scuttled in the Mediterranean and East African campaigns. Many vessels were captured on the high seas by the senior service, though some were scuttled by their crews. All came under the jurisdiction of the Ministry of War Transport and, in most cases, they were renamed and given the prefix 'Empire'. The whole operation, particularly that involving the '*Gazcon* affair', illustrates just how valuable were these merchantmen and their cargoes.

Many of those captured were old and had seen better days. There were many instances of breakdowns because of trouble to their engines, and many became convoy stragglers. Those lost to enemy action during hostilities included the following:

Uhenfels (German), renamed *Empire Ability*. 16.10.39: Sailed from Lourenço Marques, disguised as a Dutch ship in an attempt to break the British blockade and reach Germany. 4.11.39: Sighted by aircraft from HMS *Ark Royal*; captured by HMS *Hereward* off Freetown. The first (former) German vessel to arrive in the river Thames since the outbreak of war, though still wearing 'Dutch' colours. 23.10.40: Damaged by aircraft bombs, Gareloch, Scotland. 27.2.41: Convoy

OB290. Attacked by Italian submarine *Bianchi*, but torpedo missed. 27.6.41: convoy SL76. Sunk from Mauritius to Freetown by *U-69*; cargo: sugar and rum.

Teodo (Italian), renamed *Empire Airman*. 9.6.40: Sailed from Newcastle but next day taken at sea in prize, following Italy's declaration of war, and escorted to Methil. 22.9.40: Sunk by *U-100* in North Atlantic (convoy HX72).

Alster (German), renamed *Empire Endurance*. One of a series of cargo liners built for Norddeutscher Lloyd during 1927–28. Captured 10.4.40 off Vestfjord by HMS *Icarus*. 20.4.41: Sunk by *U-73* in North Atlantic, outward-bound independently for Middle East.

Gabbiano (Italian), renamed *Empire Energy*. Taken in prize in Liveprool. 10.6.40: Convoy SC52, from New York to Belfast, with maize. 5.11.41: wrecked in fog, Belle Isle Strait, Nova Scotia. Broadside to beach, resting on rocky ledge at Big Brook, 11 miles west of Cape Norman. Total loss – not on this occasion to the enemy, but to the treacherous fogs of Newfoundland.

Sturmfels (German), renamed *Empire Kumari*, 25.8.41: One of five German and two Italian merchantmen captured at Bandar Shapur, Iran. Salved by the Royal Navy, she was taken in prize. 26.8.42: Damaged by torpedo (*U-375*) north of Port Said. Towed to Haifa Bay and beached, subsequently becoming a total loss. (The landing at Bandar Shapur by British and Empire forces was to forestall enemy plans to capture the oilfields of the Persian Gulf and possible advance towards India. Abadan and its refinery together with the naval base at Khorramshahr were also taken in the assault.)

Pomona (German), renamed *Empire Merchant*. 3.9.39: Taken in prize in London docks. 16.8.40: Sunk in the North Atlantic, the first vessel to be sunk by *U-100*, one of the new class-VIIA boats.

Mugnone (Italian), renamed *Empire Progress*. 10.6.40: Taken in prize at Newcastle. 22.5.41: Bombed and gunned by German aircraft off the Needles, Isle of Wight. 13.4.42: Sunk in the North Atlantic of *U-402*.

Cellina (Italian), renamed *Empire Sailor*. 10.6.40: Taken in prize at Gibraltar. 21.11.42: Sunk by *U-518*, when with convoy ON145, with a cargo said to be phosgene and mustard gas.

Sistiana (Italian), renamed *Empire Union*. 10.6.40: Taken in prize in

Table Bay by South African Navy. 27.12.42: Sunk by *U-356*, when with outwards convoy ONS154.

Procida (Italian), renamed *Empire Volunteer*. 10.6.40: Taken in prize at Cardiff. 15.9.40: Sunk by *U-48*, convoy SC3. Loaded with iron ore, she was on passage from Wabana, Newfoundland, for Glasgow.

Homeward bound from Pernambuco and flying the Swedish flag, the 14,106-ton German *Cap Norte* was captured by HMS *Belfast* on October 1939 north-west of the Faroe Islands; she had already disembarked her passengers in Lisbon. The captain surrendered his ship in extremely rough weather. Renamed *Empire Trooper*, she carried many thousands of the armed services, and survived the war. Her sister ship *Antonia Delfino* was at Bahia, Brazil, in September 1939 and later reached Germany unharmed. She too survived the war but was taken in prize at Copenhagen upon the declaration of peace in May 1945, and renamed *Empire Halladale*.

In June 1942 British-controlled dry-cargo ocean shipping comprised some 62 per cent of world tonnage. In the second half of 1942, 72 per cent of shipping losses were of British registry. Such a rate of loss, given repairs and naval construction, was far beyond the resources of British shipbuilding. As Churchill said in 1943, 'the foundation of all our hopes was the immense shipbuilding programme of the United States'.

It was fortunate that the efforts made by the British Government in spring 1941 to encourage the US administration to build merchantmen had, by the autumn of that year, produced the first of the Liberty ships. On 27 September 1941 the *Patrick Henry* (No.2001), 10,500 tons deadweight, was launched at the Bethlehem–Fairfield shipyard in Baltimore. Three months later she was delivered to her managers.

Of simple and sturdy design the vessels measured 441 feet in length with a beam of 57 feet. With two decks, five holds, coal-fired boilers and powered by reciprocating steam engines of 2,500 horsepower, they were able to cruise at 11 knots. It was Henry J. Kaiser who revolutionized the construction of merchantmen. It was his idea to weld prefabricated parts instead of riveting, for speed of assembly was vital. A total of 2,710 were launched, of which more than 200 were sunk. Sixty-two were fitted out as tankers, twenty-four as colliers and thirty-six as aircraft transporters.

Production averaged forty-two days per ship. A record was set when the *Robert E. Peary* was completed, from laying the keel to delivery, in only eight days. The ship was built by the Permanente Metals Corporation, Todd-California (a Kaiser company), at Richmond California, where the average time for delivery was seventeen days. On 12 November 1942, the *Robert E. Peary* (vessel No.440) was launched, only four days 15½ hours after her keel was laid. She spent another three days fitting out before putting to sea.

Merchantmen whose names bore the prefix 'Sam' (after 'Uncle Sam') were American-built Liberty vessels, turned over to the British Ministry of War Transport on 'bare-boat charter'. Under the agreement made at the second Washington Conference in May 1943, 182 merchantmen of this type came to Britain. Those vessels bearing the 'Ocean' prefix were less standardized than the Sams and Empires; sixty of this type came to Britain to be managed by British shipowners.

Two new shipyards were constructed by the Kaiser organization to build the Ocean-type vessels: one near Richmond, California, that seven months before had been a mudflat; the other on the east coast of the United States at Portland, Maine. All were delivered in 1941–42 and added 633,000 tons deadweight capacity to the British merchant fleet.

The *Ocean Venture* (7,174 tons), the first of her type, was launched at the Californian yard in November 1941. At the christening ceremony Sir Arthur Salter called the event a portent of victory, and 'a decisive factor in the contest at sea – the entry into it of America as a great shipbuilder. Sadly *Ocean Venture* was not to survive 'the storms of war' for long. On 8 February 1942 she was torpedoed and sunk by *U-108* off the east coast of the United States.

With the seaborne landings in North Africa and in Europe already at the planning stage many of the American Liberty vessels were armed forward of the bridge. The US Government turned a blind eye to the discredited Geneva Convention and took a more aggressive view than the British War Cabinet. For the first in the history of battles at sea a pair of 3-inch dual purpose guns was mounted on the fo'c's'le head of merchantmen.

This additional armament was soon to include some of the Fort and Park vessels built in Canada and also many of the British-built Empires destined for work in northern Russian waters and in the Mediterranean. Examples of bow armament were to be seen on the *Fort la Have* and *Fort Boise*; on the *Empire Pride*, *Empire Tourist*, *Empire Wisdom* and *Empire Industry*; on the US-built *Ocean Messenger*; and aboard the *Behar*, *Harlesden* and *Trevider*, built for private account. The 7,840-ton *Behar*, built for Hain Steamships (a P & O company) by Barclay Curle of Glasgow, was less than eight months later blasted from the sea by the Japanese cruiser *Tone* – see Chapter 7. Most of the assault ships in Operations 'Torch' and 'Husky', the landings in North Africa and Sicily, carried bow armament.

A total of 354 Fort-type standard merchantmen were delivered from Canadian shipyards. Under the terms of the Hyde Park Agreement of April 1941, eighty-nine (later ninety) of these, designated the North Sands type, were purchased by the United States and then transferred to Britain on bare-boat charter. They were all delivered between

HMS *Snowflake* in heavy weather, North Atlantic. She also saw service with the Russian convoys

The 7,262 ton *Clan Chattan* on fire after being bombed in the Mediterranean, 14 February 1942. Photograph taken from the deck of HMS *Beaufort* which was on hand, together with the anti-aircraft cruiser HMS *Carlisle* to rescue survivors. *Clan Chattan* was carrying 200 Army personnel in addition to her crew

Operation 'Harpoon'. Convoy WS 192 of five merchantmen and the US flag tanker *Kentucky*. This general view of the convoy under air attack shows the *Kentucky* on the right.

Breconshire at Grand Harbour (Malta) after her arrival from Alexandria on 19 December 1941. Under construction for the Alfred Holt company at the outbreak of war, she was probably the hardest working unit of the British merchant fleet in the Mediterranean. Flying the white ensign she was bombed and lost off the south coast of Malta four months after this photograph was taken

Shaw Savill's 12,843 ton *Waimarama* explodes after being bombed by enemy aircraft, 13 August 1942, Operation 'Pedestal'. Only twenty of her crew of 107 survived

The 9,514 ton tanker *Ohio* (Operation 'Pedestal') is seen entering Grand Harbour, Malta, with the destroyer *Penn* on her starboard side and *Ledbury* on her port side. It was this superb feat of seamanship that enabled 11,000 tons of petrol, so desperately needed by the aircraft flying from Malta, to be piped ashore

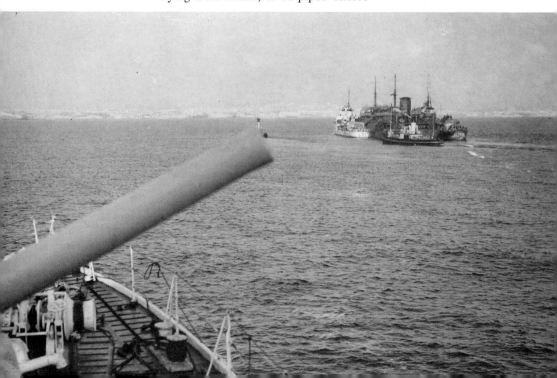

The motor vessel *Melbourne Star* of 12,806 tons enters Grand
Harbour, Malta, Operation 'Pedestal'. She was one of only
five vessels out of fourteen to survive the combined onslaught
of the enemy. *Melbourne Star* was torpedoed by U-129 and
lost in the North Atlantic, 2 April 1943

Survivors from sunken merchantmen of Operation Pedestal are seen
disembarking from the destroyer HMS *Ledbury* at Malta

The Siege Bell overlooking Grand Harbour at Malta. It was unveiled
by HM Queen Elizabeth II, 29 May 1992

The steamer *Baron Elgin* at Funchal, Madeira, October 1942. She had
brought survivors from torpedoed merchantmen of convoy SL 125
which she had rescued at great peril to herself

The Operation Torch invasion convoy. This photograph of KMF1 of twenty 'troopers' represents only a small part of what was at the time, the greatest armada in history – 352 merchantmen and 169 escort vessels. Those seen here include HMS *Sheffield* (far right), the Polish liner *Batory*, the New Zealand steamer *Awatea*, the HQ ship *Bulolo*; *Glengyle*, *Karanja*, *Keren*, *Otranto*, *Strathnaver* and *Viceroy of India*

Duchess of Richmond. Operation Torch, seen at Algiers disembarking troops and baggage, 14 November 1942. A sister ship to the *Duchess of Atholl*, she survived the war

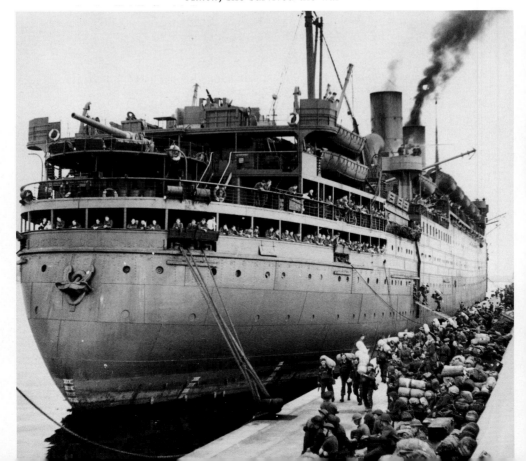

Seen here is Bibby Line's *Staffordshire*. She took part in Operation Torch, Husky and Dragoon. In the foreground an exercise is taking place involving the rescue ship *Gothland* which from February 1942 escorted forty convoys and saved 149 lives

A Sherman tank and infantry seen shortly after the Salerno landing, Operation Avalanche, 9 September 1943. Smoke from the burning US flag Liberty ship *Bushrod Washington*, struck by one of the new glider bombs, can be seen in the background

The hospital ship *Abba* of 7,937 tons. She saw service in Greece, Crete, Libya and during the 'Torch', 'Husky' and 'Shingle' Operations

The Normandy invasion fleet 6 June 1944. The greatest amphibious operation in history. In all some 287,000 men and a host of fighting vehicles had to be loaded into a variety of Royal and Merchant Navy vessels, gliders and transport planes

February 1942 and March 1943 and could be seen in great numbers in the Mediterranean during 1943 and at the Normandy beach-heads. In both theatres of war they achieved an immense amount of work.

A memorable part of my war experience was to travel to Vancouver per Royal Mail's flagship *Andes* to Halifax and thence by intercontinental train to join the steamship *Fort Fitzgerald* and thirteen months later to Baltimore, sailing in Cunard White Star's *Queen Mary* to New York to help crew the Liberty ship *Samnethy*. Both these merchantmen were managed by my employer, the Evans and Reid Group of Cardiff.

On 9 March 1943 we took delivery of the *Fort Fitzgerald*, built by West Coast Shipbuilders of Vancouver. Alas! less than seven months later this well-constructed steamer, the last but one of the ninety North Sands type transferred to Britain, was sunk by the enemy – see Chapter 10. In total thirty-one of the Fort merchantmen transferred to Britain were lost by enemy action.

West Coast Shipbuilders were, on average, launching a new ship every sixteen days, a record in the Canadian shipbuilding industry. Many were small shipyards expanded with the assistance of the Canadian Government. To avoid delay in the delivery of vessels, British crews were dispatched in good time, and ship's articles were signed at the home port before departure from the United Kingdom. A pool of crews was kept ready at Montreal and, in the case of the west coast launchings, they were sent to Vancouver some six weeks in advance of the delivery date. So to kill time and earn Canadian dollars to boot, many officers and men donned overalls and worked in the shipyards. Labour was short and many women had been recruited.

Prior to the *Fort Fitzgerald*, West Coast Shipbuilders had launched the *Fort Stager* and the *Fort Rampart*, the latter at the beginning of February, part loaded with lumber as was the custom. Topping up with aircraft engines or machine parts and foodstuffs at such ports as Seattle, Tacomo, San Francisco and Los Angeles, most home-bound Fort vessels loaded tarpaulin-covered balsa wood on deck at either Balboa or Colon during transit of the Panama Canal. This lightweight wood was much used in the aircraft industry at the time.

Sailing from New York with convoy HX233 on the last leg of her voyage, the *Fort Rampart* was particularly unlucky, for, with the Atlantic Victory in sight, she was the only vessel from this convoy to be sunk. Sighted by *U-628* south west of Cape Clear, Southern Ireland, she was torpedoed; holding up well, however, there was hope of her making port and she drifted astern. Four hours later, straggling some miles astern of the convoy, she was given the *coup de grâce* from *U-628* and also *U-226*. Less than three months from her builder's yard the *Fort Rampart* had gone to her watery grave.

Another Vancouver-built vessel torpedoed and sunk on her maiden voyage was the 7,127-ton *Fort Qu'Appelle*, which had loaded a full general cargo in Vancouver and nearby New Westminster and sailed on 3 April 1942. Many of her crew, including her captain, were survivors from the 8,800-ton *Bencleuch* who had been landed at Halifax, Nova Scotia. This merchantman caught fire in convoy whilst carrying a cargo Government stores, including ammunition and explosives, loaded at Leith and destined for the Far East via the Panama Canal. Abandoning his ship in mid Atlantic the master, Captain Murray, believed that only an act of sabotage could have caused the disaster.

The *Fort Qu'Appelle* was lost on the night of 16/17 May 1942 as a torpedo from *U-135* ripped the engine-room apart and destroyed both starboard lifeboats. Abandoning ship at daylight some 300 miles south of Halifax (where she was to have joined an HX homeward convoy) a second tragedy occurred as the port lifeboats were being lowered. A second torpedo exploded directly beneath the forward boat in which were Captain Murray and twelve officers and men: all lost their lives. Sighted by an aircraft two days later the remainder of the crew were rescued by HMCS *Melville*.

As we discovered when we boarded the SS *Fort Fitzgerald* the general armament of fourth service vessels had been greatly improved. In addition to the 4-inch stern gun we were equipped with five Oerlikons, two 'pig troughs', one pillar box, two FAM rockets and four PAC rockets. A balloon was also carried for inflation in case of air attack. In addition to a crew of forty-six, there were six naval and four army gunners.

At Baltimore the merchantman *Samnethy* (No.2332) was accepted on behalf of the Evans and Reid Company during March 1944 at the Bethlehem-Fairfield shipyard. Here were thirteen spacious slipways, three having been added at the end of 1942. It was at the same Bethlehem-Fairfield yard that the first Liberty ship, *Patrick Henry* (No.2001) was launched, and during the month of March 1944 the US shipyards were at the peak of production. Ten other ships were delivered by Bethlehem-Fairfield at this time, seven of them to British managers. They were *Samgaudie* (No.2328), *Samaffric* (2330), *Samconnon* (2331), *Sameden* (2334), *Samcolne* (2336), *Samlea* (2337) and *Samshee* (2338).

The Reardon Smith company took over three 'Sam' vessels at the Bethlehem-Fairfield yard in 1944. They were the *Samhope*, *Samlamu* and *Samwinged*. Five other North American built vessels were to join their fleet:

Ocean Pride 1942. Todd-Bath Iron Shipbuilding Corporation, Portland, Maine.
Fort Fork 1942. Burrard Drydock Company, Vancouver.

Fort Mumford 1942. Prince Rupert Drydock and Shipyard Company, Prince Rupert, British Columbia – sunk east of Cape Town (see Chapter 7).

Fort Carlton 1943. Burrard Drydock Company, Vancouver.

Fort Norfolk 1943. United Shipyards. Montreal – lost at Normandy (see Chapter 11).

Apart from the Fort, Ocean and Sam losses, 182 of the Empire vessels were lost through enemy action. The first of these was the *Empire Commerce* on 9 June 1940, off the North Foreland in the Straits of Dover, which fell prey to a warship mine; and the last, the *Empire Gold*, on 18 April 1945, a loaded 8,028-ton tanker with convoy HX348 in the South-West Approaches, which was sunk by *U-1107*. She was on passage from Philadelphia for Antwerp. The *Empire Commerce* was the former German *Christoph von Doornum* taken in prize on 4 September 1939 by the Canadian authorities at Botwood, Newfoundland, whilst loading concentrates.

Losses of the 'replacement ships' were horrendous: in 1942, for instance, seventy-seven Empires alone were sunk. However, every completed voyage – whether homewards with food, with raw materials and war cargoes, or outwards carrying consignments worldwide for the armed services – was one more step towards victory.

Even though victory in the Atlantic was assured, many more tragedies were to happen at sea. The summer of 1943, however, saw 'replacements' more than make up for the losses. The curve of new tonnage rose sharply and losses fell. Before the end of that year new tonnage at last surpassed losses at sea from all causes. During the second quarter, for the first time, U-boat losses exceeded their rate of replacement. The turnaround during 1943 was quite remarkable, particularly in view of the desperate situation during Operation 'Torch' and the early spring of 1943 when, as I shall reveal in Chapter 10, the shortage of shipping became serious.

What would have been the outcome had there been no new British and North American building on such a vast scale? Such was the situation during 1941 and 1942 that no Royal Navy vessels could be withdrawn from either the Mediterranean or eastern waters owing to the enemy onslaught. There were those who said that smaller Atlantic convoys (due to a shortage of merchantmen) would be better protected and losses would reduce as a result. There was in fact a time, during the summer of 1941, when convoys were reduced in size and sailings made more frequently; but because this happened at a time when the number of operational U-boats was increasing, little advantage was gained.

The important fact, sensed by both Churchill and Roosevelt, was that as the scale of warfare grew to encompass the world, so the countries involved would increase. And, as seaborne landings were projected to regain territories lost, so the heavy workload on the Allied merchant fleet would grow. By August 1945 as many as fifty-six nations were involved, and the death toll had risen to 57 million.

9   Combined Operations

Essential to the operations on the battlefield were the troopships, those red-ensign merchantmen which, because of their size and speed, and their passenger accommodation, were classed as transports. From the early days, in Norway and in France, they had shown that no army in the field, no airforce stations or naval establishments, nor the many auxiliary services upon which the armed forced depended, could operate without the troopship, either for invasion, occupation or evacuation. How could the Allies have crushed the enemy in so many theatres of war without the world's largest, fastest and finest fleet of passenger liners?

Few people reading of the exploits of British and Allied Forces in the many scatterd parts of the world during the Second World War have given thought to the long voyages, through enemy-infested and storm-tossed seas, undertaken to those various fields of operation. Warfare today has shown how dependent we are on trooper aircraft; during 1939-45 there was no long-range aircraft capable of moving such quantities of men and equipment.

The organization covering the movements of troopships, was by no means an easy task for armies had to be complete in every detail often necessitating the employment of cargo transports carrying a vast array of vehicles and equipment. The planning had to be carried out with the utmost secrecy and for the service personnel there were long and tedious days of waiting with many unknown trials ahead. The men whose important job was to look after the troops were the Officer Commanding troops, often an Army lieutenanet colonel of middle age with service during the First World War, as well as his staff, the master of the ship, his officers and crew.

It was by no means easy for those in command of such transports, nor the leaders of those carried, to get such fighting forces safely landed at journey's end. Nor was it any mean feat to make the travelling itself not only bearable and disciplined but even agreeable – an interval between training and battle to be remembered with pleasure; it was, above all, a time when morale must be kept high (see Appendix XIX).

In January 1942 all troopships, in Royal Naval parlance HM transports, were instructed to carry 30 per cent more troops than hitherto. Staff reporting for duty were given a personal memo from Winston Churchill: 'voyages on transports must be regarded as operations of war with all their attendant hardships'.

Apart from the passenger vessels of Belgium, France, Holland, New Zealand and Poland that were available, the force comprised some ninety British transports. These were mainly drawn from the famous fleets operated by such companies as the Anchor Line, Bibby Line, Blue-Star Line, British India Steam Navigation, Canadian Pacific, Cunard White Star, Donaldson Atlantic Line, Elder Dempster, Ellerman's City Line, Lamport and Holt, Orient Line, Pacific Steam Navigation, Peninsular and Oriental, Royal Mail Lines, Shaw, Savill and Albion and Union Castle Steamships.

In 1939 only nine transports were on charter to the Government: these were the *Neuralia*, built in 1912, *Nevasa* of 1913; *Lancashire* (1917); *Dorsetshire* and *Somersetshire* (1927); *Dilwara* (1935); *Dunera* (1937); *Devonshire* (1938), and *Ettrick* (1939). Soon to be converted for the carriage of troops were the *Queen Mary*, completed in 1936, and *Queen Elizabeth*, completed for Cunard White Star in February 1940. On 2 March that year the latter sailed from the river Clyde, bound ostensibly for Southampton, yet her voyage took her direct to New York. In November she left for drydocking at Singapore and afterwards proceeded to Australia.

During 1940, when the necessity for fast vessels capable of carrying large numbers of personnel over long distances became paramount, many ships from the fleets mentioned were requisitioned. Later came the former armed merchant cruisers, converted to passenger carrying ships, for which purpose they were built.

The first troop convoy TC1, carrying 7,400 men of the 1st Canadian Division, sailed from Halifax, Nova Scotia, in December 1939 in the transports *Andes, Aquitania, Empress of Australia, Empress of Britain, Duchess of Bedford* and *Monarch of Bermuda*. Crossing a stormy North Atlantic in thirteen days they arrived in the Clyde on Christmas Eve. The 'tail of the bank', the anchorage in the Clyde estuary, became the world's largest passenger port, an honour it held throughout the war.

Andes of 25,676 tons, launched at Harland & Wolff's Belfast shipyard six months prior to the declaration of war, was well suited as a troop transport. Designed to carry 606 passengers, she was fitted to carry 4,500 service personnel, and her fuel capacity gave her a wider range then any of her contemporaries. She undertook missions of great importance, voyaged many thousands of miles and twice circumnavigated the globe without accident or untoward incident of any kind.

En route from Australasia in January 1940 were the Commonwealth troops who were subsequently to be engaged in the bitter fighting in the Mediterranean theatre. Convoy US1, of twelve transports, arrived without incident in Suez on 12 February; *Empress of Canada, Orion, Rangitata and Strathaird* arrived from New Zealand; *Dunera, Empress of Japan, Orcades, Orford, Otranto* and *Strathnaver*, the Polish *Sobieski* and the French *Suffren* steamed across from Australia.

Convoy US2, sailing from Australia on 13 April for the Middle East, comprised the troopships *Dunera, Ettrick, Neuralia, Nevasa* and *Straithaird*. Two weeks later sailed US3, which comprised the *Queen Mary*, in company with *Andes, Aquitania* the three 'Empress' liners – *Empress of Britain, Empress of Canada* and *Empress of Japan* – and the *Mauritania*. They carried a total of 14,000 Australian and New Zealand troops for Cape Town and the Clyde. With the *Empress of Japan* left behind in South Africa, the convoy arrived without incident, dropping anchor at 'the tail of the bank' on 16 June.

Spring 1941 saw the first large movements of troops from the United Kingdom. With the Axis onslaught through North Africa bringing them virtually to the gates of Alexandria, and with the push through Greece and on to the island of Crete, the enemy threatened the whole of the Middle East. Over a three-month period, 134,320 personnel were carried in eighty-eight merchantmen of sixteen convoys to Suez via the Cape. The largest of these convoys, in fact the greatest troop convoy ever to sail from British shores, comprised twenty-three transports with a tonnage of 500,000. Some 132,000 of this tonnage were vessels of the P & O company, which at this time conveyed around 80,000 troops to Egypt.

Sailing from the Clyde on 24 March the twenty-three transports arrived in the Red Sea at the same time as convoy US10 from Sydney, Australia. In addition to *Queen Elizabeth* and *Queen Mary*, carrying 10,000 troops between them US10 included the Dutch *Nieuw Amsterdam*, the French *Ile de France* and *Mauritania*, carrying 4,000 New Zealanders. These three vessels disembarked their troops in Colombo and forthwith maintained the 'Suez Shuttle' – Bombay, Colombo, Durban and Port Tewfik at the southern end of the Suez Canal. So great was the congestion that when, on 3 May, *Queen Mary* arrived at the Port Tewfik anchorage to disembark, *Queen Elizabeth* lay off in the Red Sea awaiting her turn.

The most famous of the troop and supply convoys were those coded WS, whose letters are alleged to have stood for 'Winston's Specials' (though the great man himself was said not to have realized this until after the war). Started in June 1940 when the Mediterranean was closed to through traffic they sailed at roughly monthly intervals for the Middle East via the Cape of Good Hope. Only in June 1943 was the direct route to Egypt reopened.

Convoys WS5A and WS5B (December 1940) carried a total of 55,000 men and their equipment, 12,000 of whom were destined for

India and 43,000 for the Middle East. WS6, the following month, shipped over an estimated 34,000; WS12 in September 1941 some 33,000 (see Appendix V and VI). It so happened that I arrived in Freetown on 14 October that year when WS12 and OS7 (outwards Sierra Leone) arrived within twenty-four hours of each other. At the time I was a passenger aboard *City of Hong Kong*, having been transferred to the *City* boat by HMS *Violet* four days earlier after *Nailsea Manor* had been sunk. Never was the Sierra Leone river so congested. Never was there such a fine sight to illustrate a merchant fleet at war.

Convoy WS15, of twenty-two merchantmen, sailing in January 1942, carried 38,000 personnel; WS17 during March totalled thirty vessels with 59,000. From the outbreak of war up to July 1942 fourth service ships carried nearly one million men to the Middle East. Up to February 1943 the troopships had transported some three million military personnel all over the world with the loss of only 1,348 killed or drowned. It was a fine record of which masters, officers, seamen, and officers commanding troops could be justly proud.

The *Llangibby Castle* (12,053 tons), one of the Union Castle fleet, had perhaps the most adventurous wartime career of those vessels requisitioned as HM transports. During 1941 she was engaged on a number of uneventful voyages including voyages to New York and Halifax, Nova Scotia. In January 1942, with 1,500 troops aboard for embattled Singapore, the 1929 built twin-screw motorship was torpedoed in the Atlantic by *U-402*. Twenty-six were killed and four wounded in the incident. There then commenced a voyage of 3,400 miles without rudder or stern, even though a south-westerly gale was blowing and the seas were heavy.

Sailing without escort, steering by her engines and maintaining a speed of 9 knots, *Llangibby Castle* made Horta Bay in the Azores. She was forced to fight off an attack by a lone Focke-Wulf Condor during her three-day 700-mile ordeal. After emergency repairs she then limped to Gibraltar, passing *en route* HMS *Westcott*, which reported having just sunk *U-581* and taken forty-one prisoners. After fifty-seven days at Gibraltar, where dockyard workers patched her stern and made her seaworthy, she joined a slow convoy for the Clyde, still without her rudder.

The Union Castle mailboat was an active service in the Mediterranean throughout Operation 'Torch', where she engaged in much of the action. In the spring of 1943 she was converted to an 'assault transport', after which she was at the Sicilian landings and thereafter engaged in ferry work in the Mediterranean. She was at Normandy Beach on D-Day morning, and one of the first vessels to enter the port of Le Havre after it was freed. Finally she served South-east Asia Command as a troop transport. Not a large vessel compared with her passenger contemporaries, her service mileage was recorded at 300,265 and the number of troops and passengers carried, 152,191.

The Mediterranean war which commenced at Tobruk in January 1940 suddenly erupted with the coming of spring. In the last week of February the British Government decided to send troops to Greece, then being overrun by the enemy. Most were from General Wavell's desert army and were transported from Port Said and Alexandria. Operation 'Lustre' can be considered the start of the close association between the Royal and Merchant Navies in the Mediterranean. The work of the fighting ships and the merchantmen was closely interwoven.

Following the Italian invasion of Greece, British convoys ran regularly. In total 58,364 personnel and their equipment were transported, 11,000 being carried in cruisers of the senior service. As many as 17,125 were Australians and 16,720 were New-Zealanders. Convoy ANF24, in addition to battling against high winds and seas, was attacked by nine Junkers 88 bombers on 5 April. *Devis* was the first to be hit, and seven men were killed and fourteen injured. Later the 10,917-ton ammunition ship *Northern Prince* was set on fire, and a great pall of yellow smoke could be seen billowing aloft. Torn apart by the TNT and ammunition she was carrying, she disintegrated. Arriving at the port of Piraeus the merchantmen found much confusion and congestion. It was reported that 'every berth alongside every quay is occupied by ships off-loading'. In Phalerum Bay other vessels lay at anchor awaiting a berth.

The next day in Piraeus harbour the Dutch 11,636-ton *Slamat* lay at anchor with 500 troops on board, as did the 16,297-ton trooper *Cameronia*, *Cingalese Prince* with engine trouble, and *Devis* with a leaking hull sustained in the dive-bombing; there, too, were *City of Norwich*, *City of Roubaix*, the damaged *Clan Cumming* (from convoy MC4, Operation 'Excess' – see page 209) *Clan Fraser*, *Cyprian Prince*, *Goalpara*, *Destro*, *Benrinnes*, *Kohlistan* and *Patris*. Many masters reported muddle and delay at the discharge berths, exacerbated by the fact that many of the merchantmen were offloading dangerous cargoes.

Disaster struck the port on the night of 6 April when, at 2035 hours, the air-raid alarm sounded for the fifth time. As the minelayers came skimming over the mast-tops the gangs of stevedores ran for shelter; quickly there followed the main wave of bombers. *Clan Fraser*, unloading ammunition and high-explosive shells, was struck by three bombs, forward amidships and aft. Seven crew were killed with nine injured. Simultaneously, violent explosions erupted in the sheds and buildings on the quay. The resulting blast wrecked the bridge and upperworks. Blazing furiously, *Clan Fraser* was lifted bodily, snapping her mooring wires, and she gently drifted several yards. Four hours later, with the fire out of control, she blew up with a roar so tremendous that it shook buildings twelve and fifteen miles inland.

City of Roubaix, Cyprian Prince and *Patris* sank at their moorings close by, total losses, damaged were *Cingalese Prince* and *Devis. Clan Cumming,* offloading ammunition reeled heavily under the impact. She was abandoned after catching fire, though later her captain and five of his crew returned and brought the blaze under control. Sadly, on leaving Piraeus eight days later, *Clan Cumming* ran into an uncharted minefield and was sunk, an inglorious end to a vessel torpedoed, bombed and mined over a period of twelve weeks.

Miraculously the disaster, which caused the loss of 41,789 tons of valuable shipping together with sixty lighters and twenty-five motor-sailing vessels, resulted in few casualties. Piraeus, however, was closed to shipping for ten days and due to the magnetic mines dropped by the enemy virtually ceased to exist as a port. Those merchantmen that survived sailed for the small port of Volos, where *City of Karachi* was bombed and sunk on 13 April. Others sailed for the roadsteads at Eleusis, Scaramanga and Keratsini. *Goalpara* and *Quiloa* were both bombed and sunk in Eleusis Bay on 15 April.

It was then that the German blitzkrieg began in earnest, and within two weeks over 58,000 service personnel were at risk. On 25 April Operation 'Demon' commenced; some 51,000, leaving behind their equipment had to make their way under ceaseless attack by Stukas to the various Greek evacuation beaches. There, a great assortment of merchantmen and other craft assembled.

From his headquarters at Suda Bay on the island of Crete Vice-Admiral Pridham-Wippell directed the 'armada'. Four cruisers, HMS *Orion, Ajax, Phoebe* and HMAS *Perth*; three anti-aircraft cruisers, *Calcutta, Coventry* and *Carlisle*; twenty destroyers and three frigates; and the infantry assault vessels *Glenearn* and *Glengyle*. In addition, there were some twenty merchantmen: *Bankara, Cavallo, City of London, Combebank, Corinthia, Costa Rica, Delane, Dilwara, Dumana, Ionia, Itria, Khedive Ismail, Nicolaos Georgios, Pennland, Quiloa* (under instructions but already sunk), *Salween, Santa Clara Valley, Slamat, Thurland Castle* and *Ulster Prince*.

The *Glenearn* and *Glengyle*, built for the Alfred Holt company in 1939 and requisitioned by the Admiralty in 1940, were twin-screw motorships with a cruising speed of 18 knots. Together with *Glenartney, Glenroy, Glenorchy* and *Breconshire* and *Denbighshire* of the same class, these vessels performed tremendous work in combined operations. But for the 'Glen' ships and their landing craft employed in Operation 'Demon', only a small proportion of the 51,000 men would have been snatched from the jaws of the enemy. *Glenearn*, damaged by the attacking Messerschmidt 109s on entering the Gulf of Nauplia, was taken in tow by HMS *Griffin*.

Lieutenant-Commander P.K.Kemp RN, Admiralty archivist and head of the historical section, wrote in his *Victory at Sea 1939–1945* (1957), 'for six days Operation Demon continued and for the skill and coolness of the officers and men of the Royal and Merchant Navies it possibly surpassed even the Dunkirk evacuation. The navigational hazards, with ships having to work at night inshore, unlighted and sometimes inadequately charted waters, were extreme.'

During the evacuation German bombers sank the thirty-year old Dutch *Costa Rica*, the Greek *Pennland, Slamat* and *Ulster Prince*. Those ships that lingered beyond the dawn were quickly set upon by the Stukas – this happened to *Slamat* which lost 193 men. Although 700 men were rescued by the destroyers *Diamond* and *Wryneck* they were unable to escape. Dive-bombed, both vessels were sent to the bottom. Only one officer, forty-one ratings and eight soldiers survived, none of them from *Diamond*.

Ulster Prince, grounded off Nauplia, was attacked incessantly by Messerschmidt 110s and burned furiously; yet her gunners continued firing at the bombers until her decks were red hot. *Santa Clara Valley* had arrived at Nauplia Bay from Alexandria, where she had been refitted to carry 250 horses and mules destined for warfare in the mountains and valleys of Greece. With the animals mad with fright she was sunk by the screaming Stukas; the Greek *Cavallo* and the *Nicolaos Georgios*, both at anchor in the bay, soon followed her. *City of London* successfully embarked some 4,000 troops – British, Australian, Greek and Yugoslav – at Kalamata Bay.

Some 21,000 British and Imperial troops evacuated from Greece were landed in Crete to reinforce the island garrison; it had been occupied by the British in October 1940. From the commencement the situation was difficult; as many as fifteen merchantmen arriving in Suda Bay between 30 April and 20 May were attacked by the bombers. Eight were either sunk or seriously damaged. Facilities for unloading troops and stores were few and only 15,000 tons of stores were landed. Some 27,000 tons of war materials were consigned from Egypt to Crete but many of the vessels conveying them were forced to turn back. Less than 3,000 tons of this vital equipment was landed.

The *Glengyle* landed 700 men of the Argyll and Sutherland Highlanders at Tymbaki, an anchorage on the south coast of Crete. Two days later the *Glenroy* followed, landing 900 troops and eighteen vehicles. Sunk from air attack were the *Dalesman* and *Logician, Eleonora Maersk, Araybank* and *Rawnsley*. Damaged were the hospital ship *Aba, Scottish-Prince* and for the second time, the assault ship *Glenearn*.

In the subsequent evacuation of 22,000 battle-weary troops on 29 May, *Glengyle*, with four cruisers and three destroyers, embarked 7,000 men from Sphakia for Alexandria. Largely a Royal Navy operation, their losses were disastrous. Three cruisers, six destroyers and twenty-nine small craft were sunk; one battleship and seven destroyers were damaged.

After the crew were taken ashore from *Dalesman*, which had been sunk in Suda Bay, thirty-two were taken prisoner by German paratroops. Taken to the Greek mainland, they were then put in a cattle truck and taken by rail through Yugoslavia and Austria to Lubeck in northern Germany. In a bad state of health, many with dysentery, they were incarcerated in a prisoner-of-war camp. More fortunate were the remainder of the crew, numbering twenty-three, who followed Cadet Dobson (later awarded the British Empire Medal). Seizing an enemy machine gun he turned it on his captors; then, finding his way to a New Zealand battery he eventually boarded a landing barge where he found a mixed company of marines and soldiers. Undertaking the navigation, he brought his barge and comrades into Alexandria harbour ten days later.

At the time of near disaster in Greece and Crete the white ensign fluttered over Tobruk harbour and the wrecks of Italian transports and supply vessels; the port had been captured by the Australians on 22 January. There then followed the red ensign of the merchantmen, many of them small coasters which faithfully served the battle-weary North African coast for the next two years. During 1941 merchantmen and their crews on service in the Mediterranean faced difficulties as great as any in the world. Merchant seamen and their ships were closely linked with every landing and every evacuation; along the North African coast they became the lifeline, supporting every move of the land forces.

In these early struggles came the first appreciation of the value of MTBs and HDMLs to coastal forces and combined operations. They came from North America and the United Kingdom, secured on deck aboard the merchantmen, via that long-haul route around the Cape. Seventy-foot Elcos from the United States, Scott-Paines from Canada, UK-produced MLs, MGBs, MTBs and, later, the LCTs (landing craft tanks). My personal records show that on board *Nailsea Manor* (lost 10 October 1941) we carried an LCT Mark 11, in four sections, with a total weight of 250 tons; two sections were positioned over hatches on the foredeck and two sections on the after hatches.

At the end of March Rommel made a lightning strike in Cyrenaica following the arrival of a German Panzer division. Wavell's depleted army was driven back to the Egyptian frontier. Only the fortress of Tobruk was held. Every vessel sailing from the ports of Alexandria and Port Said had to run the gauntlet of Luftwaffe attacks. On the night of 19/20 April came the first assault on an enemy-held coast (at the port of Bardia) from ships specially equipped to carry and handle landing craft. The commandos were carried by *Glenearn* and *Glengyle*, escorted by the anti-aircraft cruiser *Coventry* and the destroyers *Stuart*, *Voyager* and *Waterhen*.

The 3,553-ton *Destro*, which had a remarkable escape from the catastrophe of Piraeus (her guns even brought down a bomber), probably withstood more attacks than any. She was working the eastern Mediterranean for sixteen months from January 1941. Suffering bombing raids on some 100 occasions there were twenty near misses and on six occasions she sustained damage. In Suda Bay she was continually bombed for two weeks; upon sailing she was inadvertently shelled by British shore batteries. On one occasion, during one of her many visits to Tobruk, she endured sixty-eight bombing raids. On 27 March 1942 whilst discharging at the port she was extensively damaged, which necessitated her withdrawal from service. She was under repair for many months.

The Luftwaffe and Regia Aeronautica made Tobruk the target in a series of determined raids, and no merchantman was safe within the vicinity of the port. DEMS and MRA gunners made determined efforts to keep the raiders at bay. The sea of the Mediterranean was in every way a part of the front line, skirted as it was by the 'desert ports' of Matrûh, Bardia, Tobruk and Benghazi. On more than on occasion, when talking of the seamen of this coast, Churchill referred to 'the professional skill of officers and men which has maintained the great tradition built up by many generations of British seamen.'

Oil was a priority cargo and one of the first consignment's delivered to Tobruk (January 1941) was by Anglo-Saxon's motor vessel *Crista*, a case oil carrier of 2,590 tons. She was the target on many occasions; on 7 February she struck a mine on the approaches, and on 17 March she was damaged when torpedoed by U-83 north-east of Tripoli. By the autumn that year it was reported that there were as many as seventy vessels of all types lying at the bottom of Tobruk harbour, thirty-three of them showing some of their superstructure above water.

It was on 16 October 1941 that Lieutenant Styles RNVR, now a prolific author of maritime novels, found himself setting out from Alexandria on a mission to salvage guns from ships sunk in Tobruk harbour. Two small vessels, escorted by the converted whaler HMS *Kos 19*, sailed with supplies for beleaguered Tobruk. The 1,208-ton Greek steamer *Samos* carried iron piping and 'sticky' grenades (for tank attack); the 758-ton British tanker *Pass of Balmaha* carried petrol. Ten hours after sailing both were torpedoed by *U-97*: the tanker was lost with all hands, including four DEMS gunners; from *Samos* eight survived from the ship's company of thirty-five.

With DEMS at Alexandria being woefully short of weapons for arming coastal merchantmen, Frank Showell Styles offered his help and applied to go to Tobruk. He sailed aboard *Samos*. Now aged eighty-four he remembers that night:

Not trusting the cleanliness of the cabin I was offered, I slung my hammock under the bridge-wing on deck. Somewhere about 0330 hours an explosion woke me just in time to writhe out of it as *Samos* rolled over and sank in a matter of seconds. When I surfaced in the starlit dark I spotted a raft with one man on it, the Greek apprentice Dmitri. I joined him and tied up his wounded leg with a piece torn from my shirt. The sea was calm, the night warm. We could make out the *Pass of Balmaha* about a mile away. After a few minutes there was a crescendo whirr and an upsurge of water between my feet, which were dangling in the water. I saw the phosphorescent trail of the torpedo rushing away towards the tanker, and after what seemed a long interval she went up in a great sheet of flame.

We could see nothing of the escort, or of any other survivors, and those on board *Pass of Balmaha* must have perished instantly. Salvaging a couple of floating pieces of wood, we started to try and paddle south towards the desert coast, but soon had to stop when the raft became exceedingly unstable. It was a Greek raft, of course, so the three oil-drums that supported its framework had been allowed to rust and were leaking. Dawn found the two of us balancing our craft with great difficulty, and when (after 4 hours on the raft) *Kos 19* came speeding over the horizon to pick us up, her officers had the amusing spectacle of two men apparently seated on the surface with nothing to support them.

The 1933-built *Pass of Balmaha*, one of several such tankers owned by the Bulk Oil Steamship Company was the prototype of the wartime-standard *Empire Cadet* class of twenty-three coastal tankers. Supplies of oil for the desert were shipped direct to Alexandria and sent forward either in the smaller tankers or in containers by a variety of merchantmen. The condemned 4-gallon tin or 'flimsy' was the commonest type, one that was universally unpopular amongst ships' crews. During May 1942 *Zealand* became a saviour of the 8th Army discharging a cargo of urgently required petrol under intense bombing from the air. The following month (28 June) she was torpedoed and sunk by *U-97* north-east of Port Said.

By the summer of 1942 when the British front line lay deep in Libya there was concern regarding tanker losses. Yet the performance of the oil carriers was something of which the fleet could be proud. Neither tanks nor aircraft were grounded to a halt through lack of fuel. Between July 1942 and June 1943 some 3/4 million tons of oil products were delivered to the forces in the Western desert. From the battle of Alamein in October 1942 to the final victory in Tunisia in May 1943, deliveries averaged 100,000 tons a month, rising to a peak of 140,000 tons in April 1943.

Only a shortage of 18-gauge steel barrels used for the conveyance of aviation spirit fell short of requirements. In March 1943 there were fears that the Air-Force in Libya might be grounded, but by the summer,

Jerrican and barrel plants at Haifa and Suez came on stream and the danger was averted, even though it was a long haul in the Mediterranean before the battle zone was reached.

A great variety of Allied merchantmen served the ports of Benghazi and Tobruk: the *Empire Patrol*, a former Italian refrigerated vessel taken in prize at Malta, June 1940; the Dutch *Trajanus* – bombed and sunk at Benghazi, she was raised and towed to Alexandria; the Greek *Elpis*; the *Sicilian Prince*, a British Mediterranean trader of the 1930s; the Norwegian *Hellas*; – bombed, she became a total loss in Benghazi inner harbour; the *Hannah Moller*, registered at Shanghai – she was also bombed and sunk at Benghazi; the *Hai Ying* of the China Navigation Company, was a frequent visitor to both ports; so, too, was the *Mirand*, a Greek trawler converted to a meat carrier; the Danish *Marita Maersk*; and the British *Bantria*, one of four Cunard vessels which in peacetime traded to the Mediterranean.

The 1,209-ton *Bantria*, with a British master and officers and an Egyptian crew served the eastern Mediterranean throughout the war carrying NAAFI stores, tanks, AGO (tank fuel in cans) and 100-octane aircraft fuel in flimsy drums. Fresh water, taken on in Alexandria, was pumped ashore at the ports for the use of the armed forces. On her return voyage she often carried German and Italian prisoners. On one occasion at Tobruk *Bantria* was damaged when she was bombed. This necessitated her being towed to Alexandria for repairs.

The hospital ship *Somersetshire* had made her name during the Saint-Nazaire evacuation in June 1940. East of Tobruk on 7 April 1942 the 9,716-ton motorship was blatantly attacked when she was torpedoed and damaged by *U-453*. The submarine commander afterwards claimed she was not marked in accordance with the Geneva Convention. Four weeks later the 3,676-ton hospital ship *Ramb IV* was bombed and set on fire by German aircraft in the Alexandria Channel. Formerly Italian, the vessel, packed with 269 wounded from Tobruk, quickly became an inferno. Although some were safely taken off, 150 died aboard the burning wreck. A total of nine British hospital ships were sunk during the Second World War.

As in many other theatres of war the lack of aircraft in the Middle East and North Africa was serious. It was not until the summer of 1942 that the Middle East Air Force reached a rough parity with the Axis air strength. That this was achieved was principally due to the operation mounted via Takoradi on the Gold Coast of West Africa. During the summer of 1940 Hurricane aircraft were dispatched in crates on merchantmen via the Cape but it soon became apparent that the supply was inadequate. And, as the U-boats were patrolling south of the Equator, there were added difficulties.

Combined Operations of the Takoradi route involved the Royal Navy, the Merchant Navy and the Royal Air Force. From as early as July 1940, just a few weeks after Italy entered the war, Group Captain H.K. Thorold arrived in the Gold Coast with an advanced party of Air Force technicians. A weekly passenger and mail service from Takoradi to Khartoum had existed since 1936, but a great deal of work was necessary: runways had to be extended, additional airfields built, new accommodation constructed, and signal communications and meteorological facilities improved. A throughput of 120 aircraft a month was planned.

The aircraft carrier *Argus* embarked thirty tropicalized Hurricanes, at Liverpool, sailed on 22 August 1940, and arrived in Takoradi fourteen days later. As a result, the first flight of one Blenheim and six Hurricane aircraft was airborne on 20 September for its 3,697-mile, six-day journey via the airfields of Lagos, Kano, Maiduguri (or Fort Lamy) to Geneina, and thence to Khartoum and Abu Sueir.

HMS *Furious* was also engaged in ferrying aircraft in the early months, but there then followed the many merchantmen sailing from Liverpool and Glasgow. The operation was not without losses in spite of the convoys being escorted and routed to as far south as Freetown from July 1941. In Chapter 5 I mentioned the loss of *Eurylochus* and her sixteen aircraft (29 January 1941) bound for Takoradi.

By the end of October 1943 over 5,000 aircraft had been sent to Egypt via the Takoradi route – a terrific achievement. They included Hurricanes, Blenheims, Wellingtons, Tomahawks and the Glen-Martin Maryland long-range reconnaissance aircraft. The Tomahawks and Marylands had already crossed the Atlantic atop the merchantmen. Many of the Elder Dempster West African traders and other steamers chartered by the company were engaged in the traffic. The motorship *Dunkwa*, sailing from Glasgow on 14 April 1941 and carrying eight aircraft, four in No. 2 lower hold and four on deck, was sunk by U-103 on 6 May, 216 miles west-north-west of Freetown. Crated aircraft were also carried by Elder Dempster's motorship *Alfred Jones*, commodore ship of convoy OB320, which was sunk by *U-107* on the first day of June, and their *New Brunswick* (convoy OS28), sunk by *U-159* on 21 May 1942.

Without these aircraft victory in North Africa would not have been possible. Those who planned the operation outwitted an enemy who considered their 'blockade' of the Cape route would throttle the Allied supply line. Those who carried out such operations, seamen and airmen alike, were the saviours of those who fought the land war. Nor should we forget those that worked in 'the white man's grave' – the technicians, the runway builders, the radio and signal men, the meteorologists. Disease and boredom, and poor living conditions were par for the course. Few complained, though there were many problems.

The supply of heavy tanks to the Middle East was not only inadequate but precarious. The losses on the 'Cape route' prompted Churchill to press the Admiralty to organize Convoy MC4, Operation 'Excess', direct to Malta, Piraeus and the eastern Mediterranean. Not only did the heavily escorted operation embrace the passage of military supplies eastward, but troops and stores from Alexandria to Malta by the *Breconshire* and *Clan MacAuley*, plus eight empty merchantmen from Malta to Alexandria. It was the forerunner of many such operations.

Sailing from the United Kingdom was the *Essex* which was carrying 4,000 tons of ammunition, 3,000 tons of seed potatoes and twelve Hurricane fighter aircraft on deck; in company were the *Clan Cumming, Clan MacDonald* and the twin-screw *Empire Song*, less than three months from the builder's yard. All three vessels were carrying heavy tanks. Whilst discharging in Malta (16/17 January 1941) the 11,063-ton *Essex* was severely damaged during an air raid, and two days later the 7,264-ton *Clan Cumming* was damaged in a torpedo attack by the Italian submarine *Neghelli*. In spite of this she was able to limp into Piraeus as part of Operation 'Lustre' during March.

The 'Excess' convoys, which sailed from Gibraltar and Alexandria on 6 January, were covered by the entire Mediterranean fleet, including the aircraft carriers *Ark Royal* and *Illustrious* and the battleships *Warspite* and *Valiant*. The fourteen merchantmen which made up the four convoys reached their destinations, but at a heavy price. The cruisers *Gloucester* and *Southampton* fell victim to the dive-bombers; *Southampton* was so severely damaged that she had to be sunk by British destroyers. Attacked by Junkers 87 aircraft, *Illustrious* was damaged by six bombs; she was hit again as she anchored in Malta's Valletta harbour. Patched up, she sailed thirteen days later for Alexandria.

Only three attempts were made to reinforce Malta by the sailings of lone merchantmen. Alas! all were destined to failure. In April 1941 the steamship *Parracombe*, unescorted and disguised, sailed from the United Kingdom. Routed via territorial waters from Gibraltar she struck a mine off Cape Bon on 1 May taking the twenty-one Hurricane aircraft she carried down with her. It was one of those horrific occasions: the mine detonated her deadly cargo of ammunition in the forward holds and the bottom of the merchantman was torn away. With the bridge and boat deck carried away, thirty officers and men were lost, and one Arab fireman later died from exposure.

October 1941 witnessed another special mission. *Empire Defender*, the former Italian *Felce* seized at Haifa on 11 June 1940, loaded stores and ammunition at Glasgow for Gibraltar. Her sixty Lascar seamen refused to sail sensing a difficult operation because of the cargo and the absence of the usual wartime grey paint. The hull of the merchantman was painted black with white topsides and a buff-coloured funnel. I must add that it is one of the very few occasions when these Asian Seamen failed their 'mother country'. The white seamen who replaced them were each awarded ten pounds in cash as inducement to accept Lascar accommodation. With her final destination 'unknown', *Empire Defender* sailed as a 'neutral', even to the extent of having all her armament removed.

Leaving her convoy off the south-west coast of Spain and intent on carrying out her secret mission the former Italian vessel passed through the Straits of Gibraltar, her crew painting the flag of the nations through whose waters she passed – first French, then Spanish and finally Italian. Due at Malta the following day, the vessel was entering the danger zone. At sunset on the evening of 14 November, some eighteen miles south of Galita Island, she was attacked by an Italian aircraft. Within minutes of the aerial torpedo striking she was on fire, and her crew abandoned ship just before she blew up and sank.

Sailing only a few hours ahead of *Empire Defender* was the 1919-built former US-tonnage *Empire Pelican*. Dawn was breaking and the coast of the island of Malta was only a few hours away. She too had sailed from Glasgow with military stores; she too was sunk by Italian aircraft. Survivors from all three merchantmen were taken prisoner by the French and later transferred to a camp near Sfax.

Only by the operation of heavily escorted convoys could Malta be supplied. As early as February 1941 General Rommel warned the German High Command, 'without Malta, the Axis will end by losing control in North Africa'. The enemy was relentless in keeping up their attacks upon the island and upon the convoys supplying it.

Operation 'Tiger' of May 1941, hastily planned by Churchill and the Admiralty, was provoked by the build-up of enemy tanks in the western desert the previous month. Convoy WS8 (via the Cape), of nine troop transports, was already assembling at Liverpool and the 'tail of the bank' when it was decided to include five 15-knot vessels, which were to be detached at Gibraltar for eastward passage to Malta and Alexandria. The Cape-bound vessels were *Abbekerk, Aronda, Dominion Monarch, Empress of Asia, Empress of Russia, Highland Chieftain, Reina del Pacifico, Sobieski* and *Strathaird*; those for the Mediterranean were *Clan Campbell, Clan Chattan, Clan Lamont, Empire Song* and *New Zealand Star*. Amongst the important reinforcements they carried were 300 new tanks, together with 180 motorized guns and aircraft.

On 6 May a slow convoy of two tankers and a fast convoy of four transports, including *Breconshire* with a cargo of oil fuel and munitions, left Alexandria. A strong naval escort included HMS *Warspite, Barham* and *Valiant*, the aircraft carrier *Formidable*, the cruisers *Ajax, Orion* and *Perth*, the fast minelayer *Abdiel* and some destroyers. Two days later there were attacks by German and Italian aircraft, but principally due to cloud cover they were unsuccessful in their assault. Approaching the Narrows between Malta and Tunisia were the vessels comprising the Gibraltar portion of 'Tiger'. Here the *New Zealand Star* was mined; although damaged, she managed to continue her voyage. *Empire Song*, however, deeply laden with munitions and equipment, including fifty-seven tanks and ten Hurricane aircraft, detonated two mines in spite of possessing paravanes. Eighteen of her crew were killed. The close escort was made up of HMS *Queen Elizabeth, Naiad, Fiji* together with destroyers.

The other four vessels, were carrying 238 tanks and forty-three Hurricanes between them; they were met by the Mediterranean fleet and escorted safely to Alexandria. The operation was considered a great success though as Captain MacIntyre wrote in his book *The Battle for the Mediterranean* (1964), 'Fortune had indeed favoured the bold, providing thick cloudy weather in the Central Mediterranean at a season when it was unprecedented.'

Convoy GM1, Operation 'Substance', fought its way eastward from Gibraltar towards Malta during July. Six fast merchantmen – *City of Pretoria* (subsequently (3 March 1943) lost with all hands in the North Atlantic), *Deucalion, Durham, Melbourne Star, Port Chalmers* and *Sydney Star* – were escorted by the battle cruiser *Renown*, the battleship *Nelson*, the aircraft carrier *Ark Royal*, four cruisers, the cruiser minelayer *Manxman* and seventeen destroyers. At the same time the *Breconshire* and five empty merchantmen, convoy MG1, returned safely from Malta to Gibraltar.

South of Sardinia during 23 July the convoy was subjected to fierce attacks from the air, in which the cruiser *Manchester* was damaged and the destroyer *Fearless* sunk. Approaching the Narrows, *Renown, Nelson, Ark Royal* and four destroyers turned and proceeded back to base. The next morning came the E-boats, the Italian MAS 532 and 533, which twisted and weaved between the merchantmen. *Sydney Star* was struck by a torpedo and, taking water forward, she suddenly took a list to port. As a consequence, the 460 troops she was carrying were transferred to one of the escorting destroyers.

Sinking slowly by the head the 1936-built 12,696-ton motor vessel *Sydney Star*, guided by three tugs, arrived at the naval dockyard in Malta later that day. She was twelve feet down by the bows, and the hole caused by the torpedo was about forty by sixteen feet with extensive tearing. Repair, which was carried out at Malta, took nearly four months to complete. Operation 'Substance' was considered a complete success, due in large measure to what Admiral Somerville called, 'the steadfast and resolute behaviour of the Merchant Navy crews.'

The 10,893-ton *Durham*, returning empty westward from Malta during August hit a mine whilst passing Cape Bon. She then discovered another entangled in the paravane, which she had been towing for some twenty-four hours. Under repair at Gibraltar she was attacked by Italian human torpedoes from the submarine *Scire*. It was twelve months before the badly damaged and beached *Durham* was made seaworthy and towed to the United Kingdom. Not until late 1943 did she resume her cargo-carrying duties. During the Italian assault the *Fiona Shell*, an oil storage hulk, was sunk and the ocean-type tanker *Empire Silver* was damaged. The latter had been completed in January 1941 as *Denbydale*, one of ten war-built tankers operated by the Admiralty (Royal Fleet Auxiliary). The 'human chariot' limpet charge broke her back while she was lying at the detached Mole. She remained at the naval base as a fuelling hulk.

At the eastern end of the Mediterranean came the incessant bombing raids by German Junkers 88s based in Crete. The sorties were aimed at shipping in the Suez Canal and the anchorage of Port Said, Ismalia and Port Tewfik. The canal was closed for a total period of eighty-two days during 1941; the longest consecutive shutdown was twenty days during February and March, after the waterway had been mined from the air.

During the night of 14 July the 25,759-ton Cunard White Star 'trooper' *Georgic* was bombed in Suez Roads and within twenty minutes she was on fire from stem to stern. At anchor nearby was the *Almanzora*, whose lifeboats assisted in rescuing survivors for many hours. Aground and burnt out the *Georgic* was later towed to Karachi, where she was under repair for nine months and did not resume trooping until early 1943. Merchantmen recruited to assist in towing the two-funnelled transatlantic liner were the *Clan Campbell* and *City of Sydney* to (as far as Port Sudan), the *Recorder* and *Haresfield* and the tugs *Pauline Moller* and *St Sampson*. The latter was lost in bad weather in the Red Sea.

The Mediterranean convoy WS11X (Operation 'Halberd') was a fast convoy including some of Britain's finest merchantmen – *Ajax, Breconshire, City of Lincoln, Clan Ferguson, Clan MacDonald, Dunedin Star, Imperial Star*, and *Rowallan Castle*. Loaded in the United Kingdom they were bound for Singapore as well as Malta, passing Gibraltar on 24 September 1941. The heavy escort consisted of three battleships, *Nelson, Prince of Wales* and *Rodney*, the aircraft carrier *Ark Royal*, five cruisers and eighteen destroyers.

Four days later all except one merchantman (*Imperial Star*) steamed into Malta's Grand Harbour to the cheers of the whole populace. It was another success for the combined services. Whilst three of the ships had narrow escapes when Italian bombers attacked, Blue Star Line's *Imperial Star* (12,427 tons) was struck by a torpedo. The rudder and both propellers were blown away, and the 300 troops she was carrying were quickly taken off by HMS *Heythorp*. Taken in tow by the destroyer *Oribi* the merchantman proved unmanageable and it was found necessary to sink her by gunfire and depth charges placed below the waterline. As her end came, 1,000 tons of high explosives, part of her valuable cargo, blew up with a tremendous explosion. During the operation four unescorted empty transports safely proceeded from Malta to Gibraltar.

In November, with the increase in the number of German U-boats in the Mediterranean there were serious naval losses. The aircraft carrier, *Ark Royal* was sunk by *U-81*; the battleship *Barham*, *U-331*; and the cruiser *Galatea*, *U-577*. The transport *Shuntien* was carrying prisoners of war from Tobruk to Alexandria. Torpedoed and sunk by *U-559* the master, four of his officers and the chief steward were killed as, eventually, were all the Italian prisoners. At first they were rescued by HMS *Salvia*, but were lost when the corvette was sunk by *U-568* shortly afterwards. There followed the loss of *Volvo*, along with twenty-one of her crew and three gunners, torpedoed by *U-75*; and, once again, *Glenroy*, hit by an aerial torpedo and beached after attempting to reinforce the besieged garrison of Tobruk (Operation 'Aggression', 23 November 1941). With her troops transferred to other vessels, she accepted a tow but it was found necessary to beach her again near Mersa Matrûh. Refloated three days later, *Glenroy* was towed to Alexandria, although the repairs necessary to enable her to undertake the passage to Britain took almost a year to complete.

The *Breconshire* was again under fire when, loaded with troops and urgent supplies for Malta, she sailed from Alexandria heavily escorted by cruisers and destroyers. During the ensuing 'First Battle of Sirte' on 17 December heavy air attacks were launched against her. These were followed by an assault by two Italian battleships, which were subsequently driven off by a superior force under Rear-Admiral Philip Vian. Two days later *Breconshire* arrived safely at Grand Harbour in Malta.

Three operations took place in January 1942; again they were designed to reinforce Malta and to return empty vessels, and again they were heavily escorted by cruisers and destroyers. The merchantmen sailing from Alexandria were *Breconshire*, *Ajax*, *City of Calcutta*, *Clan Ferguson*, *Glengyle* and *Thermopylae*; the latter was bombed and sunk off the coast of Crete, as was the destroyer *Gurkha* (formerly *Larne*) in the same action. *Breconshire*, which had left Malta on 6 January in convoy MF2, returned on 24 January in convoy MF4. A further loss was that of the *Clan Chattan*, bombed on 14 February during the passage of convoy MW9A; she was carrying ammunition and had to be sunk by her escorts to avoid an explosion. Her two companions *Clan Campbell* and *Rowallan Castle* were destined never to reach Malta either; the latter vessel, severely damaged and loaded with explosives, had to be sunk by the senior service.

Clan Campbell had returned to Suez after her epic towage of the liner *Georgic*. Ordered to Alexandria she loaded aviation fuel in flimsy four-gallon cans, ammunition and stores bound for Malta. The bomb damage was above the waterline and she managed to limp into Tobruk. There her engineers cut some plates from a sunken Italian warship and bolted them together to enable her to return to Alexandria.

During March convoy MW10 sailed for Malta. On the twentieth of the month, with the beleaguered island under intense enemy attack from the air, the now veteran *Breconshire* led the other three merchantmen – the repaired *Clan Campbell*, Royal Mail's *Pampas*, completed by Harland & Wolff's Belfast dock in January 1941, and the Norwegian *Talabot*. The convoy left Alexandria escorted by the 15th cruiser squadron and every available destroyer.

On nearing Malta, after enduring many vicious attacks, *Clan Campbell* was again bombed. Suffering a number of direct hits in bad weather and the deaths of six crew including her master, she was abandoned. The loss of the gallant *Breconshire* followed. A survivor of so many previous perilous voyages she was hit in the engine room and disabled eight miles from Valletta. The next day, a hole was cut in the side of the beached vessel as she lay on the bottom, and the precious oil she was carrying in her deep tanks was pumped out for use by the Malta garrison.

The, 9,776-ton *Breconshire* (Captain Hutchison), owned by the Glen Line, an Alfred Holt company, had been under construction at the outbreak of war. Requisitioned for service as a naval auxiliary, she made eight trips to Malta; whilst she flew the white ensign many of her original crew remained with her throughout her war service.

Talabot, with a cargo of ammunition, kerosene and aviation spirit, and *Pampas* – army stores and foodstuffs – were subjected to a series of bombing raids in Malta's Marsaxlokk harbour. Both were sunk at their moorings, though 6,000 tons of their combined cargoes of 26,000 tons had been unloaded. With the supply position now serious two massive convoys were organized for June – one eastbound from Gibraltar (Operation 'Harpoon'), the other westbound from Port Said and Haifa (Operation 'Vigorous').

Codenamed WS192, the eastbound vessels sailed from the Clyde on 5 June – *Burdwan*, *Chant* (American), *Orari*, *Tanimbar* (Dutch) and *Troilus*. At Gibraltar they were joined by the fast American tanker *Kentucky*, which had sailed direct from North America. In the opposite direction the convoy comprised the *Aagtkirk* (Dutch), *Ajax*, *Bhutan*, *City of Calcutta*, *City of Edinburgh*, *City of Lincoln*, *City of Pretoria*, *Elizabeth Bakki* (Norwegian), *Potaro*, *Rembrandt* (Dutch) and the tanker *Bulkoil*.

Operation 'Vigorous', codenamed MW11, was in trouble immediately, encountering fierce attacks by aircraft from Crete, submarines and motor torpedo boats; there were threats too from the Italian fleet, which boasted some modern ships of war. With fuel and ammunition stocks low on board the escorts, Admiral Vian decided to return to Alexandria – but the decision had been taken too late. With *Bhutan* bombed and sunk, *Aagtkirk* put into Tobruk, whence the aircraft followed, sinking her at her moorings. Following the Dutchman was the *City of Calcutta*, which suffered severe damage. Though she too took the brunt of the attack, she was later repaired. *Elizabeth Bakki* and *Potaro* were both pursued by the enemy and bombed, but were able to reach the comparative safety of Alexandria harbour.

The 'Harpoon' convoy experienced similar difficulties, being attacked by U-boats and then by German and Italian aircraft from Sardinia. After the Force 'H' escort turned back for Gibraltar upon reaching the Sicilian Narrows, the convoy was left under the protection of the cruiser *Cairo* and some destroyers. *Chant*, struck by a stick of three bombs, sank in minutes. *Kentucky*, badly disabled by a near miss, was taken in tow but later scuttled along with *Burdwan*, also seriously damaged. Later during the same day the Dutch *Tanimbar* succumbed to the mighty assault, which left only *Orari*, damaged by a mine, and *Troilus* to reach Malta. Two escorting destroyers were sunk by aircraft and three others damaged by mines as they were approaching the island.

Orari and *Troilus* with some 20,000 tons of supplies on board, were given a rapturous welcome by Maltese crowded on the ramparts of Valletta. Lord Leathers, Minister of War Transport, sent a message to the two masters: 'I congratulate you on your gallant conduct in delivering vital goods to Malta. Please convey congratulations and best wishes to all on board.' During the fifty-four days *Orari* was under repair she was subjected to 289 air raids, yet day and night the repair work proceeded.

During the summer of 1942 the plight of the people of Malta became desperate. Operations 'Harpoon' and 'Vigorous' had been failures. The Afrika Corps was only forty-five miles from Alexandria and, with the loss of valuable airfields in North Africa, the occupation of Malta by the enemy was a distinct possibility. The securing of the island, Operation 'Pedestal', is probably the best-known of any action at sea and has been well documented. It was an epic in naval history, most notable for its combined operation of the Royal and Merchant Navies.

In a supplement to the *London Gazette* on 11 August 1948 Vice-Admiral E.N. Syfret was to write:

Tribute has been paid to the personnel of HM Ships but both officers and men will desire to give first place to the conduct, courage and determination of the Masters, officers and men of the merchant ships. The steadfast manner in which these ships pressed on to Malta through all attacks … was a most inspiring sight. Many of these fine men and their ships were lost, but the memory of their conduct will remain an inspiration to all who were privileged to sail with them.

Convoy WS215 (a bogus number for secrecy), better-known for its codename 'Pedestal', consisted of thirteen fast cargo ships which sailed from the Clyde on 2 August; a 16-knot American tanker was to join them at Gibraltar. The convoy brought together 139,992 tons of modern construction, all heavily armed with up-to-date weapons manned by the DEMS and MRA. Winston Churchill personally took a hand in its formation – 'the fate of Malta was at stake and we were determined that it should not fall,' he was later to write.

Passing through the Straits of Gibraltar during the night of 10 August the merchantmen were joined by the heaviest and most powerful escort of any wartime convoy. Led by the battleships *Nelson* and *Rodney* it comprised the aircraft carriers *Eagle* and *Furious*, carrying thirty-eight Spitfire aircraft for Malta's defence, *Indomitable* and *Victorious*, seven cruisers and twenty-five destroyers. Back-up ships included the fleet tankers *Brown Ranger* and *Derwentdale*, four corvettes and the towing vessel *Salvonia*. Eight British submarines were on standby in Mediterranean waters.

The merchantmen were some of the finest cargo liners of the Allied fleet. The Blue Star vessels, *Brisbane Star* and *Melbourne Star*, members of the family of so-called food ships of the 1930s, were in convoy, as was the 1933-vintage *Port Chalmers*, owned by the Port Line, on her second voyage to Malta and now the commodore vessel with Commander A.G. Venables RN aboard. Others worth mentioning are: *Waimarama*, *Wairangi* and *Empire Hope* of the Shaw, Savill and Albion company; *Rochester Castle* (Union Castle Mail Steamships); *Dorset* (Federal Steam Navigation Co); *Deucalion* and *Glenorchy* from the Albert Holt Group and *Clan Ferguson* of the Scottish Clan line. Three vessels flying the Stars and Stripes at the gaff completed the convoy. These were: Texas Oil Company's *Ohio*, built in 1940 in Pennsylvania but now with a British crew commanded by Captain Mason – at thirty-nine years, he was the youngest master of the British-owned 'Eagle' tanker fleet; the *Santa Elisa*, a new US C2 type built for Grace Lines; and *Almeria Lykes* of the Lykes Brothers fleet (US C3 type).

The toll of ships sunk was heavy. Awaiting the convoy was a combined enemy strike consisting of Italian submarines and German U-boats, Italian naval cruisers, escort destroyers and MAS boats. Sicilian and Sardinian airfields held a total of 540 German and Italian serviceable bomber aircraft. Further, the Italians held in readiness their secret weapon: a circling torpedo or mobile mine attached to a parachute. To complete the blockade of Malta a minefield had been laid between Cape Bon and Kelibia.

From the senior service the aircraft carrier *Eagle* was sunk (by *U-73*). *Victorious* and *Indomitable* were severely damaged, thereby robbing the convoy of its essential umbrella. Two cruisers were lost; two others damaged. The fourth service lost nine of its splendid vessels totalling 91,005 tons. Five were sunk by aircraft, and four by MAS boats. Around 100,000 tons of stores, including aviation spirit and petrol in cases and drums were destroyed. The death toll of Merchant Navy officers and men climbed to 350. Those that broke through the blockade were *Brisbane Star, Melbourne Star, Port Chalmers*, the commodore ship, and *Rochester Castle*. The battered *Ohio*, torpedoed, lamed and set on fire, her boilers blown up, her engines damaged beyond repair, arrived in Valletta harbour with her gunwales awash, lashed up between two destroyers. A portion of her valuable cargo was intact and pumped ashore, though *Ohio* herself was finally written off as a constructive loss. For outstanding leadership and devotion to duty her master, Captain Dudley Mason, like the island he so well served, was awarded the George Cross.

What of the vessels destroyed? *Deucalion*, with 2,000 tons of petrol in cases each containing two four-gallon tanks, was the first casualty. Bombed, then hit by an aerial torpedo, she caught fire and blew up with a tremendous explosion. The survivors were rescued by HMS *Bramham*. *Empire Hope*, bombed and set on fire, was abandoned and *Bramham* again came to the rescue. The next day the drifting wreck was torpedoed by the Italian submarine *Bronzo*. Subsequently *Empire Hope*, a hazard to shipping, was sunk by one of the destroyers. *Clan Ferguson*, torpedoed by the Italian submarine *Alagi*, caught fire and exploded amidst a terrifying blaze. Loss of life on the 'Clan' ship was only eighteen, thirty-two survivors being taken prisoner by a Dornier flying boat which alighted on the calm sea. The master and fifteen others were rescued by an Italian Red Cross seaplane and the remainder were taken prisoner by the French in Tunisia.

Brisbane Star, also torpedoed by the submarine *Alagi*, escaped damaged. She fell out of the convoy and carried on alone. *Dorset* lost touch in the darkness and proceeded independently through the Zembra Channel, along the Tunisian coast and round Cape Bon. Two mines were detonated with the port paravane. She sustained a torpedo near-miss from an Italian MAS (motor torpedo boat); bombed, she was badly damaged and disabled. With the engine room abandoned she was towed for a short while only to be attacked by torpedo bombers. With the vessel abandoned, the crew were rescued by HMS *Bramham*.

Wairangi was torpedoed and sunk by an MAS, and all her crew were rescued by HMS *Eskimo*. *Glenorchy* was bombed, then torpedoed and sunk by the Italian 32-knot torpedo boats. *Santa Eliza* and *Almeria Lykes* were to follow, being sunk in the same manner. *Rochester Castle* was also attacked in this assault, but was later able to rejoin the convoy. Whilst survivors from *Glenorchy* were also taken prisoner by the French in Tunisia (her master chose to go down with his ship – see p.282, Chapter 12), seven were rescued by one of the MAS boats. Taken to Sicily, then to an Italian camp near Naples, they eventually (early 1944) arrived at the German prisoner-of-war camp at Milag Nord, near Bremen.

Waimarama, hit by aerial bombs in quick succession, suffered the heaviest loss of personnel of all the merchantmen. The dive-bombers came screaming out of the sun, and the ship's cargo of cased aviation spirit and ammunition blew up in a sheet of flame. *Melbourne Star* was showered with debris as the sea blazed with fire all around. Twenty of her crew of 107 were skilfully rescued by HMS *Ledbury*.

'Pedestal' was as important as the coming battle of Alam Halfa in turning the tide in the North African campaign. It paved the way for the landings in Algeria and Morocco, in Sicily and southern Italy. Overlooking the waters of Malta's Grand Harbour today stands the Siege Bell, the inspiration of the George Cross Island Association, which was unveiled by Queen Elizabeth II on 29 May 1992, an occasion at which I was privileged to be present. Fifty years before, beneath the ramparts of this harbour, came four of the nation's finest merchantmen. To the strains of 'Rule Britannia' came the British-crewed American tanker. Famous *Ohio* had broken the siege, bringing precious oil products for Malta's fighter aircraft and for its citizens.

With the victory at El Alamein setting the stamp on North Africa's future, it appeared that the years of defeat were part of history. Yet with all that was planned for the weeks and months ahead there loomed a desperate shortage of shipping, both merchantmen and escorts. Furthermore the months of October and November brought record Allied tonnage losses; 235 merchantmen totalling 1,445,587 tons. The Battle of the Atlantic was yet to be won and the routeing of ships westward from South and West Africa – even further south to the Straits of Magellan and thence by the Panama Canal and the West Indies, to join New York and Halifax convoys – added to delays and uncertainties.

Whilst the African/Caribbean crossings may have assisted the escort situation, particularly in regard to the planned invasion convoys, it meant that the merchantmen were logging many thousands of additional miles. This meant that steaming time was doubled, which in itself added to shortages. Not only that but losses of vessels carrying valuable home-bound cargoes rose. Five of Ellerman's fleet alone were sunk in the South Atlantic whilst following the new Admiralty routeing during November.

It was at this time that I found myself aboard Canadian Pacific's 20,119-ton *Duchess of Atholl*. Being a survivor from the steamship *Gazcon* I had boarded *Oronsay* (20,043 tons) at Aden and was transferred to the

CP liner at Durban. I never discovered the reason why. Also alongside the quay was *Orcades*, at 23,456 tons the newest and largest of the Orient Steam Navigation fleet. All three were HM transports and were homeward bound. Their speeds in excess of 17 knots, together with zigzagging, should have enabled safe passages.

September 1942 had seen the '*Laconia* affair' in the South Atlantic, and all merchant ship crews knew that security was sadly lacking in South African ports. Torpedoed and sunk by *U-156* 500 miles south of Cap Palmas, Liberia, the Cunard White Star transport *Laconia* (19,695 tons) was homeward bound from Suez with a crew of 692, 766 passengers and 1,793 Italian prisoners of war. Hearing cries for help in Italian as the vessel began to sink, the submarine commander Lieutenant-Commander Hartenstein, hauled some of them aboard. He discovered to his dismay that they were Italians taken prisoner by the British Army in North Africa. Summoning other U-boats in the area to the rescue, he informed Grand-Admiral Dönitz of the situation. He proceeded forthwith to arrange for the Vichy French to send surface vessels from Dakar. The rescue operation, which began with *U-156* (with 250 Italians aboard), soon included *U-506, U-507* and the Italian *Cappellini*, but was then terminated when an American aircraft from Ascension attempted to bomb the cluster of rescuing craft and ships' lifeboats. The subject of *Laconia* and of Allied brutality was raised at the Nuremberg War Trials. Loss of life was heavy, and only 975 were rescued. Captain Sharp, the master of *Laconia* who went down with his ship, was master of *Lancastria* sunk in June 1940. A total of 5,109 lives were lost in the two vessels under his command.

Lost the following month were the three transports moored at Durban:

9 October *Oronsay*, sunk by Italian *Archimede*; Position 04.29N. – 20.52W.
10 October *Duchess of Atholl*, sunk by *U-178*; Position 07.03S.11.12W.
10 October *Orcades* sunk by *U-172*; Position 31.51S 14.40E.

Captain Roskill was to write, 'these were grievous losses, for such fine ships could never be replaced during the war.'

We were forced to abandon the *Duchess of Atholl* some 200 miles east of Ascension Island, after she was struck by three torpedoes and four engineers on duty in the engine-room were killed. What I found remarkable was the calmness with which our complement of 821, including twenty-four women and children distributed over twenty-six lifeboats, behaved. This was at a time when *U-178* cruised 'peacefully' amongst us – her commander, Captain Hans Ibbeken, and his crew taking stock of their achievement. After twenty-eight hours, rescue was made by HMS *Corinthian* and we were landed at Freetown to continue our voyage in the 20,122-ton *Caernarvon Castle*, an armed merchant cruiser now 'trooping' worldwide.

The 1925-built *Oronsay* was sunk 500 miles west-south-west of Freetown. Her master, Captain Savage, was previously in command of the Orient liner *Orford*, a sister ship, bombed and sunk off southern France in June 1940. A total of 266 survivors were landed in Freetown from the much travelled *Oronsay*; a few were rescued by the Vichy French sloop *Dumant d'Urville* and taken to Dakar where they were interned.

Orcades was torpedoed west-south-west of Cape Town. She had on board a complement of some 1,300, numbering 711 passengers, some of whom were women and children and survivors from sunken merchantmen. With a moderate gale blowing and a heavy swell, great difficulty was experienced in abandoning ship. Thirty lives were lost when one of the lifeboats was upset whilst being lowered. After the fourth torpedo struck, the great liner, built in 1937, broke up and went under amidst a muffled explosion as the boilers exploded. The distress call was answered by the *Narwik*, launched as the *Empire Roamer*, a replacement ship subsequently operated by the Polish Government. Searching for many hours in deteriorating weather the heavily laden Polish-manned *Narwik*, carrying 10,000 tons of iron ore, rescued 1,021 survivors and steamed at 10 knots for Cape Town.

Another fine passenger vessel lost during October 1942 was that of the flagship, its largest at 11,330 tons, of the Elder Dempster fleet. On 29 October the 1935-built twin-screw motorship *Abosso*, serving as an HM transport and sailing unescorted at 15 knots, was torpedoed and sunk in bad weather by *U-575*, 700 miles north of the Azores. From her crew of 182 and 100 passengers 251 perished – a total which included her master and all his officers. The survivors were rescued two days later by HMS *Bideford*.

From Freetown on 16 October sailed the ill-fated convoy SL125, which I briefly mentioned in Chapter 4 in connection with Operation 'Torch'. Although the merchant seamen involved could not know it at the time, their ordeal probably saved the Allies from far worse disasters, for troop and supply convoys involved in that great undertaking were already steaming southwards from British ports and eastwards from American ports.

The escort of SL125 originally consisted of one sloop, four corvettes (*Cowslip*, *Crocus*, *Petunia* and *Woodruff*) and an armed trawler, but only the four corvettes were with the convoy when U-boat attacks started on the 26th of the month. They were inadequate to cope with the seven-day onslaught that followed. Sailing west of Morocco on a broad front of eleven columns, the thirty-seven merchantmen, heavily laden with fuel oil and foodstuffs, tea and sugar, timber, manganese and iron ore, steamed right across a patrol line of eight U-boats. Thirteen of these merchantmen, totalling some 80,000 tons, were lost.

The poorly defended merchantmen had, unknowingly, drawn the U-boats away from 'Torch'. In Volume Four of *The Second World War* Winston Churchill refers to the episode. 'By the end of October about forty German and Italian U-boats were stationed to the south and east of the Azores. They were successful in severely mauling a large convoy homeward bound from Sierra Leone and sank thirteen ships. In the circumstances this could be borne.'

Those who crewed the merchantmen during this onslaught were 'sacrificed' in the cause of war, in the cause of ultimate victory over a sadistic enemy. The cargoes, the ships and their men, were unimportant when related to what was at stake. Here was further evidence of how cruel the sea can be in time of war; yet even then one could sense the compassion that existed between those directly involved.

The compassion was shown by the master of the *Baron Elgin* and one of the U-boat commanders, whose identity remains a mystery. With the convoy in confusion the British captain turned his ship around and started to rescue survivors from those he had seen torpedoed and sunk. The U-boat which witnessed the rescue circled *Baron Elgin* on the surface whilst the merchantman, with gunners at the ready, held their fire. After some minutes the enemy withdrew, allowing the *Elgin* to proceed alone to Madeira. She arrived safely fourteen hours later, where she landed the rescued seamen.

The first casualty was the tanker *Anglo Maersk*, a Danish vessel managed by Houlder Brothers, torpedoed by *U-509*. She was damaged, and although she managed to limp along she was caught again, this time by *U-604*, which fired a further torpedo. Subsequently, she sank. The commodore vessel *Nagpore*, with Rear-Admiral C.N. Reyne aboard, was rolling heavily during a stormy night when she was also torpedoed by *U-509*. So, too, were the vice-commodore vessel *Stentor*, *Pacific Star*, *Brittany* and *Corinaldo*, the latter damaged only; she was later damaged a second time when torpedoed by *U-659*. She was finally sunk by torpedo and gunfire from *U-203* two hours later.

Breaking in two, *Nagpore* sank within ten minutes, taking her master and eighteen of her crew down with her. Nineteen survivors in lifeboat No.4 were at sea for fourteen days before landing at Puerto Orotava, Canary Islands. Lost on board *Stentor*, which had embarked 124 passengers at Freetown, were her master and Captain R.H. Garstin RNR, Retd, Vice-Commodore, the chief engineer and ship's doctor as well as all the deck officers bar the staff captain and second mate. Of the 247 persons on board, 202 were rescued by HMS *Woodruff*.

Every officer and man of the Blue Star merchantman *Pacific Star* survived to fight again. Through skilled seamanship they brought their lifeboats to the Canary Islands, although they did not easily give up their ship. After her abandonment the master and crew stood by all day in the hope that if the gale subsided and if their SOS was picked up and an ocean tug was available, *Pacific Star* could be saved. It was not to be.

On board the 17-knot 11,898-ton former French liner *Président Doumer* (managed by Bibby Bros) was a large number of servicemen. As she was torpedoed by *U-604* the explosion caused great panic among passengers and crew. Many lifeboats fell from the davits into the sea, which was full of survivors; none was seen again. Some empty lifeboats crashed 50 feet; they too were lost. It was dark, and the sea was covered with struggling people, some of whom could not swim; others clung desperately to wreckage. Although the Norwegian *Alaska*, herself seriously damaged (torpedoed by *U-510*), rescued some forty-eight survivors, the death toll was 260.

Amongst other lost merchantmen were: the *Brittany*, – with two torpedoes she sank within ten minutes taking her thirteen crew and one passenger with her; *Silverwillow* – later reboarded and taken in tow she unfortunately sank on the sixth day of her tow. The motor tanker *Bullmouth* was torpedoed, first by *U-409* and nineteen minutes later by *U-659*. She blew up in a sheet of flame, and her master and forty-seven crew perished. *Baron Vernon*, *Hopecastle* and *Tasmania* met similar fates. It so happened that the *Alaska*, after accepting a tow from a tug which set out from Gibraltar, transferred her *Président Doumer* survivors to one of the corvettes. She was thus able to reach Lisbon fourteen days later after a hazardous and frustrating voyage.

We now return to North Africa where 'the tide had turned', to those troop and supply convoys which had sailed, in great secrecy, from the United Kingdom.

10 Operations 'Torch' and 'Husky'

Codenamed 'Torch' by Churchill himself, the landings in North Africa (Algeria and Morocco) were brilliant in terms of the detail of their planning and the smoothness of their execution. The dress rehearsal for the invasion of Europe, the operation was to shape the whole future course of the war; it was the first in a series of assaults from the sea that was eventually to shatter the whole structure of the Axis war strategy.

Operation 'Torch' was the earliest example of a combined action by sea, land and air forces in which merchantmen played a highly prominent part; indeed, it was the first joint Allied amphibious operation mounted. It was the first time in the history of war that armies from two separate continents were simultaneously landed upon the shores of a third. Even fifty years later in the age of the jumbo jet, such an operation could not conceivably be accomplished without a fleet of merchantmen and naval escorts. Victory in war depends upon several factors, but without good supplies and good transport, it is impossible.

Lessons learned in early raids on enemy territory, when merchantmen were used as infantry landing ships, were invaluable. The first to carry troops and their landing craft were the converted *Daffodil* and *Princess Iris*, and the *Ulster Monarch*, known as the 'commando ship'. *Princess Beatrix*, *Queen Emma* and *Prinz Albert* took part in the Lofoten Islands raid in March and December 1941. *Prince Charles* and *Prince Leopold* were at Vaagso, Norway, during the Christmas 1941 raids. At the August 1941 Spitzbergen raid the transport *Empress of Canada* had been used. Finally, a little over two months prior to 'Torch', there was the ill-fated Dieppe onslaught.

Known as Operation 'Jubilee' (19 August 1942), the fiasco at Dieppe culminated in some 1,000 dead. The bodies of two-thirds of the Canadian troops and a fifth of the British commandos littered the French beaches; a further 2,000 men were stranded and taken prisoner. It was an operation not dissimilar to that on the beaches of Gallipoli in 1915. In spite of the scale of the disaster the Royal Navy lost only one major unit, the destroyer *Berkeley*. Evading the vicious attack of enemy forces were the converted merchantmen, the white ensign LSIs *Glengyle*, *Princess Beatrix*, *Queen Emma*, *Prinz Albert*, *Princess Astrid*, *Prince*

Charles, Prince Leopold, Duke of Wellington and *Invicta*.

Operation 'Torch' brought together the greatest armada in history: some 240 merchantmen and ninety-four naval escorts from the United Kingdom; 112 merchantmen and seventy-five naval escorts from the United States. These numbers were mustered despite the quite serious shortage of shipping – so much so that, for a time, UK imports had to be cut and industry was faced with a reduction of reserves of raw materials. Unemployment was threatened, and the lowering of living standards seemed inevitable. The six months of the ensuing campaign required the use of 106 merchantmen per month, though the estimate had been sixty-six.

The situation was aggravated by the 2½ million ton backlog of damaged vessels. The majority were lying in British ports, and although steps were taken to transfer some of the work to North America, many were insufficiently unseaworthy to undertake the Atlantic crossing. Many damaged ships were now being routed direct to shipyards in India and South Africa.

Even in spite of the uncertain situation 250,860 US troops had been brought to the United Kingdom during 1942. Of these 153,379 were carried in British-flag troopships and 129,000 were re-embarked for North Africa. British cargo ships also carried out thirty-four sailings (military equipment) on US account.

Long before the actual assault convoys left British ports for Algeria, a steady stream of convoys carrying stores, ammunition and fuel sailed in advance – the first from the Clyde on 14 October. Destinations were Oran, divided into three sectors, Algiers for the eastern and central sectors as well as the forward ports of Bougie and Bône. During the passage from Britain Force H was led by three battleships, three aircraft carriers, three cruisers and seventeen destroyers. The task force for Oran and Algiers included one battleship, five carriers, six cruisers and twenty-six destroyers.

In Casablanca, French Morocco, where the American expeditionary force made three landings, the heavy Atlantic swell caused problems, and 34 per cent of the landing craft was lost. This sector was covered by two cruisers and three destroyers patrolling deep in the waters of the Azores; close inshore were three battleships, four aircraft carriers and thirty-four destroyers.

The enemy were taken by surprise, but their underwater and air defences nevertheless proved strong, and Allied ships, personnel, servicemen and military equipment were lost. The diary kept by a merchant seaman serving as a writer aboard the P & O transport *Mooltan* gives some idea of the operation. *Mooltan*, after 'trooping' to Suez had been recalled from mid-Atlantic en route for New York. Embarking American servicemen and a small Air Force squad at Avonmouth on 24

October she sailed as one of the forty-one merchantmen which made up convoy KMF (O) 1; departure was from the Clyde estuary on the night of 26 October. On Friday 6 November at 2200 hours the convoy passed through the Straits of Gibraltar.

Saturday 7 November. Joined by another aircraft carrier and LSIs *Royal Ulsterman, Royal Scotsman* and *Princess Beatrix* about 1000 hrs. The last 3 ships named are ex cross-channel steamers equipped with LCAs. They will probably provide our assault landing craft, as our radial davits are not strong enough to support LCAs like *Viceroy of India* and many other transports, all of which have been converted with extra disembarkation ports, welded rails and scramble nets and are self-contained Landing Ships Infantry large (LSI(L)). Land visible on port side only. Catalina keeping friendly eye on us. Later joined big convoy of cargo ships (KMS 1). We are now part of huge convoy which seems to stretch in all directions. Can see 66 ships at one time without moving. Have 2 more aircraft carriers, screen of destroyers and Motor Launches, and Motor Torpedo Boats. Weather absolutely wonderful, but a little cold in the afternoon and evening.

Sunday 8 November (D Day). As soon as light could see Arzeu beach, near Oran. Most of transports laid close to land with smoke screens partially obscuring them. We were one of last to go right in close to beach. Our small contingent of RAF Regiment have already gone ashore. Until the capture of La Senia and Tafaraoui airfields our American USAF ground crews are not required ashore, no doubt our inability to carry our own assault landing craft explains *Mooltan*'s choice for this role. Two Tank Landing ships can be seen discharging lorries, jeeps, tanks and guns from pontoon to beach. Steady procession winding up roads from coast to hills. In the distance can hear steady rumble of heavy guns bombarding. At about 0800 hrs moved our anchorage to further out in bay. Landing barges coming alongside in ones and twos to take off troops. The Stars and Stripes is flying from the foremast, much to the glee of American servicemen exclaiming at 'Old Glory'. We would have preferred the Red Ensign. We are very much behind schedule. Went on watch on bridge communications at 1000 hrs and 2200 hrs. Very few signals coming through.

Monday 9 November. Cruiser *Aurora* shelled shore positions not far away. Our activity delayed through lack of landing barges. Heavy swell makes it difficult for troops laden with equipment to leave ship. At about 1400 hrs two aircraft with French markings came over and machine-gunned beach. All ships opened fire and one plane appeared to crash with smoke pouring from engine. Other plane must have got away. Later in afternoon, two more aircraft came over and are believed to have dropped bombs. No sign of any damage.

Tuesday 10 November. Another plane identified as French flew past us at deck level at 1030, swept round and machine gunned beach. Other ships opened fire at him very quickly. Actually proved to be an American plane which fired on beach by mistake. Snippets of information being constantly received, including report of sniper wiped out by hand grenade after killing 3 soldiers and wounding a fourth on shore. Big tanker converted with bow doors came alongside to take off 'baggage'. Finished Wireless Room watch at 1400 hrs and resume Bridge watch to-morrow morning.

Wednesday 11 November. Started watch on Bridge at 0200 hrs. Received news that *Nieuw Zeeland* which left Arzeu yesterday evening was torpedoed this morning on her way to Gibraltar. Also hear *Otranto* narrowly avoided 2 torpedoes fired at her on way from Algiers to Gibraltar. Big cargo convoy, we think from the States arrived to-day with destroyer escort. *Durban Castle* and *Warwick Castle* left in the evening. (Nobody recognised the significance of the date.)

Thursday 12 November. Another cargo convoy arrived about the same time this afternoon. With them was a captured French ship called *Eridan*, which with the *Jamaique* makes the fifth ship brought in here. *Ettrick, Orbita* and *Letitia* left at dusk with destroyer escort. We are the only transport left here from the original convoy, apart from the Headquarters ship *Reina Del Pacifico*. Continued discharging cargo all night into large Tank Landing ship.

Friday 13 November. Finished Bridge watches and resumed duties in office. Due to sail this afternoon, but at last moment signalled that we are to receive passengers of some sort. (Later understood that they included Naval Commandos disembarked from a British submarine by canoe who failed to reach their objective – Oran.) Shifted anchorage at dusk to just forward of *Reina Del Pacifico* – very close to Arzeu Harbour. Most of the cargo ships and the *Jamaique* and *Eridan* left during the afternoon – probably for Oran.

Saturday 14 November. Moved anchorage at 0500 hrs as in danger of going aground. Left Arzeu Bay – Z Green Beach – after a stay of a few hours short of a week at noon together with remainder of cargo ships. Learned that the *Warwick Castle* and *Viceroy of India* torpedoed and sunk. *Nieuw Zeeland* made Gibraltar with a huge hole in her side. On duty at 1400 hrs as member of 6" gun crew. In convoy with *Reina Del Pacifico* and H.M. ships *Largs* and *Bulolo* (Invasion Headquarters ships) together with 3 destroyers and another merchant ship – possibly Port line vessel. Eleven Flying Fortresses with Spitfire escort flew over. Three Tank Landing ships slowly dropping astern of us and large cargo convoy out on our starboard bow. Went in very close to Oran so that a tanker and 2 heavily laden freighters could go in. At dusk were steaming at 15 knots and taking very wide and frequent zig-zags.

Sunday 15 November. Arrived Gibraltar early morning. Finished gun watches. 'J' class destroyer with stern blown off. Continual procession of every type of aircraft flying in and out of the airfield. Trawlers with survivors coming in. Depth charges dropped outside the boom defence from blackout to daylight.

Monday 16 November. Norwegian destroyer *Glaesdale* brought *Ettrick* crew on board together with other survivors. Tanker came alongside to oil up. Survivors on board include crew members of *Viceroy of India, Awatea* and *Glenfinlas*. Also 12 naval ratings of the Escort Carrier *Avenger*, which blew up, the sole survivors from a complement of approx 500. The Purser's Clerk and I each took a typewriter into the Dining Saloon and the survivors filed past in two columns, so that we could record their particulars, and deposit typed lists of all on board with Naval Authorities at Gibraltar.

In contrast are the day-to-day notes of the Ministry of Information Officer aboard HMS *Wild Swan*, written to prepare for his coverage of the operation for the British Broadcasting Corporation:

Sunday 8 November. The great bulk of the convoy and escorts are closing in on the harbour entrance which, at this time of the morning, is shrouded with a heavy mist resembling a gigantic table-cloth. Already, we can hear the distant roar of the shore batteries. But we press on. A Cruiser is already in action in Oran Harbour; no details are available as yet, but it appears that the authorities have rejected our ultimatum for a peaceful settlement, and, according to activities at hand, intend to resist us. Landings have been made.

06.30 hours. The invasion is now in full swing unhampered by opposition. In view now is the whole panoramic coast-line which stands out so beautifully against the clear blue sky. We close in, land more tanks, lorries and weapons of destruction. From the transports, a ferry service is being run to and from the beaches where assault troops can be observed wading ashore. Inside Oran Harbour, the Cruiser which was in action has forced three French Destroyers to give up the fight, damaged and in sinking conditions. A fourth Destroyer has paid for the folly of Vichy in full; she has been sunk. Battle raging spasmodically all day. Transports in the bay are discharging their deadly cargoes with as much interruption as a luxury liner would have received in the piping days of peace.

Monday 9 November. The distant staccato of machine-gun fire can still be heard coming from the direction of the beaches. Our escorts continue to hammer at the enemy's defences as great columns of smoke continue to rise against a background of sun-baked hillocks. This morning at 10.00 hours, an armistice was signed to cease hostilities in the Algerian sector of the battle-zone, following the capitulation of the garrison. The Allied Forces, however, are still fighting with unabated fury around Oran which is slowly being encircled. We also learn with no element of surprise that

Vichy Naval Forces off Casablanca have suffered severe losses in engagements with the British Fleet, which has brought nothing but contempt from the Vichy Government.

It is interesting to note that, in spite of Vichy's rages and threats because of the Allied landings, nothing has resulted from them as yet. Indeed, the defeat of a large part of her Fleet off Casablanca, coupled with our ceaseless and heroic pursuit in the Western Desert of Rommel's Africa Corps, makes Vichy's threat of declaring war on the Allies very improbable – if not out of the question altogether.

Likewise at Algeria, negotiations for a peace settlement, this time at Oran, are now proceeding. It is unlikely, however, that a decision will be reached too hastily; at the same time it is evident that the defenders will not be able to hold out much longer against the superior skill of our troops, hammering their way into the inner and last hope of Oran's defences.

This afternoon, we herald the news of the capitulation of the French Navy and Army. Triumphantly, we also learn that the new 35,000 ton French Battleship the *Jean Bart* burns fiercely as the result of an engagement with American Naval Forces.

Wednesday 11 November. Casablanca has capitulated! News has reached us that all French resistance has drawn to a close and hostilities have ceased in French North Africa as we leave the scene of this latest Allied Battle Zone. As we steam slowly out of the bay, we also leave with the unbounded satisfaction of having done our duty, and of carrying out this gigantic task without the loss of a single ship en-route. It has now been revealed to the Public that 350 Naval ships and 500 transports took part in what has been described as the Largest Amphibian Operation in History. And to celebrate this Victory, church bells throughout the Country will be rung for the first time since the commencement of hostilities.

Upon the instructions of Prime Minister Churchill, 15 November 1942 was celebrated as Victory Sunday. Church bells rang out for the first time in three years to celebrate the passing of the risk of invasion from across the English Channel and the invasion of North Africa. The road to victory was clearing.

The twenty troopers of the first convoy included some of the finest of the P & O and Union Castle fleets – *Cathay, Ettrick, Strathallan, Strathnaver, Stratheden* and *Viceroy of India; Durban Castle, Llangibby Castle, Warwick Castle* and *Winchester Castle.* The assault convoy was led by two landing ships infantry (large) – *Keren* and *Karanja.* Also present were LSI's *Glengarry, Queen Emma, Princess Beatrix, Royal Scotsman, Royal Ulsterman* and *Ulster Monarch.*

During the first month of the campaign the losses were severe. A heavy price was paid in tonnage:

7 Nov. *Thomas Stone* (US); 9,255 tons. Torpedoed by *U-205*. (damaged).

11 Nov. *Cathay*; 15,225 tons. Bougie. Aircraft bombs.

11 Nov. *Karanja*; 9,890 tons. Bougie. Aircraft bombs.

11 Nov. *Awatea*; 13,482 tons. Bougie–Gibraltar. Aircraft bombs.

11 Nov. *Viceroy of India*; 19,627 tons. Algiers–Gibraltar. Torpedoed by *U-407*.

11 Nov. *Nieuw Zeeland* (Dutch); 11,069 tons. Oran–Gibraltar. Torpedoed by *U-380*.

12 Nov. *Browning*; 5,332 tons. ENE of Arzeu. Torpedoed by *U-595*.

13 Nov. *Maron*; 6,487 tons. Algiers–Gibraltar. Torpedoed by *U-81*.

13 Nov. *Glenfinlas*; 7,479 tons. Bougie. Aircraft bombs (damaged).

14 Nov. *Warwick Castle*; 20,107 tons. Gibraltar–UK. Torpedoed by *U-431*.

14 Nov. *Narkunda*; 16,632 tons. Bougie. Aircraft bombs.

14 Nov. *Lalande*; 7,453 tons. Algiers–Gibraltar. Torpedoed by *U-73* (damaged).

15 Nov. *Ettrick*; 11,279 tons. Gibraltar–UK. Torpedoed by *U-155* (sunk along with American *Almaak* and HMS *Avenger*).

16 Nov. *Clan MacTaggart*; 7,622 tons. UK–North Africa. Torpedoed by *U-92*.

20 Nov. *Prins Harald* (Norwegian); 7,244 tons. UK–North Africa. Torpedoed by *U-263*.

20 Nov. *Grangepark*; 5,132 tons. UK–North Africa. Torpedoed by *U-263*.

20 Nov. *Dewdale* (landing ship gantry); Bougie. Aircraft bombs (damaged).

24 Nov. *Trentbank*; 5,060 tons. UK–North Africa. Aircraft torpedo.

The *Dewdale* was further damaged by a mine at Algiers. Not until April 1943 did she arrive in Liverpool for repairs. 'Landing ships gantry vessels were equipped with four gantry crane extensions which travelled the main deck on rails and lowered fifteen landing craft in thirty minutes.)

The merchantmen were in the front line – at Oran, Algiers, Bougie (Bejaia), Philippeville (Skikda) and Bône (Annaba). In the interval between landings at Bougie on 11 November and the eventual establishment of fighter aircraft at Djidjelli two days later, there was no proper fighter cover over the port. Allied convoys were arriving at fortnightly intervals. The first on 22 November brought logistic and Air Force units, and the second at the beginning of December carried the remainder of the British 78th Division, the bulk of the 6th Armoured Division and Lieutenant-General Charles Allfrey's V Corps Headquarters. The third convoy arrived mid-December with more general military equipment. Without the back-up convoys bringing the supply and reinforcements of tanks, aviation fuel and the other munitions of war, the whole operation would have been in danger of coming to a halt.

Seven of those sunk during the early days were of the irreplaceable troop-carrying type. The LSI *Cathay* conversion, lying off Bougie and disembarking servicemen, was a fine target. Diving out of the clouds the Junkers 88s, flown by resolute and experienced pilots, attacked for many hours. Finally three bombs fell close to and abaft the engine room. With her engines wrecked and her boiler room a mass of fuel oil she listed to port and the order to abandon ship was given. Later *Cathay* took fire amidships after a delayed-action bomb exploded; she burned all night and at dawn, as the depth charges she was carrying exploded in the intense heat, the stern blew up and she disappeared.

Flying the white ensign, the LSI *Karanja* was hit by seven bombs. She blazed furiously with great loss of life and had to be abandoned. The 23-knot turbine-engined LSI *Awatea* of the Union Steamship Company of New Zealand, which was mainly crewed by New Zealanders, was abandoned soon after sailing from Bougie for Gibraltar and the United Kingdom. Attacked by six aircraft and badly damaged by aerial bombs and torpedoes she was quickly afire. Although many injured were taken ashore no lives were lost. *Strathnaver*, after enduring a heavy air-raid at Algiers, arrived at Bougie on 12 November and immediately ran into heavy torpedo and minelaying assaults. All day while unloading, she was under attack, and her gunners expended 3,204 rounds of Oerlikon and 216 rounds of Bofors with a further 750 rounds of .303 ammunition. (Surviving the war, *Strathnaver* carried a total of 129,000 troops and steamed 352,000 miles.)

With explosives in holds 5 and 6 the situation aboard *Glenfinlas* was desperate. Close by, the French liner *Alsina* was hit and caught fire. Much against their wishes, the master and officers of Glen Line merchantman were ordered by the Naval authorities to abandon ship. Salvaged from Bougie harbour in March 1943, *Glenfinlas* became embroiled in several misadventures before arriving at Sunderland for repairs as late as October. It was February 1944 before she sailed on her next outward voyage.

The master of *Glenfinlas*, in a report made to the owners of his vessel (Alfred Holt), drew attention to the defence made by her gunners during the action:

The attacks continued again on the following day, Friday 13th of November. At about 1220 hours an enemy formation of JU88's were seen approaching overhead. All effective guns that could bear were brought into action and 'pig troughs' again fired. Several large bombs were dropped on the quayside ... A JU88 was seen diving for the *Glenfinlas* at an angle of 40 degrees on the starboard side. He came under terrific fire from all ships' guns (12 pdr Oerlikons and Marlin guns). Pig troughs were again fired on the rapidly approaching track. At about 400 feet he released his bombs, possibly six. At least three of these hit the vessel on the starboard side, low down, outside Nos 1 & 2 holds.

Narkunda arrived at Bougie the next day. Disembarking troops and stores she sailed at 1600 hours. Sixty minutes later she came under heavy attack from the air, and a stick of bombs fell close to the port side, causing considerable underwater damage. By 1830 hours she had been abandoned and twelve minutes later the P & O troopship sank by the stern. With thirty-one crew members having been killed in the incident, the survivors were rescued by HMS *Cadmus*.

The enemy submarines lay in wait for the large transports. The turbo-electric *Viceroy of India*, a much-loved P & O liner built in 1929, now converted into an LSI and returning from the beachhead, was torpedoed forty miles north-north-east of Cape Caxine. All twenty-two passengers were rescued by HMS *Boadicea*; the crew suffered several casualties as a result of the explosion.

More unfortunate was the 20,107 ton *Warwick Castle*, steaming with homeward convoy MKF1 as it came under attack in heavy seas 200 miles west of the coast of Portugal. The largest of the Union Castle fleet to be lost in the war, she broke up quickly, sinking bow first with her screws still rotating. Launching the lifeboats proved a hazardous operation. HMS *Vansittart* found it particularly difficult to rescue survivors. The master, lying upon a raft, had refused all help until others had been saved, and was eventually brought aboard the destroyer in a poor condition. He died shortly afterwards and, after a brief service, was buried at sea. Sixty-three officers and men lost their lives.

The next month (21 December) the 23,722 ton P & O liner *Strathallan* was making her second voyage to Algiers as commodore ship of convoy KMF5, when she was torpedoed by *U-562*. Her passengers numbered 5,122, including 4,000 British and American troops and 250 Queen Alexandra nurses. The explosion in the engine room killed four members of the crew outright; immediately she began to list. With *Strathallan* considered to be in no danger of sinking she was taken in tow by HMS *Laforey* whilst 3,000 servicemen remained on board; other personnel were taken off by HMS *Verity*.

Later that day as fire spread rapidly, *Strathallan* was abandoned; *Laforey* and *Panther* attended to the disembarkation. With a skeleton crew left aboard, the tow was taken up by HM tug *Restive*. Just 12 miles from Oran her situation became precarious, as she began to sink lower in the water. A little later the great liner turned over and sank.

Convoy KMF5, with the 16,297-ton transport *Cameronia* as commodore ship, continued its voyage to Algiers, to which port most of the vessels were routed for discharge. However, *Circassia, Clan Lamont* and *Cameronia*, instructed to make for Bône, sustained several vicious attacks from enemy aircraft, and *Cameronia* was hit by an aerial torpedo. Damaged, she limped into Bougie harbour on one engine, carrying seventeen dead and thirty-three wounded.

On New Year's Day the Naval Commander, Expeditionary Force, Admiral Sir Andrew Cunningham (later Admiral of the Fleet, Viscount Cunningham of Hyndhope) sent a message to the officers and men of the Allied merchant vessels. In giving his good wishes he said that when victory came it would be due, in no small measure, to the courage and tenacity with which the merchantmen of the Allied nations had kept at sea in face of continued and savage attack. 'Many examples have been brought to my notice of bravery, devotion and skill which has only added to the admiration I already have for the work you have performed.' He added: 'Navy, Army and Air Force alike know how much they depend on your efforts. May success prosper those efforts in the coming years.'

Coinciding with the New Year, controversy developed between the Americans and the British regarding the transport of fuel direct to the North African coast. Atlantic all-tanker convoys from Britain had been suggested for some time but the lack of escorts had always been an obstacle. Now it was the Americans who faltered at the escort requirements, for all their newly built warships were required for the Pacific war. The British, for their part, were willing to see escorts pulled out of the Atlantic trade convoys in spite of the horrific losses that would ensue, as well as the consequent loss of dry-cargo imports for Britain. Even as the argument continued the British Admiralty took action.

Convoy TM1, a 10-knot flotilla sailed from Trinidad direct for Gibraltar and the 'Torch' battle zone under light escort. South-west of the Canary Islands and out of reach of air cover the convoy was attacked by a pack of U-boats. Seven of its nine tankers were sunk and valuable supplies of high-octane fuel lost.

It has been claimed that the enemy had been advised of the sailing of TM1 by agents in Trinidad. *U-514*, on passage to the Caribbean, sighted the tankers on 3 January 1943. After sinking *British Vigilance* by torpedo she passed through the convoy on the surface and was fired on by several of the tankers. *Otenia 11* torpedoed by *U-436*, exploded and sank on 8 January; the Norwegian *Albert L. Ellsworth* met the same fate (also by *U-436*). There followed the Norwegian *Minister Wedel* (*U-522*) and the Panamanian-flag *Norvik*, also by *U-522*. *Empire Lytton*, torpedoed by *U-444*, was subsequently sunk by two assaults from

U-442. As late as 11 January, eight days after being sighted, the convoy lost the *British Dominion* to *U-522* (three torpedoes), later sunk by *U-620* in a final *coup de grâce*. With all sinkings loss of life had been heavy and the whole episode was viewed with alarm by the Admiralty in London.

As convoy TM1 was being decimated news came of the American decision to establish 'Tortank' convoys, and on 5 February a US escorted convoy (OT1) left Aruba for Dakar. Subsequently they took over the sole provisioning responsibility for 'Torch' tanker convoys. Beginning with OT2, which sailed on 20 February, these quickly became a great success. This was the first of the 14-knot Greyhound convoys which were soon to be despatched every twenty-four days direct from the Caribbean to Gibraltar, Casablanca and the Azores.

Shipments of cased petrol continued to be transported from the United Kingdom until March, primarily because the Allied forces had no canning plants in north-west Africa. In total, 288,000 tons of petrol were transported 'packed' from Britain to the 'Torch' area during the first three months of 1943.

Subsequently 14-knot Greyhound convoys were introduced from the Caribbean direct to Britain. Convoy CU1, of nine tankers, sailed from Curaçao on 20 March. Like the OT convoys, they were organized and escorted by the US Navy. They continued throughout 1943 and 1944.

Throughout the early successes and frustrations of Operation 'Torch' the hard-pressed island of Malta was by no means forgotten, though it had received few supplies since the 'Pedestal' convoy. On 20 November four merchantmen arrived safely from Alexandria in spite of sustaining heavy air attacks en route. The next month there followed Operation 'Stoneage', a convoy one of whose five vessels was Alfred Holt's *Glenartney*. She was carrying a variety of cargo which included aviation spirit in drums – particularly hazardous in whatever manner it was carried. Shortly before sailing the Chinese crew were replaced by a full naval crew led by 'a tough RNR Lieutenant Commander in gaiters and complete with a pistol'. The convoy, whilst attracting the usual attention from enemy aircraft, did reach Malta safely, however. In the words of *Glenartney's* second mate, 'the naval crew performed splendidly throughout under the Merchant Navy officers and seemed thoroughly to enjoy their novel experience'.

North African ports like Bône, the main supply base for the First Army since 12 November and virtually on the Front Line, suffered from almost incessant air raids. Moreover each coastal convoy from Algiers had to be fought through. On New Year's Day 1943 *Novelist* and *Harpalyce* were both damaged at Bône; the day after *St Merriel* and the new 8,201-ton 'deep-sea' tanker *Empire Metal* were destroyed, and peripheral damage was suffered by *Dalhanna* and *Melampus*, moored close by. Port facilities were also hard hit, and merchantmen were required to discharge cargo with their own lifting gear.

During that Mediterranean winter there was much enemy activity. Damaged by Italian assault craft at Algiers was *Empire Centaur*; attacked by aircraft torpedo as she lay off the port was Cunard's 19,761-ton *Scythia*; at Bône, *Hindustan* and *Recorder*; at Philippeville, *Ousel* – the last three all bombed by aircraft. On the approach to the port of Philippeville, the American-flag Liberty ship *William Wirt*, carrying aviation fuel loaded in Liverpool, was bombed, and a month later was attacked again as she neared Gibraltar on her return passage. A second US Liberty vessel the *Arthur Middleton*, carrying munitions and other explosives from New York, was torpedoed by *U-73* off Cape Falcon (Oran). She exploded, with flames and debris rising to more than 1,000 feet.

Sunk in coastal convoys were the *Hampton Lodge* and *Benalbanach*, the latter with 375 servicemen aboard and a crew of seventy-four. Carrying ammunition, petrol, stores, motor vehicles and tanks, she was struck by two aerial torpedoes. In less than two minutes she broke up and sank; there were only forty survivors. The Belgian *Jean Jadot*, with eleven British gunners manning her armament, was sunk by *U-453* near Cape Tenez. She carried 323 British troops with military supplies and tanks on deck. Rescue was made by HMS *Verity*.

Among those damaged were the US-built *Ocean Rider*, the former French *Ville de Strasbourg* and the Canadian-built *Fort Babine*. The latter, towed to Gibraltar where she was under repair for over seven months, then set off for the United Kingdom towed by the naval tugs *Prosperous* and *Scheldt*. Bombed in heavy weather 250 miles south-west of Cape Finisterre (northern Spain), she had to be sunk by the senior service so that she did not remain a drifting menace to shipping. The 'Frenchman', torpedoed by *U-371*, limped to Algiers only to be subsequently bombed during one of the many raids on the harbour.

En route for 'Torch' during January two American Liberty vessels with war supplies fell to the U-boats off the Azores. They were the *Julia Ward Howe* (*U-442*) and the *Charles C. Pinckney* (*U-514*), both stragglers from convoy UGS4 (Norfolk, Virginia, to Gibraltar). US sources claimed at the time that *U-514* had been sunk by gunfire from the freighter, but, although she may have been damaged on this occasion, official sources show that she was sunk on 8 July 1943 by British aircraft of Squadron 224.

On the 11th of the month the Mediterranean island of Pantellaria was captured; obviously there were greater landings to follow, but where would the Allies strike next?

It was to Bône in June 1943 that the *Fort Fitzgerald*, loaded with military supplies from the United Kingdom, sailed. During my service aboard the Vancouver-built merchantman in the western Mediterranean

I first became aware of the Pioneer Corps, whose roots in the British Army go back a long way in history – indeed as far back as the British garrison at Calais in 1346. The North African campaign is of interest as being the first in which British Pioneer companies from the United Kingdom were sent to a semi-tropical theatre of war, and also the first in which they worked in conjunction with native labour raised in North Africa and with multiracial Pioneer companies raised from Asiatics and North Africans.

Sailing in the 'Torch' convoys between 26 October and 27 November 1942, the 7 Pioneer Group HQ and forty-nine companies were part of combined operations. With the same function, their valuable work was continued throughout the Sicilian and Italian campaigns. One of their key roles was off-loading the multitude of supplies and reloading the many merchantmen for the beach-landings which were to follow. At the port of Bône I recall the 'Pioneers' as stevedores of the highest quality, great-hearted giants, seemingly of all ages, who cleared the decks and holds of the *Fitzgerald* in next to no time. In charge was a peacetime British port official who had been carrying out this specialist work as a soldier from the very first day of the war. Bône was still an enemy target: only two weeks previously the US-flag *Daniel Huger*, discharging aviation fuel in drums, had been bombed and abandoned.

During the Grecian and Crete campaigns 80 per cent of the Pioneer Corps in the region (Cypriot, Jewish and Indian nationals) were taken prisoner. Of the 800 men of the Cypriot companies evacuated to Crete only 500 survived. Of the Jewish companies, many of them refugees from Central Europe, 2,500 were killed, missing or captured. It is a sad tale, whose story today lies buried and forgotten amidst the welter of records in some remote museum or Army archive office.

Returning westward from Bône for Pepel, Sierra Leone, with instructions to load iron ore for the steelworks of South Wales, the *Fort Fitzgerald* took aboard 1,000 German prisoners of war for disembarkation at Oran. Transport was there awaiting the prisoners which would take them to the United States. We were one of several merchantmen engaged in this 'traffic', which was not without its risks and achieved without escort from the senior service. Subsequently the US flag *Benjamin Contee* (bound from Bône for Oran), carrying 1,800 Italian prisoners of war was damaged by aircraft torpedo sixteen miles off Cape de Gardia. Some 320 prisoners were killed. Towed to Gibraltar the vessel was under repair for many weeks.

Despite the losses and the large number of vessels under repair and unworkable for long periods, Operation 'Torch' was a great success as the statistics show. Over the six-month period only 2.16 per cent of tonnage escorted had been lost. The total of Allied shipping employed was 11 million tons. At Algiers 390 ocean-going steamers disembarked men and discharged around one million tons of stores and supplies. Included were large quantities of food; some 300,000 tons of petrol, lubricant and other oils; 150,000 tons of coal for the railways and public utility services; 100,000 tons of ammunition; and some 30,000 vehicles, including tanks. On 4 February 1943 the port of Algiers was crammed with eighty merchantmen, the largest concentration of shipping since the landings.

The concise figures for five ports (between 8 November and 31 December 1942) and for Bône (between 24 November and 31 December 1942) make impressive reading:

Port	Dwt. tons discharged	Personnel	Vehicles
Casablanca	38,000	80,000	9,400
Oran	290,675	90,296	9,847
Algiers	248,048	123,559	14,746
Bougie	51,500	16,500	2,300
Philippeville	56,000	92,000	1,600
Bône	86,053	31,085	4,491

During January a further 42,000 tons was landed at Bône, 4,000 tons of which were reloaded and carried forward in naval landing craft to the small ports of La Calle and Tabarka.

Over the total period of the campaign, merchantmen conveyed 394 aircraft, 63,784 vehicles, 901 tanks, 3,677 guns and six locomotives together with their tenders. Cased petrol amounted to 239,796 tons, bulk oil 67,188 tons, barbed wire 7,000 tons, steam coal 345,713 tons, and other military stores 769,321 tons. There were, in addition, such 'comforts' for the armed services as 71,000 bags of mail, 450 million cigarettes, 9 million bars of chocolate and 500,000 pounds of soap.

The Royal and Merchant Navies successfully and continuously supplied and reinforced both Montgomery's Eighth Army and the predominantly American First Army in Algeria. The latter made little progress during the winter months, though the glorious Eighth Army advanced steadily towards Tunisia. The battle of the supply routes was the one upon which all other battles depended.

Control of the sea from Gibraltar eastwards largely overcame the formidable difficulties of keeping the two armies supplied at so great a distance from rearward bases. With the blockade of the coast complete, Bizerta and Tunis were captured on 7 May. The consequent surrender of the Axis forces five days later coincided with victory in the Atlantic. With some 150,000 German and Italian prisoners taken, King George VI was to remark: 'the debt of Dunkirk has been repaid'.

On 19 May the first convoy to reach Malta unopposed arrived in Valletta harbour. By 7 June minesweepers had cleared a passage through to Alexandria, thereby shortening the distance between the United Kingdom and Egypt by about 6,000 miles. This fact alone meant an increase in available shipping space for future ambitious projects.

On 10 July 1943 the Allies invaded Sicily. Code-named Operation 'Husky' it was the greatest seaborne force ever embarked at the time. Indeed, the number of troops and craft involved were only exceeded in the 1944 Normandy landings if the follow-up formations are taken into account. Only a shortage of sufficient shipping had prevented a landing on the underbelly of Europe before the summer of 1943. Now, even at this time, the build-up of American forces in the United Kingdom for the final action across the English Channel was being mobilized.

'Husky' was a miracle of combined operations among the four services, each dependent upon one another. Some 2,600 warships, merchantmen and landing craft converged on the south of the island, over 1,600 of which came from the British Royal and Merchant Navies. They were carrying a total of 155,000 British and Empire troops and over 66,000 American assault troops, their equipment and stores. Included were 155 British and sixty-six US merchantmen, from large troop transports to coasters. There were 14,000 vehicles, 600 tanks and 1,800 guns, with the support of 750 warships of all types and some 4,000 aircraft. The use of landing craft tanks (LCT's) and landing ship tanks (LSTs) enabled armour to be landed with the assaulting infantry for the first time. LSTs *Boxer, Bruiser* and *Thruster*, flying the white ensign, played a significant part in making the landings so successful.

Convoys sailed from the United Kingdom and the United States, from the Middle East, Algeria and Tunisia. All merged south of Malta to spearhead the operation. For the first time in the Mediterranean war Malta had become a really secure base from which operations could be launched. Close to Valletta harbour, located in one of the island's caves, was the underground operations room, from where Operation 'Husky' was co-ordinated. To ensure that the attacking force would have essential docking facilities, four out of the five drydocks were cleared of wrecked and damaged shipping.

In spite of a Force 7 gale the seaborne assault went ahead as planned; little resistance was encountered from the Italian coastal defences, which were taken completely by surprise. The covering Royal Navy force was augmented to six battleships, two aircraft carriers and twenty-four destroyers.

Assembled were some of the great names of the British liner fleet: *Ascania, Circassia, Derbyshire, Duchess of Bedford., Dunera* and *Staffordshire, Monarch of Bermuda* and *Reina del Pacifico, Orontes* and *Otranto; Durban Castle* with men of the 41st Marine Commandos;

Llangibby Castle with Canadian commando troops; *Winchester Castle* with men of the Eighth Army from Egypt.

Strathnaver, with 3,300 servicemen embarked at Port Said, joined a convoy of twenty vessels with torpedo boat and destroyer protection. *Almanzora*, a veteran of the First World War, was commodore ship of MWF37, a follow-up convoy from Port Said and Alexandria. With the convoy of twelve merchantmen, she arrived south of Sicily carrying 2,000 Army and Air Force reinforcements on 13 July. A channel had been swept, and she was able to proceed into the inner harbour of Syracuse.

Only the 19,141-ton *Windsor Castle*, which had been earmarked for 'Husky' was missing. On 23 March, north-west of Algiers, she had been torpedoed and sunk by a resolute aviator of the Luftwaffe. At the time she was travelling in convoy and carrying 2,000 troops, all of whom were brought safely to shore. Flying the white ensign off the Sicilian beaches were the LSI vessels *Glengyle, Keren, Prince Leopold, Princess Astrid, Princess Josephine Charlotte* and *Prinz Albert*. Sailing from Tripoli, carrying a total of twenty-seven landing craft, were *Princess Beatrix, Queen Emma, Royal Scotsman* and *Royal Ulsterman*.

The first batch of troops and stores for assembly at North African ports sailed from North America as early as 28 May. From these merchantmen and others assembling at Oran and Algiers were formed six of the assault and follow-up convoys. The complex convoy operation from the West began with NCS1, speed 8 knots, which left Oran on 4 July followed by the 13-knot NCF1 main assault convoy. This sailed from Algiers two days later and included twenty-two LSI vessels and seven supply merchant-men. Convoy NCF2, sailing from Algiers on 7 July, included a reserve of four troop transports which was joined by KMF19 from the Clyde.

Convoy KMF18, sailing on 28 June from the Clyde estuary, included HMS *Hilary* and twelve troop transports bound for the Bark West invasion beaches west of Punta di Formiche. Rear-Admiral Sir Philip Vian was in command aboard *Hilary*, which was also carrying Lord Louis Mountbatten, the Chief of Combined Operations, General Simonds in command of the Canadian Division, and Brigadier Laycock.

For the thirty-four convoys, with their widely varying speeds and different starting-points, to converge on Sicily in the right order and at the right time was a great achievement – not only for the planners but for the convoy commodores and their signallers, the master mariners and their navigators, the naval escorts and commanding officers, plus the crews of all vessels involved. In a letter addressed to masters of Allied merchant ships, Rear-Admiral Sir Philip Vian said 'a great part of its success [Operation 'Husky'] is entrusted to the well-proven steadfastness and seamanlike skill of the Merchant Navies of the Allies, whom I am proud to have under my command in this momentous task.'

The paymaster aboard the former P & O steamer HMS *Keren* (LSI), flying the white ensign, vividly recalls 'Husky' in his autobiography *Campaign Ribbons*.

> In the early hours of 10 July we dropped our 'hook' about a mile off the beaches of Cape Passero and the routine of assault landing commenced – boats away, scrambling nets overside, nervous troops directed to the LCP's [Landing Craft Personnel] pitching in the heavy swell, derricks creaking with the weight of cargo slings as jeeps and ammunition boxes were lowered into the waiting LCT's. Then the revving of engines as the flotillas headed in for the last mile to the beach. Would the enemy be waiting? Would shore batteries blaze into action against them and against us? It was an eerie feeling, waiting and watching as dawn broke ... By the time the sun had risen, a secure beachhead was well established.

The biggest assault which the enemy could mount at sea was against convoy KMS 18B as it passed eastward through the Straits of Gibraltar and entered the Mediterranean battle zone. Off the coast of Algeria, some 600 miles from the beachhead, *City of Venice* and *St Essylt* were lost to *U-375* on 4 July, as was the commodore ship *Devis*, to *U-593* carrying Rear-Admiral Hugh England on the following day.

KMS 18B was a slow, back-up convoy of eighteen merchantmen and one tank landing ship (LST 406) which sailed from the Clyde on 24 June. It was the second voyage to the battle zone for several of the vessels, and for the likes of *Alcinous* and *Empire Confidence*, it was the third. The latter, a former German merchantman, had been captured off Chile (December 1939) by HMS *Despatch*.

There were a great variety of vessels all carrying military supplies: *Derwentdale*, later to be damaged at Salerno, *Gudaan Maersk* and *Orestes*; five Canadian 'Forts' – *Fort Buckingham, Fort Lajoire, Fort Meduchi, Fort Nashwaak* and *Fort Stager; Empire Cato* and *Empire Elaine*; and *Benedict, Norman Monarch* and *Stanhill* of Bougie fame (the latter was alongside the quay on the day *Alsina, Glenfinlas* and *Narkunda* were bombed). A further seven tank landing ships and HMS *Roberts* joined the convoy south of Malta.

City of Venice was well known in the western Mediterranean. In November 1942 she was at Oran and Philippeville, in December and again in January at Algiers. In February she returned to Algiers for the third time. She had been present in convoy when *Grangepark, Prinz Harald* and *Trentbank* had been sunk; in December when *Bretwalda* was sunk; and in February when *Empire Webster* and *Empire Banner* were lost. Now, loaded with military vehicles and equipment for the underbelly of Europe, she herself fell victim to the enemy.

Carrying a crew of 180 and 302 servicemen (292 Army and ten Navy) *City of Venice* quickly began to settle by the head. Despite the ship's being abandoned in an orderly fashion, disaster struck as the frigate *Teviot* came to the rescue. Twenty-two were lost, including the ship's master, ten members of his crew and officer commander troops, when No.8 lifeboat capsized. Eight hours later the *City* boat, on fire fore and aft, sank; 460 survivors were rescued by the corvettes *Honeysuckle* and *Rhododendron* and HM tug *Restive*.

St Essylt, a two-year-old motorship with a complement of 401, including 300 men of the Canadian First Division, was carrying 900 tons of military stores including vehicles and two landing craft on deck. The commodore was to remark in his report, 'she was a dangerous ship'. It was her second visit to the Mediterranean having been commodore vessel of the ill-fated convoy MKS7, when three merchantmen, *Baltonia*, *Mary Slessor* and *Empire Mordred*, were sunk by mines off Bougie on 7 February.

Pitching into a short rough sea and buffeted by an easterly wind, *St Essylt* took a heavy list immediately the torpedo struck. With exploding ammunition and drums of petrol which ignited forward, there was a blinding flash. Nevertheless, she too was abandoned in an orderly manner, though many were forced to jump into the sea, where they clung hold of rafts and floats. Whilst every effort was made by the master and the chief mate, assisted by a brave MRA gunner and two Canadian servicemen, to save the ship, it was to no avail. Again it was *Honeysuckle*, *Rhododendron* and the tug *Restive* to the rescue. Eight hours after the assault *St Essylt* blew up and sank. One of her crew and thirty-two servicemen were missing.

The 6,054-ton *Devis*, owned by the Lamport & Holt company, carried a cargo of 4,000 tons of military stores, including two landing craft (LCMs) stowed on deck. Among the forty-six crew were thirteen MRA and eight DEMS gunners, plus the commodore and his staff of a Royal Navy lieutenant and five signalmen. Additionally she had taken on 289 Canadian troops at 'the tail of the bank' on the river Clyde.

After *St Essylt* had been torpedoed, speed was increased to 9½ knots and zigzagging commenced. Fifty miles east of Algiers, the sea now calm with the sun overhead, *Devis* was torpedoed on the starboard side, abreast No.4 hold which was immediately enveloped in flames. Here were stowed vehicles and petrol and immediately above in the 'tween deck were accommodated some of the servicemen. It was in this part of the vessel that fifty-two perished, with one being brought out injured. Broken in the explosion was the propeller shaft, which caused the engines to race until they were stopped by the engineer on watch. This action undoubtedly helped to ensure that no further lives were lost while the merchantman was abandoned.

Fifteen minutes after the torpedo struck, the last to leave the stricken *Devis*, Commodore England and her master, took to the water, and another vital ship in the Allied Fleet sank to the depths of the Mediterranean. Only one of the landing craft, which had floated off apparently undamaged, remained to mark the spot. The commodore, after seeing that the survivors were safely landed at Bougie, reboarded the rescue vessel HMS *Cleveland*. He then caught up with the convoy and resumed his command on board the *Fort Stager*.

Whilst Operation 'Husky' suffered losses off the beaches and in the harbour of Syracuse and Augusta they were nowhere as serious as those sustained in the early days of 'Torch'. The American Liberty ships *Robert Rowan* and *Joseph G. Cannon* were two that were struck by aircraft bombs; the latter had sailed from Haifa, carrying troops and equipment. Grounded, she was later towed to Malta for repairs. The *Robert Rowan* caught fire and was abandoned just before her cargo of ammunition blew up.

A third US Liberty ship, the *Timothy Pickering*, carrying army stores from Alexandria, was also bombed. Because she was a danger to shipping, she was shelled by one of the escorts after being abandoned and sank in shallow waters. *En route* from the eastern Mediterranean, convoy MWS36 lost the *Shahjehan*, which had been built for the Asiatic Steam Navigation Company at Port Glasgow in 1942. Torpedoed by *U-453* she caught fire and, though taken in tow, she sank a few hours later, 150 miles north-east of Benghazi.

The landing ship (gantry) *Ennerdale*, an ocean-class tanker conversion, was bombed and damaged at the time of the landings. *City of Delhi*, due to discharge at the harbour of Catania, was re-routed to Augusta as the port did not fall as planned. Here, a few miles from the front line, the anchorage was congested with merchantmen, many of them in the process of landing stores and equipment.

One of the DEMS gunners aboard *City of Delhi* remembers Augusta as some of the worst moments of his life: 'The enemy, with his JU88's and Stukas, was terrifying; every 1½ hours for three days and four nights they came at us at anchor ... We finally beached off Syracuse and discharged into DUKW's (Ducks) and floated off at high tide several days later.' After Operation 'Husky' the *Delhi* continued trading in the Mediterranean and the Indian Ocean. She was away from her home port for over fourteen months. The American amphibious all-wheel-drive DUKW vehicle was first used at the Sicilian campaign. It proved vital in maintaining the supply link between off-loading vessels at sea and land-based forces.

Augusta suffered a particularly heavy raid on the night of 20/21 July. Bombed and blown up was *Fort Pelly*, discharging ammunition; four of her officers and thirty-four crew were killed. *Empire Florizel*, hit by two bombs, exploded amidst a sheet of flame. *Ocean Virtue* received a near miss and was seriously damaged. Lying at anchor close by, but spared the worst of the assault, was *Empire Moon*. Her cargo of duff had been loaded at Immingham as early as mid-May and her duties in the

Mediterranean were to involve the bunkering of coal-burning merchantmen.

During her voyage *Empire Moon* was subjected to many problems with her cargo, which literally became 'too hot to handle' through internal combustion. *En route* she put into many ports – Bougie, Philippeville, Bône, Ferryville, Bizerta and Sousse – in order that the 'duff' could be dampened down. Only hours after receiving instructions to divert from Augusta for Malta *Empire Moon* was torpedoed by *U-81*. At the time, she was being assisted by a tug into Syracuse harbour, which at the time was undergoing almost nightly bombing, there, the harbour pilot had plans to beach her. Whilst negotiating a sandbank, a stick of bombs landed astern. She shuddered and settled on the bottom.

Syracuse was savaged during the night of 26 July. The Junkers 88s and Focke-Wulf 190s came in two waves, doing much damage to the port area. The merchantman *Fishpool*, with 4,000 tons of munitions and 1,000 tons of aviation spirit in drums still to be off-loaded, was set afire and blazed furiously for many hours. Her master, twenty-seven crew and several Army Pioneer Corps stevedores died. On 1 August the Luftwaffe switched their attention to Palermo, the city which had been captured by US forces a few days previously. Wrecked in the harbour was the Welsh trampship *Uskside* and beached whilst her cargo was unloaded was the American *James Iredell*. She had arrived from the United States in a damaged condition after being close to the French tanker *Lot* (Convoy UGS10), which blew up when torpedoed by *U-572*. Carrying aviation fuel the crew had little chance of survival.

Amidst all the hustle and bustle of 'Husky', Churchill, with his usual concern for the merchant fleet, wrote to the First Sea Lord in July concerning air attacks west and south-west of Gibraltar.

> I am shocked to see the destruction of the *Duchess of York* convoy. Will you let me have a copy of the signal from the C-in-C Mediterranean about ten days ago, warning us of the 'intolerable' (I think that was the word) dangers of the air attacks on this route too near the Spanish coast? The loss of these large ships will spoil our monthly record, which anyhow is burdened with operational casualties. Pray let me know what will be done to avoid this form of air attack in the future. Surely it is worth while going further out beyond the range of Focke-Wulfs.
>
> I see that *Port Fairy* was damaged west of Cape St Vincent. Where did the aircraft come from and how far out was she? If the enemy could reach her why could not Gibraltar air give her protection?

During the attacks off the Moroccan coast, the 20,021-ton *Duchess of York* and the 16,792-ton *California* were both sunk by Focke-Wulf Condor aircraft, which still remained a menace in the Atlantic war. Over three-and-a-half years of war service, the *Duchess* had steamed 222,600 miles, carried 73,350 troops, 5,800 prisoners of war 4,190 civilians, as well as 63,300 tons of cargo.

On 18 August the Royal Navy white ensign was hoisted over Messina harbour. On 3 September, the fourth anniversary of the outbreak of war, Operation 'Baytown' was mounted when Reggio on the Italian mainland was captured. There followed landings at Taranto (Operation 'Slapstick') and Salerno (Operation 'Avalanche'). At the small port of Salerno with its good beaches, two American and two British divisions were landed in a bid to seize the port of Naples. Stiff resistance was met on 9 September and at one point evacuation was seriously considered.

It was at Salerno that the Germans first used their new and potent weapon, the FX 1400 radio-controlled glider bomb, weighing 3,000 pounds. If released at 18,000 feet, at a speed of 800 feet per second, the armour-piercing bomb at the end of its trajectory could be neither shot down by gunfire nor avoided by manoeuvring. The smaller Henschel HS-293 bomb, carrying 1,000 pounds of explosive, travelled at over 550 mph and had a range three-and-a-half miles.

Merchantmen assembled offshore included the *Duchess of Bedford, Durban Castle, Winchester Castle, Orontes* and *Otranto*. Sailing from Tripoli came the *Devonshire, Royal Scotsman, Royal Ulsterman* and *Ulster Monarch*. Two days after the initial landings the American cruiser *Savannah* was bombed and damaged. The same fate awaited British cruiser *Uganda*, necessitating her return to Malta. On 16 September the battleship *Warspite* and HMS *Valiant* were both instructed to engage shore targets with their 15-inch armaments. *Warspite* suffered severe damage in the process and returned to Malta three days later under the tow of four tugs. There were many casualties on board. The experience of Bertie Packer, her Captain, quoted in Joy Packer's book *Deep as the Sea*, is illuminating.

> We were relentlessly attacked by German aircraft with bombs and torpedoes – intensively until midnight and then sporadically. The moonlight is a gift for determined aircraft. They attack up moon. They can see us and we can't see them. So at first sound we crack off all we've got. We've worked that up for about two months now and for about five hours whenever we felt nervous we cracked off with all we had to give them. They couldn't take it. Of course they fired torpedoes and dropped bombs but as girlishly as a timid bean-fed mare. The Gunnery Officer Hamilton … handled our considerable and varied gun armament magnificently.

Lieutenant-Commander Hamilton was in fact Lieutenant John Hamilton who, as I mentioned in Chapter 2, was the gunnery training development officer at HMS *Excellent* in Gosport.

Two American Liberty Ships were lost in Operation 'Avalanche' and one seriously damaged. *Bushrod Washington*, carrying trucks, ammunition and petrol from Oran, was struck by one of the new glider bombs. Abandoned after catching fire she blazed for over thirty hours, then exploded and sank. *En route* from Casablanca, carrying army stores, ammunition and petrol, the *William W. Gerhard* was torpedoed by *U-593* some 45 miles from Salerno. Although taken in tow she caught fire, later to explode and sink. Twice damaged by bombing while lying at anchor off the beachhead was the *James W. Marshall*. She was in the middle of off-loading military vehicles, taken on board at Bizerta – to which port she was afterwards towed for temporary repairs. She later proceeded to Scotland for drydocking.

The converted deep-sea tanker *Derwentdale* (formerly of convoy KMS 18B) was another GSL damaged by bombing off the beaches. Towed to Malta by the tug *Hengist*, she was later forced to undertake the long tow to the United Kingdom, where she was repaired. The cargo merchantman *Lyminge*, bombed by a desperate enemy at Salerno, also survived, though she too suffered severe damage. It was thanks to the senior service that there were not heavier merchantmen losses at Salerno. Fortunately the troopers and LSI's completed their work without casualties.

The 5,023-ton *Empire Confidence* (also of convoy KMS 18B) sailed without incident from Algiers and at Salerno successfully off-loaded 400 servicemen, along with their equipment and ammunition. She subsequently maintained a shuttle service between Tripoli, Alexandria, Augusta and Bari with army supplies. Other vessels engaged for many months in this work were *Empire Tana*, (formerly the Italian *Carso*), *Empire Addison, Empire Capulet, Bantria, Fort Capot River, Fort Tadoussac, Ocean Trader, Samoa, Samrich, Samsylvan*, and the American *Samuel Parker*.

With Sardinia occupied as early as 19 September and Corsica falling fourteen days later, the Italian port of Naples was workable within ten days of being captured by the Allies on 1 October. It was with some complacency that convoy UGS 18, of ninety merchant ships, from Norfolk, Virginia, steamed eastwards through the Straits of Gibraltar towards Cape Tenez.

During August that year *Fort Fitzgerald* was in New York. Still a hard-working apprentice deck officer, I watched with some awe as 6,500 tons of military stores, including 1,400 tons of ammunition for the Mediterranean, was loaded; it was to be our second visit to the war zone. As the fourth ship in the second column of UGS 18 on 4 October we steamed at 8 knots abreast the rocky promontory of Cape Tenez. Unknown to all except the commodore and his staff, the escorts and their commanding officers, this was a favourite rendezvous for enemy aircraft. Convoy arrival times were said to be calculated by enemy agents operating from Algeciras (Spain), to the west of Gibraltar.

From out of the northern sky at over 200 mph came a formation of twenty Dornier 217s, equipped with the new glider bombs, and twenty-five 111H-6s carrying two 1,686-pound torpedoes. The explosion was deafening as the torpedo struck. Clambering from the cabin through the porthole, my only means of escape, I found myself on the outside alleyway. Bleeding from head wounds, I was safely brought aboard the corvette *Lotus* thirty-five minutes later. This was my fourth escape from the enemy.

Captain Brown concluded his Admiralty report of the sinking with the following:

> The corvette returned to the ship about 0100 (5 October) by which time she was burning fiercely, the fire having spread to No4 hold. As No4 'tween deck was full of high explosives and the corvette had 200 depth charges on board, the Commander decided it was much too risky to remain alongside. He sent a party on board who reported that the deck around No4 hatch was red hot. We left the scene about 0200 and the last I saw of my ship she was heavily on fire, listing to starboard and well down by the stern, with little hope of her staying afloat much longer.

Taking five members of the engine-room staff with her, *Fort Fitzgerald* was sunk by one of the escorting destroyers. Shipped back to Liverpool aboard Cunard's *Franconia* after the *Fitzgerald* loss, I discovered I was in company with survivors from the *Fort Howe*, sunk by *U-410* on 30 September whilst proceeding westward in convoy from the Salerno landings. Three other merchantmen, including the American *Hiram S.Maxim* and the Alfred Holt-managed vessel *Samite*, had been damaged by glider bombs though both had been able to make the Algiers anchorage. The *Samite*, taken over from the Bethlehem Fairfield shipyard in Baltimore only five weeks before, had a remarkable escape. The vessel was loaded with ammunition in every hold except No3, and it was the latter which the bomb struck.

At the time enquiries were still being made by the military authorities in Algiers concerning possible sabotage within the harbour limits. In July the Norwegian steamer *Björkhaug* had blown up in the docks causing a large petrol fire. Far worse was the *Fort la Montée* disaster of 4 August, when fire broke out aboard the Vancouver-built merchantman, which was carrying a cargo of phosphorus. Towed out into the bay with the destroyer *Arrow* standing close by, nothing could quell the blaze. Suddenly there was a massive explosion, which completely split the vessel's foredeck and part of her hull. HMS *Arrow* was seriously damaged and other vessels at anchor were hit by flying debris including the cargo ship *Harpagus* and the hospital ship *Amarapoora*. The remains of *Fort la Montée* were shelled by a British submarine, though the forward section continued to burn for several days. Some 100 lives were lost aboard the 'Fort' vessel and the destroyer.

The Canadian-built 'Forts' were much in evidence in the battle zone serving as 'jacks of all trades' for the other services. As with other classes of ships they sustained losses but everywhere there was a foretaste of success and victory, a sense of what was being achieved and of what the future held.

A census of dry cargo ships and tankers taken in the eastern Mediterranean during the fourth week of October 1943 indicates how enormous the supply task was, even though the Italian campaign was now north of Naples and Bari: fifty-nine merchantmen sailed into Oran; Algiers 75; Augusta 9; Bizerta 39; Bône 26; Bougie 4; Brindisi 16; Catania 7; Malta 41; Naples 52; Philippeville 6; Sousse 2; Syracuse 4; Taranto 18 and Tunis 5 (a total of 363 merchantmen). During the last three months of 1943 a large amount of military stores and equipment was dispatched to southern Italy, some of it being transferred to smaller-tonnage vessels at Algerian, Tunisian and Maltese ports.

Before Christmas that year the Mediterranean sea war was rocked by two disasters related to the troopship *Rohna* and the port of Bari six days later. Both were attributed to weak defences and to a sense of complacency. The 8,602-ton *Rohna*, a former cargo liner of the British India Steam Navigation Company, which had been built in 1926 to carry sixty passengers, was at the time carrying 1,965 persons including 1,770 American troops. Grossly overloaded, she became the first and only troopship to be sunk by a glider bomb. Some 1,135 personnel were lost, of which 1,015 were US infantrymen.

Sailing from Oran *Rohna* joined eastbound convoy KMF26, of fifteen merchantmen, under Commodore H.D. Wakeman Colville sailing in *Ranchi*. The convoy was protected by an escort of ten naval vessels, including the anti-aircraft cruiser *Colombo*. In a Force 4 wind and rough seas the convoy was attacked by thirty Heinkel 177 twin-engine monoplanes, escorted by Junkers 88s, followed by nine torpedo-carrying aircraft. An estimated sixty glider bombs – at the time the largest number used in one assault – were released, one of which hit the troopship abaft the funnel. With the *Rohna*'s steering gear and controls completely immobilized, and with no means of pumping water to fight the fire which erupted, she quickly became a vast fireball. Liferafts were thrown overboard but great difficulty was experienced in lowering the few undamaged lifeboats that remained. Those that survived were rescued by the new *Clan Campbell*, HMS *Atherstone*, the USS *Pioneer* and the naval tug *Mindful*. From her crew of 195, *Rohna* lost five British officers and 115 Asiatic seamen.

Shrouded in secrecy for many years was the heavy air raid on the congested Italian port of Bari on 2 December. Forty merchantmen were in the harbour – some unloading at the quayside, others lying at anchor awaiting a berth; sixteen had just arrived in convoy from Augusta. As many as thirty were working overnight, discharging their cargo under floodlights. The night was dark but clear. Using a large quantity of 'Duppel', the secret radar-jamming 'tinfoil' developed by the British in 1942, and dropping flares to bathe the harbour in brilliant light a total of 105 Junkers 88 aircraft came in from the sea flying as low as 150 feet.

When the enemy departed from Bari twenty minutes later they left behind seventeen ships destroyed, eight others damaged and 38,000 tons of military supplies destroyed. Ammunition ships were blown up with great loss of life, aviation fuel was ignited and flames were raging to a height of over 100 feet. It was the worst shipping disaster since Pearl Harbor. Around 1,000 Allied personnel from the four services, along with some Italian civilians, were killed or left dying.

The reason for the huge death toll was not the German bombing itself but the cargo of the destroyed Liberty ship *John Harvey*. Stowed in her holds were 2,000 hundred-pound mustard gas bombs. Her crew, the only people who could have warned the port authorities of the clouds of deadly gas that drifted over the port, were dead. It was the only major poison gas incident of the Second World War. From 'mustard' alone there were over 600 serious injuries in Bari; and as many as 100 seamen died of the gas. It had been claimed in Washington that Hitler might resort to using poison gas if the Allies invaded southern Europe, For this reason it was to be stored at Bari to be used as retaliation if necessary. Hundreds of survivors were hurriedly shipped to other parts of Italy, Britain and the United States.

Sunk alongside the *John Harvey* was the *Testbank*. Close by, many of them blown apart by the explosive cargoes they carried, were the US vessels *Joseph Wheeler*, *John Bascom*, *John L. Motley* and *Samuel J.Tilden*; the British-flag *Fort Athabasca*, *Devon Coast* and *Lars Kruse*; the Norwegian *Lom*, *Bolsta* and *Norlum* (the latter launched as the *Empire Dunlin* in 1942). Two Polish merchantmen – *Puck* and *Lwow* were sunk and three Italians – *Barletta*, *Frosinone* and *Cassala*. Those damaged included the Dutch-flag *Odysseus*, the Norwegian *Vest* and three British – *Crista*, of Tobruk fame, *Brittany Coast* and *Fort Lajoie*.

The Allied action at Anzio, Operation 'Shingle', the last seaborne landing on Italian soil, was intended to clear the Allied path to Rome. The troops contained in the narrow bridgehead had to be reinforced and supplied by sea for more than four months. There was a regular shuttle of landing ships and craft from Naples in addition to troopships and cargo merchantmen. Anchored off the beachhead on 22 January 1944 were *Ascania*, *Circassia*, *Derbyshire*, *Durban Castle*, *Winchester Castle* and the Polish *Sobieski*. On the same day the Allied commanders conferred aboard *Bulolo*. Representing the white ensign LSIs were *Glengyle*, *Princess Beatrix* and *Royal Ulsterman*.

The US mercantile marine lost two of its Liberty vessels at Anzio:

both were discharging munitions and blew up with spectacular explosions. These were the *Samuel Huntington*, attacked by aircraft bombs on 29 January, and *Elihu Yale*, hit by a glider bomb on 15 February. Their loss hampered the Allied armies in their difficult task. A third ammunition-laden US Liberty merchantman, the *Paul Hamilton* from Norfolk, Virginia, blew up and sank north of Algiers on 20 April *en route* for the beachhead. Struck by aircraft torpedoes, she was carrying an American demolition squad for Anzio: 504 servicemen were killed.

The wounded and sick from the battlefields of Sicily and Italy owed much to the Merchant Navy crews and Royal Army Medical Corps on board the hospital ships. Regrettably the enemy did not respect the humane work upon which they were engaged. No armament nor gunners were carried and such ships were unable to fight back. On D-Day at Sicily, *Amra*, *Leinster*, *St Julian*, *Tairea*, *Vita* and *Talambra* were all in attendance, and the latter was sunk by aircraft bombs. In addition, the *Dorsetshire*, working as a hospital carrier, was bombed and damaged. Moored at Malta as base hospital ship was *Empire Clyde*, formerly the Italian liner *Leonardo da Vinci*.

Newfoundland, fully illuminated and marked in accordance with the Geneva Convention, was destroyed by aerial torpedoes at Salerno. Twenty-three wounded servicemen, plus some of the medical staff and ship's officers, perished. Anchored close by were the hospital ships *Leinster* and *Somersetshire*, both of whom took off survivors. At Anzio on 24 January the illuminated *Leinster*, *St Andrew* and *St David* were lying at anchor. All hell was let loose when *St David* was hit by a glider bomb and sunk. As the sixty survivors were rescued by *St Andrew* she too was bombed. Fortunately she sustained only light damage. *Leinster* was at the December raid on Bari with patients from the front line. Although damaged herself, she took aboard 300 casualties from the dockside. *Leinster* was at Anzio thirty-six times and evacuated a total of 17,000 wounded from the battlefield.

Even the hospital ships' base at Naples came under attack from the air. The twin-screw 7,937 ton *Aba*, owned by the Elder Dempster company, was in 1921 the world's first diesel-propelled ocean-going passenger liner. On 15 March 1944 she was damaged during a night raid on the port. In 1940 she had assisted the British 8th Army in Libya. At Piraeus she had taken on board the wounded and was the last ship to leave the devastated port, even though the Stukas tried to bomb her. Off the island of Crete, *Aba* had been raked by machine-gun fire; again during the voyage to Alexandria, while carrying 630 patients, she was attacked by Italian aircraft, their bombs resulted in severe damage and thirteen casualties.

At Naples that day, with 189 patients having been loaded at Taranto, she was waiting to embark wounded servicemen for the United

Kingdom. *Aba* carried a crew of 120, plus sixty RAMC personnel headed by Lieutenant-Colonel P.Lloyd Williams, which included a matron and fourteen nursing sisters.

In addition to the most modern medical equipment and operating theatres, *Aba* was fully equipped in the event of abandonment following enemy action. Fourteen modern lifeboats, together capable of carrying 700 persons, were each fitted with mast and sail, and radio equipment; two of them were fitted with motors, and all were kept fully provisioned.

Four rafts, each capable of accommodating thirty people, were carried; these were kitted out with self-igniting buoyancy lights, lifebuoys and provisions. A total of twenty-seven voyages were undertaken by the hospital ship *Aba* on behalf of the Royal Army Medical Corps and the Army Dental Corps.

The provision of hospital ships in time of war is something of which the Merchant fleet is justly proud. No jumbo jet, fitted out as a hospital carrier, can compare with, or take the place of, the stately cabin-wards of a converted peacetime passenger ship. A little-known part of the maritime services provided by Merchant Navy crews in the Mediterranean were the Admiralty salvage vessels. This despite the fact that their vessels flew the blue ensign. They achieved many successes during 'Torch' and 'Husky' and throughout the Italian campaign. One such vessel was the 12-knot, 200-foot-long *Salvage Duke*, managed by the Risdon Beazley company of Southampton. Carrying a complement of forty-six, including two divers, two linesmen, two gunners and a motor mechanic, she saw service in the Mediterranean and Adriatic from November 1943 until the end of the war.

Salvage Duke was involved in much of the salvage work after the disaster at Bari; she worked in the harbours of Algiers and Alexandria, Ancona and Manfredonia; and she laid mooring buoys off Ortona and the seaward end of the oil pipeline for coasting tankers. In Algeria she was made responsible for clearing and repairing the landing craft slipways at Djidjelli, and undertook a great deal of demolition work throughout the region.

My own wartime service brought me back to the Mediterranean and to Italy in particular in January 1945. Then, as I shall relate in Chapter 12, the country was returning to more peaceful days, despite being occupied by the armed forces of the victorious Allies. Following the advance northwards, Italian ports and coasts became quieter, and certain merchantmen, LSIs and a whole variety of Royal Navy vessels, proceeded to the United Kingdom where greater events were being planned and shortly to be implemented. It is to the ports of England, Wales and Northern Ireland, and the remote lochs of Scotland that we now return.

11   Normandy and the Liberation

It was due to the overwhelming support of the Fourth Service that final victory became possible. The build-up of Allied forces preparatory to the assault on Hitler's 'Fortress Europe' was chiefly the responsibility of British shipping, a process begun in 1943 but which early in the following year was greatly accelerated. On 20 January 1944 General Eisenhower began his historic task as supreme Allied Commander. Rarely is it appreciated that the success of the landings in northern France and of the 'Liberation' depended on seaborne forces.

At the end of July 1.6 million personnel were ashore, 340,000 vehicles and 1.7 million tons of stores. Military cargo carried by the merchantmen (of 4,500 deadweight tons and over) reached its peak on 8 July when it was 1.7 million deadweight tons. On 5 August it was 1.6 million tons, and the total fell to 0.8 million tons by 2 September. The number of vehicles (on wheels or tracks) carried by merchantmen across the Channel, excluding vehicles shipped direct from North America, was 121,365 to the British sector (47 per cent of total) and 130,680 to the US sector (39 per cent of total). The balance was carried by tank landing craft and landing ships.

Under Operation 'Bolero' six of the world's largest passenger liners – *Queen Elizabeth, Queen Mary, Mauretania, Aquitania,* the Dutch *Nieuw Amsterdam* and the French *Ile de France,* known collectively as 'the monsters' – became the kingpins of a huge troop transfer. Working to a punishing schedule, complete divisions of servicemen crossed the Atlantic in six days. The 'Queens', pride of the British fleet, soldiered on throughout the darkest days of the Battle of the Atlantic. The progress of their voyages were closely followed by OP20, the American Tracking Room in Washington, and OIC, the Operation Intelligence Centre of the British Admiralty. As Patrick Beesly (*Very Special Intelligence*) has written: 'the sinking of either one of them would have been the equivalent to a major defeat in a land battle.'

The greatest accolade given to the two Cunarders came from Churchill himself;

Built for the arts of peace and to link the Old World with the New, the

'Queens' challenged the fury of Hitlerism ... to defend the liberties of civilization. Vital decisions depended on their ability continuously to elude the enemy and without their aid the day of final victory must unquestionably have been postponed. To the men who contributed to the success of our operation ... the world owes a debt that it will not be easy to measure.

Together the two 'Queens' led the operation. Both could carry some 15,000 men at a speed of 30 knots. At New York on 23 July 1943 *Queen Mary* embarked 15,740 troops, which, with her crew of 943, amounted to the greatest number of human beings ever embarked on a single ocean crossing. During the period January/June 1944 she made six crossings from New York carrying over 72,000 military personnel. Between April 1943 to March 1945, *Mauretania* made twenty-one return voyages carrying as many as 7,124 US and Canadian troops at a time.

Brought into the transatlantic service were other major units of the liner fleet, such as *Dominion Monarch* and *Andes*, flagships of the Shaw, Savill and Royal Mail companies. In the first six months of 1944 nearly a million fighting men were carried across the 'western ocean', mainly in British liners. Fuel, stores and raw materials were meanwhile brought in from many parts of the world. Prior to Operation 'Bolero' *Queen Elizabeth* had steamed 230,000 miles (equivalent to nearly eleven times around the world at the Equator) and had carried well over 200,000 Allied military and naval personnel as well as 18,000 prisoners of war.

Following the success of the United Kingdom to Takoradi aircraft ferry operation came the transatlantic seaborne ferry in which the vast deck space of loaded tankers was exploited. During March and April 1944, the tanker MAC ships, in addition to their usual convoy duties, conveyed 212 aircraft over eleven voyages. As many as 1,100 aircraft were transported during May 1944 by tankers. Up until May 1945 tankers sailing to Britain carried 13,719 aircraft and 2,132 gliders as deck cargo; they also carried over 70,000 tons of vehicles. Of these sailings a total of 4,650 aircraft and gliders were carried in HX fast convoys; 679 in SC slow convoy; and the balance proceeded aboard independently routed tankers and those with Greyhound convoys.

With the build-up for the final assault came much larger Atlantic convoys, the majority crossing without loss. Sailing from New York on 17 July 1944, with the Allied armies already established in Normandy, was HX 300 of 167 merchantmen, covering an area of twenty-six square miles, the largest fleet of vessels ever to sail in convoy; a fast section of fourteen left in mid-ocean, and eighty-eight, with instructions for Loch Ewe and Oban, were detached at 21 degress West. Carrying 1,019,829 tons of supplies the freighters brought to Britain grain, sugar, lumber, oil, molasses, steel, road vehicles, tanks, locomotives, explosives, machinery, general military equipment and foodstuffs. Only one cautious U-boat was sighted and no enemy attack was made.

The commodore of HX300 was 63-year-old Rear-Admiral Sir A.T. Tillard, sailing in *Empire Pibroch*; he served throughout the war and was in charge of thirty-seven convoys. The vice-commodore, experiencing his first convoy duty and flying his standard aboard the Dutch *Gerard Dou*, was Vice-Admiral Sir B.H.O. Lane-Poole. Seventy-four of the merchantmen were of the standard 'replacement' type, and sixty-four of these, US and British-flag, were American-built Liberty vessels. In addition to the usual escort and a rescue ship (*Zamalet*), four MAC vessels sailed within the columns to protect the vast array of shipping. These were *Empire Maccallum*, *Halcyonus*, *Macoma* and *Papana*. Unexpectedly the convoy was joined by the CAM ship *Ancylus* east of Newfoundland; she had to fall out of the previous eastbound convoy (HX299) on account of engine trouble and proceed to St John's, Newfoundland, where the problem was rectified.

Mr A.V. Alexander, First Lord of the Admiralty, speaking at Bromley, Kent, said of HX300: 'When it is possible for such a mighty fleet to cross the Atlantic in safety you will realize that we do not greatly fear any enemy attempt to return in strength to that battleground, across which more than 350 million tons of shipping have been convoyed since war began.'

An extra burden on oil traffic at this time was unavoidable. Whilst the Allied tanker fleet saw an increase of about 40 per cent between June 1943 and May 1944 (see Appendix XVII), demand for the Pacific War, where chiefly US shipping was employed, became increasingly heavy. Great, indeed, were the military and air force requirements in Britain, and it was inevitable that shortages would arise. The increased demand was caused by two factors: the bombing of German cities was gaining, in momentum, and the necessary stockpiling for the European invasion was underway. It was a situation by no means helped by Britain's dependence upon refineries in the Caribbean and the Persian Gulf.

The shortage of oil was alleviated by the foresight of those who made possible the introduction of the 14 knot all-tanker Greyhound convoys and the expansion of the oil reception centres of Avonmouth and Stanlow. During the months of March, April and May 1944 eleven CU convoys, averaging over nineteen tankers apiece, arrived in Britain. One of these, CU24, was twenty-four tankers strong. Winston Churchill and his war cabinet had ensured that supplies were distributed from the west coast to where it was most needed.

By early 1943 oil was being pumped by pipeline from Avonmouth and Stanlow to Southampton Water at Hamble and Fawley. There followed a connection from Aldermaston to the East Midlands, with a second line to Kent and, later, a third line to Thameshaven. An additional pipeline supplied the East Midlands from Stanlow, thereby ensuring a good supply at the important US air bases.

The decision to mount Operation 'Overlord', the Normandy invasion in which four army corps and three airborne division were landed, was taken at the Casablanca summit in January 1943. This was the supreme offensive action of the Western Allies. The battle for Normandy and the advance into Germany lasted a full eleven months. It employed 5½ million men, 970,000 vehicles and over 18 million tons of supplies. For over two years the 'boffins' had been at work; shipyards large and small had been busily designing and building special types of merchantmen and landing craft. In all amphibious operations it is the carriage by sea of the army's land transport that presents the greatest difficulties – and it is no less a difficulty today, even though giant jumbo jets can be called upon to assist.

Laden vehicles form a clumsy and cumbersome cargo that take up far more space than men or stores. They are difficult and slow to load and unload, except for tank landing craft, which can be driven ashore. Often special slings and derricks had to be provided for handling them. It was for this reason that General Montgomery found it necessary to accept a reduction in the number of vehicles from 3,200 to 2,500 per division in the initial assault. Indeed, landing craft became the governing requirement, Some 4,000 were required, which meant that many had to be drawn from the Mediterranean and even from South-east Asia Command where Lord Louis Mountbatten had only just taken delivery of them for his own amphibious plans.

The build-up across the 'western ocean' and across the English Channel needed to be faster and more powerful than the German capacity to reinforce across the land. The assault phase of Operation 'Husky' gave proof that such an operation was technically and materially possible.

As early as 1917 whilst serving in Lloyd George's wartime cabinet as Minister of Munitions, Churchill described a project for making landing craft for tanks and also something very much like the transportable harbours used at Normandy. It was as early as June 1942 that he suggested the 'Mulberry Harbour'. From the lessons learnt at Dieppe in that year he conceived that in the Liberation action such a harbour would have to be built, after heavy sea and air bombardment. He envisaged that the operation would need to be sustained for at least three weeks without the use of a large port.

During those 'days of defeat' Churchill had shone by his fighting spirit: 'Britain will fight on, if necessary for years, if necessary alone. We shall go back,' he declared. At Normandy the Allies succeeded in exploiting sea-power just as the British had done during past European wars, and in North Africa, Sicily and Italy. Field Marshal Rommel's

Chief of Staff, General Hans Speidel, was later to comment; 'the invasion of Normandy will forever remain an event of the first order in the history of war. It was the first big operation to succeed fully in bringing together and leading the services of all services to attain one strategic goal.'

At last, Churchill 'the fighter' was to see his dream unveiled upon the enemy beaches of France. Yet as he saw victory in his sights, with the Italian capital of Rome falling to the Allies on 4 June, he was to say in a radio broadcast:

> When I look back upon fifty-five months of this hard and obstinate war which makes even more exciting demands upon the life-springs of energy and contrivance, I still rate, highest among the dangers we have overcome, the U-boat attacks upon our shipping, without which we cannot live or even receive the help which our Dominions and our grand and generous American ally have sent us.

The execution of 'Neptune', the maritime side of the 'Overlord' undertaking, was headed by its Commander-in-Chief, Admiral Sir Bertram Ramsay, KCB, MVC. Four years earlier as Vice-Admiral Dover he had rescued the British Expeditionary Force from the beaches of Dunkirk. A highly complex masterpiece of planning, as with 'Torch' and 'Husky', the operation was not without its problems – the first being a shortage of warships for escort and bombardment. 'Neptune' was responsible for the safe and timely arrival of the assault forces at their beaches, the cover of their landings and subsequently the support and maintenance of the build-up of forces ashore. The assault problems apart, the staggering task of keeping the armies continuously supplied with food, ammunition and equipment, was a daunting prospect.

Assault formations amounted to 130,000 officers and men with some 20,000 vehicles, including amphibious assault tanks – the Sherman was used for the first time on a grand scale – and engineer assault tanks. In addition, there were flail tanks for clearing a path through minefields, tanks loaded with bridges tailored for crossing anti-tank ditches, self-propelled guns, armoured fighting vehicles, bulldozers, personnel carriers and motor transport. All this was required to be landed by D-Day plus three.

The climax of all the years of bitter fighting at sea, 'Neptune' was the greatest of all combined operations. With 'Overlord' it was to become proof of the ability to transfer victory won in the oceans into its final decisive phase of a victory won across the land. For the many merchantmen and their crews this was the culmination of their work. After North Africa, Sicily, Salerno and Anzio, Normandy, though more hazardous, was the most triumphant. So successful was Operation

'Neptune' that over the first two weeks losses amounted to less than 1 per cent of the total tonnage employed.

For the assault forces the main assembly areas were the Hampshire ports, extending to Shoreham and Newhaven in the east. From westward along the Channel coast, from Weymouth, Poole and Portland, Torquay, Brixham, Dartmouth and Salcombe, came the US invasion forces. The rendezvous point off the southern coast of the Isle of Wight became known as Piccadilly Circus. Follow-up convoys with troops and equipment came from the Thames ports, as well as Plymouth, Milford Haven and Swansea. Blockships, for the construction of breakwaters, sailed from the Scottish lochs, and the bombarding Royal Navy vessels from Scapa and the Clyde. On 2 June two midget submarines slipped out of Portsmouth harbour to identify and lie off the narrow beaches of Normandy – eventually to act as markers for the assault convoys on the morning of D-Day.

On 25 May Admiral Sir Bertram Ramsay ordered all holders of the operation orders for 'Neptune' to open them. On 29 May, with D-Day provisionally fixed for 5 June, briefing of ships took place at Cowes. Some 400 Royal Navy commanders and Merchant Navy masters were present. The greatest and most carefully planned amphibious operation was about to come to fruition. The timing of the operation unravelled with oustanding precision the most complicated military plan ever conceived. As each of the ships in the nearest ports to France moved forward so the great procession followed; from ports further along the south coast, from the waterways of the Thames and the Bristol Channel, the Mersey and the Clyde, the lochs of Scotland's west coast, even the east coast to the Tay and beyond.

As far as was humanly possible every contingency had been provided for. The one thing which could not be controlled was the weather. The opening of the operation had to be postponed for twenty-four hours, which meant that, at the last moment, additional supplies of fresh water and bunkers had to be taken on by all vessels taking part. Preparation went ahead for ensuring that thousands of men, tanks, vehicles and ammunition would be landed on the beaches at times accurate to the minute. It meant landing naval beach parties, to clear not only the shore but also the shallow waters approaching it; and it meant estimating how long they would take to do their job – how soon the craft could start beaching in quantity. In addition, flak ships, gun ships and various other support craft had to be off the beaches to back up the first assault wave.

The fifty-seven blockships, twenty-six of which were British, were sunk to form the initial breakwaters at the American 'Mulberry A' sector and the British 'Mulberry B' sector – along the coast of Vierville and Saint-Laurent, Arromanches, Courseulles and Ouistreham. The blockships' function was to give shelter to the coasters and other small craft engaged in shuttling stores from the large merchantmen at anchor to the beaches. Codenamed 'Gooseberry', they were just a small part of 'Mulberry', a convenient code word used to embrace all the details of the great scheme of the prefabricated ports.

As well as the blockships, concrete caissons screened the moorings inside the harbours, so that ships drawing up to twenty-seven feet could lie at all states of the tide. The concrete caissons, the floating breakwaters and the Spud pierheads – where coasters drawing up to eighteen feet could discharge their cargoes – were assembled after what was undoubtedly the largest towing operation in history. Mass construction of the 'Mulberry' components began in December 1943 and continued day and night at a variety of sites within the United Kingdom. Initially as many as 490 tows were required to get the components into position for the Channel crossing.

Some 132 tugs towed the 'Mulberry' units across the narrow sea at an average speed of 4 knots; the Ministry of War Transport provided forty-two, some of which were Dutch-owned, the Admiralty 30, the US Navy 19 and the US Army 41. The ocean-going Navy tugs *Bandit* and *Buccaneer* stand out above all others for their splendid work at the beaches. Top of the league in towing was the ex-Dutch *Zwarte Zee*: in three-and-a-half years of war she rescued over 128,000 tons of Allied shipping, much of it from deep in the Atlantic.

Many of the tugs at Normandy had never worked outside of harbours and sheltered waters. In addition to the 'Mulberry' units, barges, lighters, dock equipment, cranes, dredgers, timber rafts and floats – all incapable of self-propulsion – had to be towed over. From D-Day onwards, tugs were working continuously. By the end of July, 295 cross-Channel tows had been carried out, many of them damaged craft being towed from the assault area.

On arrival the concrete caissons had to be sunk accurately in places selected as a result of surveys made by a special party landed on D-Day. By D-Day plus twelve more than half were in position. Similarly, advanced parties in special ships arriving on D-Day laid heavy moorings in deep water to which the floating breakwaters were attached as they arrived, an operation which was completed by D-Day plus eight. Completion of 'Mulberry' took three weeks to D-Day plus twenty-seven, mainly due to problems on towage and to the storm of 19 June. Until it was complete everything had to be landed over the beaches, with the exception of small numbers of men through the little harbours of Saint-Laurent and Arromanches.

The statistics covering the landings are beyond comprehension. Among those which delivered troops and vehicles were 1,213 Naval combatant ships, which included the battleships *Warspite* and *Rodney*, twenty-three cruisers, 105 destroyers, armed trawlers, frigates and

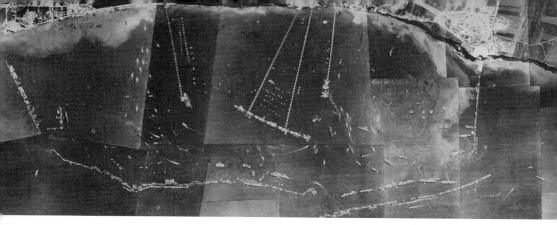

Mulberry Harbour, Operation Overlord. This vertical aerial view illustrates the artificial harbour at Arromanches. The various components were towed across the English Channel in the wake of the invasion and sunk to form a breakwater up to one mile off shore

This aerial photograph of the thousands of Allied naval craft involved in Operation Neptune was taken from a B-26 Martin Marauder aircraft of the US 9th Air Force

HMS *Warspite* is here engaged in firing on the German batteries located on the Normandy hill-top in the background

In the centre of this photograph (Sword Beach) is the liner *Letitia* now operating as a troopship. She was a sister ship to *Athenia* sunk on the first day of the war. To her right it can be seen that shells from the fifteen-inch guns of the battleship *Ramillies* are hitting their target

The Landing Ship Infantry 7,177-ton *Empire Cutlass* at Sword Beach.
Managed by Canadian Pacific she was one of thirteen such merchantmen built in the USA

The veteran dredger *Leviathan*, built in 1904. At the time she was the
largest suction dredger in the world and was engaged on invaluable
work at Normandy

The steamer *Paris* on her side in Le Havre Harbour. The port at the mouth of the river Seine was liberated by the Canadian 1st Army on 12 September 1944

OPS. 16

Form approved by the Minister of War Transport under paragraphs 6 and 7 of Regulation 47ADA of the Defence (General) Regulations, 1939.

LIBERATION OF EUROPE.
ACCOUNT OF WAGES.

Surname and initials of Seaman ___WILSON J. G___
(In Block Letters)
Dis. A. Number ___R308024___   Rank or Rating ___2nd Radio Off___

EARNINGS.

		£	s.	d.
Basic wages at £ ___12/-___ per week				
from ___22/4/44___ to ___19/8/44___ (___17___ weeks ___1___ days)		11	2	11
War Risk Money and Consolidated Rate for ___17___ weeks ___1___ days		65	14	4
Increase of Wages on promotion by £ s. d. per week				
for ___ weeks				
War Leave due ___8___ days at ___1/11d___ per day			15	4
Subsistence Allowance ___ days at ___ per day				
TOTAL		77	12	7

DEDUCTIONS.

Payments to relative		25	10	
Total Advances		35	15	
Income Tax (Code ___S___) ___17___ weeks ___1___ days at ___15/7___ per week		13	7	1
Fines and forfeitures				
Health and Pensions Insurance for ___ weeks				
Unemployment Insurance for ___ weeks				
Officers' Pension Fund : Number ___ (at 9d. in the £ on basic wages)				
N.U.S. Contribution				
TOTAL DEDUCTIONS		74	12	1
FINAL BALANCE		3	.	6

RELEASE.

I, the undersigned, having been during the above-mentioned period a member of the crew of one or more ships to which Regulation 47ADA of the Defence (General) Regulations, 1939, was applied or of the Merchant Navy Reserve Pool whilst kept for employment on such ships, do hereby release all such ships and the masters and owners thereof as well as the Minister of War Transport and the Shipping Federation Limited from all claims and demands accruing during that period in respect of any voyage, engagement or employment, except as regards the claims or demands which are set out on the back hereof.

Date ___19/8/44___   Signature ___J. G. Wilson___

And I, a Mercantile Marine Superintendent, do hereby release the said ___J. G. Wilson___ from all claims and demands accruing during the said period in respect of any voyage, engagement or employment.

Date ___19/8/44___   Signature ___[signature]___

Liberation of Europe. Account of Wages. Over a period of seventeen weeks the third radio officer of *Fort Gibraltar* earned a total of £77-12-7

Here the red ensign flown by the tanker *Empire Russell* on her entry into the harbour of Cherbourg is presented by Bob Workman (left) to Stephen Brookes, curator of the D-Day Museum at Portsmouth. Mr Workman was third engineer aboard the tanker at the time

The deck officers of the steamship *Empire Kangaroo*, managed by Donaldson Bros & Black Ltd. *Left to right* G. Howison, second mate; J. Stevenson, chief mate; Captain G. W. Cockburn and J. Field, third mate. Captain Cockburn of Aberdeen had been at sea thirty-two years

The three wartime brothers of Penarth in their apprentice days. Their father and their father's brother were both master mariners and had sailed as captain of their ship for many years. It is probable that no such British seafaring family could be found today

Captain R. J. Lee who lost his life after his ship, the *Nailsea Court* was torpedoed, 9 March 1943

Dubrovnik, March 1945. The author, third mate of the *Nailsea Moor* is on the left. The third 'sparks' to the right

The *Nailsea Moor* discharging military supplies for the forces of Marshal Tito, Dubrovnik, March 1945

The Eyes of the Convoy; air cover during the final Atlantic battles contributed more than anything else to the defeat of the U-boats

Heavily kitted troops embarking on to a converted ocean liner at the Pier Head, Liverpool

corvettes, and as many as sixty of the ubiquitous flower class. In addition, there were, 4,126 landing ships and crafts, 736 auxiliary crafts and 864 merchantmen, which included eighty troop-carrying vessels.

The Royal and Merchant Navies, gliders and transport planes landed a total of 287,000 men on D-Day, 130,000 of these across the beaches. By D-Day plus three no less than forty-seven convoys had crossed to Normandy, with 307 merchantmen sailing from the Thames ports: they alone carried some 50,000 men, nearly 80,000 tons of stores and about 9,000 vehicles.

By D-Day plus ten 500,000 personnel and 77,000 vehicles were ashore along with 150,000 tons of stores. In the first fourteen days 638,045 troops were deposited, along with 97,668 vehicles and 223,636 tons of equipment and supplies. By 6 July one million servicemen were ashore. Two days later 1,754,200 troops had been transported to France, 373,400 vehicles including tanks, and more than two million tons of supplies, had been shipped. Sailings across the Channel during the week ending 8 July averaged 10,000 men, 3,200 vehicles and 15,000 tons of supplies daily.

During the fiftieth anniversary reunions of 1994 and remembrance services for those who did not return, the Allied nations should not fail to give thanks for Operation 'Neptune', without which 'Overlord' and the 'Liberation' would not have been possible.

The main forms of enemy naval opposition were motor torpedo boats and mines. Later came 'human torpedoes', long-range circling torpedoes and explosive motorboats. The greatest nuisance was caused by a new type of mine known as the 'Oyster', actuated by the pressure of wave from a passing vessel and unsweepable at the time by any existing method. Just over a month after D-Day, out of a total of forty-three U-boats which had operated, or tried to operate, against the invasion, eighteen (or 42 per cent) had been sunk. By the end of August, Brest, Lorient and Saint-Nazaire were being evacuated by U-boats capable of putting to sea. Bergen and Trondheim, Norway, became the main bases for the Atlantic boats.

During the first month of 'Neptune' the Royal Navy lost three destroyers from mines, one damaged beyond repair and a fifth sunk by torpedo when attacked by a surface craft. Four minesweepers were lost from mines and a further three were sunk by human torpedoes. On 8 June the headquarters frigate, HMS *Lawford*, was bombed and sunk by aircraft and on 27 June the corvette, HMS *Pink*, was severely damaged when torpedoed by *U-988*.

At the head of the invasion fleet on D-Day steamed the minesweepers, sweeping a channel through the minefields – a repeat of the job they undertook in the landings on the North African coast, at Sicily, Salerno and Anzio. Built in Britain and the United States there were naval 'sweepers' and motor minesweepers, converted Admiralty trawlers and fishing trawlers, drifters and a variety of other craft. All were equipped to deal with either moored or ground mines or both. There were 'Smokey Joes', the coal-burning sweepers of the First World War, and those newly launched and still on the secret list.

Following the sweepers came the Mersey Docks and Harbour Board's veteran *Leviathan*, built by Cammell Laird of Birkenhead in 1904 and at the time the largest suction dredger in the world. She was engaged on invaluable work, dredging channels for the assault merchantmen and foundations for the concrete caissons of 'Mulberry'. With the tide running 'at a rate of knots', it was by no means an easy operation.

Leading the assault were the thirteen 7,177-ton steam turbine-engined 'weapon' class landing ships, infantry (large), of the C1 cargo-type vessels built on the west coast of the United States; they had been taken over by the Ministry of War Transport on bareboat charter and were completed as military transports in great secrecy during late 1943 and early 1944. Managed by the larger liner companies with British crews they were equipped with troopdecks to carry some 1,500 men; as they were not intended as cargo carriers, they were ballasted with concrete. With a maximum speed of 18 knots, 14 knots cruising, they carried eighteen LCAs (landing craft assault), nine on each side in two tiers. Well armed, they carried 4.7-inch guns forward and aft, a Bofors gun, numerous Oerlikons and smoke-making apparatus.

Led by experienced masters, crews were sent, first to New York, then overland to San Francisco. Before crossing to Scotland, they embarked troops at Newport News and also New York; these servicemen had been engaged in training at the naval shore bases HMS *Saker 1* and HMS *Saker 2*. A further training establishment was HMS *Asbury* at Asbury Park, New Jersey, where the senior service had taken over two hotels, the Berkeley Carteret and the Monterey.

February 1944 saw *Empire Broadsword* and *Empire Battleaxe* (Cunard Steamship Company) in the Cromarty Firth for a period of training with the white-ensign LSIs *Glenearn* and *Glenroy* recently returned from the Mediterranean. Later training took place in the many Scottish lochs along with Canadian Pacific's *Empire Cutlass* and *Empire Lance*, Blue Star's *Empire Anvil* and *Empire Javelin*, soon to be joined by P & O's *Empire Crossbow*, Furness Withy's *Empire Halberd* and *Empire Rapier*, as well as Royal Mail's *Empire Spearhead*. The remaining C1 transports, *Empire Arquebus*, *Empire Gauntlet* and *Empire Mace*, were managed by the Anchor Line and Donaldson Brothers.

Proceeding on a fifty mile front seven miles off the beaches the LSIs (L) took up their stations. 'H' Hour was between 0630 and 0745 hours in different sectors, according to the height of the tide. Continuing the build-up these fine merchantmen took less than twenty-four hours to travel from the south coast roadstead to the beaches, disembarking their troops and returning to home anchorages. Headquarters ship at Sword Beach (Lion-sur-Mer) with Force 'S' Portsmouth, was the white ensign *Largs*, at Gold Beach (Arromanches) with Force 'G' Portsmouth, *Bulolo*. Both vessels had returned from duties in the Mediterranean.

The troop transports followed in the path of the assault vessels. The hard-worked *Llangibby Castle*, attached to J Force (Juno), carried 1,590 British and Canadian troops. She was fitted with eighteen assault craft, operated by 124 Royal Navy and Royal Marine officers and ratings attached to the ship. At 0630 hours on D-Day she anchored off the beach near Courseulles. Over the following six months she was to cross the Channel more than sixty times and ferry more than 100,000 servicemen. Also at Courseulles was the Scottish *Clan Lamont*; now equipped with twenty assault craft she carried 1,400 officers and men of the Canadian army. In five Channel crossings she transported 8,218 to Normandy.

Devonshire, Lancashire, Monowai, Neuralia, Rembrandt and *Worcestershire* were all there in their capacity as troopers. P & O's LSI(L) *Monowai*, at 10,062 tons, was the largest merchantman at Normandy. Between D-Day and March 1945 she made forty-five crossings carrying troops to France without mishap. At anchor off the beachhead was the former troopship *Ascanius*. She had sailed on 10 May from Birkenhead, 'north about' to Tilbury, where she was prepared as depot ship for the Royal Navy Task Force; she also acted as barge headquarters ship. *Royal Ulsterman*, laden with over 400 personnel, was carrying out her duties as landing ship headquarters, a role in which she was well versed. A total of forty-five LSIs were involved, many withdrawn from the Mediterranean theatre, including *Prince Leopold*, now a veteran of combined operations.

Not only did *Prince Leopold* serve at Dieppe but she had also been involved in the first Allied raid on enemy-occupied France. On 28 September 1941 she carried No. 1 Commando Unit to Normandy in preparation for the D-Day landings planned for three years later. In poor visibility she mistook the beach at Luc-sur-Mer for Saint-Vaast, and the unit hastily withdrew after losing two men, one from the South Wales Borderers, the other from the Welsh Regiment. The 2,938-ton, former Belgium LSI (small) *Prince Leopold*, flying the white ensign but with mainly a Merchant Navy crew, was to end her gallant work in the waters of the Channel. On 29 July she was torpedoed and sunk by *U-621*.

Taken by surprise, the German U-boat Command immediately instructed forty U-boats to Normandy from their pens in western France. Initially as many as sixteen sailed but after six were sunk by Coastal Command aircraft between 6 and 10 June, they were withdrawn. The submarines sunk were *U-995, U-970, U-629, U-373, U-740* and *U-821*.

The first store merchantmen arrived on D-Day plus four. Work commenced immediately and the daily tonnage discharged increased as the construction of harbours was advanced. Soon, a figure of 12,000 tons a day (fifteen hours) was reached. Some delay was experienced at twilight and dusk in the early days due to the smokescreen laid by warships at these times. Delays were also experienced by the ammunition merchantmen, which, as a safety measure, had to cease work before dark to enable them to steam out of harbour. There, they would anchor in deeper water and return to their moorings the next morning. The anchoring of such vessels at night was something by no means relished by their crews.

The task set for the American harbour, or 'Mulberry A', was that it should be capable of handling 5,000 tons of supplies a day. The British harbour at Arromanches, 'Mulberry B', was to handle 7,000 tons per day. It was also agreed that sheltered waters should be provided by D-Day plus four and that the harbours ought to be fully operational by D-Day plus fourteen. As the timetable became jeopardized by the weather conditions more and more merchantmen were obliged to offload overside to a myriad of small craft including the inimitable DUKWS working to and from the beaches.

The convoys which crossed to Normandy during the first three days were made up of 753 major landing and supply vessels, excluding assault forces. Many were landing ships gantry, landing ships sternchute and the rhino ferries – these were 400-ton steel rafts used for unloading LSTs (landing ships tank) in deep water.

A total of 612 merchantmen were engaged in the build-up from D-Day to 14 June, excluding tugs and other small craft. Of the 171 vessels operating under management of the Ministry of War Transport, 97 were 'Empire' vessels, eleven of the American-built Ocean type, forty were Canadian-built 'Forts' and twenty-three were 'Sam' Liberty ships. Amongst them was *Empire Capulet*, fresh from her splendid work as a 'jack of all trades' in the Mediterranean. Arriving in the assault area within forty-eight hours of the landings, she was loaded to her marks with tanks and vehicles. On her return she took some casualties back to Southampton Water, where they were disembarked into launches for transfer to Netley Hospital. Thereafter she ran steadily to and from the Thames, surviving the flying bomb attacks on the Victoria and Albert docks.

Requisitioned by the Admiralty as HQ Infantry Landing Ship (LSI-H) was Royal Mail Line's new *Pampas*, built at Harland & Wolff's Belfast plant in 1943 to replace the old *Pampas*, destroyed at Malta the previous year. The new vessel spent much of her time at Normandy as a troop transport carrying 650 personnel.

As many as 500 coasters were employed; and during the first

twenty-three days 788 two-way voyages were recorded. Some beached upon the shore and discharged direct on to Army vehicles on the dry sand. Taking ton for deadweight ton the small ships such as *Empire Cabot* (Hull for Arromanche) put on to the beaches almost twice as much material as the large merchantmen. Their most important cargoes were petrol, in cases or four-gallon jerrycans, and ammunition. Four-fifths of these vessels had previously only carried coal. Their work was priceless.

Until blockship protection was afforded to the coasters they were successfully anchoring in 6-knot tides – a feat which could not be emulated by many of the Liberty-type vessels, because they were not fitted with long enough cables on their anchors. Smaller than the coasters were the many Thames lighters called up for service: these were fitted with diesel engines, twin screws and special ramps for unloading direct on to beaches.

Hospital ships for this vast undertaking included the *Llandovery Castle*, Royal Mail's *Atlantis* and the 1930-built *Amsterdam*, owned by the London & North Eastern Railway. She was subsequently sunk (7 August) in the Baie de la Seine an hour after sailing from the beaches. Thirty-three lives were lost, and twenty-six servicemen were brought ashore injured.

Striking a mine, *Amsterdam* was severely damaged by heavy explosions which smashed lifeboats and rafts. She took on a dangerous list and only through the efforts of the second mate who rigged up an emergency radio aerial, was a distress call sent. The port water ambulances remained intact, and later these were successfully launched, carrying many of the ship's patients. Mines also accounted for damage to hospital carriers *St Julien* and *Dinard* on D-Day plus one, but fortunately there were no casualties and both vessels reached port, where temporary repairs were made.

The wartime-standard merchantmen, in particular the 'Sams', the 'Forts' and the 7,000-ton Empire class, constructed in British shipyards, were a great advantage in that tonnages, dimensions, draughts and equipment were identical in each class. The whole question of ballasting, fuelling and loading was therefore simplified. Nevertheless some adaptation was necessary; provision in many vessels had to be made for the feeding and sanitation of troops, as well as some creature comforts. Such work was undertaken by the Sea Transport Division of the Ministry of War Transport, which shared with the military authorities the responsibility for all operational and maintenance programmes.

Merchantmen earmarked for Normandy, upon returning from overseas missions or after discharging cargoes in home ports, were given priority to ensure that adaptation was completed on time. One such vessel was the *Fort Crevecoeur*, which, upon returning in ballast from Russia in March 1944, was drydocked at Hull. There the tarmac, which had been put down as a protection against frost was removed from her decks, and the 'tween decks were fitted out for the carriage of troops, including the provision of bunks. In addition, maintenance work was carried out on her hull. The allocation of tonnage was determined at inter-Allied conferences, attended by various heads of Government departments and expert consultants. Much of the success of the enterprise revolved around what became known as the global allocation of shipping tonnage.

At one such conference it was arranged that the larger-tonnage merchantmen at 'Mulberry' should have on board a reserve of at least 3,000 tons of fresh water in their ballast tanks, and many had as much as 6,000 tons reserve. They were needed for the smaller craft and for the troops in transit. This aim was not easily achieved, taking into account the trim problems associated with bunkering, the compensating ballast in different sections of the vessel and the tonnage of cargo it was carrying. In the case of oil-burning steamers it proved impossible as tanks had to be used for fuel oil and, indeed, were held during the invasion as a supplementary source of fuel.

The supply of fresh water to an advancing army once it had broken the sea defences was an ever-present difficulty during the Second World War. At Normandy this was overcome principally by converting some oil tankers for the transport of fresh water. Several of the Shell tanker fleet, including *Goldmouth, Goldshell, Juliana* and *Opalia* were converted, enabling them to supply water to the beachhead, in addition to their task of bunkering landing craft. *Dolabella* left Southampton on D-Day plus one and continued in the role of water carrier for three months.

The forty-three Channel tankers were better known as 'the CHANTS' or the nickname given them by their crews: 'Churchill's Holy Answer to the Nazi Terror.' With their loaded draught of only ten feet, they were specially shaped for beaching. Without the 'Chant' building programme, and without the fuel they carried, the whole operation would have been in jeopardy. This was especially so, since PLUTO (Pipeline under the Ocean), an ambitious project linking the Isle of Wight to Cherbourg, failed to operate to schedule and it was not until mid-July that it was brought on stream.

Three 'Chants' were lost in the early days. 'Chant' No. 61 capsized and sank on D-Day plus two; No. 69 went down on 14 June while serving as a water supply boat – afterwards she was sunk by a senior service vessel to avoid her becoming a danger to the numerous other craft; No. 7 was driven ashore during the storm of 19 June when, in fact, several 'Chants' capsized close inshore. Whilst most were refloated and subsequently repaired, No. 7, which had loaded petrol at Thameshaven, was a total loss.

The great storm of 19 June D-Day plus thirteen, the worst at that time of the year for forty years, was to last three days. Initially from the north-west, the wind then veered north-east, reaching gale force. The waves attained heights of ten and twelve feet, and the exposed 'harbours' suffered badly with a number of breakwaters, blockships and piers becoming wrecked. Abandoned as blockships laid off Saint-Laurent and protecting the eastern entrance to 'Mulberry A' were four American 'Liberty' ships. These included the *James Iredell* and the *James W. Marshall*, last in service at Palermo and Salerno, as mentioned in Chapter 10.

The American 'Mulberry' to the west took the brunt of the storm and had to be surrendered to the elements. Discharge of cargo on to the whole fifty-mile front was abandoned during the three days; incalculable damage was wrought on coasters, landing craft and beach installations. A set-back for the advancing armies in all three sectors, it took many weeks to re-establish an adequate flow of supplies and equipment. Only the capture of the ports of Cherbourg and Le Havre on 26 June and 12 September relieved the situation.

Pluto, the aforementioned 'pipeline under the ocean', developed to pump oil under water direct from Britain to France (codenamed 'Bambi') was a sad disappointment – one that was costly in terms of time, labour, ships and materials. *Empire Taw, Empire Ridley, Empire Baffin* and *Algerian* all took part in testing and laying the pipeline. Whilst these merchantmen were taken over by the Royal Navy most of the officers and crews were red-ensign men. Later, in October that year, a second system from Dungeness to the French coast, codenamed 'Dumbo' came into operation. Sixteen pipes ran under the Channel to Boulogne, and the scheme proved much more successful; connected to the Avonmouth–Thames pipeline, there was now a line from the Isle of Grain oil terminal to the Kent coast.

The most trenchant epitaph on Pluto is perhaps provided by a few figures of comparative achievement. Until the ending of German resistance on 10 May 1945 almost 5.2 million tons of oil products were delivered through the ports of north-west Europe. Of this quantity about 826,000 tons came direct from across the Atlantic, and 4.3 million tons (84 per cent) were delivered across the Channel from Britain. Pluto's contribution was only 370,000 tons, less than 8 per cent of cross-Channel supplies. This was equivalent to an average delivery rate of under 1,800 tons a day from the time when pumping began.

By far the largest supplies of oil, which included petrol, aviation fuel and all types of lubricating oil, during the early stages of the Liberation were from such tankers as the *Empire Russell, Empire Settler* and the 8,201-ton deep-sea class tanker *Empire Traveller*, which landed 10,000 tons of petrol for the US Army at Cherbourg soon after the capture of the port. Engaged in this traffic were four tankers of the British Tankers fleet (Anglo-Iranian Oil Company): these were *British Engineer, British Faith, British Princess* and *British Renown*. All were celebrating the return to Europe after a war in which their company and employers had lost forty-four of the fleet accompanied by great loss of life.

Though Cherbourg was captured on 26 June, the port was not open to shipping until 16 July because of demolitions and mines; even then quays were not workable until early August. During the period from mid-June to mid-July *Empire Russell*, carrying a million gallons of petrol on each crossing, came within two miles of the beach at Port-en-Bessin where she would drop anchor and tie up to two large buoys. Her tanks were then connected to the shore by a 6-inch flexible hose. *Empire Russell* became the first Allied vessel to enter Cherbourg, and the first British-flag merchantman to enter a Northern European port for over four years. Subsequently she was trading across the Channel to Le Havre. There were no major oil ports capable of receiving ocean tankers between Cherbourg and Antwerp and, furthermore, these ports were unworkable and unable to receive large vessels for many weeks after their capture. This put a severe strain on the pipelines from the Kent coast, which came on stream during October.

Adding to the problems of Operation 'Neptune' was Hitler's secret weapon. The first V1 flying bombs fell on the London area on 13 June, six days prior to the storm, and built up to 244 launches during the forty-eight hours of 15/16 June, when seventy-three V1s actually exploded in London. By 15 July 2,579 of the 'doodlebugs' had been launched, of which 1,280 fell in the London area. In total there were 9,000 V1 bombs, a quarter of which failed to cross the coast. And only a quarter of those which crossed the coast, got near the capital; having reached their destination they caused mayhem, however: 6,200 were killed and 18,000 seriously injured.

Much havoc was created in London's docklands by the flying bombs. Merchantmen were delayed in loading for Normandy and convoys were stalled in the Thames estuary. Transit of convoys off the south coast of England was also affected, since fighter aircraft were engaged in shooting down the V1's instead of giving air cover to the loaded merchantmen.

For the first time in history the Merchant Navy was accorded its own special newspaper correspondents. 'A thousand ships manned by 50,000 volunteers,' headlined *The Times* on 8 June. The correspondent of the *Daily Telegraph*, who was sailing aboard *Sampep* on D-Day, was to write, 'I have been given an insight into the comradeship, courage and unfailing humour of this brotherhood of the sea. I shared with them the hazards of war. As for grit – well, every one of the 50,000 men now ferrying a thousand Merchant Navy ships with war supplies to France, is doing the job of his own free will, as a volunteer under 'V' articles he signed months ago.'

Conceived by the Sea Transport Division of the Ministry of War Transport in company with the Shipping Federation, which represented the shipowners, and societies and unions of the officers and men, the ingenious COMNO articles from the initial letters of Central Office Merchant Navy Operations. This body became concerned to ensure that every man in the Merchant Navy was taking part in the assault on northern Europe. It also made sure that wherever the men were or whatever they might be doing their families received weekly allotments of pay. It had somewhat draconian powers: crews could be transferred, if need be, from one ship to another, not unlike their brothers in the Royal Navy. They could be instructed to perform any job aboard ship, no matter in what department they were normally employed. At the same time every officer and man participating was a volunteer – thus it became known as the 'V' scheme.

The conditions in which men found themselves were very different from any which had applied to sea service in the past. The articles were signed in some secrecy and many were unaware of what was at stake. For the first time in maritime history the crews of merchantmen were regarded as constituting one operational force and not units of individual crews. At last those that manned merchant ships were accepted as servicemen, not a 'fighting service', but the 'fourth service' of the realm nevertheless. If one takes into account the fact that officers and men co-operated and assisted Navy and Army gunners in manning the ships' armaments, they also became, on occasion, a fighting service.

Another novel feature of the 'V' articles was that every man was issued with a pay-sheet which he carried at all times, and which acted as an identity card. Full records of every man were retained by COMNO, to be revised whenever needed. Some, after signing the 'V' form, were directed 'deep sea' and were disappointed at the prospect of not being able to take part in Operation 'Neptune'.

Fresh from the Mediterranean, where they had aided Combined Services so well, the Army Pioneer Corps came to Normandy. Twenty-six companies totalling 7,500 men landed on the beaches. Planning for their use in the Liberation was started in April 1942, when an assistant director of labour was appointed to join the planning staff. The work of the Pioneers in the initial stages of the invasion are often overlooked. In addition to work aboard the merchantmen, where they worked closely with officers and men, their tasks included laying flexible causeways from landing craft to shore, clearing beach obstacles, making roadways off the beaches, and forming beach dumps for ammunition, petrol, stores and supplies. They were engaged in operating the Rhino ferries from ship to shore, laying smokescreens to prevent enemy observation of the beaches, and clearing the dead and wounded. Later they carried out invaluable work in the ports of Cherbourg, Le Havre, Dieppe and Antwerp.

During the six months of 'Neptune', losses of heavy-tonnage merchantmen, whilst light in comparison with 'Torch' were nevertheless costly in terms of military equipment and supplies. Another grave consequence, in the case of the Belgian transport *Leopoldville*, was the regrettable loss of so many American servicemen. However, Allied shipping losses never came near to endangering the succes of Operation 'Overlord.'

6 June, *William L. Marcy* (US); 7,176 tons. Beaches. Torpedoed by E-boat.

7 June, *Charles W. Eliot* (US); 7,176 tons. Beaches. Mined.

7 June, *Francis C. Harrington* (US); 7,176 tons. Mined Beaches (damaged).

10 June, *Charles Morgan* (US); 7,176 tons. Beaches Aircraft bombs.

12 June, *British Engineer*; 6,993 tons. Mined mid-Channel (damaged).

24 June, *Derrycunihy*; 7,093 tons. Beaches. Mined.

24 June, *Fort Norfolk*; 7,131 tons. Beaches. Mined.

28 June, *Maid of Orleans*; 2,385 tons. Torpedoed mid-Channel by *U-988*.

29 June, *Empire Portia*; 7,058 tons. Off Selsey Bill. Mined. (On 26 February *Empire Portia* had been damaged by aircraft bombs off Murmansk.)

29 June, *Henry G. Blasdel* (US); 7,176 tons. Torpedoed, mid-Channel by *U-984* (300 troops rescued by LST 326–US Navy).

29 June, *Edward M. House* (US); 7,240 tons. Torpedoed mid-Channel by *U-984*.

29 June, *John A. Treutlen* (US); 7,198 tons. Torpedoed mid-Channel by *U-984*.

29 June, *James A. Farrell* (US); 7,176 tons. Torpedoed mid-Channel by *U-984*.

(The above four vessels were seriously damaged and taken out of service.)

2 July, *Empire Broadsword*; 7,177 tons. Beaches. Mined.

8 July, *Empire Brutus*; 7,233 tons. Beaches. Mined (damaged). (*Empire Brutus*, carrying ammunition and bombs, had been seriously damaged by aircraft bombs during 'Husky', 26 July 1943.)

24 July, *Samneva*; 7,219 tons. Torpedoed by *U-309* mid-Channel (damaged).

30 July, *Samwake*; 7,219 tons. Torpedoed by E-boat mid-Channel.

30 July, *Ascanius*; 10,048 tons. Beaches. Torpedoed by *U-621* (damaged).

8 Aug., *Ezra Weston* (US); 7,176 tons. Avonmouth/Normandy. Torpedoed by *U-667*.

17 Aug., *Iddesleigh*; 5,205 tons. Beaches. Human torpedo. (*Iddesleigh* previously damaged by torpedo on 10 August.)

19 Aug., *Harpagus*; 7,271 tons. Beaches. Mined (damaged).

25 Aug., *Orminster*; 5,712 tons. Torpedoed mid-Channel by *U-480*.

11 Nov., *Lee S. Overman* (US); 7,176 tons. Off Le Havre. Mined.

21 Nov., *Empire Cutlass*; 7,177 tons. Off Le Havre. Torpedoed by *U-978* (damaged).

24 Dec., *Leopoldville* (Belg.); 11,509 tons. Off Cherbourg. Torpedoed by *U-486*.

Damaged during the flying-bomb assault on the London area were *Empire Tristram, Fort McPherson, Samdel,* and *Viking* along with several tugs and lighters. A certain amount of controversy surrounds the cause of the damage to *Empire Cutlass*. Claims have been made that an oyster mine of the same type that sank *Empire Broadsword* was responsible, though German records show it to have been the result of action from *U-978*, which was in the area.

The Belgian-registered *Leopoldville* (convoy WEP3), with a crew of 105, was under charter to the Admiralty. On Christmas Eve, she was carrying some 2,235 soldiers of the US 66th Panther division – reinforcements for the Ardennes battle. Sunk with the loss of over 800 American lives, many were trapped when two decks collapsed. Those that survived owed much to the work and superb seamanship of HMS *Brilliant*. The night was dark and bitterly cold. The traffic to both Cherbourg and Le Havre was heavy at the time and the underwater enemy were determined to show they were still a force to be reckoned with. *Slemish* (convoy WEG14) and *Dumfries* (convoy MUS71) were sunk (by *U-772*) close by on the same night. On Boxing Day the frigate *Capel* was sunk and the frigate *Affleck* damaged, both as a result of *U-486*'s torpedoes.

On 28 December 1944 *U-772* torpedoed and sunk *Empire Javelin* (Southampton for Le Havre), carrying 1,448 US Infantry. Fortunately, only seven lives were lost. Torpedoed and damaged at the same time were the American Liberty vessels *Arthur Sewall* and *Black Hawk* (convoy TBC21); the latter was beached and became a total loss. Both submarines were later sunk: *U-772* by RCAF Squadron 407 on 30 December; and *U-486* by HM submarine *Tapir* off the west coast of Norway on 12 April 1945. There were no survivors from either boat.

Fifty years later the records and memories of those who sailed to Normandy remind us that though 'Neptune' was a resounding success, there were many days of anxiety, with the elements at times causing greater havoc than the enemy. The navigation and convoy work led to many difficulties, yet officers and men of the Merchant Navy, together with their DEMS and MRA gunners, were proud of the part they and their ships had played in such a vast undertaking.

Lieutenant Colonel R.A. Chell DSO, OBE, MC, Officer Commanding Troops aboard HM transport *Letitia* makes some pertinent comments in his book *Troopship* published in 1948:

> In July 1943 I was on the first large troopship to enter the port of Augusta in Sicily. Just as we passed through the Italian-made boom we were bombed by two daring Italian airplanes. On D Day as we steamed along inside that marvellous smoke wall between Dover and Folkestone we expected lots of things and none of them happened. No shelling from Cap Grisnez, no bombing from the air, no submarines, no odd floating mines. Yes, we were lucky, and by the afternoon of D + 1 we realized how much we owed this complete freedom from dangerous interference to our sister services. But we took no risks – the Master of our ship told me to order troops to wear Board of Trade lifejackets all the time.
>
> Everyone slept fully clothed and booted but the night was completely devoid of incident. Reveille was at 0500 hours, breakfast at 0600 and by 0700 everyone was ready to disembark. At this hour troops changed from Board of Trade lifejackets to Mae-Wests; every soldier had one of these in his invasion equipment. We found we were steaming down a channel marked out with large buoys – a perfect race-course it looked. Some of these were bell buoys and many navigators in beach convoys must have thought thankfully of the splendid sailors who marked out those channels during the night preceding D Day.
>
> We were slowly approaching one of the British beaches. Vast quantities of shipping were to be seen anchored off in lines roughly parallel to the shore. Battleships here and there (amongst them HMS *Warspite*, last seen at Salerno) busy with long-range bombardments of special targets with Allied aircraft constantly streaming overhead.

Included in convoys from the Thames during those first few days were a succession of British-managed 'Sam' merchantmen: *Samark, Sambut* and *Samholt; Samnesse* and *Samneva, Sampep* and *Samphill; Samsip, Samvern* and *Samzona*. There were Canadian-built 'Forts' too – two particularly hard-working vessels were *Fort Gibraltar* and *Fort Henley*. All these freighters were ballasted with tops trimmed level and dunnaged to take heavy army vehicles; each carried between 500 and 600 troops. One such American-flag in this category was the *Jeremiah O'Brien*, a Liberty ship now the only survivor of those 'replacements', which is today preserved and maintained as an active museum ship by the National Liberty Ship Memorial Inc. in San Francisco Bay, an American National Monument. During June and July 1944 she undertook some twelve round trips from British ports to the Normandy beachheads.

During the passage of the Thames D-Day convoy off Dover the *Sambut*, carrying 580 troops, was caught by heavy shelling from the French coast. Catching fire and covered in a dense cloud of smoke, her ammunition cargo in No. 2 hold exploded. Eighty lives were lost as the starboard side of the merchantman blew outwards. Sunk by E-boats on D-Day plus four off the south coast were the coasters *Ashanti, Brackenfield* and *Dungrange*. Mined off the beaches were the coasters *Westdale* and *Dunvegan Head* and the Trinity House vessel *Alert*.

Carrying US army supplies to the Omaha beachhead was the steamer *Freeman Hatch*. Sailing from the Isle of Wight in a four-ship convoy escorted by the destroyer *Boadicea* on D-Day plus twelve, they were suddenly attacked by enemy aircraft as dawn broke. The supply ships were safe, but *Boadicea* was cruelly raked by machine-gun fire and bombed. Finally sunk by an aerial torpedo, her survivors were rescued by a lifeboat lowered from the *Freeman Hatch*.

At Omaha beachhead on D-Day was *The President*, a coaster equipped with diesel cranes to increase the lifting capacity of her derricks. Loaded under American orders at Swansea, along with some fourteen other coasters, all were carrying deck cargo with some 100 US soldiers and eight British gunners apiece. Later *The President* loaded bombs at Fowey for Utah beach only to be damaged as she arrived on the night of the storm. She lay on the beach for six weeks as a US salvage team strove to repair her. In the end she had to be towed to Falmouth, where she lay under repair for four months before being finally declared seaworthy.

Loaded at Port Talbot with military supplies and troops was the motor vessel *Isac*, a former French wine carrier. She too had been adapted to carry small diesel cranes. With a P & O master mariner brought out of retirement she unloaded at Juno beach on D-Day plus two; at the time the sands were littered with inflatable lifejackets and crates that had each contained two flagons of rum. Subsequently *Isac*, reputedly the largest vessel to make use of the Spud Piers, made many voyages from the Thames to Normandy. During this period she was anchored off the beachhead during the night bombing of Caen, an event which was to remain with her crew for the rest of their lives. Caen fell on 10 July after 7,000 tons of bombs had been dropped by the strategic and tactical air forces. A total of 2,200 aircraft were engaged in the raids.

The 600-ton Glasgow-registered *Southport* was loaded at Tilbury in early May with 540 tons of live ammunition. For some four weeks she waited for D-Day sailing in convoy from the Solent for 'Juno'. As well as three DEMS and three MRA gunners, she carried forty-four men of the Royal Engineers and a commanding officer specially trained in handling ammunition. The Channel crossing was made in the company of some 200 other merchantmen, mainly coasters, with an escort of destroyers, corvettes and motor torpedo boats. Great care was necessary in approaching the beaches because of congested shipping. The chief mate of the *Southport* in his Operation 'Neptune' report gives some idea of the situation as seen from the deck of a small coaster.

> We were met by small naval motor boats who piloted each vessel to their respective landing area. The beaches had been heavily mined and it was a dangerous job to drop anchor. The Germans had defended the beaches by placing mines on steel tripods below the level of low water for a considerable distance off shore. Several landing craft fouled these mines before they were located and made safe by the minesweepers ... the loss of 15 DUKWS were reported by striking hidden mines resulting in many cases of landing parties being killed or wounded. Close to the beach lay one of our hospital ships and it was aboard this craft that the wounded received medical treatment.

On her second visit to the beaches *Southport* arrived at Caen Roads during the evening of 16 June. She carried medical and victualling stores as well as army equipment for the British and Canadian servicemen. Air attacks during the hours of darkness were severe, though mainly confined to the beachheads. Of the storm that followed three days later the Chief Mate reports on the difficulties experienced:

> Many of the small vessels were driven ashore where they lay on the beaches being pounded by heavy seas unable to get off until such time as the weather moderated. Eventually they were salvaged and towed to Southampton for drydocking and repair. We were at anchor awaiting convoy at this time with 75 fathoms of cable but still unable to hold ground; we had to continue steaming towards our anchor, speed 3 knots for 24 hours.
>
> On our third trip to Normandy we took another cargo of ammunition (400 tons). We made a daylight crossing on 25 June arriving 1600 hours being instructed to beach ship on a section of the shore between Courseulles and Port-en-Bessin. We steamed in slowly until ship took ground and four shackles of cable had been paid out. This procedure was for the purpose of heaving off again into deep water once the ship was discharged. The process was complete in some 24 hours, the DUKW's being solely employed in the operation.

After six cross-channel trips to the British invasion sector *Southport* was assigned to the Americans and carried bombs for the US Army. Several trips were made from Southampton to the tidal ports of Barfleur, Saint-Vaast and Isigny. On her last voyage she loaded 450 tons of live bombs from a US Liberty ship recently arrived at Southampton from North America. Upon arriving at Isigny it was found that the particular bomb loaded was no longer required. After much delay her master was instructed to return to Southampton. The *Southport* had held her deadly cargo for over fourteen days.

Another dangerous cargo was that carried by the *Jesmond*, a small red-ensign trader more used to the Mersey and Clyde waterways than the English Channel. For several weeks she was engaged in supplying the destroyers with depth charges and shells loaded aboard in Portland Harbour. It was a good example of how closely the two maritime services co-operated in Operation 'Neptune'.

On 15 August Operation 'Dragoon', the Allied landings between Nice and Marseilles, took place. A total of 103 merchantmen, including the transports *Circassia, Sobieski, Derbyshire, Dunedin, Durban Castle* and *Winchester Castle*, were employed in the initial landings, the main object of which was to capture the towns of Saint-Raphael, Saint-Maxime, Saint-Tropez, Toulon and Marseilles.

Leading the transports were the white ensign LSIs (large) *Keren, Prince David, Princess Beatrix, Prinz Albert* and *Prince Baudouin*. By midnight on 20 August eighty-three of the merchantmen had been unloaded; in another well planned operation, they had taken on troops and equipment in the Mediterranean ports of Alexandria, Algiers, Augusta, Naples and Taranto. By 31 August 184,000 troops, 39,390 vehicles and 191,230 tons of supplies had been landed.

U-230, the last enemy submarine in the western Mediterranean, ran aground and was scuttled by her crew near Toulon. This was followed by *U-407*, which was sunk north of Crete on 19 September, and *U-565* and *U-596*, destroyed in the harbour of Salamis, Greece, by the US Air Force five days later. The Mediterranean Sea was at last cleared of German and Italian underwater craft.

One French and three American divisions were landed at St Tropez. By 3 September they had captured Lyons and eight days later they joined forces with Allied troops driving east from Brittany. Brussels fell on 3 September and whilst Antwerp, the second largest pre-war European port, modern, valuable and virtually undamaged, was captured with its port facilities the following day, the enemy still held the lower reaches of the river Scheldt. At the end of August the US Army had come to a halt with the Rhine crossings only 75 miles away. Two million men and half a million vehicles had been landed; but the Allies did not possess a single major port in working order on the Atlantic or Channel coasts.

The Allied front line trailed back 350 miles to the Channel. With only Cherbourg open to ocean-going merchantmen the daily requirement of each Army division was 700 tons of ammunition, equipment and food. The US 3rd Army alone needed 40,000 tons of fuel a day, though this was restricted to 32,000 tons. Supplies were building up. The larger Atlantic convoys meant congested UK ports. Only the combined weight of Allied air forces saved the day.

Only after 9,500 tons of bombs were dropped on Le Havre during the period 5–11 September did its garrison surrender. The attack had involved some 1,863 aircraft, chiefly Lancasters and Halifaxes. Some 3,391 tons of bombs were dropped on Boulogne and on 30 September, after much heavy bombing over a period of ten days, Calais was captured. Meanwhile Dieppe had joined Cherbourg in receiving vessels carrying supplies and reinforcements for the Army. Before long it was receiving 7,000 tons of cargo daily.

During the bombing of Le Havre on 7 September the V2 rockets took over from the V1s, severely disrupting the busy London docks and Tilbury. A total of 1,050 V2s were spotted by observers, 518 of which hit the London area, killing 2,754 people and severely injuring 6,523.

The thirty-five miles of the Scheldt estuary, the great waterway to 'the prize' of Belgium was dominated by German forts. The low-lying island of Walcheren, extensively fortified, barred the merchantmen. Here, backed by the battleship *Warspite* and the monitors *Roberts* and *Erebus*, took place the last amphibious operation of the European war. The Royal Marine Commandoes had to fight every yard. For three weeks the minesweepers combed the long reaches of the estuary, the river and the docks.

On 26 November came the first convoy to reach the docks of Antwerp. A small fleet of coasters, including the *Empire Ness*, loaded at Cherbourg. She had done valuable work at Normandy, where she was storm-damaged. In the west Schelde, near Terneuzen, she collided with the US-flag Liberty *William Paca*. After an explosion of gas bottles in her cargo she quickly became a total loss. A mystery surrounds her cargo, for official sources declare this as 'confidential sea transport cargo'. From 28 November, with the arrival of an eighteen-ship convoy including *Empire Cabot*, *Redcar* and *Samarina*, Antwerp became the main supply base of the Allied armies. The city sustained them through the winter campaign with stores and oil and thereafter to the crossing of the Rhine and the advance into Germany during spring 1945. Though the naval and supply situation was not obvious to the armed forces deep inland, their dependence upon the merchantmen and their escorts never ceased.

The enemy, however, never gave up in their efforts to dislocate the Scheldt seaway and the port of Antwerp. In addition to severe winter weather in the English Channel and North Sea, the Thames–Scheldt convoys were attacked with every type of weapon. The air-raids, the E-boats, two-men midget submarines and minelaying all took their toll. *Samsip* and *Fort Maisonneuve* were badly damaged by mines in the estuary on 7 December and had to be sunk by Allied warships. *Samvern* was mined during a storm off Zeebrugge (18 January), when sixteen lives were lost; four days later there followed the steamer *Halo*. *Goodwood*, *Blacktoft*, *Auretta* and *Sampa* were all mined north of Ostend during February.

On New Year's Day 1945 the Luftwaffe, in a large-scale and low-level attack on Antwerp carried out the heaviest enemy raid of the northern European operation. They were determined to cripple the important logistical port and struck once again at the cargo-ships and tankers offloading their valuable war supplies. The port was now receiving one ocean tanker a day; smaller tankers were carrying some 2,500 to 3,000 tons a day to Ostend and comparable quantities to Le Havre. Involved in two previous incidents in the river Scheldt was the tanker *San Roberto*. On New Year's Day, with her tanks filled with aviation spirit that was about to be piped ashore, the ship's gunners shot down a German aircraft – the second credited to this Eagle Oil vessel in an adventurous wartime career.

During a third assault by one of the Messerschmidt 109F aircraft on the *San Roberto*, the enemy was brought down. The ship's Oerlikon gun crew was led on this occasion by the third mate, who was officer of the watch. His previous encounter with the Luftwaffe had been as a first-trip cadet in 1941, when the bombing attack on the *San Fabian* (See page 42) left him severely wounded. Only later were such tanker-men to learn that it was due to the continuous supply of oil, petrol and aviation fuel to the fighting-men in the Ardennes offensive that the breakthrough was achieved. To both sides the supply of oil products was imperative; and the defeat of the Germans was principally due to the destruction of their oil reserves by Allied aircraft.

Captain Roskill, in his official history, indicates that at the beginning of 1945 the First Sea Lord sent a gravely worded memorandum to the Chiefs-of-Staff, regarding a renewed offensive with new types of U-boats on a substantial scale. Some 300 flotilla craft destined for the Far East were held back and air mining and other U-boat operations intensified.

As mentioned in the final paragraph of Chapter 6, the U-boat threat was far from over during the dying days of the war. The fleet totalled 436 U-boats. The Schnorkel system enabled the U-boat to operate as a true submarine. Seventy-five such boats were based in northern waters. The Admiralty was worried that some 200 underwater craft would now operate to prevent the build-up from across the Atlantic to ports such as Cherbourg, Le Havre and Antwerp. The advent in British waters in January 1945 of type-XXIII boats with fitted Schnorkel, nullified the techniques of anti-submarine warfare evolved during the preceding five years. By April 1945 twelve of the latest U-boats, the revolutionary XXI, had completed trials, and eighty were delivered. *U-2511* became operational on 30 April, when she sailed from Bergen.

As Grand-Admiral Dönitz assumed the mantle of 'Führer' in Berlin he reflected upon his declaration that 'I will show that the U-boat alone can win this war.' Victory upon land had followed victory at sea. Yet on 8 May 1945, Victory in Europe Day (VE Day), there was less meat for the

British people than there had been a year before; during the same month it became necessary to reduce the bacon ration. In the Far East, merchantmen, with their senior service colleagues, were still fighting the enemy. The British public, forever dependent upon ships and seamen, had to be patient.

Upon the beaches of Burma 23,000 troops with stores and equipment were landed. By 15 May Rangoon was occupied. Whilst Japan surrendered on 15 August 1945 after the knock-out blow of the atomic bombs on Hiroshima and Nagasaki, there is an interesting epilogue to the Far East War, a theory that was not understood until many years later.

Over three-and-a-half years, Japan, a maritime nation, had lost the greater part of her naval and merchant fleets. Her army was unbeaten and her airforce still strong, but it was the loss of her merchant ships which created the conditions for Allied victory. Without ships, her industry and her armed forces were drained of their life-blood. With virtually no maritime strength, her dependence upon food and war materials from overseas brought about a slow but certain death.

12   The Crews

The best description of merchantmen crews during the war and possibly the one which paid them the greatest compliment was penned by that fine author of the ocean, Lieutenant-Commander Nicholas Monsarrat RNVR. In *Three Corvettes* Monsarrat pays tribute to the tanker-men:

> Imagine being on the bridge of a tanker, loaded deep with benzine that a spark might send sky-high, and seeing the ship alongside struck by a torpedo, or another torpedo slipping past your stern and doing nothing at all about it. Imagine being a stoker, working half-naked many feet below the waterline, hearing the crack of explosions, knowing exactly what they mean, and staying down there on the job, shovelling coal or turning wheels, concentrating, making no mistakes, disregarding what you know may be only a few yards away and pointing straight at you.

The words of J. Glenn Gray in *The Warriors: Reflections on Man in Battle* – 'War reveals dimensions of human nature both above and below the acceptable standards of humanity' – should be borne in mind when reflecting upon the words of Nicholas Monsarrat. As a member and survivor of the service, as one who cheated death four times within twenty-four months, I would add that by no means were merchant seamen all heroes, nor were they in any other service. But the record does display some quite remarkable instances of courage, fortitude and endurance. This was at a time when three-quarters of all merchantmen sunk by the enemy went under within 15 minutes. So fast to their grave did some plummet that many brave deeds went unnoticed. In spite of this, a total of 9,027 honours and awards were made to members of the Merchant Navy and Fishing Fleet.

Naval men had a love-hate attitude towards the sea. Your next trip was always going to be your last. As soon as you were ashore for a spell, even if you were on survivor's leave, you wanted to go back again. There was a 'people's war' aboard ships at sea in the same way as there was a 'people's war' in the air-raid shelter of a blitzed city. As in the shelter there was a great sense of comradeship between officers, seamen and gunners alike; discipline was respected regardless of whatever nationality, race, colour and creed one happened to belong to. I like to refer to it as a 'democracy' of the sea.

Discipline amongst ships' crews was imperative when boys from as young as fifteen to men older than sixty-five worked together in confined spaces on long voyages. Twenty to twenty-five days in the North Atlantic was quite common, particularly during the dark, uncertain days of 1941 and 1942, when it became necessary to route convoys far to the north with its storms, its ice-floes and low temperatures.

Certain writers have suggested that the crews were a source of trouble both in port and whilst at sea. This is by no means borne out by statistics. A safe arrival in port in whatever part of the world called for celebration. True that life was hard; that was part of the tradition of seafarers. Little had changed in the service over fifty years. In comparison with other servicemen, merchant seamen were no better, certainly no worse. Compare them with men fighting in Burma, at Tobruk and El Alamein, at Monte Cassino or Caen and Arnheim, the airmen returning from raids deep into Germany. The Atlantic frontline was established on the first day of the war. It lasted until victory was declared five years and eight months later. The survivors, from whatever frontline, needed to relax in one way or another.

Even heroes feel 'the sweat' of fear. Every member of a ship's crew experienced fear of one sort or another at some time. Courage and fortitude at a time of crisis is not easy to achieve. Whilst many find the necessary strength to overcome shock, this subsequently causes great stress, which only relaxation in its many forms and a change of environment can cure.

Whilst the enemy was rarely seen it was often known that he was there. Maybe deep in the following swell or high in a cloud-covered sky. Occasionally, as experienced by the writer during a homeward Atlantic convoy in victory month (May 1943), a corvette would pass through the convoy column, her tannoy blaring forth strains of Blake's 'Jerusalem' and Thomson's 'Rule Britannia'. What a relaxation this proved to be.

The seafaring heritage of the Celtic races, most noticeably seen in the seamen from west Wales and the Scottish Hebrides, was something which, whilst indefinable, incorporated the courage and brotherhood of merchant crews. They alone set the example for the Arabs from Aden, the Chinese from Hong Kong, the Lascars from India and East Africa and the 'coloureds' from Zanzibar and Sierra Leone.

It was this multiracial atmosphere that made the burial of a comrade at sea such a moving event. On the occasion witnessed by the writer, the vessel was stopped in the South Atlantic just before sunset, even though this was dangerous because of the presence of submarines in the area. With the ensign at half-mast all hands were assembled at the starboard side between bridge and funnel. The body, of a different colour and faith, sewn neatly in canvas and weighted with iron, lay on a hatchboard under a new red ensign. At the Captain's words 'we commit our brother to the deep,' the hatchboard was tilted and the canvas-covered body slid from under the flag into the sea.

To many young men of that era, going to sea was an adventure. War, horrific and violent though it was, provided yet another adventure. When the idiocy of the war began to make its impact, the comradeship began to mould itself together as if it were part and parcel of the curriculum of naval warfare. The smaller the ship, the more comradeship and loyalty, always providing the 'old man' – the Captain – had the right qualifications and characteristics of leadership.

There was a general grouse about poor food aboard merchantmen, particularly before the introduction of refrigerators and freezers. As late as 1941 in many of the fleet's tramp steamers, an ice-box fitted on deck was the only cold-room. Many personnel found, however, that they were better fed than their loved ones at home, even though the diet could on occasion include whale meat, which the butcher had difficulty in selling to the housewife. The chief mate of the *Tower Grange*, which was torpedoed and sunk by *U-154* in November 1942, went ashore during the 1930s slump. He was to tell his fellow officers that he only came back to sea to obtain a good meal. Those that complained most were often from poor homes, who had suffered through ill-nourishment during the Depression years.

Stewards and cooks were in short supply; many had paid the supreme sacrifice during the early days and replacements were sent to sea with as few as fourteen days' training. Whilst food was adequate, much was spoilt on occasions before it was served. Who has not heard of similar complaints from the Army canteen or the Naval messdeck.

Of more concern to the Ministry of War Transport were the high casualty rates amongst the crews; in 1942 nearly 8,000 seamen lost their lives in British merchantmen alone. Authorities became apprehensive about morale. Reports of men 'jumping ship' in foreign ports were scrutinized for any increase, and special questionnaires were drawn up by psychologists and circulated to try to discover how men were reacting to the strain. The subsequent report (mid-1942) indicated that morale remained high, that spirit and courage was quite remarkable. This in spite of the fact that many tramp steamers were out-dated and ill-equipped. Shipping companies had found life hard during the worldwide slump of the 1930s and many had gone out of business. At the outset of the war, economies were still being made in maintaining vessels and even in victualling. By July 1942, when improvements in life-saving equipment became compulsory, this brought about a general upgrading of accommodation and food.

A fine tribute to the crews was made by Captain A. Agar VC, RN, in his *Footprints in the Sea* (1959). Referring to the time he spent in escorting HX convoys from Halifax, Nova Scotia, to Britain, he wrote:

> It was the spirit that mattered most during those anxious months when we had to rely on the officers and men of our merchant ships to pull us through by taking more than a 'chance' at sea. We, in the Navy, had guns and things to fight back with. They had nothing, yet they never hesitated and we took our hats off to them.

When considering the contribution made by crews to the war effort, it should not be forgotten that there were few serious labour disputes. In comparison with the docking, shipbuilding and coal-mining industries – three other industries upon which the nation at war depended – the seamen's record was the finest.

Whilst on the north-east coast of England the shipbuilding industry was in good heart there were problems in other areas still suffering from the slump of the 1930s. Strikes and demarcation disputes continued, and the 'dilution' of jobs, by introducing extra unskilled labour to do parts of them, was strongly resisted. In the coal industry feelings of bitterness and suspicion towards the mine-owners were, if anything, more violent than during the 1930s. Wages in the industry were low, eightieth out of 100 industries in the wages table. At the end of 1943, supplies to industry had to be cut by 10 per cent and, in a hasty and desperate attempt to raise manpower and production in the pits, the 'Bevin Boy' scheme was introduced. With the aircraft industry paying record wages there was a wave of strikes. There was no such unrest in the Merchant Navy.

An amenity particularly valued by wartime merchant seafarers was the Seafarers' Education Service, which was able to provide roving ship's libraries, being privy to the information on movements of vessels. A total of 40,000 books were lost aboard merchantmen that were sunk, some of these even finding their way into enemy hands. The pocket battleship *Graf Spee* acquired such a library from one of its victims and a library was supplied to the Milag prisoner-of-war camp, with the stipulation that all books had to be new and carefully censored.

Music and song, always associated with merchant mariners, never brought the crews together as they did with the armed services or with the civilians of the blitzed cities. Nevertheless popular songs did offer comfort on long voyages and provided assurance of better times to come – such songs as 'Beneath the Lights at Home' and 'I'll Walk Alone'. Survivors will also cherish memories of the German Lily Marlene in the Mediterranean and the Japanese Tokyo Rose in Far Eastern ports when ashore relaxing.

One of the finest welcomes in the field of song was that awaiting the troopships as they berthed at Durban. There, standing on the Bluff

Point, was Perla Siedle Gibson, known worldwide as 'Durban's Lady in White'. Singing such songs as 'Land of Hope and Glory', 'Now is the Hour' and 'Will Ye No Come Back Again', she reached well over 1,000 troopships and 350 hospital ships with her voice.

Humour in war has always been a great healer. Never more so than when adrift in a lifeboat or on a raft. With the merciless sun beating down or with storm-force winds from the Arctic wastes freezing everything in its path, it was often a life-saver. All the services enjoyed this great sense of humour and it can be said that in some respects it hastened victory. We could always see the funny side of life, even the inevitable cock-ups of men and machines – a hazard of whatever twentieth-century war.

As the dust settled after the New Year's air-raid on Antwerp I was to arrive in Naples serving as third mate aboard the steamer *Nailsea Moor*, carrying military equipment and supplies. In Italy all officers and men of the merchant fleet were able to enjoy the facilities offered to the armed forces. At Naples, the San Carlo Opera House, was 'under the direction of the British Military Authorities'. At Ancona, an important supply port then fifty miles from the front line, the Alexandra Repertory Company of Birmingham was presenting *The Late Christopher Bean*, courtesy of NAAFI. ENSA brought a total of ninety-two shows for the entertainment of servicemen in Italy.

Nailsea Moor was among the first merchantmen to deliver military supplies to Yugoslavia. Just four weeks previously Winston Churchill had written to Marshal Tito: 'This alone will enable tanks and anti-tank guns and other heavy munitions, together with other necessary supplies, to be brought in the quantities which your armies require.' Discharging vehicles at Dubrovnik, loaded at Brindisi and surplus to British army requirements, we were told of 200 Jews who had been lined up in the *placa* and marched away by the Gestapo never to be seen again. To be told of such atrocities was devastating, even to those who had fought and survived a horrific Atlantic war.

When an emergency came from out of the blue, it was the radio officer upon whom the crew depended. Often he had only a few minutes in which to transmit his SOS. In the heat of sudden, unheralded attack, with bombs and bullets spreading around him, or the stench of cordite from an exploded torpedo filling his nostrils, his was the only link with the world beyond the battle. Somehow his message must get through.

Little has been written about the contribution made by radio officers or 'sparks' as they were familiarly called. Without such brave men the death toll would have been a great deal heavier. In 1940, in the light of the desperate conditions prevailing, the rules regarding the manning of the radio room on foreign-going vessels was altered from the peacetime norm of one officer to three. This enabled a 24-hour radio or signal watch to be kept on all British and Allied vessels, whether sailing in convoy or independently routed. The immediate result was to empty all wireless schools of students in training and the recruitment of young people, on a voluntary basis, to man the ships. With a training course of between five and six months this led to many young men sailing as radio officers who were well below the military age of eighteen years at the time of volunteering.

Some 46 per cent of radio officers who perished were under the age of twenty-three. One young officer on his first voyage was fifteen years of age at the time of his death. As many as 1,371 died; a further thirty-two were killed in the Royal Navy Auxiliary Service whilst serving under T124 articles. As with all Merchant Navy personnel, the peak years were 1941 and 1942 when, respectively, 365 and 394 radio officers were lost.

Decorations of radio officers for bravery totalled 247 and included two George Medals and fifty-four MBEs. The first honour bestowed upon personnel was, in fact, the OBE awarded to the 'sparks' of the SS *Manaar*, sunk by *U-38* on 6 September 1939; the OBE and BEM awarded to the chief mate and the bosun of the *Athenia* (3 September) were announced later. The King's Commendation was awarded posthumously to those officers who served aboard the 'Eagle' tanker *San Florentino* and the cargo vessel *Arabistan*. The latter was sunk by the commerce raider *Michel* in the South Atlantic on 14 August 1942, when the Chief Engineer was the only survivor.

In the loss of another 'Eagle' tanker, the *San Emiliano*, the chief radio officer managed to release the only undamaged lifeboat so enabling the survivors to get away. The official citation covering the award of the George Medal declares: 'although he was badly burnt, he crawled through the flames on his hands and knees to release the falls. Throughout he displayed outstanding courage and fortitude and but for his brave act the boat would not have got away and there would have been few, if any, survivors.' As I have related in Chapter 4, the apprentice in this boat was posthumously awarded the George Cross; the chief mate was also the recipient of the George Medal.

The second 'sparks' George Medal was awarded to the chief radio officer of the rescue ship *Walmer Castle* after she was attacked from the air and sunk whilst on duty with convoy OG74 (21 September 1941). Distress messages were transmitted but the radio officer then found himself trapped in his cabin with three others. 'As soon as the blast cleared he removed the debris and forced his way out. He returned three times to release the others, two of whom were badly hurt. By his own effort alone he succeeded in dragging them to safety.'

Of all the heroic deeds and comradeship shown by merchantmen crews, the saving of the steamer *Dover Hill* must rate as one of the finest.

She returned to her home port as one of the most decorated ships of the fleet. A vessel from convoy JW53 (April 1943), *Dover Hill* was bombed by the Luftwaffe whilst lying at anchor in Kola Inlet, northern Russia. For two days and nights nineteen officers and men dug a 1,000-pound unexploded bomb from the coal bunker where it lay buried. A mile astern lay the minesweeper HMS *Jason* at anchor ready to render assistance if the bomb should explode. For their fine example of bravery, her master Captain Perrin and four others were awarded the OBE; Captain Perrin was additionally the recipient of Lloyds War Medal. This new medal was struck at the close of 1940 to be bestowed by Lloyds upon officers and men of the Merchant Navy and Fishing Fleet in cases of exceptional gallantry at sea in time of war.

Master mariners who gained their commands during the 1920s and 1930s were a special breed of men. Fearless and modest they were used to long voyages away from home; yet they invariably had a wife and children and were homeloving men. Their wives, too, were a breed of women with special qualities. In spite of battles with the cruel sea and with the conditions that wartime brought, merchant masters were of a gentle nature. Rear-Admiral Kenelm Creighton, one of those gallant commodores, said of his merchant colleagues:

> Ordinary unpretentious people, self-contained, confident and calm. Their small talk is generally nil, their speech usually abrupt, confined to essentials and very much to the point. They uphold discipline by sheer character and personality for their powers of punishment under Board of Trade regulations are almost non-existent.

Patience was probably the least of the virtues held by masters. The *Daily Herald* of 17 April 1943 reported the case of the captain of the *Tintern Abbey*, who was relieved of his command at Gibraltar. Forty-seven years old and at sea since he was fifteen, he had sailed his vessel without instructions. 'He was anxious to catch up with a homeward convoy that had left and found it very irksome waiting in port for sailing orders.' Brought back to Gibraltar by a naval patrol launch, 'he admitted he had done a foolish thing but said owing to the shortage of ships he thought he was acting in the nation's interest'. At Cardiff he was subsequently fined £100, with 10 guineas costs, or three months' imprisonment. In his defence the merchant 'skipper' said, 'Nelson disobeyed orders and he was regarded as a credit to the Navy.'

Whenever possible masters, occasionally chief officers and chief engineers or other navigation officers, were taken prisoner by submarine commanders. This was done by the enemy to create a shortage of such qualified and experienced seafarers as well as making sure they did not report on the loss of their vessel as required by the Admiralty (in their absence such a report was then submitted by the next most senior deck officer that survived).

Being proud men, both of their ships and their command, many captains found it a great indignity to be taken prisoner with the thought of many months or years ahead in a POW camp. On occasion they could be found in the lifeboat ditching their uniform, whilst a junior officer volunteered to take his place. There were several who never reached the U-boat pens in Brittany. One such master was Captain Hime of the *John Holt*, sunk 5 March 1944, who was aboard *U-66* when she was destroyed by USS *Block Island* and *Buckley* (6 May 1944).

It is known that at least two masters refused to leave their sinking ship and in the tradition of the sea did not try to save themselves. Controversy arose in December 1940 after the loss of the 10,926-ton *Western Prince* (Captain Reed), torpedoed by *U-96*. The survivors were rescued by *Baron Kinnaird*, though six were drowned as one lifeboat capsized while coming alongside.

In twenty-one years as master, Captain Reed had never had a minor accident occur to the vessels under his command. His wife remembered that as he went to join the *Western Prince* he said, 'Goodbye Effie; if I lose my ship I shall never come back.' I asked him what he meant and he said, "I could never meet anyone if I lost my ship." ' His ship meant more to him than anyone else, even more than his wife and son. He sacrificed his life and went down with his ship. Captain Leslie of *Glenorchy* (Operation 'Pedestal'), fine sailor and gentleman that he was, chose to go down with his splendid vessel, under construction at the outbreak of war. Refusing all efforts from his loyal crew, who attempted to take him with them, and torn between the duty to his family and his 'calling' as a sailor, he died in the great tradition of those in command.

Few masters after losing their ship, along with the loss of so many personnel and passengers, could afterwards live in peace with themselves. Captain Frith was in command of the ill-fated *Aquila* when 150 lives were lost. Even in his retirement, he could never come to terms with the memory of those ninety disastrous seconds as his ship sank and the nightmare burden of appalling casualties.

There were five awards of the coveted George Cross to Merchant Navy personnel. That awarded to Chief Officer Stronach of the *Ocean Voyager* at Tripoli (19 March 1943), in the words of the official citation, 'equals any in the annals of the Merchant Navy for great and unselfish heroism and determination in the face of overwhelming odds'. Bombed during a raid by twelve Junkers 88s, the 7,174-ton *Ocean Voyager* caught fire whilst discharging petrol in drums; she was also carrying live ammunition. With her master lying dead on the bridge, George Preston Stronach, who was still recovering from being knocked unconscious, assumed responsibility. He fought the unquenchable flames, dragged

WHSmith

This voucher entitles ONE child* to

FREE ADMISSION

to any of the

SEA·LIFE
— CENTRES —

* *see reverse for details.*

SEA·LIFE CENTRES

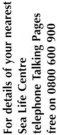

For details of your nearest
Sea Life Centre
telephone Talking Pages
free on 0800 600 900

OBAN
ST. ANDREWS
TYNEMOUTH
SCARBOROUGH
BLACKPOOL
RHYL
HUNSTANTON
BIRMINGHAM
GT. YARMOUTH
SOUTHEND
WESTON-SUPER-MARE
PORTSMOUTH
HASTINGS
NEWQUAY
WEYMOUTH
BRIGHTON

FREE
Calippo
or Twister
at
WHSmith

This voucher can be exchanged
for a free Calippo or Twister
when handed in at the front
till on your exit from this store
and must be used on the day of
your transaction. This voucher
cannot be exchanged for cash
or any other offer.

survivors to safety and threw men overboard to rafts which he himself had released. As a result of his leadership several officers and members of the crew survived. Stronach, along with the second engineer and the boatswain, were awarded Lloyds War Medals. Also sunk at Tripoli on that horrific day were the coaster *Varvara* and the destroyer HMS *Derwent*, the latter by a circling torpedo, the first use of this weapon.

Honours and awards included ten knighthoods, fifty CBEs, eighteen DSOs, 213 DSCs, 421 DSMs, forty-nine George Medals and eleven Albert Medals. Whilst masters and officers figured prominently there were many 'other ranks'. Amongst holders of the BEM and Lloyds War Medal were seamen from *Anchises*, *Benvorlich* and *British Premier; Empire Purcell*, *Empire Strait* and *Melrose Abbey; Regent Lion*, *River Afton* and *Ville de Strasbourg*. There were firemen from *Empire Avocet* and *Ocean Faith*; cooks who served aboard *Empire Eve* and *Pacific Grove*; boatswains, more often known as bosuns, the foremen of the crew, from *Port Fairey* and *Walmer Castle*; carpenters on board *Lubrafol* and *Port Fairey*; and the purser on the latter vessel received the MBE.

The carpenter and one of the able-bodied seamen of the *Lulworth Hill*, the only survivors of an epic fifty-day raft voyage were recipients of the MBE. The ship's surgeon aboard the devastated *Stentor* was awarded the Albert Medal; and the MBE went to the ship's surgeon from ill-fated *Britannia*, sunk by the raider *Thor*. George Medal recipients included able-bodied seamen serving aboard *Thistlegorm* and *Port Brisbane*, a stewardess aboard the *St Patrick* and *River Afton*'s chief steward.

Among decorated masters were Captain Harvey of the CAM ship *Empire Tide*, who received the DSO, a vessel which also collected two DSCs and one DSM. Captain Parfitt of *Narkunda* won the DSC, together with one of his engineers and the ship's carpenter; these recognized the men's contribution at Bougie on the fateful day in 1942. DSCs included Captain Morgan of *Awatea*, Captain Brown of *Deucalion* and Captain Tuckett of the *Dorset*. Amongst those awarded the CBE were Captain Rice of *Orari*, Fox of *Orcades*, Biggs of *Strathallan* and Harrison of *Trolius*.

Trying to survive in a storm-tossed lifeboat brings out either the best or the worst in a human being. John Masefield, the poet laureate and a former merchant seaman, wrote of 'a quiet English girl', one of those who drifted for five weeks in an open boat, as having behaved with a 'simple splendour'. Diana was a twenty-year-old passenger in the *City of Cairo* sunk in the South Atlantic (6 November 1942). She had all the qualities of leadership. She could never do enough – attending to the sick and injured, boat work and even actually handling the craft. Whilst she herself eventually died aboard the German blockade runner *Rhakotis*, after having been rescued by the enemy on the thirty-sixth day in a lifeboat with the chief quartermaster and ship's steward, she personally nursed many of the crew who died. They failed, both mentally and physically.

Adrift in the North Atlantic for thirteen days after the *Start Point* was torpedoed was a 22-year-old Canadian second mate. The most senior officer to survive, the captain and chief engineer having both been taken prisoner, he took charge of the two lifeboats and ensured that they kept together, navigating, attending the wounded and burying the dead. The diary that he kept vividly illustrates the paramount importance of discipline – in organization, seamanship, and in saving life. On 20 November 1942, the eleventh day, with spirits low and a gale blowing with precipitous seas and a heavy swell, he was to write:

> Tow parted again at noon. Latitude at noon 7.42 North. Greaser Mizzi in the other boat has gone mad. Several men drinking sea water. Wind continuing to freshen with heavy rain squalls. Miserable wet night with all hands soaked to the skin. Compass light continually going out and we have run out of matches. Trying to steer by the stars but some of the hands are not too adept at doing this.

In the *London Gazette* of 6 July 1943 there appeared the award of the George Medal to Vernon Gordon Allenby Upton, second officer of the steamship *Start Point*.

A remarkable lifeboat saga involves the survivors from Alfred Holt's *Rhexenor*, sunk by *U-217* in the North Atlantic on 3 February 1943, 1,200 miles from the nearest land. The seamanship and strength of her officers and senior ratings enabled her four lifeboats carrying all hands (except the fourth mate) to reach friendly shores in the Caribbean. The fourth mate, who assumed the role of ship's master, was taken prisoner and later landed at Brest.

On the seventh day after an electric storm, the young second steward made an entry in his diary. Through his ordeal, he wrote of his seventeen shipmates, led by the second mate, the torrential rain, the boat half full of water, the bailing out.

> All had a rub down with fish oil, stripped, the condition of all still quite excellent under these conditions, all worn out with loss of sleep though. Sun out making things a little more cheerful, good breakfast; 2nd Mate thought we all deserved it. Pemmican, biscuit, prune, raisins, nuts and 2 ounces of water ... Lunch with one ounce of water. Sea moderate, making 2 knots, everybody scared about the night; it rained for the last four nights. Supper with 2 ounces water.

Not until 24 February was the second mate's boat (No. 3) sighted and rescued by the American merchantman *Conqueror* and landed at St Thomas, Virgin Islands; her crew had sailed an epic twenty-one days covering 1,236 miles. Boat No. 1, holding Captain Eccles and nineteen men, landed at Guadeloupe after eighteen days. Boat No. 4, with the chief mate and sixteen men, landed in Antigua after nineteen days. The fourth boat (No. 5), with the third mate and seventeen men, landed Jost van Dyke Island in the Tobago group after twenty days.

The 5,444-ton *Medon*, also owned by the Alfred Holt company, was sunk by the Italian submarine *Giuliana* in the Atlantic, midway between Freetown and Trinidad on 10 August 1942. The disaster is likewise noteworthy for the voyages of its four lifeboats.

No. 1 boat: Captain Evans with fourteen men. Eight days adrift. Voyaged 108 miles. Rescued by the Panamanian *Rosemont*.

No. 2 boat: Chief mate with thirteen men. Thirty-five days adrift. 383 miles. Rescued by the Portuguese *Luso*.

No. 3 boat: Second mate with sixteen men. Thirty-six days adrift. 313 miles. Rescued by the British *Reedpool*. A week later the *Reedpool* was herself torpedoed and sunk by *U-515* and her master taken prisoner. The *Medon* survivors, being rescued for the second time (by the schooner *Millie M. Masher*), were landed in Georgetown, British Guiana.

No. 4 boat: Third mate with nineteen men. Seven days adrift. 40 miles. Rescued by Norwegian *Tamerlane*.

Though discipline contributed enormously to the operation of all four boats, the leadership of *Medon*'s master and his three deck officers during the voyages was unquestionably of a very high order. As Captain S.W. Roskill has written (*A Merchant Fleet in War*), 'It was surely these traditions of the Alfred Holt fleet which made the difference between success and disaster.'

The many successful lifeboat voyages made by crews of Holt merchantmen led to the creation of the Outward Bound Sea School at Aberdovey in Wales, of which Mr Lawrence Holt was one of the principal founders. It became the first of many such schools worldwide.

For the four seamen floating upon a raft for thirty-eight days in mid-Atlantic, it was eating raw fish that saved their lives. They were the only survivors from the 12,806-ton *Melbourne Star*, bound from Liverpool to Sydney via Panama. Sailing independently at the time, she was carrying a cargo of torpedoes, ammunition and other munitions of war when she was sunk by *U-129* on 2 April 1943; two torpedoes struck almost simultaneously. Famous for her successful berthing in Malta (Operation 'Pedestal'), the *Melbourne Star* sank with eighty-two of her crew and thirty-one passengers.

Sighted by an American flying boat which landed on the water and taxied alongside, the four seamen were landed in Bermuda. Sixteen months later they were awarded the BEM for 'outstanding qualities of courage, fortitude and endurance which enabled them to survive the hardships and perils of the long and hazardous ordeal on the raft'. One of them, Ronald Dunn, Ordinary Seaman, died before he could receive his award. He lost his life on the *Dungrange*, torpedoed by an E-boat off the Isle of Wight at the time of the Normandy invasion, 10 June 1944.

In addition to the stress and strain of working ships in convoy and co-operating closely with the Royal Navy in combined operations, masters, deck officers and engineering staff were forever concerned with the possibility of engine breakdowns and sabotage. Merchantmen presented a fine target to saboteurs and enemy agents in both home and foreign ports. Names of vessels and departure dates were closely guarded secrets, but whilst such posters as 'Even the walls have ears' and 'Loose lips sink ships' were displayed in public places, security was not all it could have been. It was particularly bad in South African ports and the many ports of North America's east coast.

Whilst I have mentioned such casualties as the *Bencleuch* in the North Atlantic and the two merchantmen in the harbour of Algiers, there were the mysterious losses of the armed merchant cruiser *Comorin*, the *Cape Horn* and the *Fort Stikine* holocaust in Bombay. Whilst in all three cases the necessary inquiries were set up, it was never firmly established whether sabotage was responsible.

The Canadian-built *Fort Stikine* was carrying, amongst other cargo, 1,400 tons of munitions. She took fire at Bombay on 14 April 1944 after arriving from Baltimore. So sudden was the outbreak and so quickly did it spread that little could be done to keep the flames from the ammunition. In a crowded dock the vessel blew up, creating such devastation that fifteen other merchantmen and two warships of the Royal Indian Navy were either sunk or damaged beyond repair. A total of 336 people, including many seamen, were killed and over 1,000 injured.

Cape Horn loaded 4,500 tons of ammunition and war materials in Glasgow during February 1942, and headed for the Middle East with instructions to discharge at Suez. She was already a veteran of the eastern Mediterranean, and on 14 May 1941 she had been bombed whilst sailing between Crete and Port Said, when she suffered six fatal casualties. Whilst *en route* for Suez in the South Atlantic east of Ascension Island (28 March 1942), fire broke out and an explosion took place shortly after. The blaze was believed to have been caused by a delayed-action incendiary device placed in her cargo upon loading. For some six hours the crew fought the fire but their efforts were to no avail. The after-deck was red-hot and buckling, the deck cargo ablaze. Twenty minutes after the master had given the order to abandon ship, *Cape Horn* blew up with a tremendous explosion; the crew and the twenty passengers she was carrying were later picked up by the *Clifton Hall*, there being no loss of life.

One of the armed merchant cruiser losses in the North Atlantic during 1941 was that of the 1925-built 15,241-ton P & O liner *Comorin*, crewed mainly by Merchant Navy personnel. On this occasion it was not enemy action that caused a crisis, but a fire which broke out on board. Racing to the rescue of her crew and some 400 Royal Navy recruits which she was carrying to Freetown were the destroyers *Broke*, *Lincoln* and *Glenartney*; the Glen Line vessel was *en route* for the Middle East with military stores. The rescue took place on 5 April 1941 amid a very heavy sea and with a south-easterly gale blowing. A reconstruction of the part played by HMS *Broke* was subsequently depicted in paint by Sir Peter Scott, at the time serving as master in the destroyer.

Broke was brought round at dead slow, but her bow was split wide open as she hit the *Comorin*, which was lying beam-on to the sea. From her funnel, which was belching forth smoke, the red glow from within could be seen reflected on the dark angry sea. Many were injured as they jumped from the burning inferno to the deck of HMS *Broke*, which was rising and falling in forty-foot waves. There were many casualties. It was claimed at the time that powerful incendiary devices had been planted in the boiler room of the armed merchant cruiser prior to sailing. The fire spread so rapidly that the engine room was soon engulfed, in spite of work by the ship's crew to contain the flames. The tragedy of her loss and the remarkable lifesaving work of the *Broke* has never been forgotten by survivors of her crew. (The 1,480-ton HMS *Broke* was subsequently sunk by gunfire from shore batteries in Algiers – Operation 'Torch', 8 November 1942.)

Breakdowns in the Atlantic Ocean, when crews were at the mercy of both the elements and the enemy, brought forth some epic towages, a testing time for officers and seamen alike. The *Macbeth*, whose engines broke down in mid-Atlantic, was towed by the Dutch tug *Zwarte Zee* based at Halifax, Nova Scotia. Running before a westerly gale she successfully reached a British port where she was repaired. The *Temple Inn*, bound from Durban for North America (July 1942), lost her only propeller south of the Equator. After drifting for three days on a motionless tropical sea she was taken in tow by the AMC *Cheshire*, which safely towed her to Point Noire. After lying alongside the quay for three weeks, *Temple Inn* was towed to Lagos, where a new propeller was fitted.

The *Empire Treasure*, built in 1942, received a fracture to her stern frame and lost a propeller blade *en route* for North America during a violent storm in January 1944. Dropping out of convoy ON219, the weather worsened and she lost the rest of her propeller blades. She wallowed and rolled alarmingly. For three days she maintained radio silence, knowing full well that another convoy straggler, the American *Summer I Kimball* had been sunk in the vicinity (by *U-960*). *Empire Treasure* was eventually found by the Admiralty tug *Bustler*. Tossed from trough to crest in forty-five-foot waves in storm conditions, she finally reached the Bristol Channel after a tow of more than 1,000 miles.

By far the worst which could happen to individual crew members or even to complete crews was the deprivation of captivity – to be held at the Nazi 'Milag' at Westertimkie, near Bremen, or the notorious camps in Japan like Yawata on the island of Kyushu, 200 miles north of Nagasaki, or at the small camp of Kawasaki. Whilst merchant seamen taken prisoner were covered by the Geneva Convention, they were not strictly classed as prisoners of war, being listed as civilians employed by shipowners. This fact, did not, however, stop the Japanese, who unlike the Germans, mixed merchantmen's crews with soldiers and airmen.

Captain Cant of the *Wellpark*, sunk by the commerce raider *Thor*, was the acknowledged leader of some 160 Merchant Navy men and DEMS gunners held at Kawasaki. He was greatly respected and admired by all inmates. Ironically, one of their first jobs was unloading ships; others followed in flour mills, in a soya sauce factory and attending to wagons at a railway junction. Life over the three years' imprisonment at Kawasaki was one of hard work, monotony, shortage of food and sickness. One could not reason with Japanese captors. The apparent hopelessness of the future broke the morale of many.

At Yawata, 1,200 inmates lay on bug-ridden straw mattresses, 140 men to a hut. Every day was spent shovelling coal to fuel the furnaces of Yawata steelworks. Comradeship and British humour were a lifeline. Claude Hutton, an engineer on the *Lylepark*, sunk by the raider *Michel*, was to write:

> None of us slept much that first night, the train journey from Yokohama took 27 hours. We were hungry, we'd had no meal apart from three boxes of Japanese food between 170 seamen. Most of us were like me I'm sure, worried about what was going to happen. When I did fall asleep (from exhaustion) it seemed only minutes before … Tenko! Tenko! These were Japanese words I learnt quickly enough. I was to hear them every morning at 0530.

Claude Hutton wrote of the brutality and the sickness. 'Only two skimpy meals a day and heavy work even when you weren't feeling up to it, left us wide open to disease. Dysentery hit so many that at one stage an average of six men were dying every day and of course we had no knowledge of how the war was going, to stiffen our resistance.' A young engineer who loved his life at sea, Hutton died soon after returning home from Japan. Out of the 1,200 men who had been held at Yawata some 400 died from disease aggravated by beatings.

A total of 2,985 officers and men from 211 British merchantmen were held at the Milag Nord camp in Germany. Whilst they were better fed than those held captive in Japan they also had the knowledge that they were close to home; some of the injured were later in the war in fact repatriated under exchange schemes. Red Cross parcels, too, arrived at frequent intervals and there were opportunities to pursue studies and hobbies. In general, life was more bearable under a 'European' guard than one from a little-known race in the Far East.

In the 'dark days' Winston Churchill, who never forgot the unsung heroes of those who sailed the seven seas, paid a tribute to them in the House of Commons: 'Nothing daunts the ardour of the Merchant Navy. Their toils and tireless courage are our salvation. The sea traffic upon which we, as a nation, depend for our very existence, proceeds without interruption'.

They came from the Clyde and the Thames, the north-east coast and the Scottish islands, Liverpool, Belfast and Hull, Wales and the West country. They came from just about any town in the British Isles. The smell of the sea, the sight of its waters and the ships that sail thereon have their own inspiration – men and boys who spent long hours gazing towards the far horizon were most likely to be those who sought what lay beyond.

> Eternal Father, strong to save,
> Whose arm hath bound the restless wave,
> Who bidd'st the mighty ocean deep
> Its own appointed limits keep;
> O hear us when we cry to Thee
> For those in peril on the sea.
>
> *W. Whiting*

Appendices

Appendix I

Merchant Ship Losses: British, Allied and Neutral

May 1940–May 1944

Months	British	No. gross tons	Allied	No. gross tons	Neutral	No. gross tons	Total	No. gross tons
1940								
May	31	82,429	26	134,078	20	56,712	77	273,219
June	61	282,560	37	187,128	27	101,808	125	571,496
July	64	271,056	14	48,239	20	62,672	98	381,967
Aug	56	278,323	13	55,817	19	59,870	88	394,010
Sept	62	324,030	19	79,181	9	39,423	90	442,634
Oct	63	301,892	17	73,885	17	66,675	97	442,452
Nov	73	303,682	13	47,685	5	24,731	91	376,098
Dec	61	265,314	11	70,916	7	21,084	79	357,314
1941								
Jan	44	209,394	30	107,692	1	2,962	75	320,048
Feb	79	316,349	20	82,222	1	3,197	100	401,768
March	98	366,847	32	138,307	9	32,339	139	537,493
April	79	362,471	67	256,612	8	34,877	154	653,960
May	96	387,303	24	98,559	6	14,201	126	500,063
June	63	268,634	35	142,887	10	19,516	108	431,037
July	36	95,465	6	23,994	1	1,516	43	120,975
Aug	31	96,989	9	32,010	1	1,700	41	130,699
Sept	61	215,207	13	47,950	9	22,595	83	285,752
Oct	32	151,777	14	53,434	5	13,078	51	218,289
Nov	29	91,352	4	6,260	1	6,600	34	104,212
Dec	124	271,401	44	159,276	19	55,308	187	485,985
1942								
Jan	38	146,274	65	259,135	3	14,498	106	419,907
Feb	79	341,271	69	304,804	6	33,557	154	679,532
March	107	276,312	158	531,214	8	26,638	273	834,164
April	53	293,083	76	372,284	3	9,090	132	674,457
May	58	258,273	86	410,382	7	36,395	151	705,050
June	50	233,740	110	571,254	13	29,202	173	834,196
July	43	232,718	74	350,473	11	34,922	128	618,113
Aug	58	344,763	53	281,262	13	39,608	124	665,633
Sept	50	274,952	52	266,265	12	26,110	114	567,327
Oct	60	409,519	40	224,537	1	3,777	101	637,833

Months	British No.	gross tons	Allied No.	gross tons	Neutral No.	gross tons	Total No.	gross tons
Nov	75	469,493	57	329,308	2	8,953	134	807,754
Dec	46	226,581	24	113,074	3	9,247	73	348,902
1943								
Jan	19	98,096	24	143,358	7	19,905	50	261,359
Feb	29	166,947	39	232,235	5	3,880	73	403,062
March	62	384,914	53	303,284	5	5,191	120	693,389
April	33	194,252	27	137,081	4	13,347	64	344,680
May	31	146,496	26	151,299	1	1,633	58	299,428
June	12	44,975	13	75,854	3	2,096	28·	123,825
July	30	187,759	26	166,231	5	11,408	61	365,398
Aug	14	62,900	9	56,578	2	323	25	119,801
Sept	12	60,541	15	94,010	2	1,868	29	156,419
Oct	11	57,565	17	81,631	1	665	29	139,861
Nov	15	61,593	12	82,696	2	102	29	144,391
Dec	10	55,611	21	112,913	–	–	31	168,524
1944								
Jan	16	67,112	9	62,115	1	1,408	26	130,635
Feb	12	63,411	8	53,244	3	200	23	116,855
March	10	49,637	14	104,964	1	3,359	25	157,960
April	3	21,439	10	60,933	–	–	13	82,372
May	5	27,297	–	–	–	–	5	27,297

Total ships
(May 1940–May 1944):

British	2,284	Gross tons	10,199,999
Allied	1,635	Gross tons	7,778,550
Neutral	317	Gross tons	979,146

Grand total	4,240	18,957,695

Total British, Allied and Neutral Ships sunk during the Second World War (September 1939–May 1945): 4,786. Gross tons: 21,194,000

Appendix II

Ocean Commodores Lost from Liverpool

Captain H.C. Birnie. *Bonneville* (Norge) 9.3.43 Convoy SC121 (*U-405*). Sank in 20 mins in rough sea, snow squalls. Total lives lost 36.

Vice-Admiral H.J.S. Brownrigg. *Ville de Tamatave.* 24.1.43 ONS160. Sir Henry Brownrigg was the highest-ranking officer on both sides to be killed in the war. His vessel, a former French merchantman, turned over in storm-force winds; all hands were lost.

Captain A. Dibben. *Empire Spring* 15.2.42. ON63. Convoy had dispersed when this CAM ship was sunk by *U-576*. 42 crew, 5 gunners and commodore's staff all lost.

Vice-Admiral W. Egerton. *Empire Shackleton* 1.1.43. ONS 154. Three submarines, *U-225*, *U-123* and *U-435*, involved in the sinking of this vessel. All Admiralty staff, except leading signalman, lost.

Captain J. Elliot. *Ashantian* 21.4.43. ONS3 (*U-415*). 16 men lost including the captain and the convoy commodore.

Rear-Admiral J. Fitzgerald. *Rotorua* 11.12.40. HX92 (*U-96*). 16 crew, 2 gunners and 3 Admiralty staff lost.

Captain R.H. Garstin. *Stentor* 27.10.42. SL125 (*U-509*). The commodore, having been blinded, was last seen being helped by the ship's doctor. Both were lost.

Captain N.H. Gale. *Athelsultan* 22.9.42. SC100. (*U-617*). Ship sank in 10 minutes. There were only 10 survivors.

Rear-Admiral J.C. Hamilton. *City of Bedford* 30.12.40. HX97. Ship lost in collision.

Captain H.C. Hudson. *Pelayo* 15.6.42. HG84. (*U-552*). Sank in less than 1 minute.

Captain W. Kelly. *Adda* 7.6.41. OB323 (*U-107*). Commodore last seen as he climbed over the bulwarks of the well deck.

Rear-Admiral E. Mackinnon. *City of Benares* 17.9.40. OB213. (*U-48*). The children's evacuee ship. The commodore was one of the last to leave.

Rear-Admiral H. Maltby. *Jumna* 25.12.42. OB260. The only commodore lost through action of a German surface raider. All on board lost when attacked by the *Admiral Hipper*.

Vice-Admiral D. Moir. *Trehata* 8.8.42. SC94 (*U-176*). Sank in 3 minutes. 22 lives lost, plus the commodore and his staff.

Vice-Admiral P.E. Parker. *Aquila* 19.8.41. OG71 (*U-201*). 'Whenever I think of the war I remember this convoy. It is my particular nightmare,' wrote Nicholas Monsarrat. Commodore and 5 staff lost.

Rear-Admiral R. Plowden. *Sirikishna*. 24.2.41. OB288 (*U-96*). All hands lost.

Captain E. Rees. *Empire Howard*. 16.4.42. PQ14 (*U-403*). The only commodore to be lost on Russian convoys; he was last seen in the water clutching a plank of wood and smoking a cigar. Vessel sank in less than 1 minute.

Vice-Admiral H. Smith. *Manchester Brigade*. 27.9.40. OB218 (*U-137*). A total of 52 perished.

Vice-Admiral B.G. Washington. *Harpalyce*. 25.8.40. HX65 (*U-124*). Commodore last seen on the bridge with the captain. Vessel was carrying 8,000 tons of steel and sank in 1 minute. 42 perished.

Vice-Admiral N. Wodehouse. *Robert L. Holt*. 4.7.41. OB337. (*U-69*). Last seen as this vessel dispersed from convoy. No survivors.

Captain A. Young. *Barberrys*. 26.11.42. SC110 (*U-663*). Sank in heavy seas in 7 minutes (one AB seaman was rescued after 18 days on a raft, having existed on 5 pounds of cabbage and 2 gallons of water).

Appendix III

Column 1   *Tureby* (British). *Gand* (Belgium) SUNK. *Hoyanger* (Norwegian). *New York City* (British).

Column 2   *British Prince* (British). *Edam* (Dutch). *Agioi Victores* (Greek). *Lima* (Swedish). *Orminster* (British).

Column 3   *Sommerstad* (Norwegian). *Baron Cawdor* (British). *King Edwin* (British). *Athelsultan* (British).

Column 4   *Colonial* (British), the commodore ship – SUNK after convoy dispersal. *City of Cairo* (British). *Eastern Star* (Norwegian) SUNK. *Atlantic Coast* (British).

Column 5   *City of Kimberley* (British). *Lucerna* (British). *El Mirlo* (British). *Ixion* (British) SUNK. *Ben Lomond* (British).

Column 6   *Burma* (British). *Gyda* (British). *Berhala* (Dutch) SUNK after dispersal. *Iron Baron* (British).

Column 7   *Bengore Head* (British) SUNK. *Gregalia* (British) SUNK. *Nagina* (British). *Zwarte Zee* (Dutch tug).

Column 8   *Empire Caribou* (British) SUNK after dispersal. *Chaucer* (British). *Hercules* (Dutch). *Tornus* (British).

Column 9   *Esmond* (British) SUNK. *Empire Cloud* (British) DAMAGED. *Aelybryn* (British) DAMAGED. *Nailsea Moor* (British).

Appendix IV

Russian Convoy PQ17. 0923 hrs. 4 July 1942 (see page 100)

British except where indicated.

Column 1   *Paulus Potter* (Dutch). *Hoosier* (Amer.). *Ironclad. William Hooper* (Amer.).
Column 2   *Washington. El Capitan* (Panamanian). *Bolton Castle. Troubadour.*
Column 3   *Hartlebury. Pankraft* (Amer.). *Olopana* (Amer.). *Donbass* (Norwegian). *Rathlin* (rescue ship).
Column 4   *Pan Atlantic* (Amer.). *Navarino. Bellingham* (Amer.). *Silver Sword* (Amer.).
Column 5   *River Afton* (commodore ship). *Azerbaijan* (Russian). *Alcoa Ranger* (Amer.). *Winston Salem* (Amer.). *Zaafaran* (rescue ship).
Column 6   *Peter Kerr* (Amer.). *Earlston. Empire Tide* (CAM ship). *Aldersdale* (oiler).
Column 7   *Empire Byron. Benjamin Harrison* (Amer.). *Ocean Freedom.*
Column 8   *Christopher Newport* (Amer.). *Fairfield City* (Amer.). *Honomu* (Amer.). *John Witherspoon* (Amer.). *Zamalek* (rescue ship).
Column 9   *Samuel Chase. Carlton. Daniel Morgan.*

Appendix V

Convoy WS10: August 1941

Troopships: UK–Middle East

Britannic. Indrapoera. Stirling Castle. Strathallan. Windsor Castle. Volendam. Cameronia. Highland Monarch. Nea Hellas. Orcades. Rangitiki. Reina Del Pacifico.

Appendix VI

Convoy WS12: October 1941

Troopships: UK–Middle East

Clan Campbell. Empire Trust. Highland Brigade. Sarpedon. Perseus. Almanzora. Empire Pride. Leopoldville. Strathaird. Empress of Russia. Empress of Canada. Narkunda. City of Paris. Ormonde. Samaria. Franconia. Mendoza. Duchess of Richmond. Dominion Monarch. Prince Baudouin. Royal Ulsterman. Clan Lamont. Perthshire. Highland-Princess.

Ex Avonmouth, 1 ship 29.9.41. Ex Liverpool, 7 ships 29.9.41. Ex Clyde, 16 ships 30.9.41. Rendezvous at sea 1.10.41. Commodore ship *Strathaird*. Convoy arrived Freetown 14.10 and sailed 19.10 less *Narkunda*. *Highland Princess* was detached as CT.4 (military convoys, North America). On 4.10 escorted by *Cathay* (AMC), *Agamemnon* (auxiliary minelayer) HMCS *Assinboine* and HMCS *Saguenay*.

Other escorts – Cruiser *Cairo*, as AA ship, 1.10 to 4.10. Destroyer *Sikh* 30.9 to 5.10. Destroyers *Witch, Whitehall* and *Verity*. 1.10 to 4.10. Aircraft carrier *Argus* 30.9 to 5.10 (to Gibraltar). Destroyers *Badsworth, Bradford, Brighton, Lancaster, Newark* 1.10 to 3.10. Destroyer *Beverley* 2.10 to 3.10. Destroyer *Blankney* 1.10 to 7.10. Cruiser *Devonshire* 1.10 to 12.10 (thence to Freetown). Cruiser *Dorsetshire* 12.10 to 14.10. Destroyer *Wrestler, Velox, Vimy, Vansittart* and corvettes *Armeria, Amaranthus* 11.10 to 14.10. The Dutch *Isaac Sweers* joined 7.10 and HMS *Gurka* 8.10.

Appendix VII

Catapult-Armed Merchant (CAM) Ships

A total of thirty-five: Eight were taken from private owners, and the remainder were government-owned 'Empire' tramp ships. Losses: 13.

Daghestan
Dalton Hall
Eastern City
Empire Burton – sunk by *U-74*, 20.9.41, convoy SC44.
Empire Clive
Empire Darwin – operational aircraft launch, 28.7.43 (1 damaged).
Empire Day
Empire Dell – sunk by *U-124*, 12.4.42, convoy ON92.
Empire Eve – sunk by *U-414*, 18.5.43. Mediterranean.
Empire Faith
Empire Flame
Empire Foam – operational aircraft launch, 1.11.41.
Empire Franklin
Empire Gale
Empire Heath – operational aircraft launch, 1.11.42 (1 'kill').
Empire Hudson – sunk by *U-82*, 10.9.41, convoy SC42.
Empire Lawrence – operational aircraft launch, 25.5.42 (2 'kills'). Sunk by aircraft 27.5.42, convoy PQ16.
Empire Moon – operational aircraft launch, 14.6.42 (1 damaged).
Empire Morn – operational aircraft launch, 25.5.42 (1 kill, 1 damaged). Operational aircraft launch, 18.9.42 (2 kills).
Empire Ocean – marine casualty, 4.8.42. Grounded. Refloated but sank next day on east coast of Newfoundland.
Empire Rainbow – sunk by *U-607*, 26.7.42, convoy ON113.
Empire Ray
Empire Rowan
Empire Shackleton – sunk by *U-123* and *U-435*, 29.12.42, convoy ONS154.
Empire Spray
Empire Spring – sunk by *U-576*, 15.2.42, after dispersal of convoy ON63.
Empire Stanley
Empire Sun – sunk by *U-751*, 7.2.42, independent, east of Cape Sable, Nova Scotia, on passage to Halifax.
Empire Tide – operational aircraft launch, 28.7.43 (1 kill).
Empire Wave – sunk by *U-562*, 2.10.41, convoy ON19.

Helencrest
Kafirstan
Michael E – sunk by *U-108*, 2.6.41, after dispersal of convoy OB327.
Novelist
Primrose Hill – sunk by *UD-5*, 29.10.42, after dispersal of convoy ON139

Appendix VIII

Merchant Aircraft Carriers (MAC ships)

A total of nineteen – six grain carriers and thirteen oil carriers

Oil Carriers	*Grain Carriers*
Acavus	Empire MacAlpine
Adula	Empire MacAndrew
Alexia	Empire MacCallum
Amastra	Empire MacDermott
Ancylus	Empire MacKendrick
Empire MacCabe	Empire MacRae
Empire MacColl	
Empire MacKay	
Empire McMahon	
Gadila	
Macôma	
Miralda	
Rapana	

Appendix IX

Operational U-boats in the Battle of the Atlantic

	1939	1940	1941	1942	1943	1944	1945
Jan		33	23	89	214	170	155
Feb		34	22	101	221	167	156
March		31	30	111	231	164	156
April		31	30	119	237	161	150
May		23	40	128	239	157	126
June		26	47	130	218	181	
July		29	60	140	209	180	
Aug		28	60	152	178	151	
Sept	42	31	74	169	167	146	
Oct	49	26	75	196	177	139	
Nov	38	25	81	205	163	148	
Dec	38	22	86	203	163	152	

Appendix X

Report of Ocean Escort HMS Wolfe (*formerly* Montcalm)

Convoy HX133 June 1941

June 16th   Times: Zone plus 3.
1425 Weighed and proceeded as Ocean Escort for Convoy HX133.
Ships as shown on Convoy Form less Nos.13, 44, 52, 81.
Add: No.33 British s.s. 'Scottish Trader'.
1800. Took up station in Convoy. 2030. No.83 'Emma Bakke' joined Convoy from astern after completion of Gun Trials.
Note: Ships of Convoy left well on time. Visibility about ½ mile, patchy. Fog lifted at about 1230. Ships rather bunched inside gate, but straightened out without incident. 'WOLFE' encountered fog-after passing P.W.S.S. – which lifted long enough to enable her to take station in Convoy.

June 17th   Zone plus 3.
Thick fog. Leading ships of columns on Starboard side heard sounding numbers regularly. No ships heard on port side. 2030. Fog lifted very slightly. 4 Ships sighted.

June 18th   Zone plus 3.
Thick fog. Carried out D/F programme. 1138, 1147, 1834, 1843, G.M.T.

June 19th   Times: Zone plus 3.
Thick fog. 1015. Heard apparent collision on starboard quarter. 1020. Course altered to 024 by Sound Signal. 1051. No.41 'Nailsea Manor' reported by W/T to Commodore, bow stove in, vital make for nearest port. Ordered by Commodore to proceed to St. Johns, N.F. 1112. No.32 'Dolabella' reported to Commodore that she was damaged. Ordered to return to Halifax. 1123. No.74 'Skeldergate' reported bow badly damaged – returning to Halifax. 1218. No.22 'Empire Oil' had temporary breakdown. Message 1822 addressed to S.H.X.133 from Commodore H.X.133 giving rendezvous for 0600 21st. 2237. No.42 'Havprins' reported by W/T that she had lost touch.

June 20th   Times: Zone plus 3.
Thick fog. 0255. No.71 B.H.X. 'City of Oxford' reported by W/T – bow damaged by collision. 0404. No.71. B.H.X. 'City of Oxford' and No.91 B.H.X. Norwegian s.s 'Primero' damaged by collision; ordered by 'Laconia' to proceed to St. Johns, N.F. 1200. Heard 'Ottawa' ahead passing Course signal to Newfoundland Escort. 1220. Fog lifted. Newfoundland Escort joined. 'Ottawa' (S.O.), 'Collingwood' (Port). 'Orillia' (Starboard. 1240. 'Annapolis' parted company and returned to Halifax. 1430. Convoy reformed into correct stations.

In addition to those returned damaged due to collisions. No.83 Norwegian s.s. 'Emma Bakke' and No.93 Greek s.s. 'Stylianos Chandris' had lost touch. Total ships in Convoy 22. 1746. Columns opened to 5 cables. 2045. 'Ottawa' took up station astern for the night. Disposition of Escort throughout voyage until joined by further A/S Escort was: 'Ottawa' ahead by day and astern by night. 'Collingwood', port bow. 'Orillia', starboard bow. Following ships were also damaged by collision during fog but were able to continue voyage: No.71 'Treworlas', No.82 'Kongsaard' and No.52 'Tricula'.

June 21st   Times: Zone plus 3.
0443. Sighted Convoy ahead. 0449. 'Ottawa' proceeded ahead to contact SHX and BHX section and to order them to join HX. 0707. Aircraft numbers 738 and 745 made identification signals. 0800. BHX section abeam starboard side on opposite course. Were badly manoeuvred into station by turning to port instead of to starboard – prolonging junction – and frustrating Commodore's intention of placing tankers in body of Convoy. BHX afterwards joined up in rear of SHX. BHX consisted of 15 ships – as given on Convoy form less No.71 British s.s. 'City of Oxford' and No.91 Norwegian s.s. 'Primero', who were – as previously reported – ordered to proceed to St. Johns, N.F. owing to damage through collision. 0900. SHX section turned and formed astern of HX about 3 miles, gradually closing up. SHX section consisted of 12 ships – as given on Convoy form less No.62 British s.s. 'Baltara' and No.91 s.s. 'Atlantic City'. 'Baltara' did not sail. 'Atlantic City' joined Convoy later.
1008. A.41 'Loch Ranza' was ordered to take station as No.41 of combined Convoy. 1115. Bermuda section ordered to proceed at utmost speed to gain station. 1120. Sighted and identified s.s. 'Rowallan Castle' on starboard bow. 1125. Aircraft requested to pass course to any stragglers sighted. Aircraft reported no stragglers in sight. 1330. Bermuda section in approximate station 1614. 'Ottawa' identified Norwegian s.s. 'Borgholm' on starboard bow bound for Rimouski. 2030. Dusk – 49 ships present in Convoy. 2330. Clocks advanced one hour.

June 22nd   Times: Zone plus 2.
'WOLFE' dropped back to centre of Convoy in order to facilitate signalling of changes of destination. 1500. Resumed normal station in Convoy. No.63 'Salamis' showed stern light from 0130 onwards.

June 23rd   Times: Zone plus 2.
0700. 'Chambly' joined Convoy and took station astern as A/S screen. 1015. 'WOLFE' took station in centre of Convoy to facilitate signalling of changes in formation. 1020. Norwegian s.s. 'Vigrid' dropped astern to repair engine defect. 1600. Received S/M report from Louisburg – approximate position 53 N. 41 W. 1640. Message 1757B/23 from Admiralty received and passed to Commodore. 1720. 'Atlantic City' joined Convoy from Starboard bow – ordered to take station as No.96, 1800. 'WOLFE' resumed station in Convoy. 1930. Message 2151B from Admiralty received and passed to Commodore, 2030. 'Vigrid' out of sight astern. 2230. 'Ottawa' took night station astern – 'Chambly' ahead. 2300. Course altered 40 degrees to port to comply with Admiralty's 1757B/23. 2330. Clocks advanced one hour. 2330. Submarine sighted, on surface bearing 050 degrees – distance ½ mile. 2333. Submarine submerged. Escort informed. 'Ottawa' and one other fired star shells.

June 24th   Times: Zone plus 1.
0453 'Ottawa' reported No.45 Norwegian s.s. 'Soloy' torpedoed and sunk at 0035Z. 'Traveller' picked up all hands. Submarine not seen. 1805. No.35 British s.s. 'Brockley Hill' torpedoed port side. Distress message initiated by 'Inverlee'. No.15 'Saugor' returned and picked up survivors. Crew safe but one seriously hurt, 1850. Sighted and

identified 'Gladiolus' who joined Convoy as additional escort. 1925. Sighted and identified 'Ripley', 'Fleetwood', 'Nasturtium' and 'Celandine', additional escort. 2104. 'Ottawa' reported 'Brockley Hill' did not appear to be sinking, but was on fire. 2133. 'Ripley' reported D/F bearing of U-Boat at 2200Z was 093 degrees – passed to Commodore. 2213. Convoy altered course by emergency turn 45 degrees to port, and Commodore signalled that he was remaining on that course for the night. 2330. Clocks advanced one hour. Total number of ships present 47. 'Soloy' and 'Brockley Hill' torpedoed, and 'Vigrid' lost touch.

June 25th   Time: G.M.T.
0430. 'Ottawa' reported 'Gladiolus' had sunk U-boat by gun-fire. 0555. Message 0116B from Admiralty passed to Commodore. 0708. Convoy altered course to 009 degrees to conform to Admlty. message. 0710. Leading ships ordered to resume beam bearings from Guide. Ships in column to form astern of leading ships. 1915. No.61 'Mooncrest' hoisted N.U.C. signal – engine defects – and dropped astern. Rejoined before dark. 2330. Clocks advanced 60 minutes.

June 26th   Times: Zone Minus 1.
0115. 'Nasturtium' rejoined Convoy. 0200. 'Gladiolus' rejoined Convoy. 0803. Sunderland Aircraft sighted and identified on starboard bow. 0820. 'Ottawa' proceeded away from Convoy to starboard to transmit message to C-in-C. W.A. 1000. Exchanged identities with 'Sikh'. 1013. Commodore hoisted disregard, due to defect in steering gear. 'WOLFE' took guide of Convoy. 1345. Commodore resumed Guide. 1356. 'Ottawa' reported Sunderland Aircraft had sighted submarine ahead. 1420. Course altered 60 degrees to starboard in two turns of 30 degrees each. 1428. 'Orillia' and 'Chambly' despatched to hunt submarine. 1631. Message 1350B from Admiralty passed to Commodore. 1641 course altered 45 degrees to port. 1750. Message 1522B from C-in-C. W.A. passed to Commodore. 1829. Course altered to 077 degrees to conform to C-in-C. W.A.'s. 1522B. 2330. Clocks advanced 60 minutes.

June 27th   Times: Zone Minus 2.
0100 No.52 Dutch s.s. 'Tibia' torpedoed right forward starboard side. Continued in station, later hauling out slightly to starboard. 'Ottawa' and Sunderland Aircraft informed. 0156. No.91 British s.s. 'Malaya II' torpedoed and blown up. No.81 Dutch s.s. 'Maasdam' torpedoed – believed to have sunk as was not seen after explosion in 'Malaya II'. 0203. Convoy turned 45 degrees to port by emergency alteration of course. 0214. No.82 Norwegian s.s. 'Kongsaard' reported hit by torpedo on port side of engine room, but may keep afloat. 0259. Convoy turned 45 degrees to starboard by emergency alteration of course. 0350. 'Tibia' resumed station as No.52. 1126. 'WOLFE' took Guide of Convoy owing to 'Glenpark' having trouble with compass. 1153. 'Ottawa' reported that 'Ripley' and 'Collingwood' with No.82 'Kongsaard' and No.83 'Havprins' were 16 miles astern. 1201. Sighted and identified 'Watchman' who reported relief escort group were 10 miles to northward. 1400. Details of the Convoy as now constituted signalled to 'Niger' (S.O.) for transmission to 'Malcolm'. 1430. 'Havprins' and 'Kongsaard' sighted astern. Commodore reduced to 7 knots to allow them to overtake. 1445. Hauled out of escort to port and proceeded with 'Cliona' for Reykjavik. Escorted by 'Ottawa', 'Chambly', and 'Orillia', later joined by 'Fleetwood'. 1345z. 'Cliona' escorted by two corvettes ordered to proceed to destination at best speed. 'Wolfe' escorted by 'Ottawa' and 'Fleetwood' proceeded independently. Relief Escort present on 'WOLFE' leaving: 'Niger' (S.O.) 'Speedwell' 'Watchman', 'Arabis', 'Maplin' and Trawlers. Course as for Reykjavik. 1350. Catalina Aircraft sighted. No.8 zig-zag.

June 28th
Course as for Reykjavik. 0520. Ceased zig-zag. 0602. Streamed P.V.'s. 1012. Recovered P.V.'s. 1046. Anchored Reykjavik. Discharged R.A.F. personnel. 1728. Weighed and proceeded to Hvalfjord. 1931. Anchored at Hvalfjord. 2110-0810/29. Taking oil from s.s. 'British Freedom'.

Captain

Appendix XI

Shipping Casualty Report on SS Nailsea Court

Convoy SC121 March 1943

SHIPPING CASUALTIES SECTION – TRADE DIVISION
REPORT OF AN INTERVIEW WITH THE 2nd ENGINEER, MR. H.C.C.BETTE
s.s. 'NAILSEA COURT' – 4,946 g.t.

IN CONVOY S.C.121

Sunk by 2 Torpedoes from U-Boat on the 9th March, 1943.

All Times are Convoy Times + 2 hrs. 20 mins. for G.M.T.

MR. H.C. BETTE

We sailed from New York bound for Loch Ewe with a cargo of 6,500 tons of Copper Bars, 800 tons of Nickel Ore, and Asbestos. We were armed with 1–4″, 12 pdr., 4 machine guns, and 4 P.A.C.Rockets. The crew, including 4 Army and 5 Naval Gunners, numbered 49; there were in addition 2 passengers, one a Mining Engineer, the other an Electrical Engineer, who came on board at Freetown. Of this number 48 are missing, including all officers (with the exception of myself), the gunners, and the two passengers. I cannot say with certainty, but I am of the opinion that all confidential and wireless books were thrown overboard in a weighted box. We did not carry any mails. Degaussing was off.

2. We left New York on the 27th February, 1943, and joined up with convoy S.C.121, our position being No.24, the 4th ship in the 2nd column.

3. The convoy proceeded without incident until the 7th March, when between 2100 and 2400 an attack was made and 3 ships were torpedoed. A further attack was made the following night, at about the same time, resulting in the loss of another 5 ships. On the 9th March, another attack kept us at 'alert stations' from 1945. I think a further 5 ships had been torpedoed, when at 2145, whilst steaming at 7½ knots, in position 58° 45′N, 21° 57′W, we were struck by 2 torpedoes. The weather was very bad with frequent hail squalls, visibility poor, very rough sea with a heavy swell, S.E. gale, force 7.

4. The 1st torpedo struck in No.1 hold on the port side with a dull explosion. I was in my accommodation, and at first, thought there had been a collision, so I made my way down to assist the 4th Engineer, who was on watch. When I was half-way down the

ladder, about a minute-and-a-half later, the 2nd torpedo struck. This also was a very dull explosion, but being below I do not know whether a column of water was thrown up, or if there was a flash, or smell; neither could I tell the actual dock damage sustained.

DISTRIBUTION:

C. in C. Western Approaches.
S.B.N.O. West Atlantic
I.M.N.G.
D.T.D.
D.T.D. (D.E.M.S.).
D.A./S.W.
D.T.S.D.
D.T.M.I. (Lt.Read)
D.P.D. (Cdr. Dillon Robinson)
N.I.D. (Cdr. R. Lister Kaye)
N.I.D. 1/P.W.
Lieut. Kidd. U.S.N.
N.I.D. 3/P.W.
N.I.D. (Cdr. Winn)

D.N.O. (London)
D.N.C. (Bath)
Captain Beswick.
Files (2).

The 2nd torpedo struck in the port side of No.2 hold. Both torpedoes hit forward, the hatches from No.1 hold being blown off by the first explosion. I did not hear of anyone seeing the tracks of either of the torpedoes.

5. I continued on my way to the engine room, where I found everything in order, there being no sign of water leaking through. The 4th Engineer, Mr. E.R. Dryden, and the Fireman Barnes, were still at their posts in the Engine-room, so we stopped the engines, also the circulating pump, as one lifeboat was directly over the discharge outlet and I did not wish to fill the boat up. The order was given on the telegraph to 'abandon ship' three minutes after the second explosion.

6. I went up to the boat deck, and saw that the starboard motor-boat was undamaged. During the previous day the port boat had been struck by a heavy sea, and washed inboard where it had been secured, thus leaving only the starboard boat intact and this was ultimately very much overloaded. There was some delay in lowering this boat, as the forward fall became jammed, and one of the sailors who was trying to clear it got his hand in the block. The 2nd Officer, Mr. Johasen, assisted by the crew, eventually managed to lift the boat and release the man's hand. As the falls were cleared the Captain ordered 'abandon ship' and the crew lowered the boat into the water. This starboard boat eventually had about 25 men in it, and the remainder had to get away on the rafts. Captain Lee, 2nd Officer Mr. Johasen, an Apprentice, and myself, were left on board, so all four of us jumped from the boat deck, the Captain being the last to jump as the ship sank. I saw her stern lift completely out of the water, and she finally plunged straight down by the head, without listing, 12 minutes after being torpedoed. No wireless message was sent out, and no rockets were fired, but later we flashed distress messages from the lifeboat with a torch.

7. About the same time as we were torpedoed, the Commodore's ship *BONNEVILLE* and the s.s. *COULMORE* were also torpedoed and I should think that the attacks occurred at intervals of between 3/4 minutes. The *COULMORE* was originally astern of us on the port side, in position No.15, and was struck on the port side, but she was on our starboard side when she sank.

8. I managed to get into the lifeboat, and after picking up several men from the water, some of whom I think were from the 'COULMORE', there were 37 in the boat. She became water-logged, and although we did our utmost to bale her out, with such heavy seas it was impossible to keep her dry. The Canadian Corvette *DAUPHIN* which came over to rescue us suddenly stopped when she was about 250 yards from us. The Captain shouted through his loud hailer telling us that his steering gear had broken down, and that he was unable to reach us. We signalled telling him that our boat was sinking rapidly. Again, the Captain told us that he could not possibly reach us, and that we were to try to reach him. This, of course, was quite impossible owing to the crowded condition of our boat, and about half-an-hour later it capsized. Up to this time our Captain was in the boat with us, but I do not remember seeing him afterwards. Many of the men were exhausted and washed away by the heavy seas until eventually there were only 17 left, clinging to the keel of the upturned boat. Gradually many of these men were washed away until finally there were only 7 of us left. At approximately 0200 on the 10th March, the Corvette came along for the second time. We had now been hanging on to the bottom of the boat for about three-and-a-half hours; only another man and myself were strong enough to lift our hands in order to be dragged aboard as the Corvette came along – the remaining men must have either been unconscious or too exhausted to lift their hands, or perhaps they feared that once they let go of the keel they would be washed away. There were also two men on the port raft, but only one was rescued, the other being already dead. I was in fairly good condition although obviously weak from exposure after my ordeal, but in about an hour I recovered, and was soon myself again. The 3 survivors rescued by the Corvette were the Messroom steward, a greaser named Perks, and myself. It was due to the failure of the steering gear of the Corvette that so many of our men lost their lives. We were eventually landed at Londonderry at 0800 on the 13th March, 1943.

9. Owing to the frequency of the attacks, prior to the disaster, the boat's wireless set was placed in the port boat in readiness, but this boat did not get away.

10. I would suggest that as the lifeboats frequently capsize, a rail fitted along each side of the keel would greatly assist men to hang on to the bottom of the upturned boats. In cold weather it is extremely difficult to hang on to the keel which is so wide that it is impossible to grip it tightly.

11. I would like to mention that all the crew behaved extremely well, and that there was definitely no sign of panic. Very special mention is due to the 2nd Officer, Mr. Johansen, (a Norwegian naturalised British) whose behaviour was outstanding throughout. He led and encouraged the crew during the abandoning ship operation, remaining behind in order to lower the lifeboat, and was an inspiration to all. His unselfish action cost him his life.

I would also specially mentioned the magnificent bearing and behaviour of Captain Lee, who remained behind until the end, encouraging the crew and attending to the lowering of the boat. Whilst in the boat his splendid bearing gave confidence and encouragement to everybody. Unfortunately, he was washed out of the boat and was drowned.

I would also specially mention 4th Engineer Dryden, Greaser Perks, and Fireman Barnes, who were on watch in the engine-room when the 1st torpedo struck. They remained at their posts even when the 2nd torpedo struck the ship, and still remained to stop the main engines and circulating pump, thus preventing the lifeboat from being filled with the overside discharge water.

Appendix XII

Deaths amongst Crews of Merchantmen (Enemy Action)

A Period	B Number of ships	C Gross tonnage	D Total crew	E Numbers of crew lost	F Percentage of crews lost
Sept–Dec					
1939	53	209,398	1,466	490	33.4
1940	363	1,743,751	12,206	5,553	45.5
1941	416	1,822,334	12,756	6,873	53.9
1942	427	2,561,038	17,927	7,622	42.5
1943	202	1,163,979	8,148	3,923	48.1
1944	71	339,983	2,380	1,087	45.7
1945	33	142,609	998	316	31.7
Total	1,565	7,983,092	55,882	25,864	46.3

Notes:
1. British vessels only, excluding DEMS/MRA personnel and men serving on T124 agreements.
2. Column B – Number of ships lost by enemy action in which members of the crew were lost. This excludes ships lost from enemy action in which no lives were lost and those lost from marine causes, although most losses in this category were attributable to war conditions.
3. Column C – Gross tonnage of ships in B.
4. Column D – Total numbers of crews in ships in B (based on an average of seven men per 1,000 gross tons).
5. Column E – Numbers of crew who were lost from ships in B. Does not include those lost in rescue ships or in ships on which they were being carried as passengers. They do not represent the total number of deaths in the Merchant Navy.
6. Column F – percentage of crews lost in ships sunk (proportion of D represented by E).

Appendix XIII

United Kingdom Petroleum Imports 1940–45

000 tons

Products	1940	1941	1942	1943	1944	1945
Aviation spirit	632	819	1,012	2,090	4,751	1,934
Motor spirit	2,920	3,939	3,081	3,236	4,773	4,912
White spirit	63	58	107	69	111	98
Burning oil	885	687	337	542	607	661
Vaporizing oil	108	381	519	671	764	567
Gas/Diesel oils	1,373	1,793	1,364	1,886	2,211	2,066
Fuel oil	1,193	1,445	633	1,700	1,425	1,440
Admiralty oil fuel	1,991	2,449	1,773	3,367	3,912	2,240
Lubricating oils	578	491	565	436	572	336
Crude/Process oils	1,528	1,066	867	798	1,218	1,363
Totals:	11,271	13,128	10,258	14,795	20,344	15,617

Appendix XIV

United Kingdom Petroleum Consumption: 1940–45
000 tons

Products	1940	1941	1942	1943	1944	1945
Aviation spirit	404	711	1,141	2,052	4,782	2,547
Motor fuel	3,764	4,130	3,640	3,411	4,164	3,898
Paraffin	872	943	1,012	1,067	1,134	1,263
Fuel oils –						
inland	1,572	1,553	1,414	1,241	1,413	1,367
Bunkers, civil	1,249	1,041	1,436	1,459	2,135	2,065
Bunkers, naval	2,596	2,089	2,203	2,478	4,164	2,661
Bitumen	380	348	248	177	263	243
Lubricating Oil	517·	647	628	592	699	553
Totals:	11,483	11,611	11,882	12,628	18,912	14,768

Notes:
1. Motor fuel includes motors spirit and derv fuel.
2. Fuel oils represent gas and diesel, but the figures for inland do not include derv fuel.
3. The totals shown include white spirit and industrial spirits not included under products.

Appendix XV

Tanker Tonnage by Flag: 1942–45

Allied tankers and neutral tankers (of 1,600 gross tons and over) outside enemy control or influence, excluding Great Lakes tonnage.

	August 1942 No. dw tons (000)		May 1943 No. dw tons (000)		May 1944 No. dw tons (000)		May 1945 No. dw tons (000)	
American	354	4,268	412	5,319	662	9,099	890	12,875
British	372	3,784	354	3,609	377	3,877	392	3,991
Norwegian	165	2,059	147	1,835	137	1,728	156	1,988
Dutch	70	334	69	457	69	476	66	457
Panamanian	67	827	65	758	67	765	69	796
Other flags	91	862	89	726	117	948	113	918

Notes:
1. Dates signify end of month.
2. British flag includes tankers on the register of other Empire countries.
3. Other flags include Russian and Latin American tonnage (outside Panama) and Swedish tankers outside the Baltic. Portuguese, Spanish and Turkish tonnage is not included.

Appendix XVI

Tanker Tonnage Losses by Flag: 1939–45

The table includes Admiralty tankers, whalers etc. and takes account of marine as well as war losses. Figures for 1939–41 include losses of neutral tonnage sailing in Allied and neutral trades.

	British	American	Norwegian	Dutch	Panamanian	Other
Sept 1939–41	1,469	30	430	51	63	80
1942	924	976	588	171	279	81
1943	310	262	246	10	106	41
1944	94	140	22	6	5	26
1945	91	13	13	13	–	–
Total:	2,888	1,421	1,299	251	453	228

Appendix XVII

Tanker Losses and New Building: Dec. 1941–May 1944

Tankers of 1,600 gross tons and over, including tankers owned by the Admiralty and the Royal Navy Department, whalers etc. War and marine losses are included.

	Losses: Total	New Building 000 dwt tons		
		Total	Greyhounds	other
Dec 1941–Feb 1942	712	294	145	149
March–May 1942	1,147	258	126	132
June–Aug 1942	754	339	226	113
Sept–Nov 1942	447	391	249	142
Dec 1942–Feb 1943	381	526	402	124
March–May 1943	294	720	659	61
June–Aug 1943	205	752	702	50
Sept–Nov 1943	110	1,397	825	572
Dec 1943–Feb 1944	81	1,217	857	360
March–May 1944	90	1,156	1,095	61
Total for Dec 1941–May 1944:	4,221	7,050	5,286	1,764

Appendix XVIII

Tanker Construction by Flag: 1939–45

The table includes tankers of 1,600 gross tons and over, including ocean tankers built for the Royal Navy and the US Navy.

| | United Kingdom | | United States | | Canada |
	Greyhounds	Non-Greyhounds	Greyhounds	Non-Greyhounds	Non-Greyhounds
Sept 1939–41	–	478	257	137	–
1942	–	457	909	90	11
1943	–	295	2,795	616	40
1944	106	148	3,971	54	101
1945 (Jan–May)	41	46	1,609	–	–
Total:	147	1,424	9,541	897	152

Notes:
1. 'Sept 1939–41': US construction is for 1941 only.
2. Figures for US construction, 1943 and 1944. 'Non-Greyhounds' relate to Emergency tankers, which were modifications of non-tanker 'Liberty' types.

Appendix XIX

Standing Orders on Troopships – 'Routine'

hrs	
0600	Reveille. Blankets and hammocks rolled and stored. Mattresses stored.
0630	Draw rations.
0700	Troops' breakfast.
0700	Sergeants' breakfast (first sitting).
0745	Sergeants' breakfast (second sitting).
0745	Officers' and warrant officers' breakfast (first sitting).
0830	Officers' and warrant officers' breakfast (second sitting).
0900	Guard mounting (boat deck, port side).
1000	Boat stations.
1000	Ship's inspection.
1100	O.C. troops' conference.
1130	O.C. troops' orders.
1145	Sergeants' dinner (first sitting).
1200	Troops' dinner.
1215	Officers' and warrant officers' lunch (first sitting).
1230	Sergeants' dinner (second sitting).
1315	Officers' and warrant officers' lunch (second sitting).
1600	Draw rations.
1700	Troops' tea.
1700	Sergeants' tea (first sitting).
1730	Sergeants' tea (second sitting).
1800	Officers' and warrant officers' dinner (first sitting).
1900	Officers' and warrant officers' dinner (second sitting).
2100	Cocoa (troops' only).
2215	Lights out.

Appendix XX

Total Merchantmen Casualties

United Kingdom	31,908
Royal Navy DEMS	2,713
Maritime Regiment Royal Artillery	1,222
United States	5,662
United States Navy Armed Guard	1,640
Canada	1,437
South Africa	182
Australia	109
New Zealand	72
Norway	4,795
Greece	2,000
Holland	1,914
Denmark	1,886
Belgium	893
Neutral Countries	6,500
Total:	**62,933**

Notes:
1. DEMS gunners includes those from Empire countries.
2. UK seamen include Lascars, Chinese, Arabs and miscellaneous nationalities, such as those from Empire countries and those from Europe serving on British-flag merchantmen.

Appendix XXI

Tribute by Parliament to the Merchant Navy, 1945

The Minister of War Transport has been informed by the Lord Chancellor and by the Speaker of the House of Commons of the terms of the Resolutions in identical terms passed by both Houses of Parliament without dissent on the 30th October last, of which he has been requested to communicate the following portion to Masters, Officers and Men of the Merchant Navy:

'That the thanks of this House be accorded to the Officers and Men of the Merchant Navy for the steadfastness with which they maintained our stocks of food and materials; for their services in transporting men and munitions to all the battles over all the seas; and for the gallantry with which, though a civilian service, they met and fought the constant attacks of the enemy.

'That this House doth acknowledge with humble gratitude the sacrifice of all those who, on land or sea or in the air, have given their lives that others to-day may live as free men, and its heartfelt sympathy with their relatives in their proud sorrow.'

Bibliography

Agar, Captain Augustus VC, RN, *Footprints in the Sea* (Evans Bros, 1959).

Attard, Joseph, *The Battle of Malta* (William Kimber, 1980).

Attiwill, Kenneth, *The Singapore Story* (Frederick Muller, 1960).

Barker, A.J., *Dunkirk: The Great Escape* (Dent, 1977).

Barker, Ralph, *Goodnight, Sorry for Sinking You* (Collins, 1984).

Beesly, Patrick, *Very Special Intelligence* (Hamish Hamilton, 1977).

Behrens, C.B.A., *Merchant Shipping and the Demands of War?* (HMSO, 1955).

Belfield, E., and Essame, H., *The Battle of Normandy* (Batsford, 1965).

Ben Line, *The Story of a Merchant Fleet at War: 1939–1945* (Thomas Nelson, 1946).

Bond, Geoffrey, *Lancastria* (Oldbourne, 1959).

Bone, Captain Sir D.W., *Merchantmen Rearmed* (Chatto and Windus, 1949).

Bowen, Frank C., *The Flag of the Southern Cross 1939–1945* (Shaw, Savill and Albion, 1947).

Brennecke, H.J., *Ghost Cruiser HK33* (William Kimber, 1954).

Brice, Martin H., *Axis Blockade Runners of World War II* (Batsford, 1981).

Broome, Captain J., *Convoy is to Scatter* (William Kimber, 1972).

Brown, David, *Warship Losses of World War Two* (Arms & Armour Press, 1990).

Brown, Maurice, *We sailed in Convoy* (Hutchinson, ?1942).

Bruce, George, *Second Front Now!* (The Road to D.Day) (Macdonald and Janes, 1979).

Bushell, T.A., *Eight Bells: A History of the Royal Mail Lines* (Trade and Travel Publications, 1950).

Campbell, Commander A.B., *Salute the Red Duster* (Christopher Johnson, 1952).

Caulfield, Max, *A Night of Terror: The Story of the Athenia Affair* (Frederick Muller, 1958).

Chell, R.A., *Troopship* (Gale & Polden, 1948).

Churchill, Winston S., *The Second World War* (Cassell, 1948–52).

Cooke, Kenneth, *What Cares the Sea?* (Hutchinson, 1960).

Costello, John, and Hughes, Terry, *The Battle of the Atlantic* (Collins, 1977).

Cowden, James E., *The Price of Peace: Elder Dempster 1939–1945* (Jocast, 1981).

Creighton, Rear-Admiral Sir K., *Convoy Commodore* (Futura, 1976).

Cremer, Peter, *U-333: The Story of a U-Boat Ace* (The Bodley Head, 1984).

Cross, Robin, *VE Day* (Sidgwick & Jackson with the Imperial War Museum, 1985).

Daily Post & Echo, *Bombers Over Merseyside*, reprint of 1943 edition (Scouse Press, 1983).

Dickens, Captain Peter, *Narvik: Battles in the Fjords* (Ian Allan, 1974).

Dönitz, Admiral, *Ten Years and Twenty Days* (Weidenfeld and Nicolson, 1959).

Dorling, Captain Taprell (Taffrail), *Blue Star Line at War: 1939–1945* (Foulsham, 1973).

Dorling, Captain Taprell (Taffrail), *Western Mediterranean 1942–1945* (Hodder & Stoughton, 1947).

Edwards, Commander Kenneth, *Operation Neptune* (Collins, 1946).

Edwards, Bernard, *Blood and Bushido: Japanese Atrocities at Sea 1941–1945* (The Self-Publishing Association, 1991).
Edwards, Bernard, *The Fighting Tramps: The Merchant Navy Goes to War* (Robert Hale, 1989).
Edwards, Bernard, *They Sank the Red Dragon* (CPC Books, 1987).
Falk, Stanley L., *Seventy Days to Singapore* (Robert Hale, 1975).
Franks, Norman L.R., *Search, Find and Kill: Coastal Command's U-boat Successes* (Aston Publications, 1990).
Gasaway, E.B., *Grey Wolf, Grey Sea* (Arthur Barker, 1972).
Gelb, Norman, *Dunkirk: The Incredible Escape* (Michael Joseph, 1990).
Gibson, J.F., *Brocklebanks: 1770–1950* (Henry Young, 1953).
Gibson, P.S., edited by Morley, Sam, *Durban's Lady in White* (Aedificamus Press, 1991)
Gilchrist, Derek C., *Blue Hell* (Heath Cranton, 1943).
Gough, Richard, *The Escape from Singapore* (William Kimber, 1987).
Gretton, Vice-Admiral Sir Peter, *Convoy Escort Commander* (Cassell, 1964).
Gretton, Vice-Admiral Sir Peter, *Crisis Convoy: The Story of HX231* (Peter Davies, 1974).
Halstead, Ivor, *Heroes of the Atlantic* (The Right Book Club, 1942).
Harding, Steve, *Gray Ghost: RMS Queen Mary at War* (Pictorial Histories (USA), 1982).
Harris, John, *Dunkirk: The Storms of War* (David & Charles, 1980).
Hashimoto, Mochitsura, *Sunk: The Story of the Japanese Submarine Fleet, 1941–1945* (Cassell, 1954).
Hay, Doddy, *War under the Red Ensign* (Jane's, 1982).
Heaton, P.M., *The Reardon Smith Line* (Self-published, 1984).
Heaton, P.M., *The South American Saint Line* (Self-published, 1985).
Heckstall-Smith, Anthony, and Baillie-Grohman, Vice-Admiral, *Greek Tragedy: 1941* (Anthony Blond, 1961).
Hill, John C.G., *Shipshape and Bristol Fashion* (Journal of Commerce and Shipping Telegraph, 1950)
HMSO, *British Vessels lost at Sea 1939–45*, 2nd edn (Patrick Stephens, 1983).
HMSO, *How Britain was fed in Wartime*, Food Control 1939–1945 (1946).
Hocking, Charles, *Dictionary of Disasters at Sea During the Age of Steam 1824–1962*, 2 vols (Lloyds Register of Shipping, 1969).
Holman, Gordon, *In Danger's Hour* (Hodder & Stoughton, 1948).
Hope, W.E. Stanton, *Tanker Fleet: The War Story of the Shell Tankers and the Men who Manned Them* (Anglo-Saxon Petroleum Company, 1948).
Hough, Richard, *The Longest Battle: The War at Sea 1939–45* (Weidenfeld & Nicolson, 1986).
Houlder Brothers, *Sea Hazard: 1939–1945* (Houlder Brothers and Company, 1947).
Howe, Leslie, *The Merchant Service of To-day* (Oxford University Press, 1941).
Huxley, Elspeth, *Atlantic Ordeal: The Story of Mary Cornish* (Chatto and Windus, 1941).
Infield, Glenn B., *Disaster at Bari* (Robert Hale, 1974).
Iving, David, *The Destruction of Convoy PQ17*, revised and updated edition (William Kimber, 1980).
Jackson, W.G.F., *The North African Campaign 1940–43* (Batsford, 1975).
Jones, Geoffrey, *Autumn of the U-boats* (William Kimber, 1984).
Jones, Geoffrey, *Defeat of the Wolf Packs* (William Kimber, 1986).
Jones, Geoffrey, *The Month of the Lost U-boats* (William Kimber, 1977).
Jones, Geoffrey, *Under Three Flags: the story of Nordmark and the Armoured Supply Ships of the German Navy* (William Kimber, 1973).
Keegan, John, *The Price of Admiralty* (Hutchinson, 1988).
Kemp, P.K., *Victory at Sea: 1939–45* (Frederick Muller, 1957).
Kerr, George, F., *Business in Great Waters: The War History of the P & O 1939–45* (Faber and Faber, 1951).

Kerr, J. Lennox (ed.), *Touching the Adventures of Merchantmen in the Second World War* (Harrap, 1953).

Kerslake, S.A., *Coxswain in the Northern Convoys* (William Kimber, 1984).

Konings, Chris, *Queen Elizabeth at War* (Patrick Stephens, 1985).

Lane, Tony, *The Merchant Seamen's War* (Manchester University Press, 1990).

Lewis, Peter, *A People's War* (Thames Methuen, 1986).

Lucas, W.E., *Eagle Fleet* (Weidenfeld and Nicolson, 1955).

Lund, Paul, and Ludlam, Harry, *Night of the U-boats* (Foulsham, 1973).

Lund, Paul, and Ludlam, Harry, *Nightmare Convoy* (Foulsham, 1987).

Macintyre, Captain Donald, *The Battle of the Atlantic* (Batsford, 1961).

Macintyre, Captain Donald, *The Battle for the Mediterranean* (Batsford, 1964).

McAughtry, Sam, *The Sinking of the Kenbane Head* (Blackstaff Press, 1977).

McKee, Alexander, *The Coal-Scuttle Brigade* (Souvenir Press, 1957).

McMillan, James, *The Way it Happened 1935–1950* (William Kimber, 1980).

Manderstam, Major L.H. (with Roy Heron, *From the Red Army to SOE* (William Kimber, 1985).

Masters, David, *In Peril on the Sea: War Exploits of Allied Seamen* (Cresset Press, 1960).

Miller, W.H., and Hutchings, D.F., *Transatlantic Liners at War: The Story of the Queens* (David and Charles, 1985).

Milner, Marc, *North Atlantic Run* (University of Toronto Press, 1985).

Ministry of Information, *Merchantmen at War* (HMSO, 1944).

Ministry of Information, *The Battle of the Atlantic* (HMSO, 1946).

Mitchell, W.H., and Sawyer, L.A., *The Empire Ships*, 2nd edn. (Lloyds of London Press, 1990).

Mitchell, W.H., and Sawyer, L.A., *The Liberty Ships*, 2nd edn. (Lloyds of London Press, 1985).

Morris, Eric, *Churchill's Private Armies: British Special Forces in Europe 1939–1942* (Hutchinson, 1986).

Muggenthaler, Karl August, *German Raiders of World War II* (Robert Hale, 1978).

Murray, Marischal, *Union Castle Chronicle 1853–1953* (Longmans Green, 1953).

Musk, George, *Canadian Pacific* (David and Charles, 1981).

Neillands, Robin, *The Raiders: The Army Commandos 1940–1946)* (Weidenfeld & Nicolson, 1989).

Orbell, John, *From Cape to Cape: The History of Lyle Shipping* (Paul Harris, 1978).

Pack, S.W.C., *The Allied Invasion of Sicily* (David and Charles, 1977).

Pack, S.W.C., *The Battle for Crete* (Ian Allan, 1973).

Packer, Joy, *Deep as the Sea* (Eyre Methuen, 1976).

Parker, R.A.C., *Struggle for Survival* (Oxford University Press, 1989).

Pawle, Gerald, *The Secret War: 1939–1945* (Harrap, 1956).

Payton-Smith, D.J., *Oil: A Study of War-time Policy and Administration* (HMSO, 1971).

Pearce, Frank, *Last Call for HMS Edinburgh* (Collins, 1982).

Pearce, Frank, *Running the Gauntlet: The Battles of the Barents Sea* (Fontana, 1989).

Poolman, Kenneth, *Armed Merchant Cruisers* (Leo Cooper with Secker and Warburg, 1985).

Poolman, Kenneth, *The Catafighters and Merchant Aircraft Carriers* (William Kimber, 1970).

Poolman, Kenneth, *Escort Carrier 1941–45* (Ian Allan, 1972).

Poolman, Kenneth, *Focke-Wulf Condor: Scourge of the Atlantic* (Macdonald and Janes, 1978).

Poolman, Kenneth, *The Giant Killers: Cam Ships* (William Kimber, 1960).

Poolman, Kenneth, *The Sea Hunters: Escort Carriers v. U-Boats* (Arms and Armour Press, 1982).

Porten, Edward P. Von der, *The German Navy in World War II* (Arthur Barker, 1970).

Port Line, *Wartime Experiences: 1939–1945* (Port Line, 1947).
Revely, Henry, *The Convoy that Nearly Died* (William Kimber, 1979).
Robertson, Terrence, *The Golden Horseshoe* (White Lion, 1975).
Rohwer, Jürgen, *Axis Submarine Successes: 1939–1945* (Patrick Stephens, 1983).
Rohwer, Jürgen, *The Critical Convoy Battles of March 1943* (Ian Allan 1977).
Rohwer, J., and Hummelchen, G., *Chronology of the War at Sea: 1939–1945*, 2 vols (Ian Allan, 1972).
Roskill, Captain S.W., *A Merchant Fleet in War: 1939–45* (Collins, 1962).
Roskill, Captain S.W., *The Secret Capture* (Collins, 1959).
Roskill, Captain S.W., *The War at Sea*, 2 Vols (HMSO, 1959).
Saunders, Hilary St George, *Valiant Voyaging: A Short History of the British India Steam Navigation Company in the Second World War 1939–1945* (Faber and Faber, 1948).
Schofield, B.B., and Martyn, L.F., *The Rescue Ships* (Blackwood, 1968).
Schofield, B.B., *The Russian Convoys* (Batsford, 1964).
Seth, Ronald, *The Fiercest Battle* (Hutchinson, 1961).
Shankland, Peter, and Hunter, Anthony, *Malta Convoy* (Collins, 1961).
Simmons, John R., *Campaign Ribbons* (Sunflower University Press USA, 1990).
Slader, John, *The Red Duster at War: A History of the Merchant Navy During the Second World War* (William Kimber, 1988).
Smith, J.W., and Holden, T.S., *Where Ships are born: Sunderland 1346–1946. A History of Shipbuilding on the River Wear*, revised edn. (Thomas Reed, 1953).
Smith, Peter, C., *Arctic Victory: The Story of Convoy PQ18* (William Kimber, 1975).
Smith, Peter, C., *Hold the Narrow Sea: Naval Warfare in the English Channel 1939–45* (Moorland Publishing, 1984).
Smith, Peter C., *Pedestal: The Malta Convoy of August 1942*, 2nd edn. (William Kimber, 1987).
Spooner, Tony, *Coastal Ace: Squadron-Leader T.M. Bulloch* (William Kimber, 1986).
Stewart, I., McD, *The Struggle for Crete* (Oxford University Press, 1991).
Stokesbury, James L., *A Short History of World War II* (Robert Hale, 1982).
Taylor, John P., (ed.), *The Prefabricated Port of Arromanches* (Shipbuilding and Shipping Record, February–May 1945).
Taylor, Lieutenant-Commander J.E., *The Last Passage* (Allen and Unwin, 1946).
Terraine, John, *The Right of the Line* (Hodder and Stoughton, 1985).
Terraine, John, *Business in Great Waters* (Leo Cooper, 1989).
Thomas, David, A., *Crete 1941: The Battle at Sea* (André Deutsch, 1972).
Thomas, David, A., *The Atlantic Star: 1939–45* (W.H. Allen, 1990).
Thomas, David, A., *Japan's War at Sea* (André Deutsch, 1978).
Tute, Warren, Costello, John, and Hughes, Terry, *D-Day* (Sidgwick and Jackson, 1974).
Van der Vat, Dan, *The Atlantic Campaign* (Hodder and Stoughton, 1988).
Warner, Philip, *The D-Day Landings* (William Kimber, 1980).
Waters, S.O., *Ordeal by Sea: The New Zealand Shipping Company in the Second World War: 1939–1945* (N.Z. Shipping Company, 1949).
West, Frank, *Lifeboat Number Seven: Britannia* (William Kimber, 1960).
Winton, John, *The Defence of Sea Trade: 1890–1990* (Michael Joseph, 1983).
Winton, John, *Freedom's Battle: The War at Sea: 1939–45* (vol. 1) (Hutchinson, 1967).
Woon, Basil, *Atlantic Front* (Peter Davies, 1941).
Young, John M., *A Diary of Ship Losses: 1939–1945* (Patrick Stephens, 1989).

Index of Ships

(A general index follows on page 343)

327

General Index

(A separate index of ships starts on page 327)

Sunderland, 81, 182, 184, 230
Swansea, 36–7, 59, 111, 255, 269
Sydney (Aus.), 51, 57, 65, 128, 160, 173, 199
Sydney (Cape Breton), 68–9, 74, 87–8, 114
Syfret, Vice-Adm., 215
Syracuse, 238, 241, 242, 246

Tacoma, 193
Takoradi, 110–11, 119, 133, 207–8
Tamatave, 188
Tampa, 180
Taranto, 243, 246, 248, 271
Taylor, Cdre., 146
Tees, river, 183
Thames, river, 31, 33, 37, 189, 255, 260, 269
Thameshaven, 34, 252, 262
Thomson, Sir V., 16
Thompson, R.C., 179
Tillard, Rear-Adm., 252
Tobermory, 105
Tobruk, 113, 201, 204–5, 207, 213–15

Torquay, 255
Toulon, 26, 271
Tovey, Sir J (C in C), 100

Trincomalee, 114, 166
Trinidad, 232
Tripoli, 67, 207, 238, 243–4, 282–3
Trondheim, 257
Tunis, 236, 246
Tymbaki, 203
Tyne, River, 32–3, 183, 185

Vancouver, 193–5
Vian, Rear-Adm., 213–14, 238
Vierville, 255
Vizagapatam, 167
Volos, 202

Wabana, 74, 88, 191
Washington (US), 98, 179, 247, 250
Washington, Vice-Adm., 68
Wavell, FM Lord, 162, 201
Wear, river, 182–5
Wellington, NZ, 128
Weymouth, 32, 36, 255
Whetham, Rear-Adm., 69
Wilhelmshaven, 57
Winn, Roger, 138

Yawata (POW camp), 288

Zeebrugge, 272